MASONS AND SCULPTORS IN ROMANESQUE BURGUNDY

Publication of this book has been aided by a grant from

The Millard Meiss Publication Fund
of the
College Art Association of America

MM

Prix
de la Confédération Internationale
des Négociants en Oeuvres d'Art
1983

MASONS AND SCULPTORS
in
ROMANESQUE BURGUNDY

The New Aesthetic of Cluny III

C. Edson Armi

TEXT

THE PENNSYLVANIA STATE UNIVERSITY PRESS
UNIVERSITY PARK AND LONDON

C.I.N.O.A.
Registered in Brussels
Founded in 1935

CONFÉDÉRATION INTERNATIONALE DES NÉGOCIANTS EN OEUVRES D'ART
32 East 57th Street, New York, N.Y. 10022

AFFILIATED ASSOCIATIONS

Library of Congress Cataloging in Publication Data
Armi, C. Edson.
Masons and sculptors in Romanesque Burgundy.

Includes bibliography and index.
1. Art, Cluniac—France—Cluny. 2. Art, Romanesque—
France—Cluny. 3. Art, French—France—Cluny. 4. Cluny III
(Church) I. Title.
N6851.C45A7 1983   726'.5'094443   82-42784
ISBN 0-271-00338-3

à Germaine et Marie-Claude

Contents

ARCHAEOLOGICAL APPENDIXES

Acknowledgments

Working for so many years in a foreign country, I have come to depend on the kindness of innumerable individuals. I am thankful to every one, but I cannot fail to mention Germaine Chachuat and Marie-Claude Reboux, whose help was indispensable for my research. Through their generosity I have come to relish an art and an outlook very different from my own. With my friend Florian Stuber, in this country, I have spent some of my best months reflecting on a well-nigh impossible task: translating the visual creation of Cluny into words. For sharing this experience I owe him lifelong thanks. Chris Kentera, bless him, chose to take on a profitless project for which he knew he would be roundly criticized, and Whitney Stoddard twice finely reviewed the text. My special thanks go to Linda Docherty for her penetrating criticism and care with the manuscript, to Elizabeth Smith, Sheila McTighe, Caroline Watson, and Linda Horvitz for their perceptive corrections and to Chet Brummel and Buz Sawyer for their advice on photography. J. Richard Judson, as chairman of my department at Chapel Hill, allowed me to take off a year for writing the book, and the University Research Council contributed toward its publication. I gratefully acknowledge the generous support of the International Confederation of Art Dealers (C.I.N.O.A.) and the Millard Meiss Publication Fund of the College Art Association.

Introduction

Fifteen years ago, when I began to study First Romanesque architecture in the small Mâconnais region around Cluny, I had no idea of investigating the renowned medieval abbey from the point of view of an indigenous or folkloric tradition. Instead, I was interested in churches of the year one thousand, an interest which gradually led me to explore churches of the mid-century and later. To my surprise, I discovered that First Romanesque masons had continued to work throughout the eleventh century as the principal builders in the Mâconnais and, even more significantly, that their masonry techniques had formed the basis for the construction of Cluny III. In short, I came to realize that Cluny III was the climax of a living regional architectural tradition.

The discovery of regional sources for Cluniac architecture prompted me to take a second look at Cluniac sculpture. Wondering whether the sculptors could have been local artists like the masons, I put the question to the test, and the possibility of a local sculpture tradition became a reality. I noticed that the sculpture on buildings constructed before the mother church had been created by the same artists who sculpted the ambulatory capitals at Cluny, and I realized, therefore, that the Cluniac sculptors, too, were working from a regional tradition that had begun long before they had arrived at the abbey. To answer the question of origins, then, I was forced by the nature of the art and the material itself to account for architecture and sculpture simultaneously. The resulting method of analysis, whereby the evidence from one medium becomes a standard to test the findings in the other, is to my mind as important to this book as the conclusions themselves.

The layout and organization of the chapters will follow the book's thesis: in the history of architecture, Cluny III is the building where regional masons of different traditions first combined talents to develop a new design. On the ground floor, two distinct groups of masons collaborated in unequal roles, but by the time they reached the top level they worked as full partners who together created a new "mainstream" style. This is the story the book will be telling.

Divided into three parts, the book deals first with the theory of Cluniac art and then with the architecture and sculpture. In Part I, I analyze current theories about Cluniac art, discussing their underlying consistency as well as the controversy surrounding attempts to date both the abbey and other Burgundian architecture of the period. This analysis makes clear the reasons which led me to seek a new method for exploring the changes in Cluniac style. In the section on architecture, Part II, I discuss the two groups of artisans who collaborated at Cluny: the Atelier who came from a northern First Romanesque tradition and worked with ashlar blocks, and the Mâconnais masons who came from a southern tradition and worked with stones shaped like bricks. First I talk about the Atelier and how they changed the northern First Romanesque tradition in which they were working. These innovations help to explain the complex and creative mix that occurred later at the abbey church where the Atelier joined the Mâconnais masons. Moreover, by tracing the Atelier from church to church, I establish a relative chronology among these buildings, which helps to verify the order in which the sculpture was made. Through the sequence of buildings, therefore, I show the contributions in design of individuals from a particular background and set up a framework for the discussion of sculpture in Part III.

After following the Atelier to Cluny, I turn in the last section of Part II to the southern masons and show how they came there as well. I describe the unique modifications they made within their own tradition of construction and the way in which they merged this modified style with the Atelier's latest designs at the mother church. Thus, the new aesthetic of Cluny III reflects the human situation, wherein two groups of masons from complex but separate traditions worked together on a new design.

In Part III of the book, I concentrate on sculpture. As with architecture, I here make a similar attempt to move beyond an abstract notion of style by following the changing careers of individual local artists. This section has three chapters. In the first I discuss a major Brionnais sculptor who was active before the two great Cluny artists and whose late work was contemporary with their earliest pieces. With his sculpture as a background, in the next chapter I follow the artistic careers of these two Cluny Masters before and after they worked at the mother church. I discover that together their work bridges two epochs. One began his career when the First Romanesque tradition was near its end, while the other ended his career when the Gothic period began. Showing how, when, and where these two major artists came together in their careers helps to define High Romanesque Cluniac sculpture as the creation of individual sculptors with their own preferences and peculiarities. Finally in the last chapter, I trace the influence of the Cluniac Masters' work on two late Burgundian sculptors. These three chapters outline Burgundian Romanesque sculpture as the history of individuals, with their own artistic personalities and careers, whose creative interaction resulted in the Cluniac style.

To keep my central arguments as simple and clear as possible, I place supplemental material and archaeological proofs outside the main body of the text in separate excursus and appendixes. For example, I describe theory and historiography in the first chapter but relegate the discussion of individual positions to two excursus. Similarly, to avoid complicating an already complex history of sculpture, I put the minute analysis of "hands" in excursus at the conclusion of each chapter, and I attach the archaeological appendixes to the end of the book although they contain detailed evidence of campaigns critical to the chronology and placement of sculpture. Putting the archaeological appendixes at the end of the book also allows me to devote the first part of the text to a broad theoretical discussion of the masonry origins of High Romanesque architecture. The appendixes detail the changing roles of masons in different construction campaigns and carefully discuss the sources for High Romanesque masonry techniques in the most important early Burgundian buildings. This tiered arrangement will let readers with different backgrounds, interests and needs use the book conveniently: the text can be studied by itself for theory and the appendixes and excursus can be consulted for references or specific proofs.

In this book I look for the origins of the great religious art of Cluny. By a new analytical approach which integrates the media of architecture and sculpture, I locate these origins principally among masons and sculptors who lived and worked in the region of the abbey. My approach is indeed experimental and it has all the limitations which an experiment implies. I could not investigate every issue or pursue the full implications of all my findings; if only a few find acceptance, I shall consider my work worthwhile. In a sense, too, some limitations were placed on me by previous scholarship, which, since it traditionally followed other methods and proposed other theories, could not be used as a guide. I begin by summarizing these traditional approaches, as my initial interest was stimulated in great measure by them. While it is not my purpose to advance my own theory at the expense of established figures in the field, it is only after recognizing the limits of the past that a space can be opened wherein to ask new questions and seek their answers. It is in this positive spirit that I invite the reader to turn to the first chapter and excursus.

PART I:
THEORY AND METHOD

I

On Cluniac Art

I

It is, no doubt, an odd suggestion that twentieth-century scholarship on Burgundian Romanesque architecture and sculpture may ultimately interest historiographers even more than art historians. In a field dominated by the study of regional schools, scholarly positions are known by their geography, with Parisians pitted against a group of Burgundians and Anglo-Americans. During the last seventy-five years, the two sides have disagreed on a point which has as much to do with French regional pride as with the art itself.

The controversy has turned upon the dating of Cluny III. For generations established French archaeologists of the Parisian Société française d'archéologie had fixed the locale for the rebirth of large-scale figural sculpture in the Languedoc.[1] But if, as the non-Parisians claimed, Cluniac sculpture preceded the examples in Languedoc, and if Cluniac art was revolutionary, then it was in Burgundy, and not in the Languedoc, "where [was] born the grand movement of the revolution of Romanesque sculpture."[2] When the great pioneer, Arthur K. Porter, advanced this thesis, soon supported by Americans, English, and Burgundians, the resulting furor was caused not so much by the changes in the dates themselves as by the implications of these dating changes for the origins of Romanesque sculpture.

What should have been open-eyed scholarly investigation after truth soon hardened into doctrinal opposing camps. For example, as early as 1930, a Parisian boasted that his "quite modest" contribution was actually the old "doctrine of the French savants" and not a personal theory, while in the same breath he rejected the American position as "a new doctrine which aimed at nothing less than annulling the conclusions adopted . . . by the French erudition." "The fundamental principles of this doctrine must be integrally maintained," he insisted.[3]

At times the English-speaking and Burgundian scholars, too, became more fascinated with the implications of their "findings" and their attack on the traditional theory than with visual, factual, and methodological details. Indeed, a student of Porter devoted an entire article to the "genealogy" of his own conclusions, actively searching for the origins of the two traditional positions, "the two schools" as he labelled them.[4] An outstanding Burgundian scholar branded the Parisian Société française d'archéologie as "a little cénacle," "a band of tourists pressed by time and impatient to publish their travelogue." He dismissed their position as "that antiquated doctrinal thesis" and yet in equally strong terms praised Porter's position as "the doctrine" and described Porter's remarkable student as "the disciple of the master."[5]

Considering this intensity of feeling and the fervor of the arguments, it is not surprising that no one has recognized a basic agreement between the two camps on certain essential points. The scholarly controversy, after all, revolved around the dating of Cluny and its consequences, and has had less to do with matters of theory and methodology. Both schools agreed on four points: (1) the style of Cluny III architecture and sculpture was revolutionary; (2) its new form resulted from the conscious decision of a "genius" or intellectual overseer; (3) this man selected from far and wide the elements he assembled at Cluny; and (4) lesser Cluniac buildings copied the amalgamation of these elements from the mother church. It is, in fact, this last point—which we may call "the impact theory"—which underlies the attention-getting preoccupation with dating, since according to this theory, artistic ideas were transmitted from the large Cluny III to smaller, dependent churches. The result is a domino effect, where "dependent" churches as important as Vézelay must follow the early or late chronologies of the mother church.

The effect of this full agreement and of its lack of recognition on the course of scholarship cannot be overemphasized. Preoccupied with dating Cluny, both sides have accepted the same basic theories about its origins and impact and have broached no significant methodological or theoretical alternatives. It may be worthwhile to investigate these areas of agreement further since a major conclusion of the book is to date the sculpture of Cluny after its so-called imitations, in which case the impact theory as well as the three other theories for the formation of High Romanesque art in Burgundy no longer would be tenable.

II

How the major authors individually formulated the four theories of Burgundian art is detailed in the second excursus to chapter 1. Here it is sufficient to say that all parties accepted the sudden blossoming of Cluniac sculpture and architecture, some describing it as a "spontaneous generation." The Parisians attempted to find "evolutionary" intermediaries for Cluniac sculpture, but they failed to find the "missing link" since compared to the sophisticated art of Cluny III, the early examples they found, they had to admit, were "crude" and "primitive."[6] Both sides attributed the great leap forward at Cluny to some genius like Abbot Hugh, an "architect," or a "head-sculptor," who, by a conscious, intellectual process, created a new style out of a variety of international elements. It was also assumed that the intellectual supervisor, being a member of an order with an international perspective, would have selected principally non-Burgundian visual sources over the inferior local styles. And therefore all agreed that any regional Burgundian art in the new style had been inspired by the revolutionary achievement at Cluny.[7]

On the face of it and even without new information, such theories should awaken suspicion because they are mutually reinforcing and in fact dependent on each other. The reasoning is circular. If Cluniac art is revolutionary with no immediate prototypes, then its sources must be distant in time, place, and medium, and any local art with the same characteristics as Cluny must have been copied from it. If the theory of a genius is proposed, then the wider he casts his net for non-local sources, the more selective his choice becomes, the more intelligent he is assumed to be, and the more creative or spontaneous his solution appears in light of the previous works of art in Burgundy. But such an intellectual overseer would have required an unprecedented blend of abstract and practical visual skills. He would have required the cooperation of trained workers up and down the line for him to select all the important elements of design and to mold them into a new package to be copied in turn by less inspired artists in smaller churches. No doubt a few abbots would have liked to work this way, but were they capable of doing so? and is that how things were made? Perhaps only academics, or as Morelli would say, *aesthetic literati*, have such faith in purely intellectual sources for great works of art.[8]

Without belaboring other people's opinions, I believe that the methods supporting these theories frequently are as open to skepticism as the theories themselves. Since no definitive text dates Cluny or any other important High Romanesque building or sculpture in Burgundy, scholars must turn to more formal visual methods for proof (see the first excursus to chapter 1). In this case, the methods could have been more rigorous. It is not an exaggeration to say that this abstract constellation of theories persisted because the methods for testing them often were as intellectually abstract and ahistorical as the theories themselves. The principal mistakes consist of vague, unsubstantiated comparisons and *a priori* assumptions, including non-medieval notions of quality and metaphorical "proofs."

To be constructive, I would like to illustrate specifically these main points. Perhaps the most popular method for dating Romanesque sculpture and particularly the Cluny capitals has been to apply a modern structural theory according to which "independent" figures indicate the "degeneration of a style," especially if they are agitated in movement, "commanded by nothing," and surrounded by medallions "attached to nothing." By this reasoning, the ambulatory capitals at Cluny are late because "they hang like suspended hors-d'oeuvres" (Fig. 103a).[9] Earlier in the twentieth century it was more popular to date the capitals according to a modern sense of quality and progress in art whereby the Expulsion and Sacrifice capitals preceded the rest of the sculpture at Cluny because they were "crude" and "less good" (Fig. 129a).[10] Modern notions of quality frequently were used to identify individual sculptors. The most widely accepted study of Vézelay located a Cluny master on the southern tympanum at Vézelay by the quality of his figures (Fig. 99a), which "are in truth deprived of all distinction" with "squashed bodies, the head too gross, hunched too much at the shoulders. . . . In the scene of the Visitation, Elizabeth and Mary are not better than the others and their clothing is ugly . . . the faults are so great that one does not hesitate to give the whole register to the first assistant."[11] For architectural problems, modern criteria of delicacy and symmetry often were used to distinguish medieval construction campaigns. A major study proposed that the side tympana of Vézelay were installed as an afterthought because they were "too heavy" to have been intended for the jambs beneath, and that the buttresses on the Cluny southern transept were applied later because they were placed asymmetrically beside the windows.[12]

As well as establishing patterns of medieval construction on the basis of modern tastes, theories also were justified by metaphorical comparisons to natural systems outside the artistic process. While one theory suggested that the art of Cluny "shows a completely normal progression from simplicity to ornament," another asserted that art in Burgundy developed like the roots of a tree, from complex to simple.[13] Such analogies may be confusing, but they are more helpful than similarities drawn without any standard of comparison. Americans seemed especially partial to pointing out similarities without describing the similarities. In one book sculptural comparisons frequently began and ended with the words "patently related," while without further explanation another study grouped the in situ vegetable capitals of Cluny III as all "entirely similar."[14]

When descriptive vocabulary is used, it is sometimes ahistorical in that it is not specific enough to locate an object or building in one time and place. An outstanding book on sculpture, for example, employed such generally descriptive words to date Cluny early that they can apply equally well to early Gothic and archaic Greek sculpture, both of which exhibit "naïve and schematized working of the eye," "archaic hair and beard," "unmodelled face," "simple draperies," "schematized ear," and "exaggerated articulation of the muscles."[15]

Finally, the theories generated from these *a priori* assumptions about Cluniac art often do not take into account the fragments which actually do remain; it is as if only some of the evidence had been carefully examined. For example, the major study of Vézelay architecture overlooked the paint which covers most of the walls of the nave interior and which was rendered skillfully in the nineteenth century to look like mottled masonry. This oversight leads one to suspect the analysis of the stonework beneath the paint and especially a conclusion that "no break exists" in the nave "of one perfect unity."[16] Similarly, the major study of Cluny reported that the base profiles evolved perfectly from east to west but overlooked the base profiles of the freestanding piers which would have shown a more complicated pattern of change (see appendix 4 and Fig. 68).[17]

III

Since no text exists to tell us exactly when Cluny, Vézelay, Paray, and other important Burgundian buildings were built (see Map), we can determine their chronology only by the most exact formal methods of observation and analysis. Precise dating is less important in this regard than determining a relative chronology. By simply establishing the sequence in which art objects were created, we can achieve a number of large art-historical goals. If we can spot where an influence initially appeared, we go a long way toward answering the problem of sources. If we can distinguish where changes were initiated in both architecture and sculpture, we can establish a sequence of stylistic change and begin to truly understand the interaction of artists practicing these different media. Finally, if we can clearly see which parts of which buildings were built in sequential campaigns, we can pinpoint changes in aesthetics as well as in building practices. Again, the exact dates need not be known; these major questions about Burgundian art can be answered by establishing the relative chronology of the buildings. This distinction has consequences which have largely escaped scholars.

Because we want to establish the relative chronology of objects through formal means, much more severe methods of observation and analysis are needed than have been used up to now. Ideally, the methodology should be appropriate to the materials at hand. The approach I propose to use is a combination of analytical techniques often kept separate. It will involve "hand analysis," a method originally used for identifying individual painters from the Renaissance and Baroque periods, which will be combined with techniques of archaeological and stylistic analysis to compare the traditionally separate media of architecture and sculpture. By identifying individual sculptors and masons practicing in each major building, and by establishing, through archaeology, the relative chronology of the different buildings in which the same artists worked, I observe both individual and general stylistic changes and gauge the direction and turning points of stylistic trends.

For example, the same group of masons' marks can be identified throughout the major High Romanesque buildings at Anzy, Mâcon, Perrecy, Vézelay, Montceaux, and Cluny. Significantly, in more than one case, the same marks appear on works of figural sculpture in these different buildings. Thus, the first step is to identify the masons' marks to show that in fact we are comparing different works by the same masons and not comparing apples and oranges, or works with differences explained by aesthetics and traditions of separate ateliers. The original function of a mark, whether it represented an outright signature or a "day piece" mark is largely irrelevant so long as we accept it as the sign of an individual.[18] While I criticize others for assumptions, I am hardly immune from them myself. At one point scholarship must yield to speculation, as in the case of individual masons' marks, for which texts offer no explanation in Cluniac architecture of this period. Indeed, it could be argued that the alphabetic markings typical of the Atelier (the 23 marks on the left in Fig. 36) are not distinctive enough to reflect particular individuals or a particular group of individuals. I would not accept this argument. Among the Atelier, certain letters of the alphabet never occurred; others recurred in unusually modified forms, as in the case of $\mathcal{S}$, where a line has been struck through the character. Most importantly, among the restricted alphabet of the Atelier, non-letters like the star added a decisive measure of control in most of the buildings. Moreover, in churches typologically similar to certain of the Atelier's buildings, at Bragny for example, entirely different masons' marks appeared. Perhaps most indicative of their group identity is the situation where over time they were joined by other masons, as in the nave of Vézelay (the 20

Burgundian Romanesque Sites

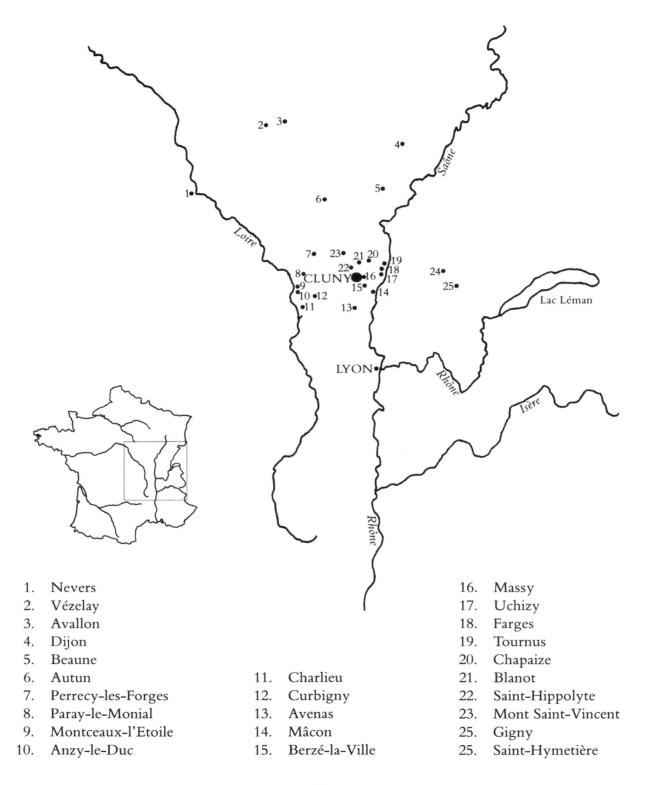

1. Nevers
2. Vézelay
3. Avallon
4. Dijon
5. Beaune
6. Autun
7. Perrecy-les-Forges
8. Paray-le-Monial
9. Montceaux-l'Etoile
10. Anzy-le-Duc
11. Charlieu
12. Curbigny
13. Avenas
14. Mâcon
15. Berzé-la-Ville
16. Massy
17. Uchizy
18. Farges
19. Tournus
20. Chapaize
21. Blanot
22. Saint-Hippolyte
23. Mont Saint-Vincent
25. Gigny
25. Saint-Hymetière

marks on the right in Fig. 36). In that case, it was the group of older Atelier masons identified by their alphabet marks who remained constant throughout, while new members joined them in two waves, in the first and after the sixth bays (see appendix 6). Significantly, all these new masons left distinctly different, non-alphabetic markings. Further evidence of the activity of the Atelier at the major Burgundian sites are the architectural motifs found on these buildings and seen, for example, on the bases in Figures 10c and 10d, 11c and 11d, and 13a and 13b.

Once we see that the same masons worked at different sites, we can use archaeological evidence to determine the order in which the buildings were built. Here I will turn to specific, and sometimes distressingly specific, archaeological evidence. Pains are taken to distinguish sutures, masonry differences, and individual parts such as bases and corbels. In spite of the pitfalls of this method, it does allow us to distinguish the individual parts of construction and, significantly, to judge precisely their change.[19]

Once we establish from marks that the same masons worked at different buildings and from archaeology that they constructed parts of these buildings in a sequence, we can return to the problem of the sculpture. After identifying the same sculptors at each site through hand analysis, and combining this with the sequence discerned from the archaeological findings, we can see how the sculptural styles individually and collectively changed. To document the archaeology of the architecture and the style of the sculpture, I have illustrated previously unphotographed details together with larger views of portals and capitals. While I tried to group photographic details with larger views of sculpture and architecture, I also arranged the photographs to follow the sequence of the text as closely as possible.

It has been traditionally assumed that architectural sculpture was carved after it was installed on the building and, therefore, that the sculpture dates later than the architecture. In the course of my archaeological investigation, however, I discovered that this is consistently untrue at the sites under consideration. For example, the jamb and column capitals on either side of the Perrecy Portal (Fig. 1a) were not only carved before the portal was constructed, they were not even intended to be placed together there. To make the left capitals (Fig. 1b) fit into the portal, a sculptor had to destroy the outer edge of the angel's wing on the jamb capital and half the acanthus scroll and a portion of the volute on the column capital. On the right capitals, the sculptor cut a right angle from the jamb capital and still had to destroy a portion of the volute and acanthus scroll on the column capital to make them fit. Similarly, a sculptor had to carve out a large portion of the Montceaux lintel (Fig. 2c) to accommodate the carved figures of the jamb capital (Fig. 2b). Clearly not enough space remains between the hole on the lintel and the capital figure to allow for the possibility of later carving in place. These two examples are typical; the problems of architecture and sculpture on these buildings are inextricably combined.[20] Because the sculpture was often made before the architecture and altered to fit it, archaeological evidence lets us see when the finished sculpture was put into place.

Now sculptural hand analysis, like the archaeology of architecture, is no substitute for a discussion of style, but simply a mechanical means of identification. But this identification together with the pattern of change discerned through archaeological analysis allows conclusions to be drawn about the order of stylistic changes. Quite obviously, much rests on the reliability of evidence. Following Morelli, I shall identify a sculptor's work by small, usually anatomical details like toes and ears. I choose these details not because they may be done as if by rote as Morelli posits, but simply because they are consistently the same in the various buildings where the artist worked.

Before I have identified a work by one sculptor I have insisted upon two criteria: (1) that a large number of minute but definable details, preferably over ten, exist in a small sculpted area, usually no larger than a square inch (e.g., Fig. 121); and (2), that these details together form a unique and complex pattern. These conditions are *guidelines* in that all details need not be present in each case and certain details may disappear over time and be replaced by others. Moreover, any observation is to a degree subjective; therefore, to increase the reliability of evidence and decrease its interpretive quality, I will use macrophotography instead of schematic drawing.[21] Thus, by combining hand analysis with my other methods, I will be able to determine stylistic changes without having to fix exact dates and without resorting to an *a priori* system like a style cycle, an evolutionary tree, or a theory of structural determinism.[22]

IV

At first, concentrating on details and even accidental marks may seem a mechanical undertaking revealing little of the "essence" of art. But, in fact, such a method for the first time reveals Cluniac art to be the individual and collective work of people rather than an expression of abstract theory. By attending to these small details, we can follow the careers of individuals; we can watch them work together as they learned from each other and changed together. Their art takes on a new level of meaning as the complex, varied, and creative activity of human beings.

A staggering number of discoveries result from applying these new methods. Specifically, the study of masons' marks and "hands" shows how small a group of masons not only built the great Romanesque churches of Burgundy but sculpted their tympana as well. The Renaissance pattern of sculptural workshops does not apply to the best Romanesque sculpture in Burgundy. Here, for example, one man executed tympana at Mâcon, Perrecy, Vézelay, and Montceaux and in addition sculpted the altar of Avenas and major apse capitals at Cluny. Masons' marks also show that principal sculptors, despite their being few in number, belonged to a "lower" and probably non-intellectual craft, since besides carving the sculpture they cut their share of ashlar blocks for masonry construction.[23] Again the Renaissance model of an intellectual and socially elevated artist cannot apply to a mason like the Vézelay Plus Master (+) who turned out masonry details for the nave arcades (Fig. 34) and massive quantities of simple ashlar blocks (Fig. 36) in addition to the important rondels he sculpted for the central portal (Figs. 33a, 33b).[24] Similarly, the work of masons ʜ and ᴇ ranged from figural jamb sculpture (Fig. 2a) and tympanum rinceaux (Fig. 30c) to plain squared stones (Figs. 24e, 31, 36).

Not only do masons' marks allow one to identify the work done by specific individuals, they also show these individuals as members of the changing group that I call the Atelier. One can actually chart the movements of this Atelier as its members travelled across the Burgundian countryside building churches. Indeed, I shall show how the sculptors and masons associated with the greatest churches, Cluny and Vézelay, had in fact joined together earlier to construct smaller local, Brionnais buildings. Therefore, the art these workers later produced did not derive from an overseeing genius or a spontaneous generation of international sources, but was solidly based on their *own* longstanding regional masonry traditions. While I do not discount the influence of international or even classical sources on the art of the local Atelier, my point is to show for the first time the *direct* impact of these individual Burgundian masons on Cluniac architecture and sculpture.

Seeing the problem of construction as a collaborative effort of individuals goes a long way toward answering other large artistic questions besides that concerning sources. As I have already pointed out, questions about the relationship between media, especially the questions of whether the style of architecture was more "advanced" than that of sculpture or whether sculpture was dominated by architecture, become somewhat academic when it is realized that frequently the same artists worked in both media. On the other hand, a new question about the rate of artistic change emerges after we recognize that the style of three sculptors shifted much more radically than previously thought possible over three campaigns at Vézelay.

Careful archaeological analysis reveals, indeed, new information about construction and building campaigns at Anzy, Mâcon, Vézelay, Cluny, and Paray. Provincials did not copy Cluny in complete "vest-pocket" editions as is so often claimed; rather, members of the same Atelier travelled back and forth from one partially completed structure to another. For example, after the side aisles were built, the chief Vézelay sculptor left to work on the Cluny capitals but he returned to Vézelay to complete its central portal. In another example, members of the major Atelier finished the Paray chevet but left a local Brionnais group in charge after completing only the lower story of the transept. We must recognize in these discoveries a completely new and complex pattern of stylistic change among the Cluniac buildings.

From the archaeological evidence, then, the "impact" theory by which Cluny is said to have inspired copies among its local dependents is largely incorrect. First of all, the Cluny "model" was never a fixed type but rather passed through a series of very different campaigns. Even more to the point, the *same* craftsmen who created the architecture and sculpture of Cluny had executed most of the so-called "inferior copies" before the "original" itself.

For the first time in the study of Burgundian art, we can establish stages of the building process and stylistic changes from the evidence of specific sculptors and groups of masons and dismiss model-copy theories based on whole building types and abstract systems of creation and impact. What results is not a diminished view of the importance of Cluny III—far from it—but a changed view of its role: Cluny III was not a fixed model but a constantly changing and experimental construction. Indeed, Cluny was important not because it was a revolutionary assembly of international sources but rather because there was merged in one building two long-standing but separate indigenous masonry traditions, the traditions of northern and southern First Romanesque construction. The traditional Mâconnais masons of the Cluny area first worked on the ground story as menial fill masons, but by the time the upper story was built, they had joined the members of the major Atelier in a harmonious working relationship wherein their distinctive construction techniques and aesthetics became one. This pattern of cooperation in the upper part of the building resulted in a new "mainstream" style which they repeated in the chevet at Paray and probably at Berzé. Abstract systems and impersonal theories of stylistic development are no longer necessary to explain Romanesque art, for it was created by men in stages reflecting their working relationship.

NOTES

1. André Michel, *Histoire de l'art*; Paul Deschamps, "Notes sur la sculpture romane en Bourgogne," 78–80, and "L'âge des chapiteaux du choeur de Cluny," 160–165; Francis Salet, *La Madeleine de Vézelay*, and "Cluny III," 235–292.

2. Deschamps, "L'âge des chapiteaux," 162.

3. Ibid., 218.

4. Kenneth J. Conant, "Deux traditions dans la chronologie du roman bourguignon," 94–99; "La chronologie de Cluny III, d'après les fouilles," 343 and note 9; "Medieval Academy Excavations at Cluny, X," 31–32. Arthur Kingsley Porter (*Romanesque Sculpture of the Pilgrimage Roads*, 3–17; "La sculpture du XIIᵉ siècle en Bourgogne," 73–74) discussed the historiography of the two positions and the role of the theory of evolution in the discipline of art history. For more historiography of Burgundian Romanesque art, see Charles Oursel, "Une grande mission archéologique américaine en Bourgogne," 58. Although scholars who have published just recently belong to many different national backgrounds, they almost uniformly support the Parisian system of dating: see, for example, discussions of the work of Peter Diemer, Carol Pendergast, and Neil Stratford in the first excursus to this chapter.

5. C. Oursel, "Comptes-rendus critiques: congrès archéologique de France—XCIᵉ session tenue à Dijon," 196; "Une grande mission," 58.

6. Deschamps, "L'âge des chapiteaux," 214.

7. The questionable assumption that artistic influence naturally goes from a major monument to a lesser one underlies other unresolved problems of medieval art, such as the relationship of Chapaize to Tournus in First Romanesque architecture, Saint-Loup-de-Naud to the Chartres Royal Portal in early Gothic sculpture, and Braine to Chartres Cathedral in High Gothic architecture.

8. Giovanni Morelli (*Italian Painters*, 6–11) described aesthetic literati in the following way: "preferring as their practice is mere abstract theories to practical examination, it is their wont to look at a picture as if it were a mirror, in which, as a rule, they see nothing but the reflection of their own minds." This is not to say that Morelli denied that the causes of certain stylistic changes were explained by the history of culture. Rather, his was simply a statement of priorities. He felt that it was almost impossible to understand the cause of visual change without first being intimately acquainted with the outward condition of the change itself. Failing that, the scholar was apt to approach a work of art with preconceived notions.

9. Focillon, *L'art des sculpteurs romans*, 153–154.

10. Deschamps, "L'âge des chapiteaux," 214.

11. Salet, *Vézelay*, 151. According to Salet, "precisely" the same faults are found in this master's work at Cluny: "D'autres paraissent *lourdes* et *quelques peu vulgaires*, l'Espérance, la Charité, la plupart des Tons de la musique. *Proportions courtes, plis soufflés, développés à l'excès*, drap souvent *confus* et entrecoupé de *la façon la plus arbitraire*, ce sont là précisément les défauts qui révèlent, à la façade de Vézelay, la main du premier compagnon" (my italics).

12. Salet, "Cluny III," 259; for disproof, see appendix 6.

13. Joan Evans, *Romanesque Architecture of the Order of Cluny*, 127, a description of windows in the churches of the Order of Cluny; Deschamps, "Notes," 79.

14. Porter, *Pilgrimage Roads*, 118: e.g., Porter's description of the sculptor of the Avenas altar: "his inferiority is, of course, patent." Conant ("Medieval Academy Excavations at Cluny—The Season of 1928," 24) described the foliage capitals in Cluny III: "One pair, minus their shafts, still cling to their places outside the blocked galilee portal at the fourth bay of the nave. They are entirely similar in character to others found in the Chapel of St. Gabriel, in the great transept, in the lesser transept farther east (surely eleventh-century work), and, in fragment, at the foot of the easternmost absidiole. They are but another proof of the homogeneity of the whole church." In easily the smoothest sleight of hand, Raymond Oursel spoke of a "ressemblance flagrante, qui

se passe de commentaire" when he compared the famous Cluny female head fragment with the head of Eve on the Cluny Expulsion capital (*Les églises romanes de l'Autunois et du Brionnais*, 92).

15. Porter, *Pilgrimage Roads*, 85.

16. Salet, *Vézelay*, 42, 49; "La Madeleine de Vézelay. Notes sur la façade de la nef," 19. While Salet observed paint on the facade, he failed to recognize painted color throughout the nave. He described "la pierre" in this part of the building as "les teintes en sont infiniment diverses . . . une extraordinaire variété, tantôt blancs, tantôt bruns, parfois même jaunes, verts ou roses. Ces pierres de mille couleurs, disposées selon la seule fantaisie, donnent à ce vaisseau une chaleur de tone, une séduction de coloris." The Monuments Historiques *Devis* of 6 September 1855, described the "Etat de travaux de peinture" of M. Caremelle, "peintre à Chablis, pendant l'exercice 1855." The document stated that he applied a minimum of two coats of paint to architectural parts, including the nave, side aisles, and facade.

17. Conant, "Excavations at Cluny, X," 32–33; Porter, *Pilgrimage Roads*, 80.

18. By the Gothic period, masons and stonecutters were separate individuals; for example, in the windows at Bourges Cathedral, they were represented by separate guilds (Jean Gimpel, *The Cathedral Builders*, 80). Whether separate workers consistently performed the two jobs in the Romanesque period or whether one or both individuals left a mark is not known. Despite these questions, simply being able to identify the marks of the same men in different buildings adds a great measure of control in comparing the masonry of Burgundian Romanesque buildings.

19. For a discussion of certain pitfalls, see appendix 4, notes 3, 13, and appendixes 2, 6.

20. Since the Cluny ambulatory capitals are no longer in their original location, it is difficult to be certain whether they were carved before or after installation. The capital most like them (Fig. 3, appendix 4), on the exterior of the minor transept chapel was clearly carved before it was installed. The evidence is definite, because the leaves at the base of the capital are severed by the astragal of the column. This makeshift change in design, or the reuse of a design meant for a different location, is an alteration which would not have occurred if the capital was originally carved in its present position. In discussing the sculpting of the Cluny capitals, C. Oursel (*L'art roman de Bourgogne*, 183) had some reason to describe the before-or-after installation arguments as "discussions byzantines, et parfaitement stériles." Conant ("The Apse at Cluny," 27) and R. Oursel (*Floraison de la sculpture romane*, 400) believed that chisel strokes continuing from the sculpture on five Cluny capitals to the area beneath their imposts prove that the carving was completed before the imposts were set upon the capitals. Aubert ("Cluny," 520) accepted Conant's evidence, but insisted that the capitals were carved in place after the completion of the choir in 1113. To accept both Conant's evidence and a later date, Aubert sophistically argued that masons worked the hard-to-reach spots under the imposts before they set the capitals in place. Only later did they carve the sculpture on the face of the capitals. Deschamps ("Notes," 68) and Denise Jalabert (*La sculpture romane*, 65), as well as Salet (*Vézelay*, 143), argued that Romanesque capitals were almost always carved in their finished form in place after installation. Deschamps ("L'âge des chapiteaux," 212) and Salet ("Les chapiteaux de Notre-Dame de Beaune," 220) described the "incomplete" capitals in the apse of Beaune (Fig. 4) as evidence of the practice of carving Cluniac capitals after they were installed. First, it must be pointed out that capitals can be incompletely carved in the workshop on the ground or in place on the building; the fact of incompletion proves nothing either way. Indeed, based on the same evidence, Conant came to the opposite conclusion from Salet. For Conant, it made no sense for workers to go through the effort of building scaffolding to carve capitals already in place and then to leave the capitals incompletely carved ("The Apse," 27). Second, the apse capital at Beaune (Fig. 4) is not unfinished as Salet claimed. It only appears unfinished because the present foliage design does not correspond to the original scratched-in eagle motif visible along the sides.

21. Conant and Salet seldom took their own pictures and almost always selected general, overall shots to illustrate their archaeological arguments. In my own work with macrophotography, I was surprised at the little effect scale differences had on the identifying characteristics and general stylistic qualities of individual sculptors.

22. While he claimed that his ideas were no more than a "thought out" version of Morelli's, Bernard Berenson altered the Master's theories on two fundamental points in *Rudiments of Connoisseurship* (pp. 111ff). He allowed for constant change in the "Grundform" throughout the lifetime of an artist: "in the case of a long-lived artist, the forms in works of his old age scarcely bear a resemblance . . . it would never do to apply a test mechanically." Second, he saw a larger grouping or context for the Grundform: "the ears—are never to be applied mechanically. The identity is in the visualization and habits of the artist. Rather than ask: 'is this Leonardo's ear or hand?' We should ask 'is this the ear or hand Leonardo, with his habits of visualization and execution, would have painted?'"

More recently, Carl D. Sheppard ("Romanesque Sculpture in Tuscany: a Problem of Methodology," 97–108) objected to the use of Morellian techniques in the study of Romanesque sculpture. He admonished historians not to explain away differences in one artist's work on the basis of fragmentary evidence, artistic maturity and immaturity, travel by the artist or the impact of different regions and "Schools." To his list of objections may be added speed of execution, the reason Zarnecki and Grivot (*Gislebertus*, 162) gave to explain the differences among what they considered to be Gislebertus's nave capitals at Autun.

While Sheppard may be right in many cases, must we abandon the attempt to identify individual artists because of incomplete information or the dearth of comparable monuments? For Morelli, perceptive visual analysis frequently made up for the lack of examples (*Italian Painters*, 34): "when two Greek scholars fail to agree about the meaning of a passage in the classics, the reason may be that one has more discernment than the other." Perhaps the problem in Romanesque sculpture lies in visual analysis and careful description rather than in the method or the quantity of evidence.

Louis Grodecki claimed that distinguishing the work of individuals is a fruitless undertaking in Romanesque sculpture because the sculptural process was a joint effort involving many different men at different stages of execution. Based on the important Cluniac sculpture, I see very little evidence for his conclusions ("Le moyen âge occidental," 22).

For the most sensitive and complex recent analysis

of the "influence" of style as studied apart from the work of individuals, see Thomas Lyman, "Terminology, Typology, Taxonomy: an Approach to the Study of Architectural Sculpture of the Romanesque Period." For a less successful treatment of the "Überpersönliche Vereinheitlichung der Formensprache," see Bernhard Kerber, *Burgund und die Entwicklung der französischen Kathedralskulptur im zwölften Jahrhundert* (p. 28).

23. It is known that at least some of the workers on Cluny III were laymen or *conversi* in 1132, for in reforming statutes in that year (Marrier, col. 1353, stat. XIX), Peter the Venerable exempted the workshops of the new church and its workmen from the rule of silence which he imposed on the other workshops and workmen of the abbey (Evans, *Romanesque Architecture*, 10). René Crozet, "A propos de Cluny," 155: "l'ignorance totale où nous sommes de la condition sociale—moines-ouvriers ou ouvriers laïcs—de la main-d'oeuvre employée."

24. When seen from the side, the + mark sometimes appears more as an "X" (Fig. 33b, and upper mark in Fig. 33a). See chapter 3 for a discussion of Master ℏ.

First Excursus: Dating Burgundian Romanesque Art

To a man, scholars insisted that Cluny-related sculpture and architecture were copied from the model at the mother church; nevertheless, two groups of scholars disputed the dates of these "dependent" buildings although most of the writers freely admitted that texts provided less than sure evidence. Indeed, Jean Virey (*Les églises romanes de l'ancien diocèse de Mâcon, Cluny et sa région*, 21) accepted only three secondary buildings as positively dated, and he "avows a great hesitation when forced to say if a church belongs to the end of the eleventh or the first quarter of the twelfth century," while Robert de Lasteyrie (*L'architecture religieuse en France à l'époque romane*, 423) resigned himself to "many of the dates (in the Burgundian School) being far from established with all the desired rigor." Victor Terret recognized "the penury of texts," "as a consequence of which" he relied "almost uniquely upon considerations of technique and style . . . to arrange sculpture in chronological order" (*La sculpture bourguignonne aux XIIᵉ et XIIIᵉ siècles*, 1). The same repeated problems with

textual material explain why no agreement exists on the dates of important Burgundian buildings and sculpture related to Cluny, including Anzy, Avenas, Berzé, Mâcon, Montceaux, Paray, Perrecy, and Vézelay.

Determining whether a document is authentic is the first important problem. This issue undermines Charlieu's consecration date of 1094, described in the undated *Mémoire manuscrit des Bénédictins contre le curé Dupont*, for that manuscript is lost and Salet has questioned the accuracy of a later reference to it in J.-B. de Sevelinges, *Histoire de la ville de Charlieu*, 1856 (Salet, "Review of Elizabeth Sunderland, *Charlieu à l'époque médiévale*," 74; see chapter 3, note 1). Many experts have agreed that the survival of the same letter types over generations makes epigraphy of little use in resolving disputes over the dates of inscriptions (Meyer Schapiro, "Review of Paul Deschamps, *Etude sur la paléographie des inscriptions lapidaires*," 101–102). For Richard Lloyd ("Cluny epigraphy," 336–337) the letters on the Cluny capitals "probably" point to an early date, although he believed that the time in dispute—thirty-five to forty years—was far too short for any distinguishing tendencies to appear.

The second problem is simply an extension of the first in another direction. If the document is authentic, did the author exaggerate or prevaricate? In his biography of Saint Hugh, written in Rome in 1113 or 1114, the monk Gilon recounted that it took the abbot twenty years to build Cluny III and the church housed one-thousand people (Marcel Aubert, "Eglise abbatiale de Cluny," 509; Dom A. l'Huillier, *Vie de saint Hugues*, 606). Salet ("Cluny III," 276) discounted the reference as "naturally, nothing but rhetoric," while Conant ("Excavations at Cluny, X," 31) accepted it almost literally as evidence for the completion date of Cluny III at the time of Hugh's death in 1109. Similarly for Paray, the monk Gilon supplied a date and even mentioned a part of the building (*Acta Sanctorum*, III, 652). But again the question arises whether we can trust the writer's version of the story told by Raimond of Semur about his uncle, Saint Hugh, who miraculously healed a novice hit by a beam falling from a tower. Raymond Oursel (*Les églises romanes*, 248–250) seized on the reference as a "sure date," "a precious foothold in the study of Cluniac architecture which allows no further discussion," while Salet ("Cluny III," 281), doubting even a monk could survive a blow from a tower, suggested that when it came to medieval descriptions of miracles, "texts of this genre are very subject to caution."

If the text is authentic and the author believable, we still have to ask whether his commentary is fragmentary or complete. For example, does a consecration or dedication refer to a partial or complete state of construction? Very often church fathers will take advantage of a pope's passing through the region to have art consecrated, and therefore the act reflects little about the state of completion. Pope Innocent III in 1130 consecrated Saint-Lazarus of Autun, whose capital style almost all scholars agree predates the sculpture at Saulieu, unknown portions of which were consecrated earlier in 1119 by Pope Calixtus II. In the case of Cluny III, it is even more difficult to relate the various consecrations to specific architecture and sculpture. On 25 October 1095, Pope Urban II consecrated the main and matutinal altars (Bibl. Nat. lat. 1716, fol. 91), and at the same time bishops accompanying him consecrated three other altars (*Bibliotheca Cluniacensis*, col 518, 519, 1368, and Orderic Vital, *Historia Ecclesiastica*, 2, 463). Also in 1095, the Bishop of Compostela consecrated an altar to Saint James, and in 1104 Geoffray, Bishop of Amiens, consecrated another altar (Jean Mabillon, ed., *Acta Sanctorum ordinis S. Benedicti*, 87; Guibert de Nogent, *Histoire de sa vie*, 200). Salet ("Cluny III," 236f.) has explained the fragmentary character of these textual dates and why they may tell us little about the degree of completeness of Cluny III. While the texts spoke of five altars in 1095, they mentioned nothing of an ambulatory or of capitals in place in the ambulatory or even of an elevation or vault above the sanctuary. Indeed, because altars frequently are movable, they do not imply definite completion of any part of the building. As we saw before, pontifical consecrations provide perhaps the least safe evidence of the state of construction, and this is true especially in the case of Urban II, who consecrated so many altars on his tour of Burgundy. Finally, from the text description "in tribus primis cancellis," we cannot be sure if the three secondary altars, consecrated by the prelates accompanying Urban II in 1095, refer to an ambulatory or transept chapel or to a chapel in a different part of the building. These seemingly specific consecrations in fact tell surprisingly little about the building and its date.

A fourth problem in dating from texts involves name confusion. To prove an early date for the Cluny III transept, Conant assigned the name "Peter" painted in the transept tower chapel of Saint Gabriel to Peter of Roda, who died in 1114 or 1115 ("La chapelle Saint-Gabriel à Cluny," 55–64; *Cluny*, figs. 114–116), while Salet ("Cluny III," 247, note 7) preferred another Peter, Bishop of Pamplona, from 1167 to 1193. Similarly, to prove the date of the Avenas altar, F. Cucherat (*Les origines du Beaujolais et l'autel d'Avenas*, 20) identified the Louis in the stone inscription as Louis the Pious, while others, including Charles Perrat (*L'autel d'Avenas, la légende de Ganelon et les expéditions de Louis VII en Bourgogne 1166–1172*) preferred the twelfth-century Louis VII.

A fifth problem in dating from texts involves the relation between media, for even with in-situ sculpture, scholars long have debated whether sculptors carved before, during or after architectural construction. Even if we accept the authenticity of a text, the word of the author, and the conclusive dating of the architecture, this means we still must ask whether the same dates apply to sculpture on the buildings. A case in point is the classic argument whether sculptors carved the Cluny ambulatory capitals before the impost blocks were installed (Aubert, "Eglise abbatiale de Cluny," 521; Deschamps, "L'âge des chapiteaux," 212; Conant, "The Apse," 27).

The lack of information surrounding accidents and disasters causes another problem in dating from texts. At Vézelay, for example, three texts described the fire of 21 July 1120, and the two most detailed chronicles agreed that "on the evening of the Feast of the Madeleine, the church being taken suddenly by fire, innumerable people, women, infants, clergy and laymen, perished in the fire" (Salet, "La Madeleine de Vézelay et ses dates de construction," 5–6; *Chronique de Saint-Marien d'Auxerre* [Bibliothèque d'Auxerre, ms. 145], an edited text of which appears in Dom Martin Bouquet, *Recueil des Historiens des Gaules et de la France*, vol. 12, 291–92; and Guillaume de Nangis, manuscript, in Hercule Géraud, *Publication de la Société de l'Histoire de la France*, 1843, vol. 1, 11). Clearly a fire burned a church, but which church—a Carolingian or Romanesque one, from 1104 or later—and how much did it destroy? Based on the same textual evidence, two quite different theories arose, because the texts typically failed to describe the visual subject explicitly. C. Oursel (*L'art roman*, 182–85) and Porter (*Pilgrimage Roads*, 88) proposed that the 1104 nave survived the disaster largely intact, while Salet (*Vézelay*, 148) believed that the fire entirely destroyed a Carolingian nave, the 1104 church never having been extended beyond the crossing. Conant ("Deux traditions," 99–103) reinterpreted the third bay rondel inscription, "I am rather covered with smoke but later I shall be resplendent," in a manner which caused him to modify the theory of C. Oursel and Porter. Based on the texts, he believed that the Romanesque masons finished the chevet and transept between 1106 and 1111, and slowly replaced the Carolingian nave, beginning with the two western bays, when the fire struck in 1120. The collapse of the vault of Cluny III in 1125 caused another round of speculation based on a text (E. Martene, *Veterum Scriptorum amplissima collectio*, 7, 1192–1193, and J.-P. Migne, *Patrologiae cursus completus*, series *Latina*, 15–27). Aubert ("Cluny," 513) and Conant (*Cluny*, 255 and 283) interpreted the words "ingens basilicae navis" as the central nave with its shallower foundations in the last six bays, while Salet ("Cluny III," 283) preferred to interpret the *navis* as the northern transept vessel. He believed that different moldings and additional windows on the northern transept illustrated by Etienne Martellange in 1617 (Conant, *Cluny*, fig. 14) reflected a wooden roof which replaced the collapsed vault.

Whether a text described a church surviving today or a different lost building is a further textual problem. An argument over one-hundred years old concerns the "pilgrims' church" which Etienne Bagé, Bishop of Autun, "blessed" during the journey to Vézelay of Pope Innocent II in 1132 (Hugues de Poitiers, *Histoire de Vézelay*, 2, Bibl. d'Auxerre, ms. 227 fol. 22). Conant and Porter accepted the narthex as the "pilgrims' church," the argument first proposed by Chérest in 1857 (Aimé Chérest, "Aperçus historiques sur la Madeleine de Vézelay," *Bulletin de la société des sciences historiques et naturelles de l'Yonne*, 11 (1857): 508–537; Conant, "Deux traditions," 94–103; Porter, *Pilgrimage Roads*, 110). Salet ("La Madeleine," 5–25, and *Vézelay*, 25f.) recognized alternative interpretations from the text. He would accept Paul Frankl's theory that the church in the text refers either to the present nave (*Die frühmittelalterliche und romanische Baukunst*, Potsdam, 1926, 165f.) or to a no-longer existing hospice chapel, freeing the 1132 date entirely from the present church complex. Another confusing question results from the fragmentary description in the *Petite chronique de Vézelay*, Bibl. d'Auxerre, ms. 227, fol. 14v. The words "dedication of the church of Vézelay built by Abbot Artaud" surely refer to a dedication in 1104 of a church built by Abbot Artaud, who governed the monastery from 1096 to 1106, when he was assassinated. The question is, which church? Conant and Porter selected the present building because, following the rules of the impact theory, its early date would confirm an even earlier one for the mother church at Cluny. Conversely, Deschamps ("Notes," 71ff., and "L'âge des chapiteaux," 175) and Salet ("La Madeleine," 18–25, *Vézelay*, 39, and "Review of J. K. Conant," 186) preferred to see only the Vézelay crossing as dating from this time.

These then are some of the major reasons why no date is generally accepted for any major building or sculpture in Burgundy. The following are the range of dates for each important building discussed in the text. Despite the differences in dating, however, every major scholar accepted each

Cluny-related sculpture as a later reflection of the ambulatory capitals of the mother church.

Anzy-le-Duc. No written documents date the construction of the church (André Rhein, "Anzy-le-Duc," 272). "In fact, no text before 1164 signals the priory church," Carol Pendergast, *The Romanesque Sculptures of Anzy-le-Duc*, 5.

While scholars disagree about the dates of the Cluny-related archivolt figures on the west facade, they settled upon a time after the Cluny ambulatory capitals. Aubert ("Cluny," 73): second quarter of the twelfth century; Gottfried von Lücken ("Burgundische Skulpturen des XI. und XII. Jahrhunderts," 106–107): the archivolt figures of Anzy exhibit a "much more advanced style" than the tympanum of Mâcon which he dated to the end of the eleventh century; C. Oursel ("Problèmes de filiation en l'histoire de l'art roman," 67–69): 1118; R. Oursel (*Les églises*, 95): 1115; Porter (*Pilgrimage Roads*, 121): 1125; Willibald Sauerländer ("Über die Komposition des Weltgerichts-Tympanons in Autun," 268, and "Gislebertus von Autun," 27, note 11): "reflex of the Cluny portal"; Stephen Scher (*The Renaissance of the Twelfth Century*, 32): 1115, after the lintel and tympanum from 1095; Neil Stratford ("Un bas-relief roman de Nevers," 304, 306, note 45): just before 1130–1140; George Zarnecki and Denis Grivot (*Gislebertus*, 28): before 1120.

Avenas. Except for Cucherat (*Les origines du Beaujolais et l'autel d'Avenas*, 1886), every major scholar who expressed an opinion followed the impact theory and placed the Avenas altar after the ambulatory capitals of Cluny. Nevertheless, their dating is hardly consistent, ranging from 840 in the case of Cucherat (*Avenas*, 20), to 1180 for J. Descroi ("Inscription de l'autel d'Avenas"); in between, Perrat (*L'autel*) and Sauerländer ("Gislebertus," 27, note 11) dated it to after 1166; a date in the early twelfth century was more attractive to Peter Diemer (*Stil und Ikonographie*, 204), Geza de Francovich ("La corrente comesca"), André Gaudillière (*Eglise d'Avenas*), R. Oursel ("A propos de l'autel d'Avenas," 204, and *Cahiers d'histoire*, 4, 1959, 98), Pierre Quarré ("La date des chapiteaux de Cluny," 160), and Zarnecki (*Gislebertus*, 68, note 4). Porter (*Pilgrimage Roads*, 118) dated the Avenas altar to the eleventh century, although he believed that the style followed the "great original." Com-

pared to Cluny, the altar's "inferiority is, of course, patent" because of its "coarseness, rigidity, jerkiness."

Berzé-la-Ville. Despite passing reference to a church in certain Berzé texts (see Virey, "Saint Hugues et la chapelle de Berzé-la-Ville"), the only one to discuss the building is the *Testimony of St. Hugh*, and typically it is more confusing than helpful. Melville F. Weber in 1926 first analyzed the text in relation to the architecture of Berzé (see C. Oursel, "La chronologie de la chapelle du Château des Moines à Berzé-la-Ville," 222–24). *La Bibliotheca Cluniacensis*, col. 496, trans. Dom l'Huillier, *Vie de saint Hugues*, 523: "Ce moûtier était bien pauvre, et presque ruiné; nous l'avons confié à notre fils Ségun pour le relever. Avec l'aide de frère Foucher, que nous avions consenti à lui adjoindre, il a rebâti la maison, acquis quelques vignes et quelques terres. Bientôt il sera reconstruit tout à fait et remis en un état prospère." The value of the text for dating the present building is doubtful because no specific reference is made to a chapel. Moreover, the text would seem to allow for different periods of chapel construction in the immediate and more distant past, in the present, and in the future—permitting any among the wide range of dates heretofore proposed. Construction in the immediate past is possible because Hugh declared that, within his abbacy, the priory was "bien pauvre et presque ruiné" such that he assigned Ségun ("nous l'avons confié à . . . Ségun") to rebuild it ("pour le relever"). As for the present, the priory was being repaired under brother Ségun who "a rebâti la maison. . . . Bientôt il sera reconstruit tout à fait." As for the more distant past and the future, we can only assume from the text that the priory, both architecturally and economically, fully prospered and will prosper, for twice in the same sentence Hugh prefaced verbs with the modifier "re": "Bientôt il sera reconstruit tout à fait et remis en un état prospère." Presumably, "tout à fait" refers to an earlier construction completed in the more distant past.

Scholars dispute the dates of Berzé like every other important Burgundian Romanesque building. Three general dates are most popular for the building, with the turn of the century suggested by Conant ("The Third Church at Cluny," 330, and "Medieval Academy Excavations at Cluny, IX," 5); Joan Evans (*Cluniac Art of the Romanesque Period*, 26): between 1103 and 1106; C. Oursel (*L'art roman*, 11, and "Berzé," 224): 1100 "sans doute possible"; Meyer Schapiro (*The Parma Ildefonsus*, 46): not after the beginning of the twelfth century; Virey ("Berzé," 449): 1100; the years around 1120 appealed to Salet ("Cluny III," 280), while the midpoint of the twelfth century held out more promise for André Grabar ("Peintures murales, notes critiques," 185–186); and Léonce Lex, who changed his opinion to this late date in "Peintures murales de la chapelle du Château des Moines de Cluny à Berzé-la-Ville," 256. For the related debate over the dates of the frescoes of Berzé and the bibliography, see Sauerländer, "Gislebertus," 28, note 23.

Cluny III. While scholars accepted the architecture and sculpture of Cluny III as the model for later copies at Anzy, Avenas, Berzé, Mâcon, Montceaux, Perrecy, and Vézelay, they divided into two camps over Cluny's dates. For a current review of the debate over the dates of the Cluny ambulatory capitals, see Eliane Vergnolle, "Les chapiteaux du déambulatoire de Cluny," 95. Briefly, one group of scholars believed that the major construction of Cluny III began and finished twenty to thirty years earlier than the other. Victor Terret ("Cluny, centre et foyer artistique," 5) perhaps first proposed the early sequence of dates with 1089 for the beginning in the east, 1095 for the completion of the choir and its capitals, and 1109 for the completion in the west except for minor details. Conant suggested that workers began as early as 1081 in the east, that they installed the ambulatory capitals by 1095 and completed the western portal between 1106 and 1112 ("The Apse," 23, 28; *Cluny*, 101). Both A. W. Clapham (*The Monastery of Cluny, 910–1155*, Oxford, 1930) and Evans (*Romanesque Architecture*, 106) agreed on the date of 1115 for the major transept, but Clapham preferred a later date, in the 1120s, for the nave. Helen Kleinschmidt ("The Cluny St. Peter," 17–33), C. Oursel (*L'art roman*, 176, and "Les étapes de la construction de la grande abbatiale de Cluny," 8), and R. Oursel (*Les églises*, 89f.) all followed Porter (*Pilgrimage Roads*, 82), who maintained that the Cluniacs began the choir in 1088, completed it and the ambulatory capitals by 1095, and finished the entire building within a few years after Saint Hugh's death in 1109, that is about 1112 or 1113. Schapiro ("A Relief in Rodez," 65; and "Review of C. Oursel, *L'art roman de Bourgogne*," 229) agreed with the date of 1088–1095 for

the Cluny capitals, but believed that the ambulatory was completed after 1095 and that the western tympanum was finished much later, before 1130. Scher (*Renaissance*, 28) tacked five years onto the sanctuary capitals, but otherwise accepted Porter's dates. J. Talobre (*La construction de l'abbaye de Cluny*, 114–115, 129) in general accepted the earlier theory of dating, assigning 1088 for the opening of the chantier, 1110 for the great transept, and 1117 for the entire structure—with finishing touches until 1135. He believed that the ambulatory capitals were carved after their installation in 1095–1097, however, and dated the western portal sculpture to 1115, before most of the ambulatory sculpture was completed ("La reconstruction du portail de l'église abbatiale de Cluny," 239). Virey ("Les travaux du professeur K. J. Conant à Cluny," 69–70) in large supported Conant's range of dating from 1088 to 1110, specifically 1095 for the ambulatory capitals, 1100 for the great transept ("Les travaux du Professeur J. Conant, à Cluny," 407), and before 1109 for the western portal sculpture ("Les fouilles américaines à Cluny, en 1928," 127). Zarnecki fell in line with these dates, accepting 1088 for the beginning, 1095 for the ambulatory sculpture, and 1107–1115 for the completion of the western portal (*Art of the Medieval World*, 234–235).

Dating the ambulatory capitals later, to about 1150, began principally with Michel (*Histoire*, 190) in 1905, when he proposed a time in the "milieu du XII siècle." Deschamps ("Notes," 69, and "L'âge des chapiteaux," 210) accepted a range of dates between 1125 and 1156 for the capitals, which he believed were carved after the choir was completed in 1109. Salet ("Cluny III," 238–247, 280) allowed that a foundation may have been laid in 1088, but denied sanctuary capitals and vaults as early as 1095. He believed that the choir was completed a little before 1120, the nave by 1132, and the western portal as early as 1109–13. Focillon (*Sculpteurs romans*, 154) and Lücken ("Burgundische Skulpturen," 115) aligned themselves with Michel's date for the ambulatory capitals, while Aubert ("Cluny," 510–514) preferred a unique compromise between the dates of the two groups of scholars. He proposed 1109 for the completion of the choir, 1113 for the finish of the last six western bays including the western portal, and 1120 for the ambulatory capitals, a date Denise Jalabert ("La flore romane bourguignonne," 194) accepted after earlier embracing Deschamps's chronology in *La sculpture romane* (p. 55). Most recently, Whitney S. Stoddard ("The Eight Capitals of the Cluny Hemicycle," 57) suggested a similar date for the hemicycle capitals "slightly later" than the Cluny west portal, which he accepted as 1109–13.

Mâcon. Scholars agreed that the portal sculpture of Saint-Vincent at Mâcon dates after Cluny, but they differed widely in the dates they proposed. Lücken ("Burgundische Skulpturen," 106–107) suggested the end of the eleventh century; Conant ("Le portail monumental en Bourgogne," 23) preferred 1118–1120; a number of scholars settled on a date around the year 1130, including Aubert (*La Bourgogne, la sculpture*, 65), Diemer (*Kapitelle*, 204), Emile Mâle (*L'art religieux du XIIᵉ siècle en France*, 418), Pendergast (*Anzy*, 358), Porter (*Pilgrimage Roads*, 122), and Sauerländer ("Gislebertus," 273). A second group hovered about the year 1150, including Stratford ("Nevers," 302) and Virey ("Mâcon, ancienne cathédrale Saint-Vincent," 469). Frédéric Girond ("Etude archéologique sur le vieux St. Vincent de Mâcon," 2) and Fernand Nicolas (*Le vieux St.-Vincent de Mâcon*) preferred an even later date of 1170.

Montceaux-l'Etoile. Following the impact theory, scholars dated Montceaux after the ambulatory capitals at Cluny. Many of those who dated the Cluny sculpture early in turn placed Montceaux about 1120: C. Oursel ("Filiation," 69), R. Oursel (*Les églises*, 233), Scher (*Renaissance*, 32). Others— Bernhard Kerber, (*Burgund*, 19) and Salet (*Vézelay*, 167)—selected a time after 1130, while Deschamps ("Notes," 76), Jalabert (*La sculpture*, 70), and Lasteyrie (*L'architecture religieuse*, 674) preferred a date closer to 1150.

Paray-le-Monial. Scholars agreed that, aside from the narthex, the church of Paray copied Cluny III, although they disputed the dates of this "vestpocket" edition. Once again, American and local scholars largely preferred earlier dates, between 1100 and 1110, although certain scholars with different backgrounds concurred: Evans (*Romanesque Architecture*, 133), Pierre Héliot ("Remarques sur la cathédrale d'Autun," 186), C. Oursel (*L'art roman*, 84: "long before 1109"), R. Oursel (*Les églises*, 248), and Talobre (*Cluny*, 109). Conant changed his opinion, "well before 1110" ("Excavations at

Cluny, IX," 5) to a later date of 1110–1130 in 1971 ("La chronologie," 346, and "L'abside et le choeur de Cluny III," 8), and Eugène Lefèvre-Pontalis ("Paray-le-Monial," 53) reduced by ten years the date he proposed in *Etude historique et archéologique sur l'église de Paray-le-Monial* (pp. 8–11). The church dated even later, to 1150, according to Lex ("Paray-le-Monial," 466), and to 1220, in the opinion of Cucherat (*Guide historique et archéologique*, 115).

Perrecy-les-Forges. Except for the reference in the *Cartulary of Marcigny* to a gift to the priory in 1108, "in galilea monasterii Parriciaci" (Jean Richard, *Le cartulaire de Marcigny-sur-Loire 1045–1144*, 290), no text directly relates to the narthex of Perrecy or to its sculpture (François Deshoulières, *Au début de l'art roman*, 104; R. Oursel, *Les églises*, 256). While proposing widely varying dates, scholars followed the impact theory by placing the tympanum and lintel sculpture after the Cluny ambulatory capitals. Scholars who proposed eleventh-century dates for the Cluny capitals also tended to date the Perrecy facade sculpture early: R. Oursel (*Les églises*, 259–263): tympanum from the end of the eleventh century, installed in 1120–1125 with a new lintel; R. Raeber (*La-Charité-sur-Loire*, 220): c. 1100. Slightly later dates are preferred by Diemer (*Vézelay*, 202): after 1120; Kerber (*Burgund*, 87, note 56): lintel and jamb capitals before 1130, tympanum even earlier; Porter (*Pilgrimage Roads*, 120): after 1120; Sauerländer ("Gislebertus," 27, note 11): after 1115; Scher (*Renaissance*, 32): 1120–1125. The latest dates were proposed by: Deschamps ("Notes," 76): second quarter of the twelfth century; Lücken (*Burgundische Skulpturen*, 115): later than the early twelfth century; Jalabert (*Sculpture romane*, 70): c. 1150; and Salet (*Vézelay*, 167): 1130–1140.

Vézelay. Following the impact theory, scholars agreed that the portal sculpture of the Madeleine reflected the ambulatory sculpture at Cluny. While concurring in the theory, however, scholars dated the portal sculpture variously, with the Americans and Burgundians again tending toward early dates. Conant ("Cluniac Building During the Abbacy of Peter the Venerable," 121) chose a relatively early date of 1122 for the portal sculpture and a late date of 1132 for the completion of the nave ("Deux traditions," 103); Evans (*Cluniac Art*, 32) dated the portal 1120–1132, and the nave to before 1120 (*Romanesque Architecture*, 78); C. Oursel ("Filiation," 67) saw the facade sculpture as after 1120, the nave along with its sculpture from 1104 to the years immediately after 1110 (*L'art roman*, 179), the same dates posited by Porter (*Pilgrimage Roads*, 88) and suggested by Pierre Truchis ("Eléments barbares, éléments étrangers," 4, note 2), who believed that the transept dated from the end of the eleventh century and the nave from the first "moitié" of the twelfth century.

Many other scholars but especially adherents of the "official" Parisian position believed that a new church largely or entirely replaced the old one destroyed by fire in 1120. Christian Beutler ("Das Tympanon zu Vézelay," 27, note 19): portal begun 1120, nave finished 1140; Deschamps ("Notes," 71–73): reused 1104 capitals in the eastern bays, entirely new nave after 1120, three facade portals 1132; Diemer (*Vézelay*, 33): crossing c. 1100, nave begun at facade in 1120; Frankl (*Baukunst*, 168): nave and facade third decade of the twelfth century, en-

tirely replacing 1104 church; Kerber (*Burgund*, 20) accepted Salet's dates for Vézelay; Jalabert (*Sculpture romane*, 60–64, and *La flore sculptée des monuments du moyen âge en France*, 59): capitals from 1104 reused in the last two bays of the nave which was almost entirely rebuilt after the fire of 1120, while the rest of the nave capitals were left uncarved until c. 1132, when the tympanum was finished; Lasteyrie (*L'architecture romane*, 425): nave of 1104 destroyed in 1120 and rebuilt almost entirely by 1132; Lücken (*Burgundische Skulpturen*, 30, 110–112): nave after 1120, facade portals after Autun; R. Oursel (*Evocation de la chrétienté romane*, 62): crossing 1104, nave 1132; Salet (*Vézelay*, 28, 148): facade portals 1125–1130, crossing 1104, nave 1140–1145; Scher (*Renaissance*, 28–30): portals perhaps begun in 1114, the nave in 1120–1140; Vallery-Radot ("Les analogies des églises de Saint-Fortunat de Charlieu et d'Anzy-le-Duc," 264) accepted Deschamps's chronology.

Second Excursus: Theory of Cluniac Architecture and Sculpture

I

Despite their well-known dispute over dating, both Anglo-Burgundian and Parisian scholars advanced the same theory of Cluniac art. They agreed on a set of abstract principles for the architecture and sculpture of Cluny III, including its spontaneous generation or revolutionary character, under the direct supervision of an intellectual overseer or artistic genius(es), who "selected" from non-local sources, and thus changed the course of Burgundian Romanesque art. These theories link and reinforce each other. If Cluny III was a spontaneous generation in the Mâconnais, then the building's sources must be distant—in time, space, and medium—and local art looking like the mother church must be a reflection of it. Similarly, the theories of spontaneous generation, non-local sources, and impact, support the concept of a genius or intellectual supervisor. The more revolutionary or

spontaneous his work, the more creative was the artist; and the farther afield he looked for sources, the more selective and inspired his choice and the more overwhelming its impact on others.

Bypassing the possibility of local sources and craftsmen in favor of the standard collection of theories, *Kenneth J. Conant* believed that Cluny itself "created the accomplished twelfth-century style as Mr. Porter believed."[1] Combining ideas of an intellectual genius, spontaneous generation, non-local sources and local impact, Conant imagined that a single "brilliant" sculptor, a "great genius,"[2] "familiar" with various media, visited distant lands and returned to formulate a "great personal creation" which he "transmitted" to "followers."

> The grace and finish of these sculptures suggest ivory carving; the rubbing pro-

cess by which the surfaces were finished is actually used on ivory. The minor sculptures were a natural place for *experiment and practice in the new style*. . . . The sculptor must have been familiar with fine *illuminations*, with *ivory* and *marble* carvings, with *stuccoes* and *metalwork* . . . it is not past belief that a *brilliant* young sculptor was *sent out* as a journeyman to form his style. Whether *German, Italian,* or *Byzantine* works lie back of his achievement, surely it was a *great personal creation*, which he *transmitted* to his fellow workers and their followers at Cluny and *far afield*.[3] [my italics]

Completing the hypothesis, the "eminent" young genius, presumably on his return, joined foreigners in an academy of talented intellects who simply outclassed the local talent.

. . . in Hugh's time there was an *academy* of outstanding artists at Cluny. The sculptors no longer occupy a precarious eminence alone, but, joined by the architects and painters, form what may be called the *Academy* of St. Hugh. They were probably *called together from a distance*. Their training *far transcended the local training available in Burgundy*, and it is infinitely likely that they were sent as journeymen to see and observe abroad.[4] [my italics]

Suggesting the same linked theories for the architecture of Cluny III, Conant proposed an innovative and intellectual genius who set the pattern to follow in Burgundy by consciously selecting sources from abroad rather than continuing the local traditions of northern and southern First Romanesque architecture. Avoiding the question of masons in the manufacture of the church, he proposed a more conceptual "functioning constructional organism which produced the building," together with a "great artist," the "first architect" Gunzo, a monk who "created" and "maintained vigorously" a "lucid program . . . in all respects ahead of its time."[5] Conant believed that Gunzo's project "entirely transcends any local style" and reveals an intellectual "integrating process" which "drew upon" the "truly imperial extension of the Order" from "all of Western Europe . . . upon the East, upon the Early Christian and upon Classic art."[6] "Quite naturally" the design "set the norm" for buildings like Paray which "repeat the plan and elevation in reduction."[7]

Charles Oursel, Conant's major ally in the dating dispute, proposed a similar set of linked theories which he refined. He maintained the spontaneous generation theory for the Cluniac sculpture although he preferred the term "renaissance" to "invention."[8] Although Burgundian sculpture "atrophied" in the eleventh century, Oursel allowed that its creators did not "forget how to use the chisel" while they lay in a kind of dormant state waiting for "the occasion to perfect their skills under an energetic impulsion through service in a large work of art."[9] Having suggested such an energetic impulsion, he explored its details more completely than Conant. Drawing parallels to literature, Oursel argued that frequently "the perfection of a type marks the beginning" of a style, and that, as in other arts, the phenomenon of simultaneous currents explains the dramatic difference between Cluniac sculpture at Cluny III and Charlieu: both being Cluniac abbeys is "no reason to make an evolutionary development between [their sculpture and] no reason to assume that the same artists worked at both places." Furthermore, because only what survived is known, Oursel allowed for "reasoning in the dark" and "the possibility of a lost artistic tradition preceding Cluny."[10] Unlike Conant, Oursel recognized "multiplicity and the reciprocal penetration" of the various centers of civilization, although like him he identified two distant and separate media as the "principal sources" for Cluniac sculpture. The "Cluniacs borrowed the style which came to renovate Burgundian sculpture" from German ivories, "issue of Rome, Byzantium, and Charlemagne," and from Italian painters.[11] Like Conant, he believed that "the atelier of Cluny" was "the only one in the province capable of furnishing expert sculptors" and therefore it transformed the style of Burgundian sculpture.[12] Indeed, he believed in a Cluniac "School" of sculpture although unlike Conant he presented his hypothesis in a carefully worded rhetorical question: "One might ask . . . if Cluny did not in fact establish or contribute to establishing an entire system of dogmatic instruction by means of sculpture. . . . In this sense, it is truly legitimate to speak of a Cluniac School of sculpture and ornamentation."[13]

Oursel proposed the same linked set of theories for architecture as for sculpture. Finding no local sources, an intellectual supervisor selected European architectural devices which he and inspired architects formulated into a new building type copied widely in the region. Except for vaults, "eleventh-century Burgundian architecture . . . was continuing along an almost one-way street. . . . It is, in one word, a primitive or primary art which on its own could hardly escape from itself."[14] The intellectual supervisor, "Saint Hugh, to realize his design, researched in all the resources which the West could offer him."[15] Among the non-local sources, Oursel considered Provence "the principal source" and the Auvergne a close second because of the family connection there of many outstanding Cluniac abbots.[16] With Hugh's research completed, "the horizon is suddenly discovered, a definitive formula is found": "he collects all the secular acquisitions into a magnificent original synthesis."[17] In a spontaneous burst, "the architects of the abbey of Cluny defined at the end of the eleventh century a style which was totally original and particular to the monument." It is this "original synthesis . . . which establishes a school" that transformed Burgundian architecture.[18] "Far from Cluny having adopted a particular model of the Burgundian school, it is the opposite, Cluny which gave the initial formula, which has been the prototype of one of the special expressions of Romanesque architecture in Burgundy."[19] "Cluny established the model."[20]

Then, regardless of his position on dating, Oursel repeated the standard linked formula for sculpture and architecture in which a genius or intellectual supervisor consciously selects international sources, formulates a new type, and transforms the regional style.

Meyer Schapiro, while supporting the early dating of Conant and Oursel, added a new level of sophistication and discrimination to the discussion. Unlike the others, he distinguished carefully between media. Because the source, creation, and impact of Cluniac architecture remained a mystery to him, he questioned the spontaneous generation and impact theories as they applied to this medium: "the antecedent architecture is unknown," and there exists "no positive evidence that the Cluny type is a spontaneous and original creation of Cluny itself and that all later forms are explicable only as copies of the first surviving examples."[21] Unfor-

tunately, Schapiro did not offer an alternative explanation and left the origins of Cluniac architecture an open question. Unlike the others, Schapiro postulated a subtle difference in the intellectual and social level between masons and sculptors, and other artists like the "disciplined monks in the Cluniac scriptorium" who created minor arts:

> Compared to older sculpture in precious metals and ivory, stone carving was virile and secular . . . imbued with something of the inventive spirit and daring of the new arts of building; its practitioners, who were most often lay artists, open to nature and common life . . . were less affected by the monastic outlook and the Italian tradition. . . . The capitals of Cluny, I believe, owe their greater freedom and naturalness to the fact that they were made by lay artists, working together with builders in marble and stone. The vigorous art of sculpture is nearer to folk life.[22]

While Schapiro subtly distinguished differences in media and the social position of sculptors, his own contribution presented the old linked theories of spontaneous generation, non-local sources, and impact, in new clothing. In the *Parma Ildefonsus*, Schapiro in effect assumed Cluniac sculpture was a spontaneous generation. While admitting a lack of knowledge of the local scene—"we must admit that we know too little of the regional art of the tenth and eleventh centuries to be able to say what is native"—he proposed several tentative foreign sources for sculpture.[23] He fell back upon the device standard to theories of Cluniac sculpture: multiple international sources, typologically vague and distant in time and place from Burgundy. He suggested certain classical sculptural motifs from Byzantine and Italian Romanesque fresco painting, and a posture stance from unclear Byzantine sources: "in earlier stone carving an older Byzantine factor may be surmised, as in the balanced asymmetrical stance of the angels of the tympanum of Anzy-le-Duc."[24] The local references he made were to anticipatory, general typological qualities found in media different from sculpture. "The style of drawing" in eleventh-century Burgundian painting included "elaborately spun folds and angular bodies that anticipate the web of lines in the great Romanesque tympana."[25] In a separate article, Schapiro added another specific non-local source, a single, fragmentary, undated tympanum from the Rodez Museum.[26] Dating the piece as early as 1040, he did not propose it as an immediate prototype, although he "suggests the possibilities of more direct connections" between the Auvergne and Cluny.[27] Schapiro believed that the Rodez relief had bearing upon the dating and source of Cluny ambulatory sculpture because "the lines on the body of the Fourth Tone at Cluny are later variants of the forms of the Rodez Christ and its Carolingian ancestors"; included in the later variants are an "incised spiral fold" on the belly, "concentric curves in diverging sets," and "discontinuous sets of rhythmic lines."[28]

Besides the methodological problem of using descriptive terms as indefinite in time and place as "spiral fold," "concentric curves," and "rhythmic lines," important theoretical questions limited Schapiro's argument. No date exists for the Rodez relief, so that it would have been helpful for him to explain why the sculpture of Perrecy and Vézelay post-dated Cluny while the Rodez relief preceded it. Moreover, while Schapiro cited the tradition of Carolingian manuscripts as the principal source for the Rodez relief, recognizing this source contributed little to dating the High Romanesque Cluniac sculpture.

I believe the 1040 date unlikely for the Rodez fragment. If the Cluniac sculptors were secular masonry artists as Schapiro maintained, and if their most immediate source was Auvergnate sculpture like the Rodez relief, then why does all in situ, contemporary masonry figural sculpture around northern Auvergne at the time—such as at Thiers, Saint-Rambert, Ris, Pommiers, Champdieu—look completely different from that of Cluny III? If the counterargument is made that early in the century the Rodez masons went beyond this "folk art," then why is there no later eleventh-century reflection of "higher" Rodez sculpture—based on manuscripts and painting—in the "lower" backwater modes of the Auvergne? And why is there no reflection in the eleventh-century lower Burgundian sites which touch the Auvergne, like Bourbon-Lancy, Souvigny I, Charlieu, and the Perrecy chevet, which share similar masonry, moldings and vegetable sculpture with the Auvergne? It seems contradictory for the Romanesque piece to stand apart from early southern Burgundian and Auvergnate masonry sculpture and act as the principal source for

Cluniac sculptors who Schapiro claimed were familiar with the masonry tradition.

Beyond the question of dating the unique and fragmentary Rodez piece, it probably was speculative for Schapiro to propose the undated work as a source for Cluny. Even more risky, however, was his attempt to move Cluny's dates back in time as a result of his conclusions about the Rodez relief. Schapiro suggested that the Cluniac masons revived the 1040 mode in 1088–95. Conceding a revival for the moment, does not the hypothesis lend itself better to 1130, when a full-fledged interest in linear sculpture was underway at Vézelay and Autun (chapter 5), than to the time of the Cluny ambulatory, when linear surface ridges only tentatively appeared (chapter 4)? Schapiro's final argument that "a work of high sensitivity and skill" at Rodez in 1040 would make more intelligible the early carving of marble capitals in the ambulatory at Cluny overlooked an important detail: the capitals at Cluny are not marble.[29]

Meyer Schapiro offered the most discriminating criticism of the theory of Cluniac art, especially when he separated the histories of different media and the varied perspectives of the men who worked in them. Nevertheless, he hesitated to propose a new theory for architecture, and his theory of sculpture, as in the past, linked a foreign (Auvergnate) source to an original, creative burst sixty years later at Cluny. His attempt to overcome the major obstacle to Porter's 1095 date, "namely, the lack of a native ancestry," probably is not achieved by his attempt "to recognize in the Rodez Christ a product of the preceding period in a line of developing art."[30]

Charles Oursel's son, *Raymond*, agreed with the early dates of his father, Conant, and Schapiro, and proposed the standard constellation of theories—varying the sources only slightly. Unlike the others, Raymond Oursel suggested Brionnais sculpture as a prototype to Cluny, but like them he denied a direct atelier connection between Brionnais sculpture and the sculpture of the Cluny ambulatory. He preferred to speak of a Brionnais "influence" or to word the relationship to Cluny in a tentative, organic metaphor: "the maturation of a foyer of art appears to be centered on the priory of Anzy-le-Duc."[31] Like the others, Oursel imagined that the same inspired artists and intellectual overseer "synthesized" the Brionnais sources from "outside" the immediate region of Cluny. According to the standard formula, he determined that the local "hiatus" in sculpture led "l'intelligente volonté" of Saint Hugh to "search out Brionnais sources."[32] "Did he not ask them to come when he began to construct his grand work? The hypothesis seems to impose itself." "The artists capable of making the synthesis which they made, and only such a group and such an abbot, could realize such a project." "Just as da Vinci or Michelangelo synthesized unto themselves a whole epoque, so Gunzo and Hézelon did so in Romanesque architecture and their unknown collaborators did so in sculpture."[33] Combining inspired sculptors, an intellectual overseer and non-local sources, Oursel extended the impact theory to Vézelay, Perrecy, and the other major Burgundian sites where Cluny's "stylistic filiation can easily be traced."[34]

In architecture as well as in sculpture, Oursel denied the influence of local southern First Ro-

manesque Mâconnais buildings—"the substrata of little rural churches"—on Cluny III, or the possibility of a synthesis of northern and southern First Romanesque architecture at the abbey.[35] Rather he believed "it is in the Brionnais," outside the local region, "where is born this exclusively Burgundian architecture. . . . architecture and sculpture knew there an equal development."[36] Continuing the standard theoretical chain, he proposed that intellectual monks Gunzo and Hézelon "synthesized" Brionnais and other foreign sources at Cluny III and then other major Burgundian buildings "proceeded directly" from the new architectural model.[37] For both architecture and sculpture, Raymond Oursel repeated the accepted formula in which higher minds merged non-local sources into a new Cluniac type, yet he stands out as the only scholar who perceived large-scale precursors near Cluny, in the neighboring Brionnais.[38]

II

The two opposing groups of scholars, the Anglo-Americans and Burgundians, and the Parisians, debated the dating of Burgundian art so continuously that they overlooked their agreement in theory. Among the Parisians, *Paul Deschamps* put forward late dates but embodied them in the standard linked theories. Although he proposed an evolutionary development rather than a spontaneous generation, he described the evolution in biological terms using metaphors of a tree ("Romanesque art normally developed like a tree of which the roots grow with the same regularity") and of a human being ("a human being never arrives at maturity except by passing through the phases of infancy and adolescence. I observe the same phases in Romanesque art"). "I propose a progressive achievement toward the simple and natural attitudes of French art of the thirteenth century, removed of all artifice and exaggeration."[39] When Deschamps presented his actual facts, however, he proposed precursors which he himself admitted were in no way close to Cluny. He then was forced to fall back upon his own version of the spontaneous generation theory, which he combined with the idea of non-local sources from

different media. "One first encounters in the eleventh century maladroit attempts by sculptors who, not having predecessors, imitated other arts of wood, metal and ivory."[40] Deschamps maintained that the Burgundian figural sculpture directly preceding Cluny belonged to this category rather than to the level of the ambulatory sculpture in the mother church. He described the reused "1104" nave capitals of Vézelay as "very crude," the "1109" south aisle capitals of Paray as "painfully misshapen," and the "earlier" Cluny Expulsion capital as "rude and without expression, the proportions are bad, the movements gauche, the vegetable décor is treated with much less talent" and in general "the execution is very inferior" to the Cluny ambulatory capitals.[41] Deschamps' Cluniac evolution exists only as a metaphor because the closest precursors he offered were, according to his own description, rudimentary.

Deschamps argued that the Cluny ambulatory capitals fit the context of post-1120 sculpture at Vézelay, Autun, Beaune, and Saulieu. But even if he dated these buildings and their sculpture correctly, he did not explain their origins and left a large gap in his evolutionary theory. In a sense, he was trapped by his own conclusions: in an attempt to eliminate the possibility of an early Cluny date, he reduced all Burgundian sculpture prior to 1109 to "rude," "crude," and "ungainly" and left no immediate prototype for Cluny and the 1120 group of sculpture. His statement that Burgundian sculpture after 1120 at Cluny, Vézelay, and Autun "permits one admirably to see the phase of evolution which Burgundian sculpture had attained in the first quarter of the twelfth century" bolstered his late dating but begged the evolutionary question because he supplied no intermediaries between sculpture he defined as pre-1109 and post-1120.

While downplaying the genius role for "the" sculptor of the Cluny ambulatory capitals, who he insisted "partakes of his time," Deschamps offered no clear antecedents for him; moreover, Deschamps believed that this sculptor's contemporary, Gislebertus, working in the same "oeuvre," could be "so independent and original."[42] Although Deschamps barely touched upon architecture, like Francis Salet years later, he believed the peripatetic intellectual supervisor Saint Hugh "went from one chantier to another" selecting ideas for a new building which other regional churches like Paray copied as "a replica in miniature."[43]

Francis Salet, the most recent spokesman for the Parisian position, added a complex new twist to the standard linked theories. Unhappy with the "dogma of the idea of an evolution, continuous and regular without brusque mutations and backwaters," he believed that evolution should never be "assumed automatically" as a law: "The biological theory of evolution, which has so profoundly—and so sadly—marked all the philosophical thought of the nineteenth century, insinuated itself even into the history of art of the Middle Ages, imposing the absurd idea of a continuous development, in a way automatic, without the possibility of jumps ahead or throwbacks."[44] Nevertheless, as a Parisian believing in the late date of Cluniac sculpture, Salet defended the evolutionary position against the possibility of a creative genius or a spontaneous artistic generation. He attacked the notion of a genius selecting the parts of Cluny III from an international pool of sources as the "desire to make out of it an exceptional work and, as a consequence, remove it

from the laws of technical and stylistic evolution."[45] And he defended the Parisian dates for the ambulatory capitals based upon an evolutionary model as opposed to the possibility of an "artistic miracle" like the birth of a Donatello or Michelangelo.[46]

Despite his on-again-off-again attraction to the evolutionary theory, when it came to the architecture of Cluny III he believed in a genius concept linked to the other standard theories. While careful to distinguish the latest Cluny III architecture as the achievement of a genius of "une longue patience," he nevertheless described the work as "remarkably audacious" and "the most prestigious achievement of Romanesque art."[47] He believed Cluny III interrupted the earlier Romanesque architectural evolution in the local region. Speaking of southern First Romanesque art, "one has difficulty believing that these relatively modest buildings, left in large part by a bypassed Romanesque art, could act as a model for architecture."[48] Instead, like other scholars, Salet discovered Cluny's sources outside the local region, although patriotically he restricted their locale to the confines of present-day France.[49] Moreover, as in the past, Salet believed that the sources were consciously synthesized, although he did not associate the selection with an intellectual academy or the monks Gunzo and Hézelon. "It is evident that everything at Cluny was thought of in terms of the French experiences."[50] He like Conant proceeded with a typological proof using as evidence the ambulatory with radiating chapels, double transepts, double side aisles, three stories, barrel vault, compound pier, and cupola on squinches, all of which he believed derived from French buildings outside the area of Cluny. And like Conant, Salet linked the concept of a break in local architectural tradition with the theory of an impact from Cluny. Cluny became the sculptural and architectural prototype for all the important dependent Burgundian churches like Vézelay, Paray, Berzé, Perrecy, and Montceaux; he disputed their dates but not the direction of artistic influence from Cluny. Although Salet argued both sides of the evolutionary issue, he vigorously supported the same group of linked theories as the Anglo-American scholars. He simply used these theories to his own end of bolstering the century-old Parisian system of dating Burgundian art.

Notes: Second Excursus

1. Conant, "The Third Church," 336; see also Terret, "La sculpture," 24: "Le système d'ornementation inauguré par l'abbaye de Cluny fut reproduit fidèlement par les maîtres imagiers bourguignons du XIIᵉ siècle"; and Lücken, *Burgundische Skulpturen*, 114. See Porter, *Pilgrimage Roads*, 84 ff.

2. Conant, "Medieval Academy Excavations at Cluny—The Season of 1928," 25: "the great genius who carved the Cluny ambulatory capitals . . . rose fully to a stupendous opportunity." Talobre, *Cluny*, 134–135, similarly believed that a single sculptor, a monk, carved the ambulatory capitals: "nul ne l'a aidé dans sa tâche."

3. Conant, "The Third Church," 338. While Crozet ("A propos," 152) saw in Conant's attempt to find the prototypes for Cluniac sculpture "générosités de sources," and Hans Sedlmayr ("Die Ahnen der Dritten Kirche von Cluny," 49) described Conant's "Stammbaum" as "fast die gesamte Geschichte der romanischen Bau- und Bildkunst aufrollen," most scholars limited the sources of Cluniac sculpture to the medium of painting. See Rufus Morey, "The Sources of Romanesque Sculpture," 20; Porter, *Pilgrimage Roads*, 100: "the sculpture of Cluny here merely translates into stone the types of . . . the miniature artists of Winchester"; Evans, *Cluniac Art*, 120: "Cluniac sculpture is Cluniac painting turned into stone"; W. Worringer, *Über den Einfluss der angelsächsischen Buchmalerei auf die frühmittelalterliche Monumentalplastik des Kontinents*; Jalabert, *Sculpture romane*, 53: "les miniatures jouèrent un rôle prépondérant"; William D. Wixom, "A Manuscript Painting from Cluny," 133. Most recently, M.F. Hearn (*Romanesque Sculpture*, 114) described "the Cluny Master" as "probably a goldsmith from the Meuse region." "Hezelo procured the sculptor" who began working shortly after 1100.

4. Conant, "The Apse," 26; Virey (*Les églises*, 14) similarly believed that "ouvriers habiles et des architectes réputés" were brought together in an international academy; "Les travaux," 75: "Au temps de saint Hugues il y avait à Cluny comme une Académie d'artistes de choix venus probablement de l'extérieur et dont la valeur dépassait tout ce qui avait cours alors en Bourgogne." Héliot ("Cluny," 185) spoke of "la collaboration d'artistes émérites" in "un milieu éminemment favorable un déploiement de leur génie." Focillon (*Peintures romanes*, 51) described Cluny as "un chantier international, où l'on avait fait appel à la collaboration des meilleurs maîtres pour édifier," and Sauerländer ("Gislebertus," 28, note 17) underscored his point: "auf lokaler Basis lösen zu wollen, ist wohl schon im Ansatzpunkt verfehlt."

5. Gunzo was "a great artist . . . the building which he created is certainly in all respects ahead of its time" (Conant, "La chapelle Saint-Gabriel à Cluny," 64); "the large lines of the project by the genial monk Gunzo," "the first architect" (Conant, "L'abside," 3, 7); the design of Cluny III was one intellectually complete project which was "maintained vigorously according to a lucid program" (Conant, "La chronologie," 342). Although Evans (*Romanesque Architecture*, 13, note 1) admitted that "literary sources are not, it must be admitted, strong evidence for the control of the design by the abbot," she found it "difficult to exaggerate the importance of the part played by the abbots of the Order as patrons." She wished to replace Viollet's "moine ouvrier," Hézelon, whom she considered nothing more than a "fund raiser" (p. 10) with a series of "abbé surintendant," erudite managers who realized the building ("Travaux du congrès à Cluny," 44). Salet ("Review of K. J. Conant, *Cluny, les églises et la maison du chef d'ordre*, 184) similarly doubted the importance of the role of the monks Gunzo and Hézelon in the construction of Cluny III.

6. Conant, "The Third Church," 327; Conant based his conclusion almost solely upon "the study of architectural motifs employed," "a method of approach which is worth much study" and which reveals Cluny III as a typological synthesis, the literal "sum of Romanesque architecture" ("The Significance of the Abbey Church," 445). He selected Italy as the major intermediary source for pointed arches, vaults, and portals, which he observed at Monte Cassino and Salerno ("The Third Church," 327). Before he deleted pilasters from his apse reconstruction, Conant declared their "only-too-obvious connection with the nave of S. Paolo fuori le Mura at Rome" ("The Third Church," 336). Moslem builders contributed major motifs like horseshoe cusping and small clerestory windows enclosed by a decorative arcade with paired columns ("Medieval Academy Excavations at Cluny" [1954], 11). For his most recent statement of the international "genesis" of Cluny III, see "Early Examples of the Pointed Arch and Vault in Romanesque Architecture," 203–209, where in addition to his previous opinions, he suggested that Cluny's straight-arris groin came from Monte Cassino. The vault can be found closer at hand in the side aisles of Anzy-le-Duc.

7. Conant, "Deux traditions," 8.

8. C. Oursel, *L'art roman*, 189.

9. Ibid., 190–191.

10. Ibid., 173, 190–191.

11. Ibid., 204–205.

12. Ibid., 180.

13. Ibid., 189.

14. Ibid., 54ff. Virey (*Les églises*, vii–viii) rewrote his introduction to reflect the point of view of Oursel. He described the Mâconnais "églises rurales d'importance secondaire, n'ont pas fourni le cadre ou les dispositions caractéristiques de la grande église de Cluny." The ab-

bey of Cluny for him constituted a "véritable révolution," as it appeared to Deshoulières ("Le rôle de Cluny," 413–434) to be a "génération spontanée." See also Talobre (*Cluny*, 91, 108), who saw in the "abbatiale de Saint-Hugues . . . le recul définitif de l'art méditerranéen du premier art roman . . . un abandon si total de traditions architecturales."

15. C. Oursel, *L'art roman*, 59.

16. C. Oursel, *L'art roman*, discussed specific typological devices without precision in time or place for their transfer to Burgundy. For relations of Cluny to Provence, see 158, and to the Auvergne, 69, 80–84.

17. Ibid., 59–60.

18. Ibid., 58–60.

19. C. Oursel, "La genèse monumentale de l'église abbatiale de Vézelay," 31–50; *L'art roman*, 97.

20. C. Oursel, *L'art roman*, 58.

21. Schapiro, "Review of Charles Oursel, *L'art roman de Bourgogne*," 227.

22. Schapiro, *Parma*, 55–58. Evans (*Cluniac Art*, 114) went even farther in Schapiro's direction: "It is more than likely that the figures were carved by a more or less illiterate sculptor." A monk or skilled scribe placed the inscription for him to carve. She found no "specific evidence for the employment of a Cluniac monk as a sculptor" (p. 4). In addition, "the literary sources are not, it must be admitted, strong evidence for the control of the design by the abbot" (*Romanesque Architecture*, 13, note 1); nevertheless, she assumed that the abbot filled the role of artistic overseer (pp. 12–13).

23. Schapiro, *Parma*, 54.

24. Ibid., 38, 57.

25. Ibid., 55.

26. Schapiro, "A Relief in Rodez and the Beginnings of Romanesque Sculpture in Southern France," 40–66.

27. Ibid., 64.

28. Ibid., 63–64. The "strong relief" and "deep undercutting" of the Cluny capitals depend upon the "intervening growth of plasticity of the capital."

29. Ibid., 65; Conant (*Cluny*, 188) stated that the apse capitals are "calcaire de grain fin; couleur de crème, et plus gras que le calcaire normand; il y a des ondes blénâtres et des rognons de silex."

30. Schapiro, "A Relief," 65.

31. R. Oursel, *Floraison*, 409. When interviewed in Mâcon 29 April 1977, R. Oursel said that "Anzy is not the place where the Cluniac sculptors first worked but where the manner of sculpture seen in the Cluny capitals was first worked out." He suggested none of the Brionnais examples I put forward in the text as possible prototypes for Cluny. Scher (*Renaissance*, 32) and Vergnolle ("Autour d'Anzy-le-Duc," 3–13) accepted Oursel's argument that the nave sculptures of Anzy were pivotal in the formation of the Cluny ambulatory style of sculpture. Perhaps the earliest statement of this position was made by Abbé Nicot (cote 726, Archives de Saône-et-Loire, Mâcon, n.d.): the nave capitals "offrent, déjà la justesse de mouvement et de proportions ainsi que la science technique de l'école clunysienne."

32. R. Oursel, "La Bourgogne dans l'art roman," 350.

33. R. Oursel, *Les églises*, 89; *Bourgogne romane*, 30–31: "l'éblouissante synthèse monumentale."

34. R. Oursel, "Mise au point," 350.

35. R. Oursel, *Les églises*, 128, 170.

36. Ibid., 110.

37. Ibid., 89, 94.

38. Another scholar, Lücken (*Die Anfänge der burgundischen Schule*), in a lucid and conceptual manner set out to trace the origins of Cluniac architecture and sculpture in Burgundy. Unfortunately, he made two assumptions which affected his conclusions. The first applied to the eleventh-century buildings he studied: he assumed that all major Burgundian churches followed Franz Kugler's abstract, linear model in which buildings became increasingly "organic" with greater "interpenetration" of "load" and "support" over the course of the eleventh century (pp. 17–18, 21, 37–38). Believing this, Lücken perceived no important stylistic differences among contemporary Burgundian buildings—for example, he entirely overlooked the separate northern and southern First Romanesque traditions of construction at the beginning of the century. Based on the Kugler system, he believed that the highly articulated crypt of Tournus reflected a late date rather than the early and unique preference of Loire Valley masons for ashlar, compound piers, classical bases, moldings, etc. (see appendix 1). Lücken applied a linear naturalistic principle to sculpture similar to the biological system he used for architecture. By his estimation, the drapery and foliage of the Autun choir capitals predated their counterparts at Cluny because of their reduced naturalistic and increased schematic character, 44–45: "das Blattwerk nur roh und schematisch angegeben, in Cluny dagegen sind die Blätter schon von naturalistischer Bildung."

A second problem beset Lücken's otherwise rare attempt to search for Cluny's roots in Burgundy. For buildings constructed after the turn of the century, he replaced Kugler's organically developing architectural system with the standard formula of a revolutionary Cluniac art derived from international sources (p. 39). As the subtitle of his book (*Ein Beitrag zum Aufleben der Antike in der Baukunst des XII. Jahrhunderts*) implied, he believed that the builders of Cluny abandoned the lessons of local small churches for international antique influences, albeit embodied in Burgundian Roman ruins, 41: "All das, was die burgundischen Bauten vom Ende des 11. Jahrhunderts der Gotik näherte, wird wieder aufgegeben, man kommt zur Mauergebundenheit der Antike zürück."

39. Deschamps, "Notes," 80; "L'âge des chapiteaux," 165.

40. Deschamps, "Notes," 80.

41. Deschamps, "L'âge des chapiteaux," 170–171, 214.

42. Ibid., 172, 206. Deschamps described the Cluny and Vézelay capitals as contemporary, and those at Autun as more likely just a few years later.

43. Ibid., 168, 173.

44. Salet, "Review of R. Raeber, *La Charité-sur-Loire*," 348.

45. Salet, "Cluny III," 273.

46. Ibid. Salet referred to Gunzo's possible participation in the enterprise as "a pious legend" (p. 271) and to Hézelon as only "perhaps one of the architects" (p. 291, note 5). It seemed to Salet that great innovative artists were restricted to periods like the Renaissance: "the style manifestly very evolved of the ambulatory capitals, which certain people prefer to ignore in favor of I do not know what artistic miracle due to the presence at the Cluny workshop of a Donatello, of a Michelangelo of the eleventh century" (Salet, "Review of K. J. Conant," 184).

47. Salet, "Cluny III," 273, 292.

48. Ibid., 249, note 1.

49. As is traditional among the Parisians, Salet ("Cluny III," 273) suggested that the most important source was Saint-Etienne of Nevers. See Lasteyrie ("La sculpture de Bourgogne au XIIᵉ siècle," 227), who described the Nevers elevation as "le véritable prototype du parti adopté par l'école bourguignonne."

50. Salet, "Cluny III," 272.

PART II:

ARCHITECTURE

2

The Architecture of Cluny III

The Cluny Atelier and the Northern
First Romanesque Tradition

I

In the first part of the chapter, I shall explore the northern First Romanesque tradition of the Atelier who dominated construction on the ground floor at Cluny. Although this tradition began more than one hundred years earlier, the traditional attitudes and techniques still influenced the ashlar masons at the mother church. In appendix 1, I describe this previous northern tradition, but here I shall concentrate on the series of changes the Atelier made in it and the particular vocabulary they developed from it. I shall attempt to prove that before Cluny the Atelier worked in order on the facade at Anzy, the narthex of Mâcon and Perrecy, and the nave of Vézelay and Montceaux. By looking at these buildings in sequence, we may come to appreciate the stylistic changes the masons achieved before Cluny.

Like a modern day construction company with a fixed number of employees, the Atelier was composed of a group of men, different members of which were sent to various sites, depending on the job. Some of the men left marks on the masonry, from which we can see that a pool of masons from the Atelier worked at all these sites (the Atelier's marks are charted in Fig. 36). While not every mason worked at each site, an overwhelming number of the same masons worked on these buildings and we can reasonably speak of one Atelier. For example, of the twelve masons who worked on the earliest building, the western campaign at Anzy, nine of them eventually completed the Vézelay first campaign (which included approximately eight courses of the aisles and facade), and seven finished the Montceaux nave. Indeed, of the three Anzy masons who did not work on the first campaign at Vézelay, two of them left their mark at Montceaux. Similarly, masons of the Atelier who worked on the second building at Saint-Vincent, Mâcon, also worked at most of the other sites. Of the seven masons identified at Mâcon, two worked at two of the other sites; three others worked at all three other buildings of Anzy, Perrecy, and Montceaux, and six of them worked on the Vézelay first campaign. In fact, five of the seven masons at Mâcon and ten of the nineteen from the first campaign of Vézelay worked at Perrecy, statistics which perhaps explain the unique and strikingly similar motifs shared by these three buildings (Figs. 10d, 10e; 13a, 13b). With the exception of mason 3 at Paray, all the masons who left marks on the first campaigns at Cluny and Paray—six at Cluny and sixteen at Paray—were part of the Atelier responsible for the construction of these other churches.

By seeing how these men worked at the different churches, we can understand artistic changes in the light of men's careers instead of attributing visual differences to new artists, provincialism, simultaneous currents, or flights of genius. To be able to link positively artistic changes to individuals working over time is a breakthrough in the study of Burgundian Romanesque architecture, yet it does not in itself reveal the order in which the churches were built. Indeed, there may not have been an order in the strict sense of the word: the same or different masons from the Atelier may have worked simultaneously at various sites or moved from one partially completed structure to another. Although many of their works, like the chevet at Paray or the clerestory and facade at Anzy, were only sections of larger structures, it is most unlikely that *all* these great works of Burgundian Romanesque could have been created simultaneously. More probably, however, the Atelier finished each project in a short time because projects usually were either small buildings like the Montceaux chapel and the first story of the Perrecy narthex, or limited sections of larger buildings like the aisle campaigns of Cluny and Vézelay.

Without being rigid or insisting on a single chain of events, I believe that we can establish a relative chronology for these buildings by using a straightforward working hypothesis. From the masons' marks I can see that different men from different traditions did not work at each site, but rather the same Atelier with the same background repeatedly worked together on the same structures. Knowing that the pool of workers was constant and homogeneous, I can establish within their buildings a consistent order relatively free from outside artistic interference. Those buildings which correspond most to earlier northern First Romanesque designs I assume come at the beginning of the sequence. Instead of relating buildings on the basis of vague notions like comparative space, I prefer to concentrate on the more routine aspects of design, such as bases and moldings, which I believe offer a more precise standard for comparison based on their numerous and complexly arranged details. I find that many specific elements of both masonry and architectural decoration change over the same sequence of buildings. I shall first look at architectural decoration and masonry details, and then examine the articulation of portals and interiors.

II

The best way to see the sequential change is to follow the same motifs as they appear in different buildings. We will use as a basis of comparison acanthus (Fig. Series 11), scroll (Figs. 10b–10f), and egg-and-dart (Fig. Series 12) base designs as well as cavet (Fig. Series 5) and cyma (Figs. 7, 8) molding profiles. It is important to realize that from the beginning the Atelier combined classical and Brionnais decorative patterns: for example, on the exterior at Mâcon (Fig. 6a) they applied a plinth molding with a purely classical scotia-torus profile upon which they set a base carved in the Brionnais manner with a grotesque Romanesque figure (Fig. 13a).[1]

Although the Atelier used classical and Brionnais motifs simultaneously, they changed them in much the same way over time. In principle, moving from Anzy, Mâcon, Perrecy, and Montceaux to the first campaigns of Vézelay and Cluny, the same masons progressively reduced the details of bases and moldings in size and compressed their shape. They shifted the overall vertical profile to a more diagonal direction and proportionally reduced the size of the fillet borders. Outside, they turned the torus from a rounded to a more segmented shape. And on the inside, they increasingly closed the scotia.

These changes in the decorative details will be seen to have occurred regardless of their function as moldings (Fig. Series 5) or bases (Fig. Series 10, 11, 12), and regardless of their motifs, classical (Fig. Series 12) or Brionnais (Figs. 13a, 13b), vegetable (Fig. Series 11) or figural. One cannot, of course, expect to see anything like a biological development in art objects or even the same degree of change between parts of each building, because the same individual members of the Atelier did not work on every building and because certain masons could have worked on two or more buildings as they were being built simultaneously. Nevertheless, because of the movement of masons among the sites, it is correct to speak of changes in a single Atelier over a sequence of buildings. Despite the inconsistencies and differences among the workers, the architectural parts of each successive campaign show a marked difference and a definite direction of change.

Let us first examine moldings. In the course of time, the members of the Atelier reduced the size of edge details. They decreased the relative size of the abacus block and the fillet chamfers; moreover, they increased the number of these edge details and inclined diagonally the profile of the molding. By these four changes—in the abacus block and fillet chamfers, the number of details and the molding profile—the masons created a cascade of small-scale details which corresponded to their changing taste in figural sculpture for smaller, less projecting drapery plates with reduced chamfer edges (see chapter 4).

Two molding types will be considered. The first type was modelled from a long-standing northern First Romanesque design where the string course is a simple cavet with or without a torus running through the center.[2] By the eleventh century this type occurs throughout Burgundy; it appears in the northern First Romanesque Tournus crypt (appendix 1 and Fig. 14a), the mid-century chevet of Perrecy and Châtel Censoir, and, significantly, in the naves of Charlieu and Anzy (Figs. 5a, 25a)—the largest Brionnais buildings preceding the formation of the Atelier. In the earliest example of the Avenas

Master's sculpture (Fig. 5b) and in the first architecture of the Atelier at Anzy (Fig. 5c), the cavet chamfers, or fillets, are relatively large, about half the size of the torus. Increasingly in later examples such as Mâcon (Fig. 5d), the chamfered fillets increase in number and are reduced to the size of diminutive border strips ("a"). In later examples like Montceaux (Fig. 5e), the size of the fillets is reduced even further to linear incisions, and they are joined by smaller tori and scotiae, which together form a multifaceted surface of small projecting parts. Similarly, the abacus reduces in relative size from the earlier (Fig. 5b) to the later moldings (Fig. 5e), fitting the pattern of smaller parts aligned in an increasingly diagonal profile.

The second type of molding, the cyma molding, was changed in a similar way. In an early example at Mâcon (Fig. 6a), the bordering tori almost equal the size of the scotia, and the profile is almost vertical compared to the later example of the molding from the first campaign at Vézelay (Fig. 7), where the fillets are smaller, the tori less round, and the scotia curves into a diagonal doucine. By the time of Cluny (Fig. 8), the Atelier frequently removed all but the abacus from the top half of this molding, leaving the beautifully simple doucine shape on the bottom. In line with the changes we have seen, they further increased the diagonal profile by extending the sloping tip of the cyma curve, and they decreased the relative size of the abacus block and the segmental curve of the torus at the base of the molding.

As they made changes in the moldings, the members of the Atelier changed six important features of the bases they carved in the series of buildings from the western campaign of Anzy to the freestanding nave campaign of Vézelay.[3] Just as the cavet chamfer narrows to fillets in the moldings, the size of the tori becomes increasingly small in relation to the size of the central decorative motif, be it acanthus (Fig. Series 11), scroll (Figs. 10b–10f), or egg-and-dart (Fig. Series 12). The workers thus gradually modified the standard northern First Romanesque design in which the base is a vertically stacked series of almost identically sized torus moldings (Fig. 9a). The standard type is found throughout eleventh-century construction in Burgundy, in the mid-century chevet of Châtel Censoir and significantly even on the portal of Charlieu (Figs. 9b, 77a), the largest Brionnais building preceding the appearance of the Atelier. Very much like these earlier models, the undecorated (Fig. 10a) and decorated (Fig. 10b) scroll bands on the bases at Avenas almost equal the size of the lower torus. After Avenas, however, at Mâcon (Fig. 10c) the scroll motif was increased about a third in relation to the tori; in the first campaign of Vézelay (Fig. 10e) it was almost doubled in relative size; and at Montceaux (Fig. 10f) it was enlarged further at the tori's expense.

The relative increase in the size of the scotia is part of two other changes: the size of the lower torus increases in relation to that of the upper torus, while the profiles of both tori take on an increasingly segmental shape. In most northern First Romanesque bases (Fig. 9a), the tori are equal in size and fully semicircular, characteristics also found in the Brionnais bases from the end of the eleventh century in the Charlieu nave and portal (Figs. 9b, 12b) and in the Anzy nave (Figs. 11a, 9c). Bases from the altar at Avenas (Fig. 10b) again retain the northern First Romanesque proportions, but the tori in the Mâcon bases are changed (Figs. 11b, 10c). The upper torus from Mâcon is only three-quarters the size of the lower, and the bottom edge of the lower torus is only slightly undercut, leaving less than a fully semicircular profile. These changes, however, are limited compared to later stages of the Atelier's work, as on the freestanding piers of the Vézelay nave (Figs. 12d, 11f) where the profile of the lower torus is more than double that of the upper, and where each is no more than a quarter circle in profile. At Vézelay the segmental shape of the tori profile is emphasized by the introduction of a fillet on the upper and lower edge of the scotia which cuts off the profile on the inside of the base. By contrast, on the bases from the first campaign at Vézelay (Figs. 12c, 11d, 10e), the lower torus is only a third again as large as the upper torus, and the profiles of both tori well exceed a quarter circle. Yet these bases show the pattern of change when compared to the even earlier bases at Perrecy (Fig. 10d)—the segmental shape of the profile and the difference in size between the tori are more pronounced.

Another change consistently occurs in the bases of these buildings. The profile of the base becomes increasingly diagonal, from almost a plumb vertical line at Mâcon (Fig. 10c) to an angle of almost forty-five degrees at Montceaux (Fig. 10f) and in the nave at Vézelay (Fig. 12d). Second, the curvature of the scotia dish becomes increasingly exposed, as shown, for example, in the acanthus series (Figs. 11a–11f). Following northern First Romanesque models, the earlier Brionnais bases like those in the Anzy nave (Fig. 11a) exhibit little undercutting in the central decorative band. The bases at Avenas and Mâcon (Fig. 11b) carry on this tradition by exposing little of the concave scotia dish: only at Perrecy (Fig. 11c) does the rounded under-surface become definitely recognizable. At Perrecy the triangular space separating each acanthus vine widens, and then widens even further in bases of the first campaign of Vézelay (Fig. 11d), so that each acanthus motif stands out as a separate undercut form in front of the scotia dish. The scotia dish becomes more pronounced at Montceaux (Fig. 10f) until finally in bases of the freestanding pier campaign of Vézelay (Fig. 11f) it projects into a fillet at its curved top and bottom.

In a final significant change, the surface of the bases becomes more regular and finished throughout these buildings. The evidence is clear although erosion and damage in many cases make this quality difficult to see. For example, the earliest tori at Avenas and Mâcon are uneven and irregular; the profiles vary in circumference and sag as much as an inch around the base (Figs. 10b, 11b). By the time of the Vézelay freestanding campaign (Fig. 12d), the Atelier seem to have employed primitive templets to regularize the profiles of tori and scotiae around the base. In addition they polished the decorative surfaces, replacing the irregular and marked surface of earlier bases (Fig. 10a) with a smooth and shiny finish seen in the egg-and-dart motif (Fig. 12d).

To sum up: the Atelier made four notable changes in the moldings in their building sequence: the relative size of (1) the abacus block and (2) the fillet chamfer decreases, while (3) the number of fillets and (4) the diagonal profile of the entire molding increase. They made six notable changes in the bases: (1) the central decorative band increases in size in relation to the tori; (2) the lower torus increases in size in relation to the upper torus; (3) both tori take on an increasingly segmental shape; (4) the entire base profile becomes more diagonal; (5) more of the scotia dish is exposed; and (6) the regularity of profile and polish of the finish increase. The changes in the moldings and bases are analogous in that the relative size of the tori and fillets diminishes while the profile becomes increasingly diagonal. Moreover, all the changes occur sequentially in the same series of buildings. In establishing this pattern of change in moldings and bases from building to building, we see the first concrete evidence of the sequence of the Atelier's career.

The simultaneous changes of these many architectural details indicate that the Atelier's origins are primarily in the northern First Romanesque masonry tradition, from which the Atelier gradually formed a distinctive vocabulary. In their earliest works, the Atelier largely followed the northern First Romanesque pattern of treating the decorative motifs and their framing elements equally (Figs. 9a, 10a): they created tori and scotiae of the same size and diameter and stacked them vertically. The carving is shallow, with little difference in depth between undercut background and surface design; and both are finished with irregular chisel strokes. By the time they completed the nave of Vézelay, however, the Atelier seemed to have come to appreciate the effects of projecting, undercut decoration. They no longer stacked parts equally but changed the proportion of torus to scotia while creating not a vertical but an increasingly diagonal profile. They distinguished the size, circumference, and proportion of border elements from the central decorative motif. These changes in detail correspond to changes in masonry and in larger architectural parts, as will be seen in the next two sections.

III

In analyzing the architectural decoration of the Atelier, we observed a series of changes. In arranging these changes in a sequence, we assumed that the Atelier first worked on buildings with bases and moldings most closely resembling northern First Romanesque models. Now we will look at the masonry of the Atelier, and again we shall note a series of modifications in the northern First Romanesque model. These changes become increasingly marked over the same sequence of buildings we established according to changes in architectural details, thus making more viable our assumption about the Atelier's career.

The largest remaining Burgundian northern First Romanesque construction is the crypt of Tournus, a structure built in sharp contrast with the southern First Romanesque narthex (appendix 2). Unlike their southern counterparts who applied mortar sparingly in even courses, the masons who built the crypt came from the Loire Valley and revelled in mortar almost as a separate medium (see appendix 1 for a full description of northern First Romanesque construction). In their hands, mortar frequently occupied half the wall surface and disrupted courses of fill masonry (Saint-Philibert, Tournus, Fig. 19; Saint-Michel-sur-Loire, Fig. 20; Saint-Wandrille, Fig. 21; Saint-Laurent, Tournus, Fig. 22b). Besides using mortar constructively, the northern masons also applied it imaginatively to decorative areas. They left the wooden grain of slats impressed on the surface of freshly poured vaults (Fig. 14a). While they let the mortar project between masonry joints (Fig. 18), the masons frequently added an extra layer of mortar to joints which they then smoothed into rounded and pointed peaks (Figs. 17, 18), and they even created the illusion that these joints continued into the abacus block by carving false mortar joints in the stone (Figs. 14b, 15, 16).

Unlike the southern masons who chiseled and chipped the surface of brick-like stones well into the eleventh century (Figs. 41, 42, 43, 44a), Loire Valley masons from the tenth century used the axe to create swirl patterns on large ashlar blocks (Figs. 14a, 17, 18). Instead of running the uniform brick-like stones in courses across wall bays in the southern technique, they divided and outlined parts of the building (Figs. 20, 21, 23) by placing ashlar blocks in strips, up buttresses, responds and windows. Brick or brick-like stone (Figs. 19, 22a) they reserved for a unique, petite type of opus spicatum ("a"), or for a single vertical filler or "blade" ("b"), as the French describe it.

At Charlieu and Mont Saint-Vincent, among the largest churches built in the Brionnais before the Atelier worked there (chapter 3), masons used the specific northern First Romanesque techniques of extra pointing ("1" in Figs. 24c, and 78b), vertical "blade" fillers in brick or brick-like stone ("2" in Figs. 24b, 24c; Figs. 78b, 79), swirling axe strokes ("3" in Figs. 78b, 79, and Fig. 77a), and irregular rubble set in oversized mortar beds ("4" in Figs. 24a, 24b).[4] While following the northern First Romanesque techniques, masons who built the Anzy nave aisle (Fig. 24d) varied the tradition in that they extended framing stones into the area of filler masonry ("a") and they used fewer "blade" stones.

The Atelier continued to use the northern First Romanesque techniques found in these later eleventh-century Brionnais churches but refined them in building their own series of churches. Beginning with the western bay clerestory and facade at Anzy (Fig. 24e), and extending to the upper story of Cluny (Fig. 66), the Atelier gradually worked their masonry into larger more horizontally proportioned ashlar, cut with sharper corners, finished with a more even and less deep axe stroke, and set in more regular courses between smaller mortar beds.

The Atelier's work on the facade and clerestory at Anzy (Fig. 24e), when compared with the Anzy aisle campaign (Fig. 24d), shows how much more wall surface the Atelier devoted to ashlar framing stones.[5] They increased the size of these stones, in the horizontal direction especially, and as a result needed fewer of them to line windows and buttresses. The Atelier also made the filler stones increasingly even, rectangular, and smooth (Figs. 24f, 24g), placing them in smaller, more uniform mortar beds. To eliminate northern First Romanesque rubble fill, the Atelier extended the larger framing ashlar completely across the filler course area, tentatively with smaller courses in the first campaign at Vézelay (Fig. 226c) and then with full-sized framing stones at Montceaux ("a" in Fig. 24g).

In a similar way, and in the same sequence of buildings, the Atelier gradually changed the appearance of the plain ashlar used without fill stones. In the western campaign of Anzy (above the dotted line in Fig. 25b) and at Mâcon (Fig. 26b), they followed the older northern First Romanesque pattern found in the Tournus crypt (Fig. 14a) and Anzy nave (below the dotted line in Fig. 25b); they used predominantly squarish or even vertical ashlar—irregularly sized, unevenly shaped, roughly finished—which they set between wide courses of mortar dotted with vertical "blades." As they slowly increased the size and horizontal proportion of the stones at Perrecy (Figs. 27b, 27c), the first campaign of Vézelay (Fig. 28, the lower courses "A" as described in appendix 6), Montceaux (Fig. 24g), and the first campaign of Cluny (Fig. 64a), they evened courses, narrowed mortar beds, reduced axe strokes to faint lines, and almost eliminated vertical "blades."[6]

When the Atelier reached Cluny, they continued their own longstanding tradition of northern First Romanesque ashlar construction but blended it with an unfamiliar southern First Romanesque technique. The new combined masonry type set the standard for Cluniac architecture. How and why it was brought about will be discussed in detail in the context of southern architecture in the second part of chapter 2. What is important here is to understand the role of the members of the Atelier, as masons, in the design process. Two important questions, one about the relation of masons to sculptors, and the other about the origins of Cluniac architecture in regional design, can be answered by observing the role of the Atelier in the initial Cluny campaign. Members of the Atelier worked the ashlar on buttresses, jambs, and responds all around the ground story of Cluny as can be seen by identifying marks placed on the stones (Fig. 8). But no marks appear on the fill masonry of the ground story. In the minor transept, for example, their marks skip from the ashlar of the chapel voussoirs (Fig. 62c), to the southern portal jamb (Fig. 8), to the western dosserets (Fig. 63a). Thus, a hierarchy or distinction in task between a fill and frame mason, unknown in the Atelier's previous buildings, appears for the first time at Cluny.

Before Cluny—that is, on the facade at Anzy (Fig. 25a), at Mâcon (Fig. 26b), Perrecy (Fig. 27b), Vézelay (Figs. 24f, 28), and Montceaux (Fig. 24g)—the Atelier's marks are left on all types of stones, even the filler stones connecting ashlar blocks; moreover, the marks which appear throughout these buildings on a simple frame and fill construction recur on tympana sculpture. Master **B** signed a voussoir on the Mâcon central tympanum (Fig. 29b) and in addition worked as a simple mason in the buildings at Perrecy and Paray (Fig. 36). Of the two masters who signed the southern tympanum voussoirs at Vézelay (Figs. 30b, 30c), Master ⋊ carved at least forty-one plain blocks of Vézelay stone while Master **E** more than doubled that amount (Fig. 31). In addition, Master **E** , a most active mason, signed fifty stones at Anzy (Fig. 24e), fifteen at Perrecy, six at Paray, and strategic jamb stones on the portals at Vézelay (Fig. 32) and Cluny (Fig. 8). In this context Master ⱨ and the Plus Master are perhaps most important: Master ⱨ left his mark on figural jamb sculpture, at Montceaux (Fig. 2a), as well as on simple ashlar blocks at Anzy (Figs. 24e, 36); and the Plus Master not only signed (+) three figural sculptures in the central portal of Vézelay (Figs. 33a, 33b), but he also contributed a great quantity of plain ashlar to the Vézelay nave (Fig. 34) and four other Atelier sites (Fig. 36). By means of these marks, then, we can understand for the first time that the later-medieval and Renaissance distinction between a sculptor and a mason did not exist in the major Atelier before they encountered southern masons at Cluny. Moreover, because these masons frequently were sculptors, it will hardly come as a surprise to see in chapter 4 that the different media of sculpture and architecture underwent markedly parallel changes.

Finally, we can now definitely say that the technique of ashlar carving and decorative architectural details used at the mother church had a local origin or source since the Atelier that worked on the first campaign at Cluny had worked on a succession of buildings before it. This we know by observing parallel changes in moldings, bases, and masonry in buildings where the Atelier's masons' marks reappear. Moreover, careful examination of the architectural details makes it clear that the members of the Atelier worked out of a longstanding northern First Romanesque masonry tradition and did not require the guidance of overseeing intellectuals inspired by foreign sources to design their churches.

IV

From the architectural details and masonry of the Atelier, let us turn to the relationship of parts as seen in the articulation of their buildings. Like their handling of other architectural elements, the masons moved away from northern First Romanesque prototypes in the same sequence of buildings. Around the year 1000, both northern and southern First Romanesque masons used details and construction techniques especially appropriate to their different systems of articulation. In the second half of this chapter we shall see that in southern architecture, with its uniform, brick-like masonry courses, masons articulated the exteriors of their churches with the Lombard system of continuous corbel tables and Lombard bands (Fig. 38a): corbel tables extend continuously in the horizontal direction between bays, and Lombard bands run uninterruptedly, vertically between stories. Similarly, within these buildings continuous bands or orders—usually without the interruption of bases, moldings or capitals—connect transverse arch, dosseret and compound pier, and in effect erase the visual distinction between these parts (Fig. 41). The continuous articulation of southern First Romanesque architecture quite suited its uniform brick-like material.

In contrast, northern First Romanesque masons from the Loire Valley used different construction materials to create an almost opposite articulation (Tournus, Figs. 14a, 19; Saint-Wandrille, Fig. 21). Instead of using one stone shape in continuous courses, they used different stone types and distinguished ashlar from rubble, frame from fill, and veneer from wall. These differences in construction lent themselves to a different sort of articulation. Instead of creating a continuum of parts, the northern First Romanesque masons accented the points where parts separated; these points were defined by joints, moldings, bases, and for the first time on a wide scale, punctuated with figural capitals and compound piers.

The northern worker employed these different materials and articulating devices in an interior elevation and plan that was likewise broken into separate parts. While the southern mason stressed the vertically continuous elements of the elevation, his northern counterpart emphasized horizontal divisions. Usually he preferred the horizontal line of a wooden roof to a vault, as in Saint-Wandrille (Fig. 21). When he selected a vault he chose a groin or a broken barrel which ended in pointed webs instead of a tunnel vault which continued into the wall plane (Fig. 14a); for added measure he accented the bottom edge or springing of each web, formeret, and order with a molding or a capital (Figs. 14a, 15, 16). With these two decorative devices together he capped the dosserets and responds at their summit while he terminated them below with bases and socles. In addition to horizontal interruptions, the northern mason preferred low and wide interior proportions to the high narrow bays which complemented the vertically continuous orders of the South. And he selected a horizontally spread and broken-up ambulatory plan with radiating chapels for almost every major northern First Romanesque cathedral (e.g., Chartres and Auxerre).

At the end of the eleventh century, if the Atelier had looked for models among the major Brionnais churches in the vicinity of their first projects—the facade at Anzy and narthex at Mâcon—they would have found naves articulated in the traditional northern First Romanesque fashion at Anzy and Charlieu (Figs. 25b, 77a). In the naves of both of these buildings, the wall is a single plane framed at the top by pointed webs of groin or broken barrel vaults, and at the bottom by pronounced moldings.[7] A horizontal molding links the stepped archivolts at the springing of each arcade and separates the figural capitals, columns, and bases from the wall above them. In other respects, however, the horizontal articulation of these buildings is less than fully explored, perhaps due to the influence of continuous orders from southern First Romanesque in Burgundy: string courses are almost unknown; moldings rarely continue horizontally from the imposts onto the wall plane of the nave; and the impost moldings are usually limited to individual orders—in the Charlieu portal (Fig. 77a) the imposts support only every other order, and in the naves of Charlieu and Anzy (Fig. 25a) they support the orders of the arcade but do not extend around the dosseret and colonnette on the face of the pier;[8] the archivolts in all these examples remain rectangularly stepped orders undecorated by carvings. The result is a horizontal articulation, interrupting the elevation at key, isolated spots. But the elements of division, the moldings themselves, do not form a continuous, linked horizontal system on the surface of the buildings.

Just as they modified northern First Romanesque moldings, bases, and masonry techniques in the series of buildings they constructed, the Atelier pushed the horizontal northern articulation found at Charlieu and Anzy to new limits. They lined the wall surface with more horizontal, projecting decorations which were complemented or highlighted by the increased undercutting and faceting of detail described before. And they increasingly coordinated these decorations horizontally and vertically, creating a correspondence between the parts. Let us chart the sequence of change in the articulation.

In completing the facade and upper story of the western bays at Anzy, the Atelier continued to build in the manner of the early nave campaign, although they left their own mark on the exterior portal design.[9] In the older style, they finished both sides of the facade without horizontal string courses and they left both interior openings—the portal door and clerestory window—as undecorated, square reveals (Figs. 25a,b). On the openings of the exterior, however, they added elaborate decorative orders, although they carved these very much in the older tradition (Fig. 84b). Like the earlier bases and imposts of the Atelier, the parts of the orders are relatively equal in size. Two cavets of the same dimension are each bordered by two tori of the same dimension—the only difference being that the cavet on the inside order is filled with figures of the elders and the cavet on the outside with a continuous foliate motif. As in earlier northern designs, the fillets separating the parts are relatively large and uniform, and bare surfaces abound: uncarved tori and large undecorated masonry reveals line the orders, and squat columns and undecorated jambs surround the door opening. Moreover, such rounded and flat undecorated forms are not only adjacent to each other but approximately the same size, reflecting earlier northern First Romanesque designs where a balance exists between frame and field elements.

The isolated placement of the horizontally articulating members recalls the earlier treatment on the facade of Charlieu and the nave at Anzy. The portal decoration does not continue horizontally around the buttresses on the front of the building or around the jambs in the interior. And within the portal itself, the connections are disjointed. The decoration on the side portals later built at Vézelay (Fig. 30a) is more coordinated. There, the jambs and the pilaster supports are each reflected in a separate stepped impost and the steps correspond to the three tiers of the archivolts and tympanum. Here, at Anzy, the projecting edge of the jamb collides with the receding corner of the impost molding, setting up a discoordination and juxtaposition further emphasized by the receding edge of the archivolt above the jamb; moreover, because the impost begins halfway up the lintel, it covers part of the sculptural panel and is not aligned with the division between the carving.

In their second building at Mâcon (Fig. 29a), they completed only the central bay above the level of the exterior plinth, yet the narthex is finished enough to show important changes.[10] For the first time the Atelier supported their bases on the interior and exterior with socles of a classical cyma profile (Fig. 6b). And they outlined the exterior plinth with a continuous cyma molding and applied en délit fluted pilasters to the wall surface on the interior (Fig. 26a). This use of applied ornament seems tentative, however. They left the wall bare behind the interior pilasters, and the plinth beneath them is an undecorated square step (Fig. 26a). They left the wall beneath the tympanum as an uncarved surface, using only one slight vertical reveal instead of pilasters or columns to support the two jamb capitals, and they carved only one decorative order around the tympanum (Fig. 29a). As at Anzy, the articulation recalls northern prototypes, with large areas of uncarved surface and few parts that are simple in type and relatively equal in size. The single order around the tympanum is based on the traditional northern First Romanesque cavet, divided in the middle by one large decorated torus and bordered above and below by large fillets with bare reveals. In a refinement of their work at Anzy, however, they introduced smaller, more irregularly sized and more numerous parts in the impost (Fig. 5d), and they extended the molding horizontally across the portal. But as at Anzy, the advances and recessions of the string course do not directly correspond to the support system below or the articulation above. The door jamb and its capital recede slightly, the impost above them projects, but neither edge is continued in the single plane of the tympanum. In contrast, the column and its projecting capital do continue as a separate order in the impost and archivolt.

By the time of Perrecy, the Atelier noticeably increased the amount of horizontal articulation in the narthex (Figs. 1a, 27a,b,c). They applied a plinth molding on two sides of the building's interior, and they added one decorative order to the archivolts on the exterior, another on the first central bay of the interior, and a third around the tympanum. While carving the orders at Mâcon, the Atelier closely followed the northern First Romanesque practice of using a few, balanced, and equal parts; at Perrecy, however, they multiplied these details, reduced them in size, and began to combine irregularly sized parts. On the exterior, for example, although the central portal arcade (on the right in Fig. 27c) still has the older square-edged profile as well as the decorated torus and cavet molding found in the Mâcon tympanum, the lower portion of the cavet has been all but eliminated, marking a change in the careful balance between these parts. A more dramatic shift can be seen on the other portals (on the left in Fig. 27c), where the Atelier replaced the single square-edged arcade with a double torus and scotia molding analogous to the standard impost design used on the interior (Fig. 27b). As well as increasing the number of smaller parts on the exterior arcade—especially classically based details—the Atelier ornamented all four interior transverse arches in the central bay with an extra doucine molding (Figs. 1a, 27a). Extending the horizontal articulation, they brought this transverse arch molding over to the facade, where it continues on the same level and with the same profile and diameter as a blind arch around the tympanum. Besides this extra order, the Atelier added another classical molding—an egg-and-dart torus—to the plain torus surrounding the tympanum. The narthex at Mâcon is simpler than that at Perrecy, where the Atelier multiplied the number of orders and parts within the archivolts and arcades, added columns and recessions to the supports beneath the tympanum, and extended the outside order of the tympanum into the transverse arches of the central bay.

Despite these changes, the masons did not carry the horizontal decoration to the extremes found in their later work. They left the archivolts on the other interior bays with the earlier square-edged design (Fig. 27b), and they continued to isolate the decorative devices of archivolts, plinths, and imposts: buttresses divide the decorative orders of the exterior archivolts, and columns interrupt the horizontal plinth molding (Fig. 27c); imposts at Perrecy (Fig. 27a) do not extend as string courses across large expanses of wall surface (the tympanum impost, for example, does not continue into the side bays of the facade, Fig. 27b);[11] and while there is a new coordination between the string course and the embrasure of the central portal—the inside jamb and column are echoed in the two steps of the impost molding—the outer edge of the jamb is not reflected in an extra stepped impost and none of these projecting supports is continued directly in the orders above. Similarly, despite the added number of classical motifs in the torus and scotia (Fig. 27c), egg-and-dart (Fig. 1a), and doucine moldings (Fig. 27a), the details hardly approach the quantity and irregularity of the Atelier's later architectural decoration. The moldings are still relatively equal in size to each other and to the plain tori and square-edged orders which accompany them, and they are separated by large distinctive fillets (Figs. 27a, 27c).

Their next buildings were small or left incomplete. While the Atelier finished the first campaign (Figs. 28, 226c) at Vézelay only to the approximate level of eight ashlar courses on the nave facade and aisle walls, they joined the portals with a string course and outlined the base of all these walls on the exterior and interior with a horizontal cyma plinth molding, a feature which becomes standard in their important later buildings at Cluny and Paray (Figs. 67, 68). By adding a third step to the impost molding on each side of the portals (Fig. 30a), they complemented these horizontal connections on the facade with vertical correspondence within each portal. Unlike at Perrecy, where the three recessions of the embrasure beneath the molding are not reflected in the steps of the

46

molding or the orders of the tympanum, at Vézelay the three recessions correspond to the steps in the molding and to the three tiers of the tympanum and archivolts.

Their next construction at Montceaux is more of a wayside chapel than a church, and for this reason it seems that the Atelier concentrated their energies on the tympanum (Fig. 2c), circling it with a record number of decorative orders while leaving bare all but the eaves. In spite of its small size, the details and arrangement of the orders distinguish Montceaux as a late work. Unlike the previous portals at Anzy and Mâcon, very small reveals separate the tori and appear to be narrow fillets rather than plain and flat horizontal and vertical surfaces. Unlike the simple, balanced, and repeated decorations on earlier portals, these archivolts include a wide variety of sizes and shapes, including a motif that looks like a diamond-shaped apple turnover with its rounded points folded toward the center and indented on the sides. Three fillet profiles are interspersed between differently shaped tori, and no longer are these flat and round forms carefully balanced, for the larger tori clearly dominate, as they do in the later bases as well.

Similarly, the sophisticated articulation of the parts is typically late. In a three-dimensional tour de force, the concave mandorla and the apostles are carved from the same stone and set against a deeply recessed cul-de-four, which on the sides (Fig. 2b) actually overlaps these figures and projects over their heads. The shift within such a small space from overhanging foreground to deeply receded background is emphasized by the impost block, which divides the archivolts from the supports at this horizontal level. Unlike the repeated and regular shapes of earlier designs, the impost is stepped irregularly to match the corresponding difference in size between the small square jamb and column below, and between the single outside and double inside tori above.

By the time the Atelier began the aisles of the second campaign of Vézelay they were ready to expand the use of decorative courses into a linked system of projecting horizontal and vertical moldings. On the exterior (Fig. 226b), they lined the top with a rosette cornice and the bottom with a classical plinth molding, and enclosed the horizontal space between with squared-off buttresses. Inside they divided each bay into two smaller horizontal areas by running an extra string course below the window (Fig. 37); in most cases they made this string course into a classical cyma profile analogous to the formeret, transverse arch, impost, and plinth molding, thereby creating a continuous border outline which framed the parts of the aisle wall. They further increased horizontal divisions by isolating structurally different parts: three analogous moldings—the transverse arch, formeret, and string course—converge at the point of the groin web, severing the vault from the wall; a string course separates the transverse arch from the capital and column beneath it; and a running plinth cuts off the column at its base.

These decorative courses not only divide the surface of the wall and the structural members into horizontal parts, they frequently seem to have a life of their own, independent of the elements to which they are attached. While the decorative orders of the transverse arch and arcade correspond to the dosserets beneath them, the formeret simply rests on the projecting string course, and together they form an independent encrusted decoration above the wall plane. At Vézelay, then, the Atelier pushed the northern First Romanesque system of articulation to new limits.

In the sequence of buildings that we have established, the Atelier complemented the older design with improved ashlar and refined classical border details and they set them in a new type of facade with horizontally and vertically linked, multi-portal sculptural programs. On the elevation they created ever smaller horizontal units by means of moldings which frequently projected from the wall plane as an independent system of decoration, and they designed orders with more numerous, irregular and smaller parts. While a crew of the Atelier continued to work in the nave at Vézelay (see appendixes 4 and 6), the group who built Cluny III combined these new effects with the vertically continuous system of planar articulation from the South, a development I shall discuss in the context of their working relationship with southern First Romanesque masons.

To summarize, we learned about formal changes in parts of Anzy, Mâcon, Perrecy, Montceaux, Cluny, and Vézelay by relative rather than absolute dating. First we determined that the same Atelier of masons worked at each site. Then within the same sequence of buildings we observed simultaneous developments in architectural details, construction, and articulation. We identified as earliest those churches where the Atelier followed most closely the tradition of northern First Romanesque design. In the next section, we shall study the Atelier at Cluny where, for the first time, they worked with southern masons who had a different approach to design.

Later, in chapter 4, we shall see another use for the relative chronology established here. The same two sculptors carved tympana and capitals in most of the Atelier's buildings; therefore, understanding the buildings' relative chronology reveals the sequence of the sculptors' careers, the direction of the change of their sculptural style, and the close relation of this change to architectural design.

Cluny III and the Southern First Romanesque Tradition

V

At the special moment when the Cluniac Order was at the height of its wealth and power under Abbot Hugh, two traditionally separate groups of artisans united to create a new artistic tradition at Cluny III.[12] The construction of a single building in a series of campaigns brought them together to form a new synthetic art which was much more than the sum of the individual styles they had practiced before. So far, we have seen that the Atelier, far from being revolutionary, took few risks in refining its architectural style before it came to Cluny. Similarly, we shall see now that the other group of masons at Cluny III simply continued working in the southern First Romanesque tradition of construction indigenous to the area around the abbey. Despite their long and separate histories and an initial reluctance to adapt to each other's ways, their close working relationship at Cluny III forced an exchange of ideas, and in the course of construction they achieved a new synthesis of art that influenced notable Cluniac buildings in southern Burgundy. Most properly, however, we can speak of a new mainstream or standard aesthetic only if we restrict our use of the term to the specific parts of Cluny and Paray that the two groups of masons created jointly.

It would be quite another matter to speak of an intellectual or even conscious search for a joint style. Besides the obvious wealth and power it took to bring two large pools of masons to one site, there is no evidence that anyone in the Cluniac Order set out to unite two traditions or recognized the aesthetic consequence of bringing them together. In fact, judging from the archaeology—and there are dangers in judging intentions from results—the union seems to have sprung from necessity: the Atelier went through a kind of "shotgun wedding" with the southern masons, at first having wanted little to do with them.

Before coming together at Cluny, groups of masons from the northern and southern First Romanesque traditions practiced independently for one hundred years in Burgundy.[13] At the beginning of the eleventh century, they even had worked separately, although almost simultaneously, on the same buildings at Tournus and Dijon (appendixes 1 and 2); by the second half of the century, southern masons were installing northern sculpture in the cloister of Tournus, although the capitals there (Fig. 52a) were isolated examples possibly shipped from distant sites like Meaux and Venasque.[14] By contrast, outside of Burgundy, between the paths of the Loire and Saône Rivers, masons went beyond juxtaposing separate, isolated elements; at Ris in the Auvergne, for example, masons had already adapted the southern barrel vault and system of continuous orders to strictly northern bases, capitals and imposts by 1050. By merging the two systems this early, however, they were limited to a strictly First Romanesque vocabulary, unlike the particular blend of developed northern and southern First Romanesque forms which distinguishes the later achievement at Cluny.

How and why did the two traditions merge at Cluny? My primary goal is to answer "how," by showing that the builders of Cluny III increasingly accepted the eleventh-century changes in Burgundian southern First Romanesque architecture. Like so many causal questions, to explain why this happened is largely impossible without supporting textual evidence. However, we can attempt an answer by observing how the Atelier treated the southern masons when they first worked together (see appendix 4 for campaigns) and then relating this knowledge to what we know about the size of the project, the resources, and the available work force.

At Anzy (Fig. 25b), Mâcon (Fig. 26a), Perrecy (Fig. 27b), Vézelay (Fig. 24f), and Montceaux (Fig. 24g), the Atelier worked and signed both the framing stones and the fill masonry. During the first campaign at Cluny III, the Atelier masons continued to sign the ashlar framing stones *but not the fill masonry* in the lower story of the aisle wall below the windows. In fact, as we shall see, this fill masonry is totally different from their previous work because the stones are shaped and laid like brick in the southern tradition. They were not signed because they were not carved by the Atelier but by the southern masons with whom they were now working.

Why the Atelier changed its building practices to include southern masons is not known, although indications point to the need for extra laborers. Clearly, the Atelier had never before built on such a large scale. Indeed, Cluny III was the longest church in Europe before Saint-Peter's was built four centuries later. If we can trust texts, the undertaking was fully funded and accomplished with speed, a great portion being finished during the last twenty years of Abbot Hugh's life.[15] Moreover, except for the Mâcon narthex on the southern tip of the Mâconnais, the Atelier had never worked before in this region of Burgundy where masons practicing southern First Romanesque techniques had built the only large-scale buildings, the naves of Tournus (Fig. 156a) and Mâcon, and the vast majority of churches. Pressured to complete such a large building quickly and having the money to do it, the Atelier probably resorted to the available local talent for the lesser masonry tasks. Necessity makes for strange bedfellows.

Whatever the reasons for working with the southern masons, the Atelier, with its long tradition of ashlar and sculpture, took a while to appreciate masons who did not sculpt and who cut stone to look like brick.[16] It was only in the upper stories that the two traditions merged into a new, and what became a standard Cluniac style. To understand this synthesis, it is necessary to look at the history of the southern First Romanesque style up to the time the southern masons joined forces with the Atelier at Cluny.

VI

In the Mâconnais, as in areas of the Mediterranean littoral, masons at the turn of the eleventh century built with brick or stones in the shape of bricks (see Chapaize, Figs. 38a, 41; and Blanot, Fig. 39). Unlike the technique of frame and fill practiced in the North, this masonry created two equally clear patterns. One consists of continuous, horizontal beds which are a result of the brick-like laying of the stones. This uniform pattern of brick-like stones creates a continuous construction in which courses of identical size run straight through doors and windows without the interruption of larger jamb ashlar. These uniform courses extend even into arches, orders and windows (Chapaize, Fig. 38a; Blanot, Fig. 39), architectural elements which in the North were made up by specialized stones like trapezoidal voussoirs (Figs. 20, 21). This pattern I shall refer to as *continuous coursing*.

The second pattern concerns articulation and is actually an extension of continuous coursing, since the uniform brick shape lends itself to an uninterrupted articulation of larger parts. This pattern is created by the vertical and horizontal bands found both in the interior and exterior. Rarely broken by carved moldings or capitals, the bands have narrow proportions with a width of usually no more than two stones and a reveal of one stone. Vertically the bands line the corners of towers and horizontally run across their face as narrow corbelled tables (Chapaize, Fig. 38a; Blanot, Fig. 39). Narrow bands, without moldings or capitals, connect parts of the interior so that it also reads like a series of analogous, brick-like rectangular edges. In the Chapaize nave and Tournus narthex (Figs. 41, 42), for example, the pier necking, transverse arch, groin springer, and formeret—in addition to the bases at Tournus (Fig. 44a) and the arcade archivolt at Chapaize (Fig. 41)—are all formed from brick-like reveals without any molding, capital, or ashlar separating the analogous parts.[17] The pattern of continuous southern First Romanesque beds and bands marked by projecting reveals became an important part of High Romanesque style, contradicting the claim that southern First Romanesque was a "folkloric dead end" (for a discussion of the theory of southern First Romanesque architecture, see the excursus to this chapter).

As the century progressed, Mâconnais masons subtly but importantly altered southern First Romanesque brick-based construction and its square-edged reveals. Although they still used continuous courses of brick-shaped stones between structural parts and openings, they began to work the stones with an axe, increasing their size and widening the bands in relation to the wall. This change over time can perhaps best be seen by comparing the ground and upper stories of one building, Tournus (Figs. 43, 171). On the nave piers at the ground level, southern First Romanesque masons chipped the surface of brick-like stones, while at the top of the same piers, masons from the latter part of the eleventh century axed two-foot wide stones ("3") with long, parallel, superficial blade strokes (Fig. 44b). On the exterior of the nave (Fig. 45) and upper story of the narthex ("a" in Fig. 46b), the masons extended these worked stones into wide projecting strips almost equal to the wall area between them. A similar transformation can be seen in the bands on the tower of Massy (Fig. 40).

Looking at the effect in both these buildings, one may well ask whether the wall recedes or the bands project in the original southern First Romanesque sense. The fact that a wider projecting band could appear to be a wall plane was not overlooked by mid-century masons, who began to experiment with it in this new context. For example, on the northwestern corner of the Tournus nave (Fig. 45), what appears in the older context as a projecting strip ("a") on the side wall continues as the primary and only wall surface on the western face ("b"). Similarly, on the round piers, the lower molding that simply circles the pillar as a band of continuous brick construction in the First Romanesque narthex (Fig. 42) extends as the projecting lower edge of the wall plane on the later upper story of the Saint-Michael chapel ("a" in Fig. 47).

The apse of Anzy-le-Duc is one of the most spectacular examples of these developments in southern First Romanesque masonry before Cluny III.[18] While masons created the standard southern First Romanesque bands and corbel tables from uniform brick-like stones (Fig. 48), they converted these forms to a series of analogous wall planes with vertical square-edged reveals. They turned the narrow southern First Romanesque corbel table into a wide plane in the quarter-barrel vault ("1"), and they extended the Lombard band into a spandrel plane ("2") concentric and analogous to other reveals in the apse ("3"). Indeed at times, masons abandoned specific reference to the southern system by eliminating the decorative corbel table from Lombard bands and widening them into wall planes, which they then continued as analogous, undecorated reveals all the way to the floor, as on the interior of the apse chapel of Anzy ("4") and on the exterior of the Tournus nave (Fig. 45). By the end of the eleventh century, the tradition of southern First Romanesque architecture had developed into a sophisticated planar system, and as the only large-scale building tradition in the Mâconnais it profoundly influenced Cluny III and the other High Romanesque Cluniac churches built in the region.[19]

In the High Romanesque church of Saint-Hippolyte, a Cluniac building only a few miles from the mother church, masons used southern planar surfaces extensively (Fig. 49a). Here, masons worked brick-based forms with different functions into analogous square-edged reveals without corbels. What begins as the major surface on the apse ("2a") continues into the side of the choir as a narrow reveal of the front wall ("2b") and extends around the window of the choir as a recessed plane ("2c"). Compounding the planar confusion, the dimension of the window face ("2c") is repeated in three places: on the edge of the parapet ("2b"), on the projecting reveal ("3b") of the choir wall which covers over the plane ("2c") of the window, and on the face of the window ("1") in the first plane of the apse. By making reveals of projecting and receding surfaces into uninterrupted edges of the same dimension, the masons created ambiguity between the different wall planes or between the same wall plane at different points, and they transformed the southern First Romanesque system of bands on walls into a continuous articulation based on planar reveals.

The masons at Saint-Hippolyte treated the interior, too, as a system of analogous, revealed planes (Fig. 49b). Except for the corbelled string course in the choir, the wall reveals, regardless of individual function, remain virtually continuous and identical. For example, plane "3" projects the same width as a transverse arch ("3a") in the crossing, as a dosseret ("3b") in the choir, and as an arcade ("3c") in the apse; therefore, it reads as analogous and continous wall reveals in each case. The same is true for plane "2," which projects identically to plane "3" and appears vertically continuous and analogous regardless of its separate "functions" as a dosseret ("2a") in the crossing, a pilaster ("2b") in the choir, and a window jamb ("2c") in the apse.[20] The remaining parts of Saint-Hippolyte, as well as the nave of Tournus and the chevet of Anzy, epitomize the developed southern articulation based on analogous plane reveals that survives in High Romanesque Cluniac buildings.

VII

In the preceding section, I have shown how the southern First Romanesque tradition in the Mâconnais became increasingly distinguished by the use of planar reveals which masons carried to new extremes, as in the Cluniac church of Saint-Hippolyte. In this section I intend to show that masons extended the southern First Romanesque tradition in High Romanesque buildings constructed by the Cluniac Order, and that they combined it with the Atelier's northern tradition to create a new mainstream Cluniac style. We have already seen how, having started from a diverse local Brionnais tradition, the Atelier gradually came to prefer and, by Cluny, to use practically only classical models for their bases, moldings, imposts, and capitals. Despite the resulting purity of classical elements at Cluny, these motifs were combined with southern techniques to such an extent that by the upper stories of the abbey the two traditions had come to exist as a new and indistinguishable whole.

Cluniac masons could call upon the two complementary traditions and merge them as they saw fit. On the interior three-story elevation, where horizontal division, ashlar framing, and projecting decoration dominate, they deemphasized the vertical articulation, brick construction, and non-figural sculpture of the South. In other areas, as in the large infili sections on the exterior of the transepts (Fig. 59), they preferred an uninterrupted surface of uniform material, and here they exploited the techniques and materials of southern First Romanesque architecture. On the exterior, at the northwestern corner that joins the nave aisle to the western face of the great transept, masons created the most complex variations on the southern system: four exterior wall planes, from two different parts of the building, read as identical square-edged reveals where they come together (Fig. 50). The first reveal ("1a") of the transept extends up from the wall plane above the filled-in western door, and its dimensions match the width of the first row of voussoirs on the door and the window above it ("1b"). The second plane extends down from the primary wall plane of the great transept, and its dimensions ("2a") correspond to the width of the second row of voussoirs above the window ("2b"). The third plane ("3") extends down from the arcaded wall surface of the nave aisle, and the fourth plane ("4") continues up as the aisle's primary wall surface.[21] Regardless of its function in the elevation, each plane appears as an identical square-edged reveal as is typical of developed southern articulation in the Mâconnais.

The exterior of Saint-Hugh's Chapel at Berzé-la-Ville also follows this pattern of articulation based on analogous plane reveals. Perhaps because the chapel was small and aisleless, masons chose to emphasize the continuous vertical articulation of the South.[22] At first glance, they recreated on the exterior an actual southern First Romanesque design (Figs. 51a, 51c) with brick-based bands, corbelled tables, and soffits lined with tile-like stones. The southern system dominates the small chapel, especially along the exterior flanks which have the distinctive continuous coursing without ashlar framing. In this part of Berzé, the masons applied southern techniques including a special variation found at Laizé and in the Saint-Michael chapel (Figs. 46a, 46b) and cloister at Tournus (Fig. 52a): as there, a unique semicircular white stone (Fig. 51c) frequently is fitted to the curved soffit below each corbelled arch; and where the arches come together, they are formed into a "T" made of a horizontal and vertical stone, supported by a corbel shaped like a projecting wide, flat wedge. Typical of the changes within the southern system, the mass of the Lombard bands (Fig. 51a) is increased and they are used more like buttresses; as in the apse of Anzy and nave of Tournus (Fig. 45), the corbel table is eliminated or reshaped into pointed arches, and the wall is divided into a series of squared-off reveals which run uninterruptedly to the roof. At Berzé, as at Anzy and Tournus, masons transformed these analogous reveals from southern First Romanesque bands into a series of planar surfaces, some of which, regardless of individual functions, look the same (Fig. 51a): for example, the nave wall reveal ("1") duplicates the projecting edge of the "band" above it ("2").[23]

Such play with planar reveals also occurs on the interior of Cluniac buildings, and like the articulation on the exterior is derived from traditional southern First Romanesque uses. Indeed, it is highly possible that the medieval bay division was created by the linking of continuous vertical square-edged orders from the pier through responds to the transverse arch;[24] yet, the Cluniac masons, in line with the more recent southern practice, expanded such vertical orders into continuous vertical planes. To continue using uninterrupted narrow orders on the interior of High Cluniac buildings, as seen in the retardataire Mâconnais examples at Mellay and Culles, would have been like using simple Lombard bands on the exterior. Let us again turn to Berzé and Cluny to see how the Cluniac masons developed these southern planar forms on the interior.

It is easier to see than to describe the complex effect obtained on the interior of Berzé, so please refer to Figure 53a, where I have labelled the separate planar surfaces. Three planes, marked "1," "2," and "3," extend from the nave through the apse as analogous square edges and dominate the northern ashlar, bases, capitals, and columns. What appear to be narrow southern First Romanesque bands or dosserets in the High Romanesque sense at points "A" and "B" in the crossing are in fact the extended edges of planes "2" and "3": the arcade apse wall plane, "3," extends down into band "A," and the nave wall arcade, "2," extends down into band "B." Although molding "x," to the left of the column, helps make "B" appear to be a dosseret rather than the revealed edge of a plane, it is actually the revealed edge of plane "2," as can be seen at the right of the column where the molding disappears and the "dosseret" turns into a wall plane revealed again in the square-edged arcade "C" around the crossing window. Typical of the developed southern First Romanesque system, the exposed wall planes around the crossing window perform different traditional functions—plane "1," the jamb splay; plane "2," the archivolt; and plane "3," the apse arcade—but all read as analogous and continuous square-edged reveals along the side of the window.

Although the southern masonry, motifs, and planar treatment dominate the exterior and interior of Berzé, a closer look reveals that these elements have been combined with northern and classical devices and articulation to create the particular High Cluniac style. Indeed, the ashlar elements correspond to the upper stories of Cluny and likely share the relatively late date of its final campaign. Like their late Cluny counterparts (Paray, Fig. 56), the Berzé masons consistently veneered the inside (Fig. 53a) of the brick-based stone exterior, extending ashlar from its original use as single framing stones, as in the first campaign on the ground floor of Cluny (Fig. 62a). Moreover, on the apse exterior of Berzé (Fig. 51b) they interrupted the southern articulation of continuous vertical bands with a projecting doucine molding. Such instances of the merging of classical detailing with southern masonry are steps the Atelier took only after the first campaign ground story of Cluny, as seen, for example, in the later ground story of the Paray choir (see appendixes 4 and 5).

Besides the veneered ashlar and horizontal articulation, the Berzé masons also carved exterior details in a northern technique. They worked the lower apse corbels from ashlar, sculpted swans and other figures on their faces ("a" in Fig. 51b), and entirely eliminated Lombard corbels on the upper bands, substituting a cavet molding with billet corbels in their place ("a" in Fig. 51a). Similarly on the interior (Fig. 53a), the Brionnais and classical details they combined in the capitals and bases (Fig. 53b) correspond closely to the latest stages of Cluny III and specifically to the tower chapel of Saint Gabriel.[25] The classical scotia profile of the apse base matches the late freestanding pier campaign of Cluny (Figs. 53c, 68); also, the accompanying decoration of the bases—for example the ovals (Fig. 9d)—although seemingly revived from classical models, in fact continues the northern First Romanesque devices then in use on Brionnais buildings at Vézelay, Perrecy, and Charlieu (Figs. 9b, 9c).[26] As I showed in the first part of the chapter, the Atelier did not revive classical motifs at Cluny, as is so often claimed, but increasingly emphasized them in their earlier buildings. When they joined with masons from the South, as at Berzé, the ashlar-trained masons adapted the classical vocabulary to brick-based construction in a subtle synthesis of northern and southern motifs and articulation.

While northern features are evident in a small Cluniac chapel like Berzé, they are especially prominent on large vertical constructions like the interior three-story elevation and crossing tower of Cluny III, where masons apparently desired ashlar detailing and a high degree of articulation. Initially, the tower of Cluny III appears overwhelmingly southern in design (Fig. 54). It owes its brick-based filler construction ("2") and its specific and complex motif, the recessed Lombard band and corbel table framing a column set between a double arcade window, to southern First Romanesque towers in the Mâconnais like Chapaize (Fig. 38a) and Blanot (Fig. 39). In addition to these, the tower reflects the new emphasis within the southern First Romanesque tradition toward multiple plane reveals. Taking their cue from the southern system of planes, the Cluniac masons seemed to add extra planes through the artifice of trompe l'oeil. In the case of the Cluny transept tower, they created an effect of increased planes by seeming to repeat elements from the lower story in the upper story where in fact they treated them differently. The lower level has two actual planar depths: the first, a constructive brick-like wall with plug holes ("1"), and above it a second constructive wall supported by an ashlar spandrel arcade with columns ("2"). The upper story, however, is lighter in appearance because more planes and pilasters seem to be exposed around a larger opening. While the ashlar arcade molding on the lower story recedes almost a foot between the constructive spandrel wall and the plug-holed wall of the first plane, the arcade molding on the upper story barely recedes and is carved on the same ashlar blocks as the arcade above and the voussoirs beneath. Even though the molding is practically flat, from a distance it seems to recede because the shadows cast by the projecting ornamental buttons on the molding make the arcades of the two stories look alike from a distance. The wall depth not used or "saved" by the apparent recession of the arcade molding was then added to the sides of the corner pilasters. With the extra depth, the masons continued a separate projecting plane from the surface of the pilasters to the corbel table. The effect of another plane apparently was intended, since the pilaster continues on the bottom story where it does not project but is flush with the second wall plane ("2")—the same plane they originally projected as a separate constructive wall with a receding arcade molding above the plane of the first plug-holed wall ("1"). The whole planar effect can be compared to the *mille feuilles* of a baklava pastry which add delicacy, complexity, and lightness to a rich cake.

Despite the southern fill masonry and planar features, however, the structure of the tower is distinctly northern. We can see that the brick-like southern bands and corbels now assume the shape of oversized framing blocks at the corners and on the top, while the once continuous southern vertical articulation is divided into stories. Projecting string courses interrupt the vertical bands and create separate horizontal levels where orders are caught by classically derived capitals, columns, and bases. The masons even turned the standard Lombard band and corbel table found on the outside corner of southern First Romanesque towers (Figs. 38a, 39, 40) into fluted classical pilasters (Fig. 54). On the tower of Cluny III, masons combined the northern articulation refined by the Atelier with developed southern planes which they took to new decorative extremes while incorporating classical motifs and characteristically Cluniac devices like buttons. The result was a new synthesis of preceding currents—a standard or mainstream style which buildings at Berzé and Paray shared.

Even in the interior elevation of Cluny III, where the masons used predominantly northern and particularly classical motifs, they modified them with southern designs which they expressed more explicitly on other parts of the building. This is true of the ashlar pilasters separating the triforium arcades on the interior (Cluny, Fig. 57; Paray, Fig. 58), which on the surface seem simply to copy classical detailing—like that on the triumphal arch of Saint André at Autun—but in fact owe much to the southern tradition of the brick-based pilaster construction which can be seen on the exterior windows of the upper stories (Fig. 59). Indeed, for over one hundred years southern masons as close as two miles away at Massy (Fig. 40) had combined windows and arcades with continuous orders separated by pilasters, the very features which dominate the brick-based construction on the exterior of Cluny (Fig. 59). In fact, towers were the only large-scale, multi-storied structures that southern masons produced in the Mâconnais and which the Cluniacs immediately could have turned to for a source. Like each bay of the interior elevation of Cluny and Paray (Fig. 58), the tower of Massy has three stories lined on the sides with orders. The center story is pierced by round-headed windows surrounded by arcaded pilasters, and the upper story of arcaded columns, capitals, and bases is outlined by a string course molding above corbels. So, when we look for the sources of the standard three-story Cluniac elevation, we cannot exclude southern First Romanesque precedents despite northern and indeed classical articulation and motifs.[27]

Suggestions of *purely* classical, foreign, or "higher" prototypes for the elevation of Cluny III do not take into account Mâconnais models close at hand and the local origins of the masons who created similar forms in southern techniques on the exterior of the same building.[28] In the largest sense, the question of the sources for the elevation is part of the general problem of classicism in the architecture of Cluny. These influences are complex, being both indirect and direct, long-term and immediate. In addition to the complicated and indirect influence of the Roman ruins in Burgundy and the direct contact of Cluniac monks with Rome, we should consider the traditions of the builders themselves: the Atelier on the one hand, with its longstanding practice of classical detailing, and the southern masons on the other, practicing an originally Italian system of brick-based arcading, orders, and articulation.

Although the question of sources for Cluny III is complex, the actual construction of the interior elevation is clear: in practice, the masons merged the southern planar system with northern ashlar and horizontal articulation. Like the crossing at Berzé, on the ground level of the northern bay of the Cluny transept (Fig. 57) what appears on one side of a column to be a typical northern dosseret ("C")—with a horizontal molding and stepped archivolts caught by moldings and capitals—on the other side continues in an uninterrupted vertical reveal to the springing of the vault ("B") as a plane separate from the main surface of the transept ("A"). Combining the virtues of both systems, the masons broke up the face of the wall plane with capitals and moldings on the east and west ("C"), while on the south side they allowed its planar reveal to rise without interruption ("B").

In a system where masons revealed planes as analogous square edges, they also transformed the traditional role of the dosseret. Usually just a small corresponding member, the dosseret becomes a vertical surface which extends or reappears elsewhere on the same plane. On the southeastern side of Cluny's great transept, for example (Fig. 60), they turned the corner dosseret ("3a") into the outermost arcaded plane of the barrel vault ("3b"); the outside portal dosseret ("2a") into a spandrel ("2b")—the principal wall plane which also continues around the second story window ("2c"); and the inside portal dosseret ("1a") into the archivolt surface ("1b") which reappears as the inside plane of the window above ("1c"). In this way, the three orders or dosserets ("1," "2," "3") which appear as analogous squared edges on the ground may also be seen as the tips of advancing and receding wall planes. By having the dosseret act in two different ways at once— as a storied corresponding member articulating horizontally, and as a sheer continuous wall plane rising vertically—the Cluniac masons successfully blended two traditionally separate but complementary systems. While the refinements in horizontal articulation can be seen in the sequence of buildings the Atelier erected in Burgundy before Cluny III, the treatment of the elevation as revealed vertical planes can be traced back to the experiments in continuous articulation which local masons conducted with southern First Romanesque bands in brick-based buildings like the nave at Tournus and chevet at Anzy after the middle of the eleventh century.[29]

VIII

In order to establish the sources for Cluny III, we analyzed the refinements the Atelier made in their buildings compared to northern First Romanesque antecedents and the progress southern masons made in their architecture over the eleventh century. Then we described the nature of the synthesis of these two traditions in a new High Romanesque Burgundian style. Now we can focus more closely on the construction of Cluny III to see exactly how the northern and southern systems were brought together in one building.

It is fitting that Cluny III was the first important church where the northern and southern traditions were united, and that its construction today vividly shows this process of assimilation. I shall attempt to personalize the design process, to explain in human terms how the Atelier accepted the developed southern First Romanesque taste. The impact of the brick-based style can be measured best by contrasting the earlier work of the Atelier with the work they did after joining with southern masons on the first campaign of Cluny. Therefore, the buildings we will look at are the ground story of Cluny, the later campaigns of its upper stories, the nave of Vézelay (built at the same time as these upper stories but without southern masons), and finally the chevet of Paray.

During the first campaign, Cluny's exterior walls were completed up to the level of the aisle windows (see appendix 4). The parts of this campaign that remain standing today prove that southern and northern masons worked side by side but barely merged their styles. It is as if southern masons were called upon to produce quantities of infill masonry without expressing the articulation and design possible with their brick technique. We know they worked the first campaign infill masonry because it is completely brick-based (Fig. 62a), with radiating and laterally placed brick-like stones replacing trapezoidal voussoirs over the doors of the choir (Fig. 63b) and western transept (Figs. 50, 64d). With the exception of one notable planar reveal on the northwestern corner of the great transept (Fig. 50), the southern masons did not surround openings with the continuous orders typical of the later upper-story windows (Fig. 59). It is as if they sacrificed or suppressed their talent for articulation on Cluny's exterior in order to provide quantities of sheer uninterrupted, brick-based infill masonry on all parts of the ground floor still standing—on the walls (Fig. 62a), and windows (Fig. 62e) of the minor transept; the choir (Figs. 63a, 63b); eastern (Fig. 64a) and western great transept (Fig. 64d); and nave aisles (Fig. 65). This treatment contrasts sharply with the upper stories, where southern masons formed brick-based fill into a series of continuous reveals around wall openings (Fig. 59).

The southern masons not only failed to express or were kept from expressing their native design, they were literally isolated from the work of the Atelier. While in their previous practice the Atelier veneered smaller exterior fill masonry with ashlar on the inside—for example at Anzy (Fig. 25b) and Perrecy (Fig. 27b), and later in the upper stories of Cluny (Figs. 57, 59, 60)—throughout the lower story of Cluny they never covered the brick-like fill stones (Figs. 62a, 62d). Moreover, in their previous buildings, such as Montceaux (Fig. 24g) and the Vézelay aisle campaign (Figs. 24f, 226c), the Atelier mixed frame and fill masonry, frequently continuing courses of fill directly into dosseret framing stones; in the first campaign of Cluny, however, the Atelier abruptly distinguished between ashlar and fill (Figs. 62a, 62b), and they never extended ashlar or even the flagged ends of dosserets horizontally into the filler beds over the entire first campaign, from the minor transept (Fig. 63a) to the nave aisles (Fig. 65).[30] This treatment contrasts with the upper stories of Cluny (Fig. 66), where the Atelier recalled their earlier practice. Ashlar from the buttress ("b") extend continuously through the fill masonry into the window jamb, and fill courses ("a") extend directly into the sides of the ashlar buttress stones. This is a distinct change from the lower story construction.

While the Atelier clearly carved the ashlar framing stones, signing them in noticeable spots, as on the minor transept portal (Fig. 8), they restricted any real contact with the southern masons during the first campaign to isolated and marginal areas. The voussoirs and billets (Fig. 62c, 62f) carved by the Atelier on the minor transept chapel are no more than isolated ashlar details surrounded by southern brick-like voussoirs above and below. A majority of the windows (Figs. 64a, 62e) are of purely brick-shaped construction, lacking ashlar jambs, voussoirs, or moldings, and none of the corbelled and encrusted ashlar decoration which marks the Atelier's later contribution to the Cluny three-story elevation exists in the first campaign.

By examining the work of the Atelier in the nave of Vézelay, we can see from another angle the way in which their style changed at the mother church. Despite standoffishness during the first campaign at Cluny, the Atelier joined with southern masons there and increasingly worked with them during the later campaigns. At Vézelay by contrast, although members of the Atelier built the nave at the same time as the later campaigns of Cluny (see appendixes 4 and 6), the Atelier never encountered southern masons. Even with the addition in the nave of new masons to the core of eighteen from the first campaign (see Fig. 36) and the notable changes in their ashlar, bases, and sculpture described previously, the masons at Vézelay remained well within the northern First Romanesque tradition.[31] Indeed, the church of Vézelay stands as the culmination of northern design. In its nave (Fig. 61), they pushed to the limit the basic northern First Romanesque ingredient of framed ashlar, horizontal articulation, and flat elevation.

The masons exhibited none of the planar play of Cluny in the flat exterior and interior nave and aisle walls at Vézelay. They only interrupted the walls with pilasters and string courses, and they projected these forms without altering the principal surface plane. Indeed, repeating the relationship of the formeret to the projecting string course on the aisle wall (Fig. 37), they rested the fluted nave pilaster directly on the corbelled rosette string course, encrusting the nave surface without changing its wall plane.[32] As we have seen, this contrasts with the treatment of High Cluniac buildings in southern Burgundy, where the Atelier combined northern pilasters, colonnettes, corbels, and string courses with a system of continuous vertical plane reveals.

The members of the Vézelay Atelier did not adapt ashlar decoration to square-edged vertical plane reveals; rather, they used it in the northern tradition to emphasize the horizontal articulation of the building. Unlike Cluny (Fig. 57), where dosserets and string course moldings frequently appear on only one side of a pier leaving the other side an unbroken vertical plane, in each bay of Vézelay a colossal dosseret and colonnette project from the flat wall and moldings continue around the entire horizontal surface on three levels, creating three separate horizontal zones. An impost molding wraps completely around each nave compound pier at the springing of the arcade, a projecting rosette string course runs continuously below the pilasters, and an undulating formeret molding extends the length of the nave above them.

Within these stories, separate architectural parts create further horizontal divisions in each bay. At both the arcade and clerestory level, each stepped recession in the horizontal molding marks the junction between two separate architectural parts, such as between the formeret and pilaster in the clerestory, and between the inside order and pier column in the arcade. By contrast, at Cluny a single continuous vertical plane may join these distinctive parts so that where it is not interrupted by a stepped horizontal string course molding these differences are eliminated ("B" in Fig. 57, "3a" in Fig. 60). Within the upper story of Vézelay, the projecting pilasters join the formeret and rosette molding on each side of the bay, creating an enclosed, corbelled decorative framework around each window. Similarly, on the aisle walls (Fig. 37), analogous and projecting formeret and string course moldings frame the interior window, while on the exterior (Fig. 226b) a rosette molding, a cyma plinth, and ashlar buttresses form a continuous outline around the flat wall of each bay. By contrast, on the exterior at Cluny, individual corbels punctuate the southern masonry only· at intervals (Fig. 64b). At the vault level, the groined webs of Vézelay disappear to a point above the intersection of each formeret and transverse arch molding, emphasizing the vault as a separate horizontal division which is repeated in each bay; this is different from the barrel vault at Cluny (Fig. 60), which frequently extends over many bays and continues directly into the plane of the transept wall.[33]

Thus, we can see that ashlar masons on the upper stories of Cluny and in the nave of Vézelay carried the traditionally northern qualities to new limits: they emphasized classical pilasters, moldings, and bases and the correspondence between these separate parts, and they multiplied horizontal divisions, framed bays with corbelled moldings, and refined the shape of ashlar and its finish. At Vézelay, they used these new devices to extend the century-old northern single-plane design, but at Cluny they joined them to the southern system of vertical reveals to create a new complementary *parti*. Appreciating this difference is critically important for understanding the final architecture of Cluny III as the special product of two groups of men who worked together for the first time. Although later masons would turn to Cluny as a model for imitation, the original builders created it from two long-standing but constantly changing traditions of construction—the northern one epitomized by the nave of Vézelay, and the southern one by the buildings at Anzy, Tournus, and Saint-Hippolyte.

During the first campaign at Cluny, the relationship between the northern and southern masons was distant: each group revealed little of its special capabilities and hardly made an effort to learn from the other. Although the southern masons practiced a brick technique, their work showed few signs of the vertical articulation normally associated with that tradition; similarly, northern masons, while contributing ashlar stones, created almost none of the encrusted moldings, horizontal divisions, or ashlar veneering associated with a developed northern building such as Vézelay. But by the final stories of Cluny the relationship between the two groups had become a partnership through which they assimilated the most developed articulation and masonry techniques from each other. The result was a style in which the two traditions are virtually indistinguishable.

To further explain the design of Cluny III as the creation of individuals, and especially to understand the role of the Atelier in the collaboration on the upper stories, we turn from the earlier first campaign of Cluny, where both groups of masons worked almost independently, and the contemporary nave of Vézelay, where the Atelier did not come in contact with masons from the South, to Paray, which was built later and probably contemporary with the final western campaign at Cluny (see appendix 4). Thirteen of the original Brionnais masons who worked at Anzy, Mâcon, and Perrecy constructed the chevet of Paray (see Fig. 36, and appendix 5). Among that number are included all but one of the masons who left their marks in the first campaign at Cluny, a fact which gives us a firm basis for comparing Paray with the mother church. Construction of the chevet of Paray was begun well after the ground floor of Cluny had been completed. At the beginning of construction on the ground floor at Paray, the Atelier showed the complementary blend of northern and southern features which they had worked out only in the second and third campaigns of Cluny. The diagonal, compressed, and low bases of the Paray columns (Figs. 67, 69), and their capitals, correspond to those in the Cluny upper story and facade (see appendix 4 and Figs. 70, 71, 72, 73). Paray's flagged exterior buttresses (Fig. 67), corbelled horizontal string course moldings (Fig. 58), superimposed pilasters and arcades, as well as its planar reveals, are typical features only on the upper stories of Cluny.

Clearly, Paray is a copy of Cluny III in type, technique, and articulation, but the copy is of a unique kind not heretofore understood. Provincial builders did not replicate a mainline structure; rather, the same masons continued to work out the techniques they had previously mastered. In fact, falling back upon their northern tradition, the original Brionnais members of the Atelier cut filler stones of ashlar and signed them (Fig. 67), creating in spots a more uniformly finished building than Cluny, from which it was "modelled." Moreover, they "copied" from only a part of the mother church, the complementary blend which was achieved on the upper stories of the Cluny elevation; therefore no complete Cluny model exists. Indeed, just as Cluny is not a complete model, Paray is not a complete copy: the Cluniacs seemed to have employed the original Atelier at Paray only to complete the chevet, the most important part of the building. No sign of their work appears in the transept above the horizontal suture (Fig. 74) or in any part of the nave elevation. This pattern of construction in which the Atelier first laid out the plan of the building with low horizontal walls in the transept (Fig. 75) and side aisles (Fig. 76) is not exceptional but repeats the local practice found in the transept of Anzy (see appendix 4, note 1, and Figs. 198a,b), the nave of Tournus (Fig. 156a), and most importantly, in the first campaign at Cluny (appendix 4 and Figs. 64a, 65).

The merging of northern and southern techniques, motifs, and articulation into a new synthesized style appears throughout the chevet campaign of Paray, for example on the north transept portal (Fig. 55). There, the masons built the wall (Fig. 75) with brick-shaped stones, but typically they used more northern features for the decorated portal (Fig. 55). They framed the portal with ashlar, and to the southern corbel table and band they imaginatively added Cluniac buttons and rosettes, as well as classically fluted pilasters, cavet moldings, and billets. Similarly, inside the Paray choir (Fig. 56), they blended southern motifs and articulation with northern designs. They employed the distinguishing devices of a Lombard band ("a") and table as well as continuous articulation, extending the principal dosseret through the arcade level ("b") without interruption.[34] As on the Cluny transept tower, the masons created the impression of more plane reveals than actually existed: in the choir the egg-and-dart molding ("c") recedes between stepped archivolts, but in the apse the molding ("d") only appears to be recessed; similar to the button molding on the Cluny tower, it actually projects from a flush wall, leaving the dosseret beneath the molding ("e") free to support the extra plane from the Lombard band. In this way, the masons blended traditions: they simultaneously added planes and transformed southern motifs with northern construction, framing the corbels with oversized ashlar and "catching" the Lombard band with a corresponding dosseret and horizontal molding. Moreover, although they vertically extended the principal dosseret through the arcade level, in northern fashion they divided it and the entire elevation into two horizontally unbroken string courses, creating three distinct stories in the choir.

The chevet of Paray exhibits the same complementary blend of southern and northern techniques found in the chapel of Berzé and interior elevation of Cluny. To understand this new achievement as an expression of individuals and not an abstract style, I have distinguished the parts of Cluny and Paray which were built first and then interpreted them as the work of masons from different traditions who learned from each other. While I cannot overlook the possibility of a creative visual role for abbots or even architects, I take the position that we have no evidence that they participated or even that the design process was centralized or organized from above the atelier level. The emerging picture shows that the Cluniacs used the available local talent, and these masons in the course of construction worked out a new relationship among themselves. Their work at Cluny reflects a creative moment when masons not only applied their distinctive techniques and aesthetics to large-scale religious architecture, but merged two previously separate masonry traditions into a new design. The result is something new, containing all the subtleties and complexities of late eleventh-century ashlar and brick-based construction.

But the architecture is not new in a way standard to Cluniac theory—in the sense of an architectural revolution engendered from foreign designs by an overseeing intellectual. In spite of an overlay of classical devices, the core of the building is a survival of masonry traditions from the local regions of the Mâconnais and Brionnais. This revision of theory, however, does not mean that the important role of Cluny is diminished. Far from it. The role is simply changed. Cluny is the point of synthesis—a unique, exceptional experiment—but not the revolution from outside heretofore thought. The experiment was eclipsed suddenly as artistic centers like Charlieu, Dijon, and Autun sprang up outside the Mâconnais after 1120 and masons turned for inspiration to the Rhône Valley, Ile-de-France, and Lyon, sites far from Cluny.[35]

NOTES

1. Cluny III may not have been a classical watershed of revolutionary importance because the Atelier had employed antique vocabulary long before in different contexts like bases and moldings, as seen in the continuous exterior cyma molding at Mâcon. While at Cluny they largely stopped combining local base and molding designs with classical decoration, in a process quite different from a classical revival the Atelier distilled the antique features from the wide range of motifs they had used before. Indeed, the role of Cluny in a classical revival is further reduced in light of the Gallo-Roman motifs which northern First Romanesque masons introduced earlier in Burgundy. See note 28.

2. Deshoulières, "Essai sur les tailloirs romans," 18, 31. Although he denied any "règles fixes," Deshoulières recognized an evolution in the Romanesque "tailloirs à baguette centrale": "ce quart-de-rond ou cette baguette mal dégagée devient un véritable tore allégé par des onglets, des cavets ou des gorges." In general, Deshoulières believed that Romanesque imposts followed more of a "véritable évolution" than bases, although he admitted exceptions, anomalies and regional differences. He limited his views on the evolution to general statements (p. 45): "the luxurious exuberance increased while the proportions and profile of the imposts decreased."

3. By contrast, it is standard theory that the Brion-

nais base type used by the Atelier is considered to be too varied and fanciful to be used as a measure of change. Deshoulières ("Essai sur les bases romanes," 83) described the Brionnais bases as "trop fantaisistes" for measuring an "évolution," a position repeated by R. Oursel (*Les églises*, 70): "les types des bases de colonnes sont variés et la plus grande fantaisie y règne." In describing the bases of Vézelay, Salet (*Vézelay*, 50) believed that "comme ces divers profils se distribuent au hasard, on n'en saurait tirer argument pour la marche des travaux." While I distinguish the wall bases from the freestanding bases at Vézelay, I also believe that certain of the later bases were added to the wall after the destruction of 1120, especially in the southern aisle; moreover, a few of the earlier bases were reused in the freestanding western bays. Complicating the issue are the recarved bases of Viollet-le-Duc as well as the bases with a classical torus-scotia profile. These latter bases confuse any straightforward comparison between the Brionnais base types on the freestanding and aisle piers.

4. A second and later atelier executed the second-story facade of Charlieu. The dimensions, proportions, finish, and lay of the remaining masonry are different, as are the type and treatment of bases, capitals, moldings, and archivolts. See chapter 4, note 1.

5. The distinction on the interior between the Ate-

lier's work and the construction of the previous nave at Anzy is discussed in chapter 4, note 2.

6. At Montceaux, the interior dosserets, capitals, and bases, as well as the exterior buttresses, masonry, and corbels on the crossing bay are different and earlier than the nave construction. The masonry probably is the work of the same masons who built the heretofore unrecognized first campaign at Châteauneuf. That campaign extends horizontally to just above the level of the southern nave portal. The details on the Montceaux crossing corbels relate directly to the corbels above the chevet at Iguerande. See chapter 3, note 5.

7. Elizabeth Sunderland, *Charlieu*, 44.

8. The evidence from the crossing piers at Vézelay indicates that a similar system existed there on the earlier church. A remarkable similarity exists between the size, shape, finish, and lay of masonry on the Vézelay crossing piers, and the construction of the first-story facade at Charlieu and the nave piers at Anzy.

9. For a campaign description, see chapter 4, note 2.

10. For a campaign description, see chapter 4, note 3.

11. The second story of the Perrecy narthex was completed by different Brionnais masons. Above the ground floor the original Atelier's masons' marks disappear; a later, low and compressed classical torus-scotia base type appears; brick-based filler stones surround some of the windows; and diamond-shaped imposts and Brionnais capital foliage, absent from the work of the Atelier on the ground floor, appear on the second-story arcade. See chapter 4, note 4.

12. According to Conant ("Excavations at Cluny, IX," 6), instead of assimilating two traditionally separate groups of masons, the Cluny III atelier grew from a single, specifically Cluniac work-force: "the works of Abbot Hugh at Cluny in the eight years 1078–85 clearly involved a great continuous chantier with all the implied concomitant systems of design, control, and supply. This organization, capable of being transferred at once to the great church, explains the rapid construction of Cluny III." Again in 1971, Conant ("La chronologie," 341, 347) described an "équipe permanente" "continuellement en fonction" at Cluny.

13. In the two undated, unpublished, and uncatalogued manuscripts in the municipal library of Dijon discussed in appendix 1, Pierre Truchis probably first outlined these separate traditions of eleventh-century Burgundian architecture ("Architecture-romane-lombarde en Franche-Comté"; "Ecole de Bourgogne, ancien évêché de Mâcon—architecture romane primitive dans le Département de Saône-et-Loire").

14. The capitals and bases in the Tournus cloister were cut on the sides to fit the outside wall. These alterations indicate that they were not designed for their present location, and I believe (appendix 2) that capitals from before 1050 were reemployed in a second cloister cam-

paign, dating from the last half of the century. The stylistic relationship of the capitals from the cloister at Tournus to capitals in the so-called baptistry of Venasque and Saint-Pierre at Montmajour has been recognized since P.-A. Février ("Venasque," 348–364). Alan Borg further suggested, correctly in my opinion, that the same workshop produced these three groups of capitals (*Architectural Sculpture in Romanesque Provence*, 21). See also, John B. Cameron, "Early Romanesque Sculpture in Provence and the Dauphin Capitals," 15. These discussions of the sculpture overlook the important connections between the Saint-Michael and cloister capitals from Tournus and the sculpture from the crypt of Meaux Cathedral, suggested by Maurice Berry in conversation about his article, "Tournus l'abbaye de Saint Philibert." See also Jean-Michel Desbordes, "La troisième campagne de fouilles sous le choeur de la cathédrale de Meaux," 27–33.

Another isolated example of "Loire Valley" sculpture in Burgundy, in this case dating very early, to the year 1000, is cited by Louis Grodecki ("La sculpture du XIᵉ siècle en France," 98–112). He maintained that capitals in the crypt of Saint-Bénigne at Dijon are closely connected to First Romanesque capitals at Bernay, Saint-Germain-des-Prés, and Saint-Aignan at Orléans. I believe that the ashlar detailing in the rotunda, like the capitals on the cloister at Tournus, were isolated elements applied to a fabric of southern, brick-based construction (see appendix 1).

Pierre Truchis thoroughly investigated the simultaneous practice of northern and southern First Romanesque architecture in Burgundy and published his findings in 1921 (see note 13 and appendix 1, especially note 4). However, the lack of dissemination of the literature has caused oversights in major recent publications on Saint-Bénigne at Dijon, as discussed in appendix 1, note 31.

The chevet of Anzy is an example from the last half of the eleventh century in which northern and southern masons worked simultaneously—even on the same part of one building. A northern atelier created the ashlar details, including moldings, corbels, bases, and capitals, and their work probably affected the southern atelier to the extent that ashlar quoining began to frame the southern-based stones toward the top of the transept. See chapter 3, note 6.

15. Conant, *Cluny*, 80ff. Gilon in Dom A. l'Huillier, *Vie de saint Hugues*, 605–7.

16. The relief of Burgundian southern First Romanesque figural sculpture, in the few cases that exist, is extremely shallow, barely projecting from the surface of the architecture. The statue column, usually thought of as a creation of the Gothic period, actually developed in this southern First Romanesque context. The origin of the statue column within southern First Romanesque

architecture is understandable from the unpublished example in the Chapaize tower (Fig. 38b) where the figure projects little from the architectural column and continues its vertical lines. By contrast, sculpture in northern First Romanesque architecture is part of a horizontal articulation where orders are caught by projecting moldings, capitals, columns, and bases. See Armi, "Orders and Continuous Orders in Romanesque Architecture," 178–181.

17. Exceptionally, as described in note 14, an isolated northern ashlar detail is implanted in the brick-based fabric of the building. See also the impost on the southwestern corner of the nave at Chapaize.

18. Certain of the interior pilasters were reconstructed in brick when Jean-François Maurice restored the painting in 1857. For a description of the painting restoration, see Rhein, "Anzy," 283.

19. R. Oursel attributed a few limited features of Cluny III to southern First Romanesque architecture. These included the type of vault and "petit appareil uniforme" ("A propos de la 'reconstruction' de l'abbatiale Saint-Martin d'Autun au XVIIIᵉ siècle," 70). Similarly, his father recognized a few "secondary" features such as arches and vaults as originating in the "Lombard Style," although he believed that their impact died out: "l'architecture bourguignonne du XIᵉ siècle, celle de la première période romane, était engagée dans une voie a peu près sans issue" (*L'art roman*, 54f).

20. The confusion in the wall planes, to the right of the choir window in Figure 49b, is perhaps the result of a slight advance in the wall surface which corresponds to the projection of a horizontal molding immediately below it. Not being trained in the northern system of projecting moldings, southern masons in their own manner may have built the wall out as a plane to correspond to this decorative molding. As a result, this extra projecting reveal overlapped the normal wall plane ("2b") where the two met at the right of the window. My thanks to Debbie Bedford.

21. The arcade on the outer surface of the aisle is largely restored.

22. For the bibliography and dates of Berzé, see the first excursus to chapter 1, as well as Virey, "Berzé," 91–93; R. Oursel, "Berzé-la-Ville," 1–8. The first surviving photographs made by the Commission des Monuments historiques date from the classification and restoration of 1893 [*Bulletin archéologique du comité des travaux historiques et scientifiques* 3 (1893): 420].

23. Fernand Mercier ("Berzé-la-Ville," 489) proposed that the two floors of the chapel were created in separate campaigns because of the difference in painting technique—fresco below and tempera above—and differences in stone construction—irregular "gros appareil" below and "perfectly worked stones of large dimensions" above; and because of the non-correspondence of the exterior bands from the two stories. Salet ("Cluny

III," 280f.) agreed that the top story is "mal liée à celle de la chapelle basse." Straightforward errors and inconsistencies undermine these observations. First, paint was applied after the architecture and therefore should not be used to date the building. Second, only the bands on the apse do not correspond; the bands on the side, visible on the south, continue to the ground without interruption. Third, there are many examples, such as the narthex of Tournus, where vertical bands do not align within a single campaign. Indeed, on the eastern face of the three-story transept at Cluny, the two bands on the top story veer noticeably to either side of the bands below them—yet Salet overlooked these discrepancies when he described this bay as the uniform work of a single campaign. Fourth, the interruption of bands in the apse of Berzé does not simply involve bands but the larger issue of northern and southern masons working together. A discrepancy is almost to be expected in this case where northern masons, trained in horizontal articulation and ashlar technique, interrupted the continuous brick-based stone construction of Lombard bands with a classical doucine molding and sculpted the Lombard corbel tables with figural reliefs (Fig. 51b). Fifth, in a situation where masons of two different traditions worked this closely together, it is incorrect to assign a portion of their building to one group or to evaluate one element of their work, such as the masonry on the lower story, as "clumsy" and "irregular." Rather, qualities of both masonry traditions appear throughout the construction of Berzé: as I pointed out in the text, within the predominantly northern details of the upper story, certain elements like the exterior corbels are worked almost entirely in the brick tradition of the South; but while the corbels on the first story are Lombard in type, their execution with a doucine profile and ashlar figural representation indicates a distinctly northern presence.

24. Armi, "Orders and Continuous Orders," 173–188. In explaining the origin of the high medieval bay system, Walter Horn skipped the vaulted bays of southern First Romanesque architecture and turned to wooden prototypes ("On the Origins of the Medieval Bay System," 2–23).

25. For the different characteristics of the early and late bases of Cluny III, see appendix 4, and Fig. 68.

26. C. Oursel (*L'art roman*, 93) described the Berzé apse arcade as "à peu près identique" to the one at Mazille. At Mazille, the ashlar details of the apse, including the string course, bases, and capitals, are closer to Berzé than to any building in the Mâconnais. In comparison to Cluny III, the exterior corbels and socle moldings of Mazille are comparable to the latest phase of construction. The squared profile of the tower string course is standard only in the latest examples of Mâconnais First Romanesque construction at Chissey, Taizé, Clessé, and Chazelle. See also A. Lorton, *Mazille et Sainte-Cécile*.

27. The southern First Romanesque tower, to the best

of my knowledge, never has been suggested as a source for the elevation of Cluny III. See especially the Burgundian tower studies of Marcel Aubert ("Les clochers romans bourguignons," 38–70); A. Margand ("Les églises et clochers Mâconnais: région du sud-est," 35–36, 63–64); Evans (*Romanesque Architecture*, 130–131); Virey (*Les églises*, 49–57), who, far from seeing a source in the Mâconnais First Romanesque towers, labelled their constructors "médiocrement préoccupés." Robert Branner suggested that Gothic builders used the exterior elevation of Romanesque towers like Bury Saint Edmunds as the model for the 1160–1180 interior *parti* ("Gothic Architecture 1160–1180 and Its Romanesque Sources," 92–104).

28. It is a standard theory that Roman ruins in Burgundy inspired the Cluniac elevation: in describing the triple story and superimposed orders of Cluny, C. Oursel (*L'art roman*, 138) referred to the mother church as "une véritable colonie de Rome en Mâconnais," just as Evans (*Romanesque Architecture*, 86) observed that "this characteristically Burgundian arrangement seems ultimately to have been derived from a Roman tradition." See also Jalabert, *Sculpture romane*, 64. Many scholars specifically credited the Roman arches of Autun with inspiring the Cluniac three-story elevation: Lasteyrie (*L'architecture*, 430) pointed to "la porte d'Arroux qui a inspiré le triforium d'Autun, comme celui de Cluny et tous leurs dérivés"; and Lefèvre-Pontalis ("Etude historique et archéologique sur l'église de Paray-le-Monial," 333) believed that the classical elements in the elevation of Paray were "explained by the impact of the Autun portals." In a seminar in the Department of Art, University of North Carolina, Chapel Hill, in 1979, Anne de Forest distinguished between the application of isolated classical motifs at Cluny III and the interpretation of an entire classical model, the Roman portal, at Saint-Lazarus of Autun. She rejected the close dependence of Autun on the elevation of Cluny. Héliot ("Autun," 191) suggested another possible source for the pilasters in the nave of Autun: the interior decorative pilasters common in the apses of parish churches in the Brionnais, Mâconnais, Beaujolais, and Lyonnais.

Typically, Meyer Schapiro subtly refined the problem of classicism (*Parma*, 38), proposing that perhaps classical traits first appeared in the minor arts: "the introduction of classical forms from Italy through painters in the late eleventh century stimulated the builders and sculptors in Burgundy to study and adapt elements of Roman art still visible in ancient remains in France"; when classicism did appear in architecture, he proposed that it modified a predominantly local style ("Review of *L'art roman*," 228): "did not the architects in the late eleventh century and in the twelfth modify a native style, itself unlike Roman art, by imposing on it visible Roman forms of the region?"

29. From the evidence in this chapter, I disagree with Evans' conclusion (*Romanesque Architecture*, 119) that Berzé appeared unusual or alien in the Mâconnais and that bands coupled to arcades were rare in High Cluniac architecture: "Berzé . . . has a slightly alien air in the Mâconnais, and it is easy to recognize other than local influence in it. Pilaster strips and multiple arcades are, indeed, rarely used on the nave walls of Cluniac churches."

30. The only example of flagging in the first campaign is an exterior column on the minor transept chapel, and it is flagged only on one side and only part of the way up the column. In this case the courses of the flagging stones in most instances do not correspond to the beds of the filler stones. For the curious case of the ashlar on the choir portal, see appendix 4.

31. See note 33.

32. The most common Cluniac motif, the rosette, dominates the architectural decoration at Vézelay as well. Rosettes appear on the interior on the central string course molding in the nave and on the exterior on the corbel molding—the only noticeable carved decoration along the flanks of the building. This is but another repetition of decorative masonry at both buildings and is another example of the lack of substance to the theory of a "Martinienne" resistance to Cluny at Vézelay (see note 33).

33. Following Truchis ("Eléments barbares, éléments étrangers"), C. Oursel ("Les églises Martiniennes de l'école romane de Bourgogne," 293, and *L'art roman*, 100) and his son R. Oursel (*Les églises*, 19) correctly recognized Vézelay's northern First Romanesque origins. Extending this theory, however, they incorrectly believed that Vézelay's groin-vaulted nave represented a political rejection, a "volonté d'autonomie" from Cluny. Instead, I maintain that in vaulting, masons at each building continued the tradition with which they were most familiar. The Atelier modified the groin vault standard to northern First Romanesque architecture, adapting it to a domical construction at Anzy and using it without completely crossing the arris at Vézelay (Robert Vassas, "Travaux à la Madeleine de Vézelay," 56–61). They only rarely employed a barrel, and when they did they treated it like a groin, placing it laterally in a separate compartment as at Perrecy. By contrast at Cluny, when the southern masons joined the Atelier, they introduced the standard southern First Romanesque nave barrel into the Atelier's work for the first time. Despite just criticisms of the "Martinienne" theory—that Vézelay was a dependency of Cluny during the period of Romanesque construction (Salet, *Vézelay*, 104), that Cluniac sculptors worked at both Vézelay and Cluny (Schapiro, "Review of Charles Oursel," 227), and my own claim that the same masons worked at both sites—the theory of the northern origins of the architectural style, when stripped of political implications, is fundamentally sound.

34. The local Brionnais atelier who completed the nave (appendix 5) used no continuous orders or Lombard bands in any part of their construction. This difference in the work of the two ateliers confirms the campaign differences I discerned through archaeology (appendix 5).

35. For the twelfth-century sculptural links of Burgundy to the Rhône Valley, see Neil Stratford, "Chronologie et filiations stylistiques," 7–12; for the contacts of Tournus and the Dombes buildings to the Lyonnais, see Vallery-Radot, "La limite méridionale de l'école romane de Bourgogne," 295, 302. R. Oursel ("Mise au point,"

353) suggested that two "axes" emerged in Burgundy in the course of the twelfth century. The double axes of Cluny, Charlieu, and La-Charité, as opposed to Langres, Dijon, Avallon, Vézelay, and the Ile-de-France, expressed the "political evolution" of the area in which Cluny, spiritually and materially impoverished, "passe la main." Lücken ("Burgundische Skulpturen," 123) recognized that in the first half of the twelfth century, the "stark vorhandene Stileinheit des ganzen Gebiets hört auf" and was replaced by "eine Vielsprachigkeit des künstlerischen Ausdrucks."

Excursus: Southern First Romanesque Terminology

Isolated in Spain, Puig i Cadafalch felt he could say, "Je n'ai guère de prédécesseurs."[1] But earlier nineteenth-century French architectural historians Anthyme Saint-Paul, Courajod, Enlart, Lefèvre-Pontalis, Lasteyrie, and Truchis were in substantial agreement with two of his major conclusions about the architecture which preceded the Romanesque: that it (1) existed throughout the southern littoral of Europe, and (2) was folkloric and unprogressing (unlike Puig, these scholars maintained that Lombardy was the source of the pre-Romanesque style).[2]

Underlying these two conclusions about Lombard architecture is an aesthetic outlook shared by Puig and his followers when they described First Romanesque architecture. The chief spokesman for Lombard architecture, A. K. Porter, suggested that the style was a "failure" because it "attempted what it could not carry to completion."[3] The concept of an architecture unable to lift itself up by its own boot straps, so to speak, becomes also the standard explanation for the "unprogressing" character of First Romanesque architecture. In the introduction to *La géographie et les origines du premier art roman*, Puig held a transfixing, primordial law, a sort of aesthetic determinism, responsible for the static character of this widespread architectural style:

> Il y a des sauts, des éclairs de génie; les caractères architectoniques ne se déroulent pas toujours suivant une loi de continuité. Mais ces objections perdent quelque portée, quand il s'agit de ces arts

primitifs, pleins de saveur populaire, où l'initiative individuelle n'agit pas sur le fond du style. Aujourd'hui il nous est difficile de nous rendre compte de ce qu'était cet art si lent à évoluer, où les disciples recevaient intégralement l'héritage de leurs maîtres, les préceptes empiriques d'un métier régi par des formules, comme le sont les oeuvres populaires. L'époque moderne a introduit dans l'évolution de l'art la prédominance anarchique de l'individu et accéléré le rythme de son évolution. Nous approchons du temps où chaque aspect de l'art architectonique, oeuvre individuelle, ne sera plus qu'une mode éphémère. Dans cette ambiance, il nous est difficile de comprendre un art dont l'élaboration dura des siècles, qui se mouvait lentement, avec une solennelle majesté, obéissant à des lois que tout homme suivait inconsciemment, comme les prescriptions d'un canon sacré.[4]

Mâconnais First Romanesque Architecture. C. Oursel and Virey, the two authorities on Mâconnais architecture, took the case of "aesthetic determinism" a step further. Like Puig and the French architectural historians before him, Oursel described early eleventh-century Mâconnais architecture as (1) an unprogressing, folkloric style (2) present in the same form throughout the southern littoral of Europe.[5] Also, like Porter and Puig, he found the style an aesthetic "dead end": "Au reste, malgré la multiplicité et l'ingéniosité des méthodes . . . l'architecture bourguignonne du XIᵉ siècle, celle de la première période romane, était engagée dans une voie à peu près sans issue." The distinguishing feature of this form of aesthetic determinism is that it is defined structurally; in the tradition of Franz Kugler, structure expresses aesthetic choice or demand: "Or nos architectes du XIᵉ siècle demandaient essentiellement l'équilibre à l'entassement des matériaux. Peu leur importait d'avoir à remuer un grand nombre de ces matériaux, petits et de cube réduit."[6] This aesthetic preference produced a structure that was self-defeating: "Les murs sont donc énormes, les piles volumineuses, les arcs épais et grossiers, les portées assez réduites par un compartimentage multiple, les percements timides par crainte de compromettre la solidité des murailles. L'ensemble est lourd et pesant, et si l'on veut faire grand, on risque aussi de le faire plus lourd et plus pesant, d'augmenter les poussées, donc la masse qui les doit contenir. C'est un cercle vicieux." Severe structural limits were imposed therefore by the aesthetic demands: "Mais sa technique, emprisonnée dans la masse, ne pouvait se rénover par elle-même." A new aesthetic was needed to overcome the structural impasse. "C'est, en un mot, un art primitif ou primaire, qui ne peut guère, par ses propres moyens, sortir de lui-même. Mais à la fin du XIᵉ siècle, grâce à Cluny, l'architecture bourguignonne va réussir à s'en évader rapidement."[7]

Virey also described eleventh-century Mâconnais architecture as an unprogressing, folkloric style present throughout the southern littoral of Europe.[8] Like Oursel, Virey found that the structure of Mâconnais First Romanesque architecture expressed an aesthetic of "l'entassement des matériaux"; only the Cluniac "renaissance" brought relief from this sad state of affairs: "Longtemps et surtout pendant la première moitié du XIᵉ siècle, nos constructeurs, comme l'a justement remarqué M. Oursel, ont demandé l'équilibre à l'entassement des matériaux: murs énormes, piliers encombrants, arcs épais et grossiers, portées réduites, percements timides . . . et ce n'est que vers la fin du même siècle, grâce à la construction de l'abbatiale de saint Hugues à Cluny que l'architecture bourguignonne prit son essor."[9]

The men who have written of Lombard or First Romanesque architecture, then, have held that throughout the littoral of southern Europe was found an architectural style which could not catapult itself beyond the level of folk art. Although Oursel was the first Frenchman to give this "aesthetic determinism" a structural definition, he had in fact been anticipated by the German Gottfried von Lücken who, in 1913, applied the structural theories of Kugler to Burgundian Romanesque architecture.[10]

Like Oursel after him, Lücken assigned an aesthetic to a specific group of buildings which had been constructed within a definite time period. The first chapter of *Die Anfänge der burgundischen Schule* was entitled "Die flächenhafte, ungegliederte Architektur am Anfang des 11. Jahrhunderts" because Lücken saw the aesthetic of the first phase of Burgundian architecture expressing an unarticulated, flat surface character. Like Oursel, Lücken's next step was to give a structural definition to this aesthetic. Using the Kuglerian formulae, Lücken described the structure of the architecture as at the very beginning of the *Wechselwirkung* between *Last* and *Stütze*, an interchange that was worked out in the course of the development of medieval architecture. This beginning stage was characterized by a total lack of expression of the architectural forces (load and support):

> Alle die Errungenschaften, die die römische Kunst sich erworben hatte, um die Wand zu gliedern und die Last auf wenige Punkte zu verteilen, sind aufgegeben. Der Mauerkörper wird als einheitliche, gleichartige Masse aufgefasst. Ebenso ist der Pfeiler, der die Mittelschiffsarkaden trägt, ein unartikuliertes Glied. Die Funktion, die er ausübt, ist in keiner Weise betont. Basen und Kapitelle sind zu schwachen Profilierungen zusammengeschrumpft. Der Körper des Pfeilers bleibt ungegliedert, er ist im Querschnitt ein einfaches Rund oder Rechteck und ist nicht mit Rücksicht auf das gebildet, was er zu tragen hat. Tragende und lastende Glieder stehen einander neutral gegenüber. Etwas unvermittelt sitzen die Arkaden, zumal wo die Pfeiler runde Formen zeigen, auf diesen auf. Es fehlt jede Betonung der Struktur.[11]

Using a very similar method, Oursel would later arrive at almost the same conclusions: an aesthetic of bound masses gave rise to a cumbrous, under-developed structure. For both Lücken and Oursel, there existed in the Mâconnais a base group of buildings defined by an undeveloping structural aesthetic.[12]

French First Romanesque and "Schools". With the exception of a Germanic interest in the structural limitations of First Romanesque architecture in Burgundy, Oursel and Virey resembled modern architectural historians writing on French First Romanesque. These scholars repeated the formula established a generation before for Lombard architecture: the double concept of First Romanesque architecture in France as (1) an unprogressing, folkloric architecture, (2) present in the same form throughout the southern littoral of Europe.[13] For the modern generation of French architectural historians, such an explanation in no way contradicted the traditional concept of regional "Schools": since the First Romanesque architecture in France was nowhere unique—in no region showed signs of repeated and developing original forms—regional "Schools" could have come about only after the mid-eleventh century, as had always been maintained. However, there were some regional differences among First Romanesque buildings. In order to continue using the traditional "School" theory, a new vocabulary had to be developed to accommodate the *lusus naturae.*

The new vocabulary was used to describe architecture which was not strictly speaking First Romanesque but which did not approach a "School" type. The apparent object of such vocabulary was to maintain the distance between First Romanesque and "School" architecture, to retain the uniform, unprogressing quality of First Romanesque architecture on the one hand and the regional quality of the "Schools," distinctly separate, on the other. A good recent example of the new terms is *mi-chemin,* a word recently used by Jacques Thirion, a specialist in Provençal First Romanesque architecture, to describe the church of Saint-Donat: "Ainsi l'église de Saint-Donat nous apparaît à mi-chemin entre les églises alpines et les églises provençales. . . . l'église de Saint-Donat, au coeur des Alpes de Provence, semble donc constituer une sorte de lien entre les édifices du premier art roman conservés surtout dans les montagnes et les grandes églises rhodaniennes du stade des écoles."[14] The word *mi-chemin* is typical of all these

new terms. It keeps two closed systems closed, while allowing exceptions to run in between.

A New Vocabulary for Mâconnais First Romanesque Architecture. A few scholars saw no trace of local originality in the First Romanesque architecture of the Mâconnais. They, of course, needed no new vocabulary to describe differences which they did not see. Virey was one.[15] Vallery-Radot believed that architectural irregularities which were thought to be of local type (he called them *jeux d'appareil*) were actually standard throughout southern Europe.[16] Similarly, Puig found no such thing as a variant or a uniquely local First Romanesque device.[17]

The other writers who ascertained a degree of independence in Mâconnais architecture found new means to fit these buildings into the universal formula of First Romanesque architecture. With the aid of a new vocabulary that eliminated regional First Romanesque types, these writers bolstered the endangered French "School" theory.

To retain the definition of an unprogressing First Romanesque architecture, Bréhier established a new category of early Romanesque; besides the architecture north of the Loire and the architecture of the First Romanesque in the south, he established a third type: the tenth-century "School" type of the Basse-Auvergne. Here were concentrated all the creative efforts of early Romanesque architecture, whereas the variants of Burgundy were merely *tâtonnements, prototypes, formules,* and *tendances.* In this way, the "School" superstructure remained intact, First Romanesque universally remained uninterrupted by regional variations,[18] and the date of formation of a single "School" was simply pushed back.[19]

Similarly, Oursel introduced the term *variantes* to describe the unique qualities of Burgundian First Romanesque architecture. Only with the architecture of Cluny III was a real "School" type discovered:

> . . . type lombard. Ils ont marqué à l'origine un progrès considérable; puis l'art s'est en apparence à peu près stabilisé, et les variantes introduites, si appréciables qu'elles soient, manifestent une marche lente dans une voie tracée, un peu monotone, et sans grande perspective.
>
> Avec Cluny et saint Hugues, à la fin du

XIᵉ siècle et au commencement du XIIᵉ, l'horizon se découvre soudain. Une formule définitive est trouvée.[20]

Francastel also found any distinct character of Mâconnais First Romanesque architecture to be of an incidental variety. He applied the terms *nouveauté* and *formules* to differences not sufficient to establish a regional stylistic "School."

> . . . le premier emploi d'un procédé ne constitue pas un témoignage chronologique ni esthétique absolu. Aucun déterminisme ne préside à l'évolution de l'art, du moins aucun déterminisme matériel. Certaines formules, comme celle de Tournus ou de Romainmôtier auraient pu—la seconde l'a prouvé plus tard—donner naissance à un style. Elles ne l'ont fait à l'époque romane. L'art roman n'était pas préfiguré, pour ainsi dire, par le parti du voûtement total de l'édifice. Il ne suffit pas qu'à une époque, on voit surgir une nouveauté pour que l'on puisse déclarer, aussitôt, qu'un nouveau style existe. Comme celle d'école, la notion de style implique l'idée de groupement, de série. Elle suppose non l'identité, mais la parenté des solutions.[21]

For Francastel, "School" Romanesque began after 1070 and First Romanesque (as defined by Puig) was only one of a number of international styles present in Burgundy in the year 1000.[22]

Focillon asked questions about the significance of the variants of First Romanesque architecture in Burgundy: "At an early date it had produced buildings like Saint-Bénigne at Dijon and Saint-Philibert at Tournus. But, thus dignified by the authority of powerful tradition of its mediterranean borrowings, was it at the same time capable of devising new forms in western art or of foreshadowing the great Burgundian Romanesque which was to follow?"[23] His answer was hardly precise. He saw that two architectural elements were created in Burgundy—the so-called Benedictine plan, and the combination of stone vaults and direct lighting in the nave. For Focillon these Burgundian developments did not constitute a local "School," they simply revealed the creativity

within the international style of First Romanesque. Focillon's point was that "In Provence . . . and still more in Burgundy, it [First Romanesque] has representatives whose stylistic purity does not preclude the most profound originality."[24] As Bréhier applied the term *tendances* and Francastel *formules* to the incidental variety in Burgundian First Romanesque architecture, so Focillon invested the architecture with a turn of phrase: "modifications of an obsolescent academism."

Although Deshoulières regarded Focillon's early dating of Burgundian vaults as incorrect, he agreed that the First Romanesque international style was capable of greater individualism than Puig allowed. "Donnons une part un peu plus grande à l'individualisme."[25] Like other modern French writers, Deshoulières did not think that this "individualism" provided the basis for local "Schools." Rather, First Romanesque was itself a totally international "School," separate from the other *école primitive* of northern France.[26]

Like the French writers, Conant coined his own words for what he considered to be the incidental variety of First Romanesque architecture in the Mâconnais: "Burgundian Developments" he entitled the section of his recent book dealing with the architecture in that part of France between 950 and 1050.[27] Although "progress was early made towards the Romanesque ideal in Burgundy," the progress was within the context of the international First Romanesque style. Conant considered regional "Schools" a phenomenon separate from the "Burgundian Developments" and discussed it apart in his fourth chapter.

In connecting the early architecture of the Mâconnais to English Romanesque, Jean Bony employed the term *chantier* to describe the Tournus type of construction. Cylindrical piers "semblent dénoter toujours l'influence du chantier de Tournus."[28] Whether by professional caution or choice, he went only so far as to define the local style in terms of a *chantier* from the one church; English comparisons were made to this *chantier* and not to later possible derivatives (e.g., Farges, Jura types, or Combertault); in addition, no mention was made of the concept of First Romanesque architecture. Again, Mâconnais architecture fell short of being defined as a local regional "School." Like a *tendance*, a *chantier* is an incidental variety—it does not evince a larger local style.

One group of modern writers, Puig, Virey, and

Vallery-Radot, discovered that every element of Mâconnais First Romanesque architecture existed elsewhere; therefore, no "School" or local style existed in France at the time. Other authors, while agreeing that no regional First Romanesque "School" existed, pointed out that variously named but incidental local variations were unique to the Mâconnais.

NOTES

1. Puig i Cadafalch, *La géographie et les origines du premier art roman*, 7.

2. For the origin of "the theory that, far from constituting merely the local style of North Italy, Lombard architecture was widely disseminated through northern Europe," see Alice Sunderland, "The Legend of the Alternate System at St. Bénigne of Dijon," 2–3. While the earlier writers, A. de Caumont and Jules Quicherat, left Lombard architecture out of their architectural systems, French architectural historians at the end of the nineteenth century included it in their theories. LOUIS COURAJOD outlined the change of theoretical position in *Leçons professées à l'Ecole du Louvre* (p. 392). ANTHYME SAINT-PAUL (*Annuaire de l'archéologie française*, vol. 1, 96) spoke of a communal type within the "région germano-italienne et lombardo-allemande." The type consisted of the division of the exterior wall by Lombard bands which were joined under the cornice by small round arcades. Louis Courajod, although he disagreed with Caumont, Quicherat, and Viollet-le-Duc about the ultimate origin of Lombard architecture, agreed with them about the basic principle of the style ("Etude de l'art lombard," *Leçons professées*, 391): "Il y eut certainement au Xe siècle, et surtout au commencement du XIe siècle, un style d'architecture en pierre qui fut en quelque sorte international. C'était le style lombard." The influence of Lombard architecture was "énorme" in France (p. 394); he cited Saint-Bénigne of Dijon as a French example left by the *magistri comacini* ("La pénétration lombarde," 379). ROBERT DE LASTEYRIE disagreed with Courajod about the ultimate origin of Lombard architecture, yet cited the international similarities of the style's bands and arcades (*L'architecture religieuse*, 22). CAMILLE ENLART (*Manuel d'archéologie française*, vol. 1, 201–202) posited an international unprogressing style: "Les premières années du XIIe siècle produisirent des édifices semblables à ceux du XIe siècle: il ne paraît pas qu'alors aucun progrès appréciable ait été réalisé depuis cent ans, quand, tout à coup, l'art prend un essor prodigieux et réalise en quelques années la transformation la plus complète. . . . L'architecture romane peut être l'objet de deux grandes divisions chronologiques, XIe et XIIe siècles, et de deux grandes divisions géographiques: l'Ecole germanique et lombarde et les Ecoles françaises." The "Ecole de Bourgogne n'est réellement formée qu'au XIIe siècle"; in the meanwhile "le Mâconnais lui échappe en partie pour s'en tenir à la première manière bourguignonne, apparentée à celles du Languedoc et de la Lombardie." And PIERRE DE TRUCHIS also described Mâconnais churches as Lombard in style ("Les influences orientales dans l'architecture romane de la Bourgogne," 465): "C'est une équipe de bâtisseurs ravenniens qui en fut chargée [Saint-Bénigne at Dijon], tendis qu'un atelier de la même école reconstruisait la nef de Saint-Philibert de Tournus et surélevait son narthex à l'appel de l'abbé Bernier. . . . Tournus, Dijon, et Cluny peuvent revendiquer l'honneur d'avoir été le foyer d'où rayonna en Bourgogne l'école lombardo–proto-byzantine." Later Truchis was the first to formulate the differences, most notably reformulated by Plat, Francastel, Deshoulières, and Grodecki, between a First Romanesque architecture of the south and a First Romanesque architecture of the north ("L'architecture de la Bourgogne française sous Robert-le-Pieux," 37). On one side of a "barrière naturelle" stood a French architecture in the Carolingian-Roman tradition, progressive ("aboriginally" creative), varied, and the wave of the future; on the other side, entirely isolated, endured the unprogressing, folkloric ("vulgar"), alien Latin-Lombard architecture (defined p. 20). Deshoulières recorded the final opinion of EUGENE LEFEVRE-PONTALIS on Romanesque "Schools"; Lefèvre-Pontalis attached an eighth "School" to Choisy's seven, the "école lombardo-rhénane" ("La théorie d'Eugène Lefèvre-Pontalis sur les écoles romanes," 229): "L'école lombarde, qui a été constituée dès le XIe siècle, a régné dans l'Italie du Nord d'où elle est descendue jusqu'à Naples en créant des édifices d'un intérêt considérable. Dans le courant d'influences qu'elle a produit en France elle a suivi une double voie: la première s'est dirigée sur le versant des Alpes pour gagner la rive gauche du Rhin en passant par Tournus, tandis que l'autre côtoyait la Méditerranée pour parvenir dans le Roussillon et la Catalogne, mais après s'être échappée dans l'île de Corse.

"On a dit avec raison que cette marche avait été conduite par des maçons migrateurs, les *maestri comacini* qui, partis de la Lombardie, apportaient dans les différentes régions où ils allaient travailler les méthodes architecturales de leur pays d'origine. Nous avons vu en effet que Guillaume de Volpiano s'était fait accompagner en Bourgogne par des maçons."

3. Porter, *Medieval Architecture*, 221: "Lombard architecture, although it showed much attainment on its decorative no less than on its constructive side, still fell far short of being a truly great, or even a satisfying art. There is no monument of the Lombard Romanesque capable of affording deep esthetic enjoyment. Although the charm of age, the glamour of history, the thought that these monuments are the parents of the stately cathedrals beyond the Alps, lend them an undeniable interest; although there is a grace that cannot be gainsaid in such a design as that of S. Lazaro, Pavia, the daintiest of all Lombard constructions; yet we turn away from Lombardy towards Pisa, or Venice, or the Rhineland, or France, or Spain, with the feeling that Lombard art, after all, was only a failure; that it was an art which attempted what it was unable to carry to completion." Such aesthetic reservations are surprising from the man who wrote a four-volume work on Lombard architecture. While Porter was unable to derive deep aesthetic enjoyment from the later Lombard buildings such as S. Lazaro, Pavia, he found the earliest examples of the style even less satisfying; e.g., he dated the crypt ambulatory of Ivrea cathedral to the year 1000 on the basis of its "very absence of architectural character" (*Lombard Architecture*, 475).

4. Puig, *La géographie*, 8–9; see also Puig, *Le premier art roman*, 7–8.

5. C. Oursel, *L'art roman*, 57.

6. Ibid., 54–55.

7. Ibid., 57.

8. Virey, *Les églises*, viii–x.

9. Ibid., 13.

10. Lücken, *Die Anfänge*. See chapter 1, second excursus, note 38.

11. Ibid., 26.

12. With the exception of Bourbon-Lancy, the base group of buildings defined by Lücken in chapter one are all located in the Mâconnais; while he included Bourbon-Lancy for its date, he excluded it from his definition of first-phase architecture in Burgundy (*Die Anfänge*, 18): "Nirgends, ausser an der Vierung von Bourbon-Lancy, ist der Kern plastisch gegliedert." Lücken differed from C. Oursel and his French contemporaries by suggesting that an intermediary development existed between buildings of this base group and buildings of the Burgundian Romanesque "School" (see the excursus to chapter 1, note 38).

13. This note includes modern architectural historians who have said that First Romanesque architecture is (1) a folkloric, unprogressing style (2) present in the same form throughout the southern littoral of Europe. BREHIER ("Les origines de l'art roman") believed that

among three architectural types that existed in France at the beginning of the eleventh century, only the "School" of the Massif-Central exhibited original and lasting features. Whereas the churches built north of the Loire "sont restées fidèles, jusqu'au XIIᵉ siècle, aux principes de construction et de décoration élaborés par les clercs de l'entourage de Charlemagne" (p. 134), the churches of the "sud-est," built by the "maîtres lombards," employed even older traditions (p. 133): "Alors que, dans le reste de la France, l'architecture se transformait, ces provinces ont gardé, jusqu'à une époque très avancée, les plans archaïques et les systèmes d'équilibre importés d'orient. C'est ce qui explique qu'en face des écoles régionales du XIIᵉ siècle, l'architecture religieuse du sud-est apparaisse comme une survivance d'un passé déjà lointain." For Bréhier, this Lombard architecture lacked regional qualities (p. 136): "Les églises construites dans ces régions dérivent, soit d'une importation étrangère, soit d'une adaptation artificielle d'éléments antérieurs. Ce n'est pas encore, à proprement parler, une architecture régionale." For PUIG (*Le premier art roman*, 7–8) southern First Romanesque architecture had the stylistic uniformity of folk art: "Le premier art roman, quoique réalisé par des peuples différents apparaît partout avec une grande uniformité. Les lois qui régissent et qui sont observées dans des terres même très lointaines, témoignent d'une force inconnue dans d'autres arts. C'est un art qui pénètre dans le peuple et qui a l'uniformité et la permanence du folklore, et les formes dont il use ont la permanence des choses populaires." The art, in his mind, hardly changed (*La géographie*, 8–9). VIREY (*Les églises*, viii, ix–x) followed Puig's opinion that the style of First Romanesque architecture was international and unprogressing: "Les belles études de M. Puig y Cadafalch, et notamment son ouvrage *Le premier art roman*, nous ont fait voir dans quelle mesure nos églises les plus anciennes, depuis la fin du Xᵉ jusque dans la seconde moitié du XIᵉ siècle, ne se distinguent pas de celles de la même époque construites dans l'aire très étendue reconnue par cet archéologue, en n'ont rien de spécifiquement bourguignon." "C'est seulement à la fin du XIᵉ siècle et au début du XIIᵉ que l'architecture romane bourguignonne prend son caractère, grâce à l'abbatiale de Cluny dont la construction opère une veritable révolution." VALLERY-RADOT ("Le premier art roman de l'occident méditerranéen," 153), spoke of a solid "bloc préroman" conditioned by a special geographic and politial situation. The unprogressing block was undistinguished by local types and was supplanted by the Romanesque "Schools," the "écoles romanes proprement dites." In the "Introduction" (*Congrès archéologique* 121 (1963): 20), he again described the cleavage between the First Romanesque style and the "constitution" of the Romanesque "écoles." In *Eglises romanes, filiations et échanges d'influences* (pp. 17–18), he noted that "les éléments distinctifs, qui doivent constituer les types régionaux, ne sont pas encore pleinement dégagés" in southern First Romanesque architecture. "Alors règne, en effet, une architecture religieuse qui, avant d'être particularisée comme elle le sera plus tard en écoles bien définies, revêt au contraire dans certaines régions—et ces régions sont parfois fort étendues—un caractère d'uniformité très remarquable et pour ainsi dire international." In *Saint-Philibert de Tournus* (p. 22) he speaks of "l'universalité du premier art roman, art interrégional, art sans frontières qui s'était propagé dans la vaste superficie de son aire de diffusion, dont Puig i Cadafalch a précisé la 'géographie'." Vallery-Radot ("Le premier art roman," 166), unlike Cadafalch and Oursel, preferred Lombardy as the source for the international diffusion of First Romanesque architecture. C. OURSEL (*L'art roman*, 55–57), described Burgundian First Romanesque architecture as primary and primitive; it did not appreciably progress and it was supplanted by Cluniac architecture. Oursel believed that only the superficial elements of the Lombard style were picked up in Burgundy; instead, the essential parts of Burgundian early Romanesque architecture derived from the southern First Romanesque buildings in Catalonia. Taking the opposite position from C. Oursel, DESHOULIERES stated that only superficial elements of French First Romanesque architecture came from Catalonia ("Le premier art roman d'après M. Puig i Cadafalch," 102–103); the essential ingredients of the style came from northern Italy. Like Truchis and Plat, Deshoulières described two large-scale "Schools" of early French Romanesque architecture, the southern "School" extending from Lombardy ("Séance du 15 Decembre," 150): "On trouverait alors en France un groupement scindé en deux seules écoles, celle du domaine royal, formée d'éléments nationaux et d'éléments étrangers introduits jadis par les conquérants, Rome et les Barbares; la seconde, composée d'apports venus de l'Italie du Nord et qui demeurera plus sobre, parce que les architectes se contentèrent d'échaffauder une architecture que jadis Ravenne avait su rehausser par des enrichissements abandonnés sur la route. Ce n'est que plus tard que ces deux écoles primitives se multiplièrent pour former celles que nous connaissons sous le nom d'écoles romanes. Mais ce n'est pas sans peine que disparurent les vieux errements lotharingiens. . . ." GABRIEL PLAT (*L'art de bâtir en France*, 192), like Truchis before him, divided French early Romanesque architecture into two groups. He believed that the Lombard group was alien in origin and was so uniform and constant (submitting to a "canon rigide" with "traditions immuables") that it could be called rightfully an international "School": "cet art, estimable par sa technique, barbare par son aspect et monotone par son uniformité." PIERRE FRANCASTEL (*L'humanisme roman*), like Truchis and Plat, distinguished two types of architecture in France at the beginning of the eleventh century. However, unlike these other writers,

Francastel cited both types as unprogressing and traditional. The northern variety was not "aboriginally" creative (Truchis, "Robert-le-Pieux," 23) nor "original and vital" (Plat, *L'art de bâtir*, 193), but was a "Carolingian Renaissance," replaced after 1070 with a truly original architecture deserving the name "Romanesque." Like the other writers charted here, Francastel described the southern type as repeating international folkloric formulas; however, the internationalism was not network-like but congealed around specific and widespread centers (pp. 80, 87): "l'art folklorique naît de la vulgarisation et de la répétition dans un cercle étroit de formules mises au point par un petit nombre de grands hommes ou de grands centres." Although GRODECKI (*L'architecture ottoniene*) pointed out the importance of First Romanesque architecture for later styles (p. 313, note 4, and p. 318), he defined it as an international bloc, as a widespread style, circumscribed in time and space by a "front de résistance," and separate from a "second art roman" as well as from a "premier art roman du Nord." "Elle [Ottonian architecture] fait partie du même bloc stylistique de l'architecture charpentée, formée à partir des prototypes carolingiens, sorte de 'premier art roman du Nord,' distinct, et symétriquement opposé au 'premier art roman' méridional. . . . on peut se demander si nous ne serions pas autorisés, et même obligés, en refusant le cadre fourni par l'histoire politique de l'an mil et en ne retenant que des classements fondés sur l'analyse de style, à grouper dans un même ensemble formel tous les 'styles régionaux' depuis l'Océan jusqu'à l'Elbe, et depuis la mer du Nord jusqu'aux Alpes et jusqu'à la Loire" (pp. 314–315). Grodecki explicitly included the Mâconnais within the orbit of First Romanesque architecture of the South. The region he defined as the "area of contacts" falls to the northeast of the Mâconnais (pp. 63–64, 70). See appendix 1.

14. Jacques Thirion, "L'église de Saint-Donat," 278, 292.

15. Virey, *Les églises*, ix–x; see note 13 above.

16. Vallery-Radot, *Saint-Philibert*, 22–23: "Le narthex de Tournus est l'une des manifestations les plus saisissantes en Bourgogne de l'universalité du premier art roman, art interrégional, art sans frontières. . . . Autour de lui, se groupe toute une famille d'églises mâconnaises de même parentage . . . sans doute, on retrouve, dans le narthex de Tournus plus d'un de leurs caractères distinctifs, grosses piles maçonnées de plan circulaire de Chapaize, de Farges, de Saint-Vincent-des-Près, jeux d'appareil qui semblent la transposition dans la pierre d'un décor de briques, des églises de Blanot, de Farges, de Massy. Mais aucun de ces détails n'est spécifiquement bourguignon. Ils appartiennent à un répertoire de formes très largement disséminées dans le vaste domaine du premier art roman."

17. Although Puig allowed that climate, geography and topography determined differences between build-

ings of the First Romanesque style, he believed that no strictly local aesthetic existed and that no architectural device appeared uniquely on one local group of buildings (*Le premier art roman*, 137). Again in *La géographie*, Puig did not discuss the geographic variants of the style, but rather, by chapter: the topographic range of First Romanesque, the international stages of the style's development, churches ornamented on all sides, simple and transepted basilicas, the migration of the cupola in Europe, analysis of the architectural devices of the style, and the origin of the style. Nowhere were any local variants of the style discussed outside of an international context; in *Le premier art roman* for example, Mâconnais First Romanesque architecture was discussed under these international categories: the transformation of the vaulted basilica (structural problem of vaulting as related to unarticulated piers), cupola basilicas, and the chronological and geographic extension of the First Romanesque style.

18. Bréhier, *L'art en France des invasions barbares à l'époque romane*, 153: "A vrai dire, entre l'art carolingien et l'art roman il n'y a pas de véritable solution de continuité. Une école régionale se forme en Basse-Auvergne dès le Xᵉ siècle, et l'on peut voir dans la curieuse église de Tournus comme un prototype de l'art roman de Bourgogne." Bréhier, "Les origines," 143: "Des églises entièrement voûtées s'élèvent en Bourgogne . . . ne représentent pas encore une architecture régionale. Les berceaux transversaux à la mode persane et les piliers cylindriques de Tournus ne feront pas école en Bourgogne. . . . En un mot, entre 1000 et 1050, le développement architectural a franchi une nouvelle étape, quelques tendances locales se manifestent, mais il n'y a pas encore d'écoles régionales." "Cet architecture ne représente pas une école régionale comme celle du Massif

central, mais une formule antérieure à toutes les écoles régionales . . . " (Bréhier, *L'art en France*, 148).

19. Similarly, Plat pushed back the date of the "écoles romanes du sud-ouest" into the tenth century, "La Touraine berceau des écoles romanes du sud-ouest," 375–377.

20. C. Oursel, *L'art roman*, 57.

21. Francastel, *L'humanisme roman*, 126.

22. Ibid., 133: "Dans la première partie du siècle, où règne, là comme ailleurs, le carolingien, on rencontre en Bourgogne plusieurs types, d'ailleurs internationaux. Il y a des rotondes, comme Saint-Bénigne de Dijon, parallèlement avec des basiliques, comme le second Cluny. Il existe aussi une quantité de petits édifices qui rentrent dans les catégories, décrites par M. Puig i Cadafalch, des types populaires issus du carolingien: les uns utilisent la voûte d'arêtes sur les bas-côtés et la coupole, les autres le berceau plein cintre. Les influences les plus contradictoires se coudoient sans se fondre: la Bourgogne est une des terres d'élection de la dernière Renaissance carolingienne dont l'un des traits les plus remarquables est l'éclectisme. C'est alors qu'on pourrait parler de l'existence d'une Bourgogne triple et davantage sans qu'il soit d'ailleurs possible de dire en quoi consistent très exactement les caractères généraux du style bourguignon."

23. Focillon, *The Art of the West*, 41.

24. Ibid., 32.

25. Deshoulières, "Le premier art roman," 105.

26. Deshoulières, "Séance du 15 Decembre," 150.

27. Conant, *Carolingian and Romanesque Architecture*, 80.

28. Jean Bony, "La chapelle épiscopale de Hereford," 38.

PART III:
SCULPTURE

3

Sculpture in Burgundy
Before the Cluny Atelier

efore members of the Atelier carved the figural sculpture at Cluny, they had had, in my opinion, a long career. But even before the Atelier was formed, another earlier atelier, working even more closely within the northern First Romanesque tradition, had sculpted large-scale tympana in Burgundy. The work of this atelier preceded the work of the Cluniac Atelier, and in fact the Cluniac sculptors worked alongside this earlier group in their first building at Anzy. The purpose of this chapter is to describe the Brionnais sculptural tradition of the earlier atelier. Significantly, just as we know from masons' marks that sculptors of the Cluniac Atelier worked as masons, we learn that these earlier sculptors began from a masonry tradition.

In the past, scholars either have dismissed the early tympana at Charlieu and Mont Saint-Vincent (Figs. 77a, 78a) as provincial, backwater art or they have dated the sculpture to approximately 1094 on the basis of a disputed and unspecific consecration of the church at Charlieu.[1] In either case, the northern First Romanesque style of the sculpture and architecture have consequently been overlooked. Charlieu is located near the Loire River of northern France, and the portals of both Charlieu and Mont Saint-Vincent are northern First Romanesque in style and very likely the earliest large-scale sculptural programs in Burgundy.[2] While the sculpture is not identical to the earliest examples of the Atelier's work at Avenas and Anzy, its style is close, perhaps a starting point; and as in the Atelier's work throughout its career, these earlier portals combine similar figural and architectural decoration.

I

I date the tympana of Charlieu and Mont Saint-Vincent early, shortly before 1080, and dismiss the possibility of a twelfth-century artistic backwater, because the northern First Romanesque portal masonry reflects no trace of influence from High Romanesque architecture. The bases (Charlieu, Figs. 77a, 12b; Mont Saint-Vincent, Figs. 78a, 12a) at both sites share the same motif, an oval bordered by tori and outlined by double strips, which, in a unique twist, hook beneath the oval. Like northern First Romanesque bases at the turn of the eleventh century (Saint-Benoît-sur-Loire, Fig. 9a), upper and lower tori are fully semi-circular, have the same circumference, and are almost half the size of the oval fill. Such characteristics contrast with the later, unequal, segmented tori whose top torus occupies only a fraction of the infill area (e.g., Vézelay nave, Fig. 12d). Moreover, like the standard northern First Romanesque base, the overall profile of these bases is almost plumb; their central decorative bands are nearly the same height as the framing tori; and the socles are almost as high as the bases. Seldom is even one of these characteristics of northern First Romanesque bases found in later works of the Atelier (Fig. Series 12) and never are they found all together or without the addition of later features.[3] Furthermore, despite their presently eroded condition, the bases show deep and uneven strokes unlike the regular, shallow, and frequently polished marks on the Atelier's bases (see chapter 2).

The impost moldings of the Charlieu portal and nave (Figs. 77d, 77a, 5a) manifest typical northern First Romanesque qualities in torus size, profile, and circumference, all of which indicate an early date for the accompanying tympanum sculpture. As in the bases, a fully semi-circular torus occupies at least one third of the impost and aligns vertically with the abacus, unlike the later Atelier's segmental torus (Montceaux, Figs. 5e, 2a), which makes up a fraction of the impost design and slants diagonally from the plumb face (see chapter 2).

The masons of these architectural details demonstrated their early northern First Romanesque training in the finish of the stonework as well. They created an ashlar block (Figs. 77a, 79) smaller but more vertically proportioned than the later Atelier type (Perrecy and Vézelay, Figs. 27b, 28), and they worked its surface with deep and swirling axe strokes, leaving uneven corners and inserting slivers of vertical brick ("2" in Figs. 78b, 79) or brick-like stone ("2" in Figs. 24b, 24c) between large built-up mortar beds ("1" in Figs. 78b, 24c). Their use of highly irregular fill masonry with a concentration of square stones laid in barely coursed mortar beds often as large as the stones themselves (Figs. 24a, 24b) is just another indication of their northern First Romanesque background.[4]

II

The architectural details in the portals of Charlieu and Mont Saint-Vincent (Figs. 77a, 78a) are clearly typical of northern First Romanesque art. Significantly, the tympana sculpture is closely analogous to these details and is built into the architecture itself. Thus, the sculpture too is early, dating near the beginnings of Romanesque art in Burgundy.

The execution of the sculpture on both portals shows little sign of undercutting or twisting surface planes (Figs. 80, 78a; 81, 77a). Rather, it fits the northern First Romanesque taste for isolated, built-up ridges of decoration, seen in the First Romanesque crypt of Tournus (Figs. 14b, 17) and in the masonry details of Charlieu and Mont Saint-Vincent. The isolated ridges occur in the full semi-circular tori of bases and moldings (Figs. 9b, 77a); in the uninterrupted meander on imposts (Figs. 77d, 77a) and looping series of parallel ridges along and between the tips of leaves; and in the built-up mortar joints of ashlar and fill (Figs. 78b, 78a). Similarly, the sculptors built up drapery into isolated rounded surface ridges which do not cross. The drapery pattern of the lintel sculpture at Charlieu (Figs. 81, 82a, 77e), like that on the tympanum sculpture at Mont Saint-Vincent (Fig. 80), almost duplicates a pattern found on a small unidentified figure (Fig. 83) on the masonry base of the left jamb portal at Charlieu. In addition to the technique of execution, the location of this figure on a base is evident of the masonry character of the portal sculpture.

Almost invariably, one fold begins where another ends without overlapping or undercutting; for example, in the Charlieu tympanum crescents of drapery on the skirt of the angel (Figs. 77b, 77a) peter out to points ("3," "4") just at the edge of the neighboring vertical pleats. In the Charlieu lintel (Fig. 82a), folds run parallel ("1") or come to a point ("2") without overlapping. Emphasizing the surface quality of the drapery, etched grooves or rills surround the edges of each fold, separating the crescent pleats ("3") on the Charlieu tympanum angel (Fig. 77b), and the parallel drapery strips ("1") on the lintel apostles (Fig. 82a). These individual grooves then frequently join each other on the surface as one continuous line. As a result, the linear quality of each fold is extended into a continuously inscribed linear pattern. For example, in the drapery of the tympanum angel (Fig. 77b), the rills around each crescent pleat ("4") continue down the front of the skirt as a vertical line ("5") which then extends horizontally as an inscribed rill ("7") along the edge of the hem.[5] On the chest of Christ (Fig. 77c), these inscribed folds form a continuous linear pattern which is not undercut at the edges but surrounded by flat, narrow tubes of drapery on the cuff, collar, and around the arm and stomach.

Besides exhibiting similar techniques of execution, the portal sculpture of Charlieu and Mont Saint-Vincent share identical motifs. These resemblances are striking in the tympanum of Mont Saint-Vincent (Fig. 80) and the lintel of Charlieu (Fig. 81), which I assign to the same master (see the excursus to this chapter). In both cases, the master created a skirt from parallel, evenly spaced vertical pleats ("a"), and bordered them on the sides with a triangular flaring or curling fold ("b"). He ended these pleats not with a border but simply with a straight horizontal cut at the ankles ("c") and across the shins ("d"). Over the lap of the seated figure, he carved increasingly smaller parallel "V" folds ("e") and continued their central point to a "box" pleat ("f") which has vertical sides, a horizontal base, and a triangular center. On either side of the "V" folds on the skirt, the mason created a single strip of drapery over each knee. On either side of each knee, the folds are shown as parallel vertical lines ("g"). He carved the top of the fold as a semicircle above the knee ("h") and extended the bottom of the fold to a point ("i") along the horizontal line of the drapery at the shins. This lowest point also forms the bottom tip of a smaller pleat, set in the shape of a parallelogram at the base of fold "j". In this pleat, an incised central line ("k") connects the bottom point ("i") to a symmetrically placed point ("j") at the top of the parallelogram. Clearly, the master shows a remarkable consistency in the drapery details of his sculpture at both sites.

Another master created the tympanum sculpture at Charlieu (Fig. 77b). As we have seen, he shared the northern First Romanesque taste for isolated, linear surface folds, although he executed his drapery differently than the lintel master. He carved the folds ("3," "4," "5" in Fig. 77b) into a series of gently rounded profiles which contrast with the flattened and diagonally chamfered rills of the other master (Figs. 81, 82a). This difference carries down to details of anatomy such as toes (Figs. 77b, 82b) which are more rounded on the surface and less severely chamfered on the sides.

The master of the Charlieu tympanum discriminated between the types of ridges: he frequently distinguished drapery pleats from hands and toes by carving them subtly into asymmetrical triangles ending in extended crescent-shaped points. By contrast, the artist of the lintel created minimal formal difference among features, cutting all the toes and fingers, sleeves and hem, horizontal and vertical pleats, to the same approximate width and dimension (Fig. 82a). Although he used a rill technique similar to that of the lintel mason, the Charlieu tympanum master infused the line with greater variety; on the right angel (Fig. 77b), he extended a crescent pleat into a "piping" edge ("2") next to the fold ("1") and lined both hems ("10," "11") with a running border; on the zig-zag skirt pleats, he distinguished the two sides of the material, adding a border outline below the horizontal folds on the front (e.g. "7"), but not on the diagonal back side of the skirt; and with rare exception, he carved the vertical skirt folds only from the tips along the upper and lower edges of the diagonal hem ("6," "8," "9"). He carved subtly, with a complexity and variety missing from the works of the lintel master.

III

While the master of the Charlieu tympanum worked differently from the master of the Charlieu lintel and Mont Saint-Vincent tympanum, both men practiced the traditional northern First Romanesque manner of architectural sculpture. It is extremely important for understanding the origins of High Romanesque sculpture in Burgundy to realize not only that their sculpture is located in buildings of northern First Romanesque type but also that both masters worked in a technique characteristic of northern First Romanesque architectural decoration. Clearly, documenting the position of these two early sculptors within this architectural tradition goes a long way toward confirming the masonry origins of large-scale figural sculpture in Burgundy.

Perhaps even more important, understanding their position explains the masonry context of style and technique within which the Cluny Atelier began to create High Romanesque sculpture in Burgundy. For when a sculptor from the Atelier of Cluny first worked in situ on a building, it was in the Anzy archivolts (Figs. 84b, 89b; see chapter 4, note 2), side by side with the Mont Saint-Vincent master, who carved the lintel there (Fig. 84a). Besides the identifying characteristic of the ear (see the excursus to this chapter and Figs. 85a, 85b, 85c, 85d), the master of the lintel at Anzy repeated other important features from his work at Mont Saint-Vincent (Figs. 80, 81).[6] In a grotesque exaggeration, he again created feet ("1" in Figs. 80, 84a) almost the length of the shin bone and extended them into a narrow point. While by this time he may have copied certain features of the Charlieu tympanum master such as the crescent pleats along the leg ("3" in Figs. 84a, 77b), those folds have none of the variety of the tympanum master. Likewise, vertical folds on the shoulder and skirt lack variety and fall in repetitive parallel lines ("m" and "a" in Figs. 81, 84a). The master nowhere used an incised border, but as before he cut off the parallel vertical folds of the skirt with a straight horizontal hem ("c"). He carved the same parallelogram pleat ("j") over the knee and curled the fold on either side of the skirt ("b").

What made this master's lintel at Anzy later than his work at Mont Saint-Vincent and Charlieu and like the earliest examples of the Atelier's work was that he no longer simply isolated folds by inscribed grooves but began to undercut and overlap them, so that the parallel pleats read like stacked narrow strips of drapery, one on top of the other (Fig. 84a). The parallel curved shoulder folds ("m") and the hanging vertical pleats on the outside edge of the skirt ("n") have a stepped and even slightly undercut profile in contrast with the flat relief of similar folds ("m" and "g" in Fig. 81) on the Charlieu lintel. Whether the lintel master copied the Cluniac Atelier or vice versa is of secondary importance compared to the fact that the change in the Mont Saint-Vincent mason's work corresponds to the most outstanding characteristic of early in situ sculpture of the Cluny Atelier (see chapter 4, and Figs. 89b; 88a,b).[7] Thus, a late work of the earlier atelier and an early work of the later Atelier overlap stylistically and appear simultaneously on the portal of the same building. While the Anzy portal may not mark the point of departure for the Cluniac Atelier, it highlights the Atelier's beginnings within the context of the northern First Romanesque masonry tradition in Burgundy.

NOTES

1. A consecration of 1094 for the church of Charlieu is cited by J.-B. de Sevelinges, *Histoire de la ville de Charlieu*, 1856, who refers to the lost document, *Mémoire manuscrit des Bénédictins contre le curé Dupont*. One group of scholars believed that the date referred to the completion of the entire church and portal sculpture: Deschamps, "Notes," 64; Lücken, "Burgundische Skulpturen," 107; Porter, *Pilgrimage Roads*, 71; Vallery-Radot,

"Les analogies," 259; Sunderland, "Charlieu," 87; Jalabert, *La flore sculptée des monuments du moyen âge en France*, 60. Other scholars believed the lost text to be a questionable document: Salet, "Review of E. R. Sunderland," 74; Pendergast, *Anzy*, 103; Vergnolle, "Autour d'Anzy," 12, note 2; or they believed that the 1094 date referred to the church and not to the later portal sculpture: Rhein, "Charlieu," 243, 252; C. Enlart, "Le porche de Charlieu," 232, 234. For a comparison of Charlieu to the later nave at Anzy, see Vallery-Radot, "Les analogies," 259, and the response of C. Oursel, "Les églises Martiniennes," 293–99.

2. In speaking of the type of northern First Romanesque portal architecture at Charlieu (Fig. 77a) and Mont Saint-Vincent (Fig. 78a), I distinguish it from the construction on the second or clerestory level in both buildings. At Charlieu, the upper-story masonry and especially the sculpture change in ways closely parallel to the work of the Atelier (see chapter 4, note 1), while at Mont Saint-Vincent the construction undergoes extensive changes. The fill masonry between the aisle and clerestory becomes larger, more rectangular, and less mortar is used with it. The corbels largely change from a cavet to a classical doucine. The change to a more truly ashlar construction occurs in the buttresses and in the windows. Fewer, larger stones are used for the voussoirs, which reduce in number from an average of 14 in the aisle to 9 in the clerestory, and in the window jamb stones, which reduce from an average of 5 to 3.5. The ashlar surrounding the central portal on the lower story do not join the porch ashlar at the ground level, although the facade clerestory ashlar and buttresses course with the quoining stones on the second story of the porch. Clearly, the central portal existed before the ashlar of the porch was affixed to it, while the clerestory of the nave and second story of the porch were constructed at an identical but later time.

While attempts have been made to establish an atelier and even a hand connection between the Anzy lintel and nave capitals, and the capitals in the Vézelay eastern nave, Tournus crossing, and the sculpture on the western portal of Charlieu, no one suggested that the Mont Saint-Vincent portal preceded the group or that its architecture or sculpture exhibited northern First Romanesque characteristics. Pendergast ("Anzy," 117) intimately linked the western portal of Charlieu with the lintel and corbels of Anzy, but placed them in a twelfth-century context; Deschamps ("Notes," 72) cited the parallels between the nave capitals of Anzy and Charlieu, and the reused eastern-bay capitals of Vézelay; Lücken ("Burgundische Skulpturen," 105–6) and Vallery-Radot ("Les analogies," 256–57) drew the same parallels and observed similar foliage in the lintels of Charlieu and Anzy. Based on her impression of "une certaine incompréhension de l'équilibre interne," Vergnolle ("Anzy," 7) recently cited what she described as the "dépendence" of certain Charlieu nave capitals on comparable capitals in the nave at Anzy. See also Vergnolle, "Recherches sur quelques séries de chapiteaux romans bourguignons," 55–79.

Salet ("Review of E. R. Sunderland," 74) correctly summarized the stylistic analysis of the Charlieu portal sculpture as "à vrai dire, n'a jamais été faite sérieuse-ment"—and no one suggested that it followed the tympanum at Mont Saint-Vincent. Deschamps ("Notes," 74) dated Mont Saint-Vincent parallel in time with the Charlieu consecration of 1094, while most others saw it as a provincial reflection. Porter (*Pilgrimage Roads*, 76ff.) granted that on first impression Mont Saint-Vincent seemed "more primitive" than Charlieu, while a second look and its "mountain" location indicated a later "retarded art," "merely a crude and retarded echo." He remarked upon the analogy of the portal capitals and console figures at the two sites. Similarly, Pendergast (*Anzy*, 290–91, and "The Lintel of the West Portal at Anzy-le-Duc," 139) recognized that Mont Saint-Vincent's "archaizing character . . . stems from an unskilled craftsman . . . and not from an early date," and together with R. Oursel (*Les églises*, 124) and M. and C. Dickson (*Les églises romanes de l'ancien diocèse de Chalon*, 210), she placed it after the lintel of Anzy and the Charlieu portal. Earlier, turn-of-the-century scholars also maintained that the sculpture of Mont Saint-Vincent was a workshop reflection (see Pendergast, *Anzy*, 291).

Elizabeth Sunderland is unique in recognizing astutely the early date of the bases and decoration of the Charlieu western portal ("Charlieu," 87; *Charlieu*, 46): "at an early time and long before the actual completion of the church." However, she believed that these elements along with the lintel were reused in the later construction when the tympanum was carved ("Charlieu," 87). "Certainly the lintel was not designed to be used with the tympanum" because "the two central arches and the band of stone above them have been bevelled back to permit an unobstructed view of the feet of Christ." Previously Porter (*Pilgrimage Roads*, 73) suggested that different sculptors carved the lintel and tympanum, although he believed that both men worked at the same time. Salet, ("Review of E. R. Sunderland," 74) also believed the lintel and tympanum to be contemporary, a point of view I think a number of archaeological details support (Fig. 77a).

The incised lintel border line which curves below the feet of Christ (Fig. 77e) continues uninterrupted into the borders on all four sides of the lintel ("A"). If one argues for a recarving, then one must admit that the masons very carefully hid the transition between the line beneath Christ's feet and the older border line, or that they carved an entirely new line around the old lintel. Corresponding to the curved cornice, the back wall of the lintel bows slightly behind the central arcade figures. If the cornice above the figures was carved away later, and the changes were made to correspond to it, then why do the figures and the lintel wall show no sign of recarving? Perhaps most telling are the two central lintel arcades ("B"), which not only are larger than the others but overlap the curved cornice. Logically, if one argues for the curved cornice being carved later, then one must date the overlapping arcades to the time of the remodelling or after it, despite the fact that the halos ("C") on the wall behind the figures conform to the present circumference of the arcades, and the fact that the halos and arcades show no sign of recarving.

Taken together, these three arguments point toward a lintel carved entirely at one time. Because of the connections cited in the text between the sculpture and the architecture, and the stylistic similarity of the lintel to the tympanum and to the figure on the base of the portal, I believe that the entire portal was carved at one time.

3. In addition to the bases in the crypt of Saint-Benoît-sur-Loire (Fig. 9a), other notable examples of this type of northern First Romanesque base appear in the crypts of Notre-Dame-de-la-Couture at Le Mans and in the nave of Beaulieu-les-Loches.

4. An unusual feature found at both sites is the occasional narrow and rectangular filler stone which marks the junction between the fill and frame masonry ("a" in Fig. 24a).

5. Many of these characteristics were exhibited by the sculptor, heretofore unrecognized, who carved the central portal capitals and southern portal lintel at Châteauneuf (Figs. 87a, 87b) as well as a number of capitals reused in the northern nave arcade at Souvigny (Fig. 86). See chapter 2, note 6; P. Pradel, "Les sculptures de l'église de Souvigny"; Deshoulières, "Souvigny," 182–223; and Virey, "Excursion à Charlieu et a Châteauneuf," 287–93.

6. Extending the comparison of ears, I am sure that the Anzy lintel Master completed most of the Anzy nave capitals as well as the related crossing sculpture at Tournus and Mont Saint-Vincent. His unique eye and facial type also can be seen in these works. Perhaps the earliest examples by him are the Virgin and Child on the interior western face of the Anzy transept and the corbels on the eastern exterior of the same transept.

7. Anatomy of the Anzy lintel Master's jamb figures—especially the treatment of the corners of the mouth and eye—reflects his contact with the Avenas Master.

Excursus: Identifying Characteristics of the Master of the Lintels of Charlieu and Anzy, and the Tympanum of Mont Saint-Vincent

EAR

The (1) tapered end of the helix leg (2) hooks around the top, inside edge of the tragus—(3) spherical in appearance—and the leg extends to (4) a point at (5) the edge of the ear hole. A (6) deep V-groove separates the helix from the antihelix, and (7) stops at the lower level of the tragus. The (8) ear hole is practically a circle with diagonal sides set (9) in the center of the ear. On the

Figures 85a, b, c, d, e

bottom, the hole is (10) directly bordered by the ear lobe, which (11) measures over three-eighth's the length of the ear, (12) has a flat surface, and (13) forms a straight diagonal line on the facial side. This line (14) runs in the direction of the facial side of the tragus and helix leg, and (15) the curved end of the lobe touches the lower edge of the tragus.

4

The Avenas and Perrecy Masters: The Principal Sculptors of Cluny

I

In periods of history when artists' names are known, questions about art and its creation are asked in personal terms: Who was the artist? What was his background? How did his art change over the course of his career? In the past, Romanesque art in general and Cluniac sculpture in particular have been studied not as the work of individuals but as an anonymous style described in abstract terms such as "evolution," "cycle," or "revival."

However, by combining techniques of archaeology and "hand" analysis, it will be possible for the first time in the study of Burgundian Romanesque sculpture to ask and answer questions about individual artists. Hand analysis enables us to identify two sculptors whom I shall call the Avenas and Perrecy Masters, after the sites where their work first appears. Further, by arranging their works in chronological order according to the archaeological findings of chapter 2, it will be possible to investigate stages in their artistic careers. In this way, the origin of the sculptors and where they worked before Cluny will become clear, as will the impact of their individual styles on each other at different points of their careers. Moreover, by combining the architectural and sculptural methods of analysis, a stylistic relationship between the two media can be discerned, as can the relative "speed" of stylistic change.

Before we can answer or honestly ask the larger questions, individual artists must be identified. This can be done by turning our attention to the complexly interwoven patterns of small details found in minute peripheral areas of the sculpture—the toes, fingers, ears, eyes, and hems; such sculptural patterns are distinctive—indeed idiosyncratic—for each individual artist. Only after examining these details and determining that we are dealing with distinct personalities can we go on to answer larger questions by making broader comparisons of style. While some of these broader stylistic differences and similarities appear in details of sculpture—indeed, often the details correspond to overall tendencies of an artist—our major conclusions about an artist's career must come from analyzing major parts of his work. To spare the reader some of the drudgery of hand analysis, I put in the excursus to this chapter the analysis of minute but tedious details that is necessary to distinguish the two separate individuals. In the text itself I shall go on to describe the significant differences between the Avenas and Perrecy Masters.

Once we compare the important stylistic differences between the two men's work, we can judge how their styles changed together and how they differed over the course of their careers. Certain features appear in both sculptors' works. In each case, sculpture followed the direction of change of the architectural decoration described in chapter 2. Moreover, the direction of change in each case was away from the northern First Romanesque prototypes like the tympana of Charlieu and Mont Saint-Vincent described in chapter 3. At Anzy and Mâcon, the Avenas Master began by dividing drapery into narrow strips. However, by the time of the construction of Perrecy and the first campaign of Vézelay, both sculptors overlapped drapery as plates of folds analogous to the new projecting architectural moldings and bases at these sites. Moving to Cluny, the sculptors changed these stacked plate folds to linear incisions or small cuts into a single surface plane, perhaps in accord with the new architectural preference for smaller and more numerous details and for continuous vertical surface reveal. Finally, in the Vézelay central tympanum, the Perrecy Master reduced drapery folds to patterns of linear surface design that were paralleled by the changes in Cluniac architecture at Autun.

The differences in the styles of the Avenas and Perrecy Masters are most pronounced where they worked separately. The Avenas Master worked alone at Avenas, Anzy, and Mâcon, before working with the Perrecy Master at Perrecy, Vézelay, and Cluny;[1] the Perrecy Master worked alone in the nave and in the last two facade campaigns of Vézelay. In the case of the Avenas Master, his early contact with northern First Romanesque sculpture, specifically on the portal of Anzy (chapter 3), seems to have formed the character of his individual style. However, he was not caught up in the past but initiated major changes which influenced the Perrecy Master's style. For example, although the Avenas Master did not participate in the final linear style of the Vézelay tympanum, he tentatively explored its techniques at Cluny. The Perrecy Master, while seemingly less innovative and less varied in technique, worked at fewer sites but changed more dramatically. He reduced stacked plate drapery at the Perrecy lintel to inscribed surface lines by the end of his career at Vézelay.

Although both sculptors created a distinctly Cluniac style at Perrecy, Vézelay, and Cluny, the work they completed apart from each other represents the two extremes of High Romanesque sculpture. Before the Perrecy Master joined him, the Avenas Master at Anzy brought the Atelier in early contact with northern First Romanesque sculpture; after the Avenas Master departed, the Perrecy Master, with two newcomers, the Plus Master and Gislebertus (described in chapter 5), formed a linear style continued in Gothic sculpture at Chartres in the Ile-de-France. In sum, the Avenas Master began his career with a style close to the northern tradition of First Romanesque, while the Perrecy Master's late style coincided with the emergence of Gothic.

II

Avenas Master. The Avenas Master probably was the principal stone mason of the small chapel at Montceaux who signed 7 ashlar stones with ꜧ (Fig. 36) and who also incised this initial on the primary western face of the left jamb capital (Figs. 2a, c). It is unlikely that another mason prepared this block and left his mark before the Avenas Master carved the sculpture because the serifs at the base of the letter rest precisely on the vertical line where the sculptural carving begins. This correspondence in all probability would not have occurred had the block been hewed and signed previously.

Characteristics of the Avenas Master's style may have resulted from his early collaboration with the lintel master at Anzy (Figs. 84a, 84b) or from other early contacts with sculpture carved in the northern First Romanesque tradition at sites like Charlieu and Mont Saint-Vincent. He seems to have been affected by the continuous surface design of that earlier tradition (described in chapter 3). Although he shared important stylistic changes within the Atelier—for example, the progressive taste for strips, plates, and delicate surface cuts in drapery—the northern First Romanesque concern with continuous surface design remained constant for the Avenas Master. This concern underlies the four basic elements which define his style throughout his career. He pushed to the limit the northern First Romanesque interest in surface line (1) by confusing distinctions between drapery and body parts; (2) by joining individual strands of folds which in real drapery would fall separately; (3) by confounding the distinction between receding and projecting drapery edges; and (4) above all, by taking one drapery pleat or anatomical part and branching it out into many pleats or parts, a process of divarication I shall call "branching." In contrast with the Avenas Master's sculpture, that of the Perrecy Master shows opposite qualities; the Perrecy Master seized opportunities to sever forms with a chamfer cut, to end planes of drapery where they touched, and to cover openings between planes.

Throughout his career, the Avenas Master often used a motif of two opposed concave folds in the drapery on his figures. With this motif he created an effect of a continuous drapery by simultaneously pulling together edges of drapery and branching them apart, frequently without cutting or otherwise interrupting the folds. On the kneeling figure from Avenas (Fig. 88b), by means of this motif ("I") he channeled a border strip and numerous edges of drapery from the back into a narrow strip ("3") over the arm, indeed branching one back fold ("2") into a narrow piping edge ("a") before finally merging it into the new strip ("3"). After narrowing the motif ("I") at the new strip ("3") he spread its upper concave fold ("4") on the shoulder in the direction of the neck and branched the lower concave fold ("5") over the arm into a series of narrow hanging strips of folds on the stomach ("6").

The Avenas Master achieved an effect of continuous drapery by joining individual strands of garment which in real fabric would fall separately. In the Avenas figure (Fig. 88b), he merged the upper curve of the motif ("I") into the surface of the shoulder drapery ("4") and then extended that surface beneath the original motif ("I") on the arm (at point "b"). In a third constant quality of the Avenas Master's sculpture, he confounded the distinction between recessed and projecting edges. In the second example of the motif ("II") in the Avenas figure, he extended the lower concave curve of the motif over a back fold ("2") on the left ("1"), but passed it beneath the same fold on the right (at point "a"). And in a fourth continuity, he confused the surface of the body and drapery in the third motif ("III"), on the hip in the figure: is it possible to tell if the drapery on the stomach ("6") continues as the surface of this motif ("III") beneath the band ("7") or as the actual stomach plane ("8") below and above the motif? Thus, the Avenas Master used the drapery motif of two opposed concave edges in these four ways to multiply folds and connect them unnaturalistically to each other, to confound the surface of the folds as well as to manipulate the folds' recessed and projecting edges.

The drapery on the facade capitals and archivolts at Anzy again shows the Avenas Master's use of the double concave motif ("I") to achieve the same effects of continuity (Figs. 89b, 84b). In the bulbous thigh area above the upper curve of the motif ("I") he confused the surfaces of drapery and flesh, while on the lower curve of the motif he branched the drapery edges into new folds ("1," "2"). Unnaturalistically stretching the drapery, he has the same motif falling over vertical pleats ("3"), then joining to them ("4"), and in a play on projecting and receding folds, tucking beneath them (at point "a").[2]

At Mâcon (Figs. 90c, 90a, 29a), the Avenas Master used the motif in the same ways to radiate new forms and to connect normally separate parts on the figure.[3] He extended the standard motif ("I") from the skirt on the hip in a separate strip across the stomach and then he continued the "fabric" onto the surface of the shield. In an example of branching, he carved chest folds ("1") and ("2") in gentle curves from the same point ("a") next to the cloak of the left arm. In another typical continuity, he connected folds unnaturalistically, first extending the tip of the fold ("2") in a long narrow ridge along the edge of the cloak, turning it into a wide chest fold, and finally, branching it above into the curve of a neck tab ("3") and below into another wide fold on the other side of the chest ("4"). He unnaturalistically rendered the edges of the drapery as well, by first projecting a fold ("5") on the stomach and then receding it at the chest ("6"), in analogy to another chest fold ("1"). Moreover, he blurred the distinction between body surfaces and drapery fabric by carving an unspecific large, round, and fleshy protrusion in the area of the stomach.

At Perrecy (Figs. 91b, 91a, 1a), the Avenas Master again used the standard concave motif ("I") to channel complex folds of drapery without interrupting them. In addition, at Perrecy he increased his tendency to branch and link strands of drapery and to confuse their planes and edges.[4] Following the continuous, and what turns out to be endless, path of just one edge of the motif, we can see how in his stone carving he distorted the actual properties of cloth. Stretching the natural limits of fabric, he extended the curved surface of the motif ("I") underneath a loose belt strap ("2") with which the motif in fact merges at a point ("1") where the strap begins; on another level, he branched the strap at the center of the chest into a fold ("3"), simultaneously wrapping the strap around the fold's top surface ("4"); he merged this new chest fold ("3") into a neck tab ("5") and shoulder fold ("6")—a fold he then tucked beneath the original strap (at point "7"), continued below as a skirt pleat ("8"), and finally in a loop (at point "b") returned to the original surface of the motif where the strap begins (at point "1"). Thus, with the concave motif ("I") the Avenas Master connected most of the drapery folds; he also used it to channel other folds at the hip. He continued a vertical skirt fold ("9") directly into the lower concave curve of the motif and merged almost all the shoulder and arm drapery into the motif's upper left curve under the chest fold ("3").

By the time the Avenas Master worked at Vézelay on the facade capitals and the left half of the upper and all of the lower register on the north tympanum (Figs. 92a, 93b, 94a), he included new forms of drapery in his sculpture. Yet while he rendered (Figs. 92b, 92c) narrow strips ("1," "6"), plates ("2"), and even large surface planes of drapery ("3," "5") with greater delicacy of edge, the four principal features of his style are clearly present. Most striking is a change in the rendering of the body. Whereas before he seemed to play at confusing drapery and body surfaces, now he fully reveals large parts of the body. Instead of confusing the outline of the stomach and thigh with the surface of the drapery as at Mâcon (Fig. 90c) and Anzy (Fig. 89b), he exposes at Vézelay large parts of the anatomy like the leg. The outline of the leg, for example, is revealed ("4," "5" in Figs. 92b, 92c; "10" in Fig. 94b) through narrow strips of hem drapery ("1," "6," "7" in Figs. 92b, 92c; "8," "9," in Fig. 94b).

In light of the increased variety of drapery folds, it hardly comes as a surprise to see that he both expanded the number of branching parts and increased the unnaturalistic connections between them. As in the past (Fig. 94b), he channeled the continuous folds through the double concave motif ("I"): on the left he merged the upper curve of the motif into a staff ("1") and branched the lower curve into a plate fold ("2"), a hem border ("3"), and a "windswept" edge ("4"); on the right ("I"), he continued a skirt fold ("5") as a raised ridge on the hem ("6"), and twisted it into yet another surface on the underside of the central pleat ("7").

At Montceaux (Figs. 95a, 2c), the Avenas Master articulated folds in the same continuous manner, channeling them through the double concave motif, although he largely reduced the variety of folds to one drapery plane (Fig. 95b). Again confusing the surfaces of the fabric and body, he extended the curves of the buttocks ("1") into the concave curves of motif ("I") on the drapery. Unnaturalistically merging different sorts of drapery, he stretched the motif ("I") into a narrow border on the side ("2") before branching it into radiating folds along the back ("3").[5]

The Avenas Master appears to have last worked at Cluny, where in an updated style he again achieved the effects of continuity characteristic of his manner. In a figure from the first of two Tone capitals he executed for the ambulatory (Fig. 96), the Avenas Master entwined the thin pleats on the chest by unnaturalistically crisscrossing them ("1") and by looping one chest fold over itself ("3"); he represented cloth stretched beyond its natural limits by extending three sets of folds from the chest onto the upper arm ("2") and, in line with a new interest in the surface quality of sculpture, he branched inscribed folds ("4," "5," and "7") on the skirt, and exposed fleshy areas through the thin openings of drapery on the stomach ("3," "6").

Similarly on the second Tone capital he worked at Cluny (Figs. 97a and 97b), the Avenas Master achieved characteristic effects of continuity as can be seen by analyzing one ("I") of two ("II") standard double concave motifs. In rendering drapery, he again stretched the real limits of fabric, extending the front surface of the skirt ("1") through the motif as a narrow strip ("2") to a new series of radiating folds on the opposite side of the dress ("3"); in the process, he created a whole series of folds ("4") from the bottom curve of the motif, finishing one of them ("5") where he began the set on the front plane of the skirt ("1").[6]

In rendering smaller details of anatomy, the Avenas Master also used the four characteristics of his drapery style. Branching details in tight spaces such as in hands and feet (Fig. 124), he ran a small shelf or lateral process between each finger and toe at their tips ("10") (see the excursus to this chapter for the identifying characteristics of the Avenas and Perrecy Masters). He unnaturalistically merged parts of the face together (Fig. 121) by joining the ear directly with the jaw through an elephantine lobe ("1"); by interrupting the jawbone line and dropping what appears to be a sack of flesh (Figs. 115c, 115d, 115e) from the cheek directly into the neck ("18"); and by curving down both corners of the upper lip ("20") almost half the distance to the chin. Continuously connecting these small parts of the body, the Avenas Master took liberties with real anatomy as he had with the real properties of cloth. He bent the outside toes on the same foot concentrically inward ("1" in Fig. 124) and he prolonged the ear tragus up the side of the forehead and even into the hair ("10" in Fig. 121).

Perrecy Master. Certainly the Perrecy Master was an equally great sculptor, although his execution and style lacked the complexities of the Avenas Master. Indeed, the most important characteristics of the Perrecy Master contrast with the typical features of the Avenas Master's style. In drapery, the Avenas Master typically branched folds away from a point; the Perrecy Master usually continued folds parallel to each other. Their contrasting styles can clearly be seen in their rendering of foliage: the identifying characteristics of the foliage of the Perrecy Master (Figs. 102c, 112c, 113) are almost opposite to the small continuous details of foliage carved by the Avenas Master (Figs. 2b, 88c, 89a, 90b, 93c, 97c).

The Perrecy Master inscribed leaves as relatively parallel lines ("1") on the surface of the plant (Figs. 102c, 112c, 113). Continuing the length of each leaf ("2") lower than the Avenas Master (Fig. 93c), he reduced the relative size of the drill hole at the base of the leaf ("3"), and narrowed the leaf tips so that their width at the widest point ("4") approximately equals the length from that point to the tip. The Avenas Master did not extend his leaves by inscribing parallel lines but rather by drawing the leaf lines in toward each other at the base ("1" in Figs. 90b, 93c, 97c), thus expanding the relative width of the leaf at the top ("4") and increasing the relative size of the drill hole at the base ("3").

Unlike the Perrecy Master who carved the leaf stem as a parallel stalk ("5") and ended it with a drill hole ("3"), the Avenas Master in his typically continuous fashion branched the stalk into a wider surface ("5") and continued this face onto the sides of the leaves next to the drill opening ("6"). In another continuity, he bent the tips of the bottommost leaves toward the base of the capital ("7"), frequently aligning the tops of leaves with the curved edges of neighboring leaves ("8"). By contrast, the Perrecy Master rarely pointed leaves toward the base of the capital ("7") and so only touched them to neighboring leaves without aligning their surfaces ("8").

The comparison between the Perrecy and Avenas masters has to do with their distinctive use of parallel lines and continuously branching forms. In designs larger than foliage, such as drapery, and in smaller details of anatomy the Perrecy Master paralleled and severed forms. These forms are rendered by means of a different motif from the Avenas Master's double concave fold. The Perrecy Master avoided branching folds from a single spot by carving each fold from separate, evenly spaced points along the front of the leg, usually in two separate series at the thigh and shin (Figs. 101b, 101a, 102b, 102a, 104d, 107, 108, 110b, 110a, 111b, 111a, 112b, 112a). He completed this motif by having the edge of the top shin fold overlap each parallel thigh fold, thereby dividing rather than merging these two sets of folds. In the bottom of the hem in a variation of the motif, (Figs. 98b, 98a, 100b, 100a) he closed each parallel fold with a separate, scooped trough instead of merging them together.

The Perrecy Master consistently severed rather than merged forms, even in the smallest anatomical detail. While the Avenas Master linked toes (Fig. 124) through lateral processes ("10"), the Perrecy Master divided the foot (Fig. 125) into a series of flat chamfer cuts. He made these chamfers on the foot above the toe ("12"), and on the side and top ("9") of the toe where it attached to the foot; the cuts are also made on the surface of the toe itself, around ("2") and including the nail ("1") and its posterior margin ("3"), and on the top ("6") and sides ("7") of the joint. He similarly separated the parts of the ear (Figs. 122, 123) into a series of chamfer wedges that, for example on the rim, demark the flat top ("9"), diagonal side ("11") and pointed tip ("10") of the antihelix.

While hardly a naturalist, the Perrecy Master rendered fabric more plausibly and simply than the Avenas Master. He avoided the impression of branching it in unnaturalistic directions or stretching it in implausible ways. While he billowed drapery at the edges (Figs. 108, 107, 106, 105b, 105a), he rarely overlapped a surface across itself. By avoiding connections of this kind he rarely blurred the distinction between receding and projecting edges. And he distinguished between the surface of the body contour and drapery, unlike the Avenas Master, who seemed to delight in confusing their appearance. From his earliest stacked drapery plates at Perrecy (Figs. 98b, 98c, 98a) through smaller projecting folds at the Vézelay facade (Figs. 99b, 99a) and Cluny (Figs. 103b, 103a), to the final linear surface of drapery in the central tympanum (Figs. 114c, 114a) and nave (Figs. 112b, 112a, 111b, 111a) of Vézelay, the Perrecy Master distinguished fabric from flesh, usually by carving projecting edges of drapery which hid the outline of the body. By contrast, the Avenas Master revealed the body through openings in the drapery or created an ambiguity between the body and the surface of drapery itself.

III

From details discussed in the excursus to this chapter, the works of these two sculptors can be identified at different sites. With this information, the consistent personal styles of major Burgundian Romanesque sculptors can be documented for the first time. Using the chronological sequence of buildings established through archaeology in chapter 2, we now can go a step further. Following each sculptor from building to building, we can discern reactions of the two masters to each other's style. We will also see what stylistic changes they shared, where and with whom the first changes occurred, and how these changes corresponded to stylistic shifts in architecture.

The pattern of change in the art of both sculptors helps to confirm the relative chronology we established from architectural decoration in chapter 2, for, despite consistent stylistic differences, the sculpture of both men changed in remarkably similar ways throughout their collaboration, ways which parallel changes in the architectural decoration in the same sequence of buildings. And indeed, we would expect parallel changes in architecture and sculpture from an Atelier whose members, masons like **B** , **ᚷ** , and **E** , carved both ashlar blocks (Figs. 31, 28, 36) and decorative tympanum voussoirs (Figs. 29b, 29a, 30b, 30c, 30a). For example, from Avenas and Mâcon to Perrecy and Vézelay, a major change in sculpture paralleled a similar change in the architectural decoration of these buildings. At Avenas and Mâcon, the drapery of the sculpture is made up of isolated, single narrow strips with chamfered edges but little twisting or undercutting; at Perrecy and Vézelay, the drapery has changed and is made of stacked projecting planes of folds, with deep spaces between the costumes of the figures. The change in figural sculpture corresponds to a similar change in architectural decoration. The interior wall of the Anzy facade (Figs. 25a, 25b) and the lower portion of the Mâcon narthex (Fig. 26a) are bare ashlar, undivided by string moldings and unframed except for a plain rectangular plinth at Mâcon. While an interrupted cyma molding lines the exterior below the arcade level at Mâcon, this feature is expanded in the next construction at Perrecy (Fig. 27a). Classically based moldings appear on three levels—in certain plinths, arcade supports and archivolts—and on both the interior and exterior. These projecting moldings are used as isolated decoration, however—on the bays closest to the tympanum, for example—and no string or plinth molding interrupts the plain surface of the wall. By the first campaign of Vézelay, the facade is carved in high relief on both faces: continuous plinth moldings line the bottom, string moldings project across the middle, and encrusted orders of archivolts surround the tympanum in every bay.

As the sculptors moved on to Montceaux, Cluny, and the second campaign at Vézelay, they decreased folds to small edges in a uniform surface of drapery, and the Atelier paralleled these effects in their architecture. The masons created moldings and architectural decoration with more numerous and finer details, and they coordinated more closely the decorative parts on the different levels of the facade and elevation. At Cluny the Atelier collaborated with southern masons, and therefore we might expect the correspondence between architecture and sculpture there to be less direct and specific. While this is true, the southern masons at Cluny created an architecture with small plane reveals of uniform, brick-like material, which extend between many stories, qualities which complement the increased detail and correspondence in the decoration of the Atelier, and parallel the smaller folds and uniform surface of the ambulatory sculpture.

Even the workmanship of sculpture ran closely parallel to the changes in architecture.[7] As they emphasized the surface decoration of their architecture by increasing the number of projecting moldings and undercutting the bases, the Atelier gave the surface of these details a more polished finish. At Avenas and Mâcon sculpture and decoration have a rough texture. The stones were axed with relatively deep and irregular strokes, leaving chisel lines trailing from the eyes (Fig. 116a) and circling the bases (Fig. 10b). Details are irregularly carved; the torus bases are wobbly (Figs. 10a, 11b) and the nostrils and eyelids have uneven surfaces (Figs. 116a, 116c). By the nave of Vézelay, however, both sculpture and masonry have a smooth finish: the ovals of bases (Fig. 12d), foliage (Figs. 112c, 112a), and facial details (Fig. 123d) have been sanded or polished. Inscribed lines on statuary are a regular and frequently symmetrical part of the overall design (Figs. 110b, 110a), and while slight variations on the bases show that advanced templets could not have been used (Fig. 12d), each torus has yet been rounded to a uniform circumference and the ashlar has been finished with regular and extremely superficial axe strokes.

In analyzing the changes which occurred in sculpture, we must first look at the sites of Avenas, Anzy, and Mâcon, where the Avenas Master worked before the Perrecy Master joined him. In these earliest works, the Avenas Master continued and elaborated certain characteristics of northern First Romanesque art. For example, very much in keeping with the earlier tradition, he reduced hair and facial features to rounded surface ridges. Even in small anatomical details like the ear (Figs. 121a, 121b, 116b, 121c, 118b), he exhibited the early style, continuing rounded forms along the surface, while later he would carve these with chamfered planes and precise edges (Figs. 121h, 118e). Similarly in drapery, the Avenas Master repeated the continuous and analogous qualities of northern First Romanesque drapery ridges, although he adapted them to continuous strips of drapery. These new drapery strips are typical of the first sculpture of the Atelier, and the Perrecy Master used them when he first appeared at Perrecy. Compared to the later work, the early drapery (Figs. 88b, 88a) stands out for its quantity of evenly carved narrow strips whose edges are cut straight down at a right angle to the surface, and whose entwined "byzantine" folds are isolated at the sides of the skirt. If occasionally, as on the back ("2") of this figure, he spread a strip into a wider plane, he chamfered its thick edge instead of rolling it, tucking it under as he later did with thin folds at Montceaux and Cluny (Figs. 95b, 96).

After Avenas, at Anzy and Mâcon—that is, even before he worked with the Perrecy Master—the Avenas Master increasingly modified the northern First Romanesque technique of rounding surface ridges. He projected features such as the upper lip and hair further from the face (Figs. 116a, 116b, 84b, 116c, 29a) and reduced the number of isolated drapery strips (Figs. 88b, 88a, 90c, 90a). Key to the future of Cluniac sculpture, he began slightly to undercut folds ("1" in Fig. 90c), an effect he occasionally emphasized by rolling their top edges. In comparison to his later work at Perrecy (Figs. 91b, 91a), however, the drapery of statuary at Anzy and Mâcon show fewer overlapped and stepped folds; and instead of fading out at their edges, folds usually continue around the side of the body (Figs. 89b, 84b, 90c, 90a).

The sculpture of both masters appears in one building for the first time at Perrecy.[8] Fresh on the scene, the Perrecy Master offered a startlingly new approach to sculpture which became basic to their later style; and yet it seems that at Perrecy he largely followed the experienced Avenas Master and the characteristics found in previous work at Mâcon and Anzy. The sculpture at Perrecy marks an important transition from the Avenas Master's work alone, based on an earlier tradition, to the more uniform collaborative work of both men, their "High Style," at Vézelay and Cluny.

From the largest parts to the smallest details, the work of the Avenas Master at Perrecy confirms the sculptural position of Perrecy between Mâcon and Vézelay. On the leg of the right jamb figure at Perrecy, in a change from the raised strips at Mâcon, he created a large, sharp plane edge ("a" in Fig. 91b) and in the ear (Figs. 121e, 115c) he continued the antihelix as a plane into the lobe, although he did not bevel the plane into a series of small chamfers as later at Cluny (Fig. 121h). In his drapery, too, he stopped short of his later work at Vézelay, multiplying the drapery strips of Mâcon (Figs. 90c, 90a, 91b, 91a) while failing to undercut them extensively or to interpenetrate body forms. And yet compared to his work at Mâcon (Fig. 90c), at Perrecy (Fig. 91b) he largely succeeded in pushing the drapery strips to the outside as framing elements around the neck ("5"), chest ("2"), waist ("1"), and elbow, leaving larger areas as wide plates of drapery. Moreover, at Perrecy he further reduced the separate narrow strips of drapery by fading out their edges into points, as in the thigh and arm, and by slightly increasing the undercut ("c") and stepped quality ("d") of the folds.

The arrival of the Perrecy Master at Perrecy provides us with another measure of control for the role of each individual and for the interaction of their styles within the history of Cluniac sculpture. As a newcomer, the Perrecy Master contributed projecting, pronounced stepped folds (Figs. 98b, 98c, 98a, 99b, 99a) and these changes, although modified at Vézelay, altered the stylistic direction of the Atelier. While the type of drapery folds he introduced were significantly new, the refinements to them—the techniques which modified the stepped profile to its later form at Cluny, including undercutting the edges, rounding tucks and eliminating strips—were devices the Avenas Master had experimented with at Mâcon before he worked with the Perrecy Master at Perrecy. Moreover, despite the Perrecy Master's fresh approach, in large measure he practiced techniques the Avenas Master had already abandoned. Perhaps he was a young artist who lacked a personal vocabulary. He did not get rid of narrow strip folds or restrict their use to outside borders as the Avenas Master did at Perrecy; rather, he made them the principal element of his stepped profile drapery, creating a series of small parallel banded strips laid on in steps (Figs. 98b, 98c, 98a). He carved folds with the old straight chamfer technique used at Avenas, showing hardly a trace of the subtly undercut edges the Avenas Master began to carve at Perrecy. And he made little attempt to stretch the parallel strips into planes; instead, he extended each narrow fold intact around the limbs ("a") or into the border margin ("b").

Being exposed to each other's work at Perrecy seems to have affected their styles in some mutual ways. By the time the two masters carved the lower Vézelay facade, both were undercutting projecting folds and widening them in a new planar treatment. At Perrecy, the Perrecy Master rarely had the edges of drapery fade out to a point (Fig. 98b);

at Vézelay, however, in the south tympanum, the upper right register of the north tympanum, and the lower jamb capitals, he frequently merged the edges of strips into one plane at the edges of the body by means of small hooked points ("a," "b," "c," "d," "e" in Fig. 100b, "a" in Fig. 99b). The effect is as if the succession of stacked narrow strips were reduced to folds cut into one fabric. By undercutting the straight chamfered edges with diagonal slices ("a" in Fig. 101b), he further reduced the effect of a stepped series of folds to that of a sectioned but relatively flat single surface. Similarly, in the smallest anatomical details the Perrecy Master moved away from the few, large chamfers at Perrecy (Figs. 123a, 125a) to an increased number of smaller, diagonal cuts at Vézelay (Figs. 125b, 100a) that leave the surface a series of facets.

The work done by the Avenas Master shows that he had learned something from the Perrecy Master while still keeping a step "ahead" of him moving in the direction of Cluny and High Burgundian style. In the facade capitals, and in the left half of the upper and all of the lower register on the north tympanum, he further undercut the details of folds, anatomy, and foliage. And taking a cue from the Perrecy Master, he projected limbs and pleats ("a" in Figs. 94b, 94c) into knife-like edges, using the open spaces between folds and figures to "insert" parts of the body. For example, on the north tympanum he placed the feet of one apostle between the legs of another (Fig. 94c), a quality of interpenetration he later extended in the figural group on the right in the Montceaux lintel (Fig. 2b).[9] The changes the Avenas Master made in the carving of drapery were like those he made in the carving of foliage: the carved relief of leaves and stems as well as the width between them are increased in the foliage sculpted at Vézelay (Figs. 93c, 93a), Montceaux (Fig. 2b), and Cluny (Figs. 97c, 97a) when compared to that of Avenas (Fig. 88c), Anzy (Figs. 89a, 84b), and Mâcon (Figs. 90b, 90a). He also increased the relative size of drill holes at the base of each leaf cluster, the encrusted projection of the leaves at the tip, and the degree of twist on their face.

Both masters increasingly projected and undercut forms while expanding drapery from strips into planes. But the difference in the Avenas Master's approach foreshadowed many of the changes the Perrecy Master made afterwards. While the Avenas Master occasionally merged a parallel series of folds into a single plane on the edge (Figs. 94b, 94a), he more frequently widened each fold surface so that it reads like a separate plane. And while he extended the planes into long edges across the body at Vézelay (Figs. 93b, 93a), at times he reduced them to thin sheets ("3" in Fig. 93b; "2" in Fig. 94b; "8" in Fig. 92c), foreshadowing his later play on surface folds at Cluny. At Montceaux he consistently tucked, shortened, thinned, and intertwined these edges (Figs. 95b, 95a), creating a continuous, crisscrossed surface pattern of folds so minute that their rolled edges dissolved into the body plane, as on the buttocks in Figure 95b.

At Cluny, both masters used techniques which heightened the effect of a continuous surface of wafer-thin drapery which the Avenas Master had himself explored at Montceaux. The Perrecy Master simply left more drapery uncarved and emphasized this plain surface by polishing it to an even finish; he frequently carved folds only where drapery would appear flat, leaving the curved drapery around limbs as continuously smooth surfaces (Figs. 102b, 102a, 103b, 103a). He emphasized that these surfaces were smooth by making the transition to folds less abrupt; he carved each pleat so that its chamfer only gradually disappeared into the smooth surface by means of a long and extended tip ("a" in Fig. 102b). And like the Avenas Master, he emphasized the continuous surface by reducing the edge of each fold to a minimal cut ("b" in Fig. 102b). He even began to make the depth of the cut of a fold equal to the distance on the surface between each fold ("a" in Fig. 103b). As a result, he created a series of identically pointed wedges on the surface which he multiplied into a formal style by the time of the second campaign of Vézelay (Figs. 104c, 104b, 104d, 108, 107, 104a).

Similarly, the Avenas Master largely abandoned the built-up drapery plates of Vézelay for an almost continuous surface of small incised folds at Cluny. While he occasionally carved drapery with large plate-like projections, he usually reduced the length, projection, and chamfer of folds in his Cluniac drapery so that the folds are tightly spaced, with rounded edges projecting barely above the surface (Figs. 96, 97b, 97a). Personal conventions aside, both artists worked remarkably in step at Cluny, down to the smallest anatomical details. Carving ears for example, both masters reduced the design to a series of surface facets by decreasing the size and angle of the chamfers. These characteristics are pronounced on the side ("7") and the exaggerated point ("6") in the Perrecy Master's work (Fig. 123b), and in the numerous shaved secondary planes (Fig. 121h) of the Avenas Master's sculpture (e.g., on the helix role, the antihelix plateau, and around the fossa between the helix and lobe).

In some figures at Cluny, the Avenas Master further reduced the drapery from barely raised edges ("1," "2," "3" in Fig. 96), to inscribed linear folds ("4," "5," "7" in Fig. 96). From the built-up planar edges at Vézelay to delicate reveals along a continuous surface, the Avenas Master took "the next step" to inscribe folds as lines on the surface. Although like him in so many ways, the Perrecy Master did not practice this technique at Cluny but adopted it later while carving figures for the nave capitals of Vézelay (Figs. 110b, 110a; 111b, 111a). By that time, however, he had worked out his own system of surface folds based on the series of pointed ridges he began at Cluny ("a" in Fig. 103b).

Then, if intentions can be judged from results, one could say that between Vézelay and Cluny both masters sought to create the effect of a single surface by decreasing the pronounced planar relief of drapery folds. At Cluny, the Avenas Master occasionally reduced superficially incised folds to scratched lines while the Perrecy Master reduced minimally planed edges to a series of pointed surface ridges.

When he returned alone to Vézelay (see appendix 6 and the excursus to this chapter), the Perrecy Master used this pointed ridge technique almost exclusively as he carved the folds of the Christ figure of the central tympanum (Figs. 109, 104a), the figures on the lintel (Figs. 108, 107) and most of the central portal jamb figures (Figs. 104c, 104b, 104d, 105b, 105a, 104a). Although the overall effect of this drapery is startlingly new, the Perrecy Master actually developed these pointed ridges from the incised folds on a continuous surface he carved at Cluny. Indeed, he experimented with pointed ridged drapery at Cluny, but only in a very few and isolated spots (as in point "a" of the capital of the Liberal Arts, Fig. 103b). At Vézelay, moreover, he updated another Cluniac drapery technique, the alternating pattern of fold surface and edges, by raising the level of every third or fourth ridge ("1" in Fig. 105b) while carving new, smaller linear ridges between them. Among the second campaign figures the Perrecy Master carved for the central portal of Vézelay, the tympanum Christ (Figs. 109, 104a) appears most like his figures on the earlier ambulatory capitals at Cluny. For the Christ, he widened the space between the pointed ridges of drapery and occasionally undercut them diagonally in the older technique (Fig. 101b).

While other artistic media from distant cultures may have contributed to the appearance of the linear style of High Burgundian sculpture, these outside causes could not have affected an immediate or wholesale change. Rather, as we have seen over a series of buildings from the lower Vézelay facade, to Cluny, and through the later construction at Vézelay, the Perrecy and Avenas Masters successively reduced the drapery in their masonry sculpture to a linear design.

Perhaps because of a fire at Vézelay, the Perrecy Master stopped carving figures for the central portal and proceeded to sculpt capitals for the nave (see appendix 6). His work on the nave capitals (Figs. 110b, 110a; 111b, 111a; 112b, 112a) shows neither the rounded tube profile (Fig. 114f) nor the flat, almost uniform tube pattern (Figs. 114c, 114e) of the work he later finished on the Vézelay central tympanum (Fig. 114a). As on the earlier jamb and lintel figures of the portal, on the nave capital figures he recalled the alternating pattern of Cluniac folds and projected every third or fourth ridge (Figs. 111b, 111a; 112b, 112a), occasionally pointing the chamfer edges ("d" in Fig. 110b). Yet in the nave sculpture he increased the linear quality of the folds. Usually (Figs. 110b, 111b, 112b), he shaved off the points of ridges leaving a flattop surface ("a") or, in many cases, nothing more than a scratch. While still indenting every third or fourth fold, he often replaced its pointed profile with a rounded edge ("c").

Even in the details of the nave capitals, the Perrecy Master turned from small-scale chamfers to linear incisions. In the ear he eliminated facets on the rim (specifically from the helix leg and tragus, Figs. 122e, 123d) and reduced the elongated depression, or scapha ("8"), to a line. In foliage he added lines around drill holes ("a" in Fig. 112c) and extended leaf lines further down the face of the acanthus than before.

After completing the nave capitals, the Perrecy Master returned to finish the work that had been interrupted on the central tympanum. Archaeological details confirm that he carved the left apostles of the central tympanum after the Christ, lintel, and many of the jamb figures (see the excursus to this chapter and appendix 6). The drapery on these apostle figures also indicates a later date because of the marked increase in tubular surface quality.[10] Occasionally in these apostle figures, he carved a less projecting version of the older chamfer plates ("e" in Fig. 114d) or reverted to the flattop fold with inscribed lines which he used in the nave ("a" in Fig. 114d), but the majority of folds he carved to a new low profile, round on the top and curved convexly on the sides ("c" in Figs. 114d, 114f; 114a). And while he projected every third or fourth drapery tube, faintly recalling the alternating pattern at Cluny, he made the difference so slight ("f" in Fig. 114e) that the drapery appears like a tubular network on a continuous flat surface. He heightened this effect by eliminating deep spaces between limbs;[11] attaching the drapery tubes on the chest and arm together as if there were no anatomical break ("g" in Fig. 114e); forming individual parts of the body, such as the outline of the eye, the rim of the ear, and each strand of hair into the rounded shape of a tube (Figs. 114b, 114a); and joining many of these analogous parts, so that on the shoulder, for example, tubes of hair and drapery are not only virtually indistinguishable from but literally connected to each other ("h" in Fig. 114c). In this way the Perrecy Master created a unified design on one surface from parts normally separate in real space.

IV

In conclusion, strong evidence supports the theory that Cluniac masons and sculptors worked closely together and often the same individuals worked in both capacities. For example, the same individual mason's mark appears on ashlar, decorated voussoirs, and figural rondels. The career of the Avenas Master is another indication of this close tie between sculpture and masonry since his early style is marked by characteristics of the northern First Romanesque masonry tradition. In addition, changes in the sculptural techniques of both the Avenas and Perrecy Masters seem to correspond to changes in the architectural decoration in the sequence of buildings where they worked. Over time, both masters gradually reduced the planar folds of sculpted drapery to linear ridges without any sudden or wholesale inspiration from any "higher" medium other than masonry sculpture.

Even without direct outside influence, both artists changed constantly and, considering the quantity and quality of their work, with remarkable speed. Despite their strong personal styles, the Avenas and Perrecy Masters changed their approach to sculpture in essentially similar ways when they worked together at the same buildings. By the time the Cluny capitals were carved, the two men had achieved a remarkably similar style. The Avenas Master is unique in that his early contact with northern First Romanesque forms seems to have affected his personal style throughout his career; moreover, although he apparently began his career earlier than the Perrecy Master, the Avenas Master stayed "ahead" of the Perrecy Master at almost every step along the way, particularly by undercutting plate folds at Perrecy and incising linear folds at Cluny. The Perrecy Master's career extended farther ahead in time, until the third facade campaign at Vézelay, and the style of his drapery sculpture approached that of early Gothic at Chartres. Yet the style which characterized his last work he had developed from the Cluniac tradition; over a sequence of buildings, he gradually reduced the earliest stacked folds he introduced at Perrecy to a series of linear tubes at Vézelay.

In the next chapter we shall see that the change in the Perrecy Master's sculpture at Vézelay, a change from incised flattop folds in the nave to tubes of folds with a rounded profile in the apostles of the tympanum, occurred at Autun in the drapery from the chevet Infancy cycle capitals (Fig. 134) to the western tympanum (Fig. 135).[12] Thus, the sculpture of the Perrecy Master and Gislebertus shows that two of the three principal masters who worked at Cluny III underwent the same stylistic changes at the end of their careers. The technique they created was used on all parts of the body and drapery and was elaborated from the small-scale experiments with linear surface design which the Avenas Master, working with the Perrecy Master, introduced in his last project on the ambulatory capitals at Cluny.

NOTES

1. Besides working at Avenas, Anzy, Mâcon, Perrecy, Vézelay, Montceaux, and Cluny, the Avenas Master carved certain of the second-story facade capitals at Charlieu. His identifying characteristics are evident in the faces and ears of the figures on these capitals (Figs. 115b and 121d), although comparison with his other works is difficult because of the lack of drapery in the Charlieu capitals and their restricted quantity and scale. While the original exterior western archivolt decoration on the second story of the facade is closely parallel to the Anzy portal voussoirs and the original interior archivolt decoration is similar to the lower exterior arcades at Perrecy, the lack of original masonry and masonry marks surrounding the Charlieu voussoirs makes relative dating with other Atelier works uncertain at best. In addition, certain of the Charlieu second-story bases never appear in any of the Atelier buildings, leading one to suspect that masons outside the original Atelier joined in the construction of the upper story. Comparing the finish of anatomical details and the execution of the foliage with other carving of the Avenas Master, I would place these and similar arcade capitals at Illiat (Dombes) between the Avenas Master's works at Anzy and Mâcon, and his portal sculpture at Perrecy.

2. The portal sculpture is part of a new western campaign which descends on both sides of the nave from the clerestory window of the second bay (Figs. 24e, 25a, 25b). The older nave campaign, however, includes all the western bay arcades including their imposts, capitals, and bases. On the facade it descends in a stepped fashion below the level of the capitals (Fig. 25a). R. Oursel's theory of a completely new vertical campaign in the western bay (*Les églises*, 151), based on Rhein's observation of a changed impost block at that point ("Anzy," 280), is probably incorrect for a number of reasons. First, a clear suture runs from the clerestory of the second bay (Fig. 25b) on both sides of the nave; at regular intervals, plug holes mark the descending suture line ("A") indicating the starting point of construction along the wall. Second, the consistent use of the Atelier's masons' marks appears only above the suture line (Figs. 24e, 25b). In fact, with the exception of the alphabet tablet in the southern aisle, only two definite letters ("C" and "E") can be sighted below the campaign suture, while over one hundred appear above it (Fig. 36). In explaining the meaning of the alphabet, F. Cucherat (*Hugues de Poitiers*, 109) drew certain analogies to calendars, while F. Ginet-Donati ("Notes épigraphiques," 117) saw it as letters meant to "guide" the masons, or simply as the gratuitous markings of a mason. Third, a distinct ashlar difference separates the stones above and below the suture line (Figs. 24e, 25a, 25b): above it, stones change to larger, more horizontally proportioned ashlar, cut with sharper corners, finished

with more even and less deep axe strokes, and set in more regular courses between smaller mortar beds. These differences also distinguish the stones of the transverse arch between the first two western bays from the stones on the transverse arches in the rest of the nave: masons' marks consistently mark the ashlar blocks which are larger and therefore fewer in number, and are joined with less mortar, finished with sharper edges and smoother axe strokes, and are arranged in two stepped arcades with much wider reveals. Fourth, the capitals and imposts of the facade course to the new campaign wall but their accompanying bases and plinths do not join the older campaign wall on the facade below the stepped suture. Indeed, the supposition that the portal with its archivolts and buttresses was added later to the facade is disproved by the prerestoration photographs in the Commission des Monuments historiques, Dossier 1121, and by Lefèvre-Pontalis photograph 8493, which show that the buttresses originally coursed directly to the wall jambs. Fifth, the argument that the existence of a classical torus-scotia base on the first southern nave pier indicates a completely new vertical campaign in the first bay, is inconsistent. The same type of base occurs on the second southern pier, which Oursel assigns to the older campaign. And the older Brionnais type of base seen throughout the nave occurs on the first northern bay, which he claims belongs to the new campaign. Moreover, the capitals and imposts on the arcade level of the first bay reappear throughout the nave; for example, the northernmost arcade capital appears again on the easternmost north clerestory, while new corinthian capitals and imposts like the ones on the portal (Fig. 5c) first appear between the first and second bays at the clerestory level, the point in the second bay where I claim the new campaign begins.

By comparing other works of the same masons and sculptor who worked at Anzy, I conclude in the text that the portal archivolts and capitals preceded the ambulatory capitals at Cluny. Previously, all scholars maintained that Anzy's Cluny-related archivolts and portal sculpture followed the ambulatory capitals at the mother church. Within this theory, one group believed that the sculpture on the Anzy portal was created in at least two stages. Already in 1923, Lücken ("Burgundische Skulpturen," 106) distinguished the "weit fortgeschrittenen Stil" of the archivolts from the tympanum, which he believed reflected the "gleichen Stil" of the tympanum at Mâcon, dating from the eleventh century. R. Oursel (*Les églises*, 78, 95, 149, 151) believed that the Anzy lintel was created before the Cluny capitals in a dissimilar style and was installed when the Anzy archivolts and portal capitals were created in a style reflecting the capitals at Cluny. Oursel believed that the master of this later sculpture also carved the Cluny western portal archivolts (p. 93), the Perrecy lintel and portal capitals (p. 95), and the Montceaux portal sculpture, but Oursel maintained that the artist did not carve Vézelay's southern portal, as Salet claimed (*Vézelay*, 98, note 1). Oursel's opinion that the Anzy voussoirs and portal capitals followed the carving of the tympanum and lintel by over fifteen years is supported by Raeber (*La-Charité*, 227) and Scher (*Renaissance*, 32).

A second group of scholars agreed that the Anzy archivolts and portal capitals followed the Cluny ambulatory capitals, but they maintained that the archivolts and portal capitals were stylistically related to the Anzy tympanum and were carved by the same master at the same time. They believed that as part of this single campaign, a separate master created the lintel in an archaistic style. Pendergast, *Anzy*, 317; Quarré, "Cluny," 160; Salet, *Vézelay*, 167; Sauerländer, "Gislebertus," 27, note 11; Stratford, "Nevers," 306, note 45.

3. Virey ("Mâcon," 469) believed that the central bay of the Mâcon narthex was revaulted in the first quarter of the thirteenth century. In conversation at Mâcon in the summer of 1973, Stratford proposed that the capitals above the first string course belonged to a second campaign closely connected to the Charlieu narthex. Indeed, the masonry of the upper story is distinctly different and the moldings and capitals there directly relate to those at Châteauneuf and Semur. However, the distinction he drew I believe corresponds to a second and third campaign, with the Atelier responsible for a first campaign built to the level of approximately the exterior dado ledge. Compared to the second campaign masonry (for example, visible around the arcades in Fig. 26a), the ashlar below the dado is almost twice as large, more vertically proportioned, and coursed with uneven and wider mortar spacing. A specific characteristic of the masonry is the repetitive pattern of chisel teeth marks, seen in the right side of Figure 13c. This campaign includes the innermost jambs of the tympanum portal, with its surrounding columns and capitals, as well as the small-diameter bases that support the outermost order of the exterior arcade (for example, on the right in Fig. 13a). All of the larger-diameter bases placed in the innermost order of the exterior arcade (and visible from inside the narthex, Figs. 26a, 13c) belong to the second campaign, with the exception of the southwest bay of the facade (Fig. 6b).

All of the large-diameter bases from the inside order of the arcade are classical in type, with a torus-scotia-torus profile set upon a squared-off plinth (visible on the left in Fig. 13a). By contrast, almost all the bases from the outside order of the exterior arcade (seen on the right, Fig. 13a) and from below the dado level on the interior of the narthex (Fig. 26a), are the standard Atelier type common in the Brionnais (Figs. 10c, 11b). Corresponding to this difference in base type is a distinction in the type of socle molding: a cyma profile beneath the orig-

inal bases (Fig. 13a,) turns into a squared-off profile beneath the later bases. Significantly, in the exceptional case of the southwestern bay of the facade, where the original base type is kept on the inside order, the original socle type also continues beneath it (Fig. 6b), showing a consistency of workmanship that is confirmed by other archaeological evidence. For example, this is the only bay where certain columns on the inside order are fluted, are not monolithic, and where the lower beds of the shafts are coursed into the narthex wall. From this evidence, I conclude that walls on this bay were sufficiently finished in the first campaign to warrant the completion of interior column bases. In all the other bays of the exterior arcade, the new square-profile socle and torus-scotia bases are built directly over the remains of the earlier campaign (especially evident on the north side, Fig. 13a). Not only did the second-campaign masons abut the older molding with a square socle, they covered it with the torus of the new bases (Figs. 13a, 13c). After they carved away the cyma profile of the older socle, they frequently buried or overlapped it with the new base (Fig. 13c).

There is nothing in the tympanum to distinguish its construction from the first campaign, which also includes the capitals, columns, and bases beneath. Porter (*Pilgrimage Roads*, 122) proposed that the frieze and Last Judgment were added later to the original tympanum from 1130, which was smaller in size and represented the Majestas Domini, apostles, and two witnesses to the Apocalypse. The tympanum underwent two major restorations (Virey, "Mâcon," 470). According to Virey, the tympanum was removed in 1848, and was found to be damaged on the parts which projected. The tympanum then was reassembled with questionable accuracy. Recounting his restoration to the narthex in 1848, the architect Guillemin (*L'annuaire de Saône-et-Loire*, 1856, 298) described the destruction: "il s'agissait de consolider les piles de la porte. . . . Pour arriver . . . nous avons dû démolir le tympan" (Sauerländer, "Weltgericht," 291–92). See also the Commission des Monuments historiques, Dossier from the year 1843, which contains the *Devis* of Guillemin from 1 May 1857, entitled "Restauration de la façade du narthex du Vieux Saint-Vincent"; see also the Commission's *Rapport* from 14 May 1938 by P. Gelis, who in the course of removing the stucco ("le piquage des enduits") and rejoining the masonry in the narthex, failed to mention the effect these restorations might have had on the sculpture. Older descriptions of the nineteenth-century restorations include F. Lacroix, "Le vieil évêché de Mâcon," 46–51; Lex, "Congrès archéologique de France—Mâcon," 447–92; and L. Decloitre, "Les véritables dimensions de la cathédrale Saint-Vincent de Mâcon," 63. See especially the discussion of the original plan by the architect Guillemin (Archives de Saône-et-Loire, serie Q, registre 30, folio 8 to 15).

4. On the basis of anatomical details and drapery (chapter 4 and its excursus), I assign the tympanum and innermost jamb capitals to the Avenas Master, and I assign the lintel and outermost jamb capitals to the Perrecy Master. As explained in chapter 1, the innermost and outermost jamb capitals (Figs. 1a, 1b) were not designed to be grouped together, and each had to be partially destroyed in the process of installation. In addition, on both sides of the portal the running abacus changes motifs between each capital. Lücken ("Burgundische Skulpturen," 115) and R. Oursel (Les églises, 261) observed that the circumference of the tympanum is significantly smaller than the surrounding archivolts; a filler on the left side was inserted to augment the original size of the tympanum. Importantly, the increase to the circumference size of the archivolts corresponds to the width of the central lintel span before it projects on the sides. In the text I claim that the lintel is the work of a separate master from the tympanum sculptor, the Avenas Master. The smaller circumference of the tympanum would have fallen directly above the Avenas Master's coursed innermost jamb capitals which together with the tympanum perhaps formed an original ensemble created alone by him. In this regard it is important that the bases (Fig. 11c) beneath the outermost, freestanding column capitals by the Perrecy Master are later in type than the rest of the bases in the narthex (Figs. 10d, 13b): their upper torus is relatively smaller, their profile more diagonal and their overall height smaller. Indeed, they come closest to the original bases on the Vézelay facade (Figs. 10e, 11d, 233), which I believe immediately followed the work at Perrecy (chapter 2; appendix 6).

In spite of disagreements over the authorship and date of the Perrecy sculpture, scholars agreed that it, like the other major works described in chapter 4, followed the ambulatory capitals at Cluny. For the tympanum of Perrecy, R. Oursel proposed a date directly following Cluny, at the "end of the eleventh century"; however, he believed that the tympanum was installed later in a single "jet" when the sculptor of the Montceaux portal and the Anzy archivolts carved the Perrecy lintel (Les églises, 261). Kerber (Kathedralskulptur, 18, 87, note 56) reiterated Oursel's theory that a previously carved tympanum was installed as part of a later portal. The date he proposed was "after" Cluny but before 1130.

Lücken ("Burgundische Skulpturen," 115, 122) believed that the tympanum only superficially resembled a style as early as 1100, while the bearing, folds, and "schwingende Linien" date it to the much later time of the lintel. He broadly compared the styles of Perrecy and Montceaux. Similarly, Salet argued for a single campaign dating 1130–1140, after the Vézelay facade (Vézelay, 48–49). He believed that the sculptor of the tympanum carved nothing at Vézelay but could have created the western portal of Anzy, while the "médio-cre" sculptor of the southern tympanum at Vézelay directed the lintel carving at Perrecy. Sauerländer ("Gislebertus," 27, note 11) supported Salet's theory of authorship and style, maintaining that Perrecy's sculpture reflects the ambulatory capitals at Cluny. For Diemer as well, Perrecy unquestionably ("steht hier nicht zur Diskussion") followed Cluny, although he believed that the "schematisch und leblos" quality of the Perrecy sculpture ruled out the possibility of the same sculptors who worked at Vézelay (Vézelay, 98, 200–2).

The architectural restorations to the Perrecy narthex are clearly spelled out to the Commission des Monuments historiques in Selmersheim's "Rapport de l'architecte sur la nature et l'importance des travaux prévus" of 15 May 1891. Both the "descriptif et estimatif" Devis of 15 February 1883, prepared by the architect on 14 July 1890, and the final Devis of 22 April 1898, give no indication of any restorations to the portal sculpture; and Monuments Historiques photograph 22744, taken before the restoration in 1892, shows the tympanum, lintel, and jamb sculpture in their present condition. For a history of the restoration, see R. Oursel, Les églises, 254; Lesaing, "Le prieuré de Perrecy-les-Forges," 251; and H. Barrès, Perrecy, son prieuré, son église, 64–65.

5. The architect Sauvageot's 0.01 scale drawings of the exterior elevations "vu par l'inspecteur des travaux sousigné Paseyk" pinpointed each stone which was replaced between 1898 and 1907. Sauvageot's report of 9 August 1898, approved 15 March 1902 by the Commission des Monuments historiques, described the wall masonry which he planned to replace, notably the "porte bouchée" on the second southern bay, while his Devis, accepted 15 December 1901, described his intention to demolish the porch as well as to undertake the "nettoyage à fond des chapiteaux, colonnes, basses, arcs, moulures, etc." of the facade. From surface inspection, I do not think that this cleaning included scraping or other surface alterations. For a photograph of the porch facade before restoration, see Monuments Historiques cl. 284.292.

While all scholars agreed that Montceaux sculpture was created after the ambulatory capitals of Cluny, they disagreed about the source and stylistic connections of the portal sculpture. For R. Oursel (Les églises, 233) Montceaux "n'est que l'expression évoluée mais toujours fidèle au mode original." Lasteyrie (L'architecture, 674) saw the closest connections to the porch sculpture of Charlieu. Kerber (Kathedralskulptur, 19) believed that the Montceaux sculpture derived from and dated after Perrecy. Porter (Pilgrimage Roads, 170) cited the style as "close to the tympanum of the side portals of Vézelay." Within the context of the Vézelay side portals, Salet (Vézelay, 167) narrowed the connection to the same "médiocre" master who carved the southern portal tympanum, a choice with which Sauerländer ("Gislebertus," 27, note 11) concurred. Diemer (Vézelay, 99–

101) preferred a connection to the upper register of Vézelay's north tympanum, although he believed that the Montceaux portal preceded the works at Vézelay and the "lebendiger und spontaner" character of the Montceaux sculpture excluded the same artist working at both sites.

6. In the most sensitive attempt to distinguish the works of two sculptors in the ambulatory capitals, Whitney Stoddard assigned the Tone capitals to separate masters ("Eight Capitals," 57).

7. Clearly, the workability of different materials plays a role in stylistic changes. The ambulatory capitals at Cluny are made of a fine-grained calcium stone, the portal at Montceaux of a porous calcium stone, while the sculpture at Mâcon and Perrecy is carved from a harder rock.

8. At Perrecy, the Avenas Master may have carved the tympanum and two jamb capitals before the Perrecy Master created his sculpture. See note 4.

9. On the Vézelay north portal, the right group of figures on the upper register are the work of the Perrecy Master. On the south portal, the Avenas Master carved the two Annunciation figures. Among the apostle fig-

ures on the lintel at Montceaux, one among the right group of six apostles was isolated to the left, which meant that the remaining five figures had to be imaginatively intertwined to compress them into the remaining lintel space.

10. In addition, new masons from the final nave construction to the east of bay six helped build the masonry surrounding the tympanum on its eastern face (see appendix 6). The central tympanum, then, is different from the jamb sculpture on the side portals (below the string course molding), which is surrounded by ashlar created entirely by masons from the original Atelier (see Fig. 36).

11. For this observation I thank Caroline Watson, graduate student in the Department of Art, University of North Carolina at Chapel Hill.

12. The most basic comparison of anatomical details from the chevet Infancy capitals and the western tympanum shows that they were created almost entirely by the same sculptor. Salet's contrary view was presented without any detailed proof ("La sculpture romane en Bourgogne," 325–343).

Excursus: Identifying Characteristics of the Avenas and Perrecy Masters

AVENAS MASTER	PERRECY MASTER

FACE Figures 115a, b, c, d, e, f, 116a, b, c, d

The top of the nose above the septal cartilage, the dorsum nasi, is a flat, planed off ridge (1) with parallel edges (2), especially sharp at the upper end on each side. A straight chamfer (3) extends at an angle from these chamfer edges to end in a rectilinear depressed groove (4) at the base of the lateral nasal cartilage. Each nostril is a triangular opening with an acutely pointed tip (5) and straight sides of the base (6), the outside margin (7) and the septum (8)—which is a flat ridge (9), with parallel (10), sharp edges (11), chamfered diagonally on both sides (12). Unlike the philtrum of the Perrecy Master, the philtrum ridges of the Avenas Master remain rounded and the philtrum base occupies almost half the length of the upper lip (13). In contrast to the Perrecy Master's work, the top lip (14) of the Avenas figures remains horizontal and the bottom lip (15) turns down on the sides. The bottom lip reveals less inside surface at the

FACE Figures 117a, b, c

Unlike the hair on the head of the Avenas figures, the first strand to either side of the central part on the Perrecy figures is undercut by a straight chamfer (1) almost three times the depth of the other hair rills. The front of the forehead (2) is practically a flat plane and it pitches at an obtuse angle from the nose. Unlike the flat dorsum nasi, chamfered nasal sides and straight lateral grooves of the Avenas figures, the Perrecy nasal ridge is round and the alar cartilage (3) frequently is encircled by a line. Instead of beginning on the corner or inside the nostril, the nasolabial groove (4) often begins from the lesser alar cartilage along the side of the nose. In contrast to the pronounced asymmetry of the Avenas lips, on the Perrecy figures the corners of the upper lip (5) turn up and the corners of the lower lip (6) turn down, exposing (unlike the Avenas figures) the full surface of the lower lip (7) at its corners. A straight chamfer with a vertical corners than in the center of the philtrum (16). The bottom of the chin (17) is fully rounded, unlike the flat undersurface of the Perrecy sculptures, and it is surrounded on either side by a fold of the cheek which curves into the neck (18). Frequently folds (nasolabial) begin inside the nostrils or at the base of the nose (19), and then extend as triangular wedges pointing downward from the corner of the upper lip (20). On bearded figures, the strands of hair usually are flat ridges (21) which extend directly into the plane of the face (22). The sides of the ridges are formed by parallel (23), diagonal (24) chamfers which slope to a line (25), creating a series of V-shaped grooves often as wide as the flat ridges of hair.

EYE   Figures 118a, b, c, d, e

Unlike the iris of the Perrecy Master, the iris (1) is only a fifth the length of the globe, and it is shallowly carved (2). Frequently, a pupil formed by a deep hole (3) occupies less than a sixth the central area of the iris. Unlike the Perrecy's globe, which typically is fully rounded and ends in a vertical line on the medial side, the globe of the Avenas Master flattens, especially at the base (4); it extends to points (5) on both the medial and lateral sides, and stretches in width (6) almost twice the distance of its height. Unlike the medial canthus which ends in a vertical line with square corners in the Perrecy eye, the Avenas medial canthus (7) projects laterally straight and ends in a point (8). The point of the medial canthus is formed by the two symmetrical curves (9) of the lid margins. In contrast, the lateral canthus (10) is asymmetrical, for it continues the downward curve of the upper lid margin, while it turns the lower lid margin into an S-curve (11). Unlike the Perrecy eye, in the Avenas eye there is no sharp brow ridge, no chamfered brow wedge, no groove at the base of the brow, and no superior marginal strip of definite size and shape. At Avenas and Mâcon, a sulcus (12) runs parallel to the interior margin and ends at the point of the lateral canthus (13).

EAR   Figures 121a, b, c, d, e, f, g, h

The Avenas ear is most distinctive for its treatment of the lobe and tragus. Unlike the Perrecy ear, which is made without a lobe, and where the helix turns back toward the center of the ear at the base, the Avenas helix continues downward into a lobe (1) almost the same length as the rest of the ear combined. The border of the lobe next to the face (2) is almost a vertically straight line. The bottom of the lobe (3) is a wedge, chamfered diagonally toward the back of the ear, and the back side of the lobe (4) is a diagonally straight line, extending to a point (5) at the base of the helix. Unlike the Perrecy ear, where the helix leg touches the tragus at its top, a distinct channel separates these parts in the Avenas ear and leads to the concha. The channel (6) has parallel sides, and is bounded on the one side by the straight, diagonal outside line (7) of the helix leg which ends in a point (8). On the other side, the channel is bordered by the upper edge of the tragus (9), which also is straight and

outside line closes the mouth opening on each side (8); the chamfer extends beneath the underside at each corner of the lower lip (9); at each corner of the upper lip it forms a triangular wedge (10) before it frequently continues as a bevelled strip (the nasolabial groove) to the lesser alar cartilage (11). The philtrum (12) usually occupies no more than a quarter of the length of the upper lip. The philtrum is made up of two sharp ridges (13) with sloping chamfers forming a shallow V-shaped groove in the center (14). Unlike the rounded modeling on the Avenas chin, on the Perrecy figures the underside of the chin (15) extends as a flat plane which curls up at the end.

EYE   Figures 119a, b, c, d

Compared to the eye of the Avenas figures, the Perrecy iris (1), where it exists, occupies more than twice the area on the globe. Moreover, the iris (2) is much deeper and has no discernible pupil (3). Typically the globe is fully rounded (4), extending as a ball into the eye socket. The globe is particularly rounded and undercut immediately above the inferior margin (5). Unlike its Avenas counterpart, the globe never disappears at a point on the medial side (6). The globe often ends in a straight vertical line (7) parallel to the medial canthus (8), which appears also as a straight vertical line bounded above (9) and below (10) by square corners formed by the intersections of the upper and lower lid margins. The brow (11) is a straight chamfer wedge, ending in a sharp ridge (12) above, and below in a depressed grooved line (13) which forms the upper edge of the superior marginal strip. On the lateral side, the brow wedge comes to a point (14) separate from and above the termination of the superior marginal strip. The superior marginal strip begins as a straight vertical line (15) with a square corner (16) above the medial canthus and extends as a parallel, narrow strip (17), no wider than the orbital margin at its largest.

EAR   Figures 122a, b, c, d, e, f, 123a, b, c, d

In contrast to the helix leg which is separated from the tragus by a channel in the Avenas ear, the straight diagonal lower edge (1) of the Perrecy helix rests directly (2) upon the top of the inside curve of the tragus (3). From there, the helix leg extends into a point (4) which touches the antihelix wall on the inside of the ear (5). Unlike the protracted upper edge of the Avenas tragus, the Perrecy tragus narrows to a small point (6) at its upper facial edge; the tragus rises as a spherical shape (7), distinct from the flat surface of the face.

The treatment of the helix at the base of the ear is substantially different from the Avenas ear. The inside edge of the helix is demarcated by a linear groove (scapha) (8), which borders a flat ledge (9), that parallels the curve of the helix and extends into a small pointed or triangular plane (fossa triangularis) (10) where it meets the helix leg at the front of the ear. The side of the antihelix is a straight, inclined plane (11), which, contrary diagonal. In analogy to the treatment of the lobe at the base of the ear, the channel extends (10) into the forehead at least twice the distance of the tragus itself. The top edge of the helix is cut diagonally to a flat (11), triangular (12) wedge, with the point on the summit of the ear.

to anatomy, is encircled at the base of the ear (12) by the fully rounded helix (13) and its accompanying linear groove (8). At the base of the ear, the tip of the helix (14) turns entirely around toward the concha and the inside edge of the helix comes to rest against the antihelix wall (15).

TOES   Figures 124a, b, c, d

Unlike the Perrecy toes, which are built up through a series of separate, flat chamfers, the toes of the Avenas Master are carved as part of a continuous whole. The toes on both sides of the foot point toward the center: the outside three toes (1) are curved in a single direction toward the center, and the large toe (2) curves toward the center in the other direction. Unlike the series of chamfers on the Perrecy nails and toes, a sharp ridge (3) often runs down the length of the toe, and frequently it extends into the nail (4). Sometimes the ridge even continues to the ground at the tip (5) of the digit.

The cuticle margin (6) often is joined to the surface of the nail by curved pointed wedges on each side at the base of the nail. The toes connect to each other at a small straight base (7) perpendicular to the toes, with square corners (8), one on each toe. And the toes connect at their tips by merging or overlapping their edges (9), or by a lateral process (10) that extends around the edges. And the toes connect with the foot by a sharply chamfered V-wedge (11) which sometimes extends from the top surface of each toe to a point (12) on the top surface of the foot.

TOES   Figures 125a, b, c, d, e, f

Almost all the forms of the toes are created from distinct, flat chamfer cuts. Unlike the pointed nail ridges of the Avenas Master, the nails are made of a flat surface (1), and frequently the tips of the toes (2) are bevelled down in three or four separate chamfers. When a cuticle is carved, it intersects the nail as a flat surface (3), straight on the bottom (4), and asymmetrically rounded on top (5). Also the joints are outlined as distinct planes (6), built up on their front by small, irregular flat chamfers (7).

Unlike the toes of the Avenas Master, which are joined on the surface of the foot through a series of V-shaped wedges, the Perrecy toes remain distinctly separate. The three outside digits (8) are straight and parallel in contrast to these toes which are curved in the same direction in the Avenas foot. And a continuously bevelled edge (9) runs between the ends of the toes, separating them from the foot. On the foot, a sharp ridge (10) extends on either side above each toe, and continues parallel (11) often as long as the toes themselves. Parallel concave troughs (12) run next to the ridges, dividing the surface on top of the foot.

5

Gislebertus and the Plus Master: The Heritage of Cluny

I

We have seen that in a sequence of buildings constructed by the Atelier, the Avenas and Perrecy Masters gradually completed a "cycle" of drapery styles beginning with narrow strips, moving to planar folds, and ending with linear tubes of drapery in the Perrecy Master's work on the nave and central tympanum of Vézelay. The change in drapery from strip to tube not only ended a "style cycle" but also ended a "geopolitical phase" in which the two men dominated the medium of sculpture by carving almost all the important projects in greater Burgundy from 1080 to 1120. From another point of view, however, the final heritage of mainline Cluniac sculpture, as represented by the linear tubes of Vézelay sculpture, can be seen to have inaugurated a new phase of localized Burgundian sculptural centers. To the north after 1120, sculptors continued carving linear tubes of drapery at Vézelay, Autun, Saulieu, Chalon, and Beaune, while different sculptors practiced other styles and techniques in widely separated Burgundian sites such as Charlieu, Dijon, Donjon, Savigny, and Souvigny. Gothic artists who worked on Chartres in the 1140s looked to new local centers like Autun rather than returning to the older mainstream Burgundian style prevalent before 1120.

This chapter explores the careers of two major sculptors, the master of the tympanum of Autun, who is called "Gislebertus," and the master of three rondels at Vézelay (Figs. 33a, 33b) who signed each of them with a + and so will be called the Plus Master. The styles of both of these men underwent changes similar to those in the Perrecy Master's style in the final stages of his career. Indeed, the Plus Master not only changed his style in the way the Perrecy Master did, but the later sculpture of both men appeared together in the same locations at Vézelay. The simultaneous changes in both masters' works confirm the sequence of sculpture and construction established from drapery technique, archaeology, and the additional new masons' marks in the nave and behind the central tympanum sculpture (Fig. 36). The coincidence of the careers of the Perrecy and Plus Masters also will help us understand the career of the third artist, Gislebertus. To seek the origins of Gislebertus's career and the formation of his linear style solely in media other than sculpture is to disregard the parallel direction of the Perrecy Master's sculptural style from Cluny to Vézelay (chapter 4) and the similar and simultaneous changes in the work of the Perrecy and Plus Masters at Vézelay. For the first time, we may follow precisely the careers of three Burgundian artists and see how their styles underwent similar patterns of change. Together the three men created a technique that literally rounded out that of mainline Cluniac sculpture. At the same time, it became the basis for a new, local Burgundian taste important for the future of Gothic sculpture.[1]

II

While pieces of Gislebertus's work remain only as fragments at Vézelay, sculpture by the Plus Master left in situ offers an accurate index of the location and sequence of stylistic shifts at Vézelay. By identifying his work (see the excursus to this chapter) in places where we identified the Perrecy Master's sculpture, we can observe the stylistic parallels and confirm a relative chronology of the work of each master. The sequence of stylistic change of both men in turn supports the chronology of building campaigns suggested by archaeology and masons' marks.

The style and inscription on one of the Plus Master's last works, the Ecclesia rondel in the nave arcade spandrel of the third southern bay, tell us much about his career (Figs. 128a, 128b, 142). Scholars largely agree that the inscription on the rondel—"I am rather covered with smoke but later I shall be resplendent"—refers to a fire that took place in 1120, a convenient *post quem* for dating the drapery of this figure.[2] The drapery (Fig. 128b) has the same flattop folds as the Perrecy Master's work in the nave and even shows signs of the tubes the Perrecy Master used on the left apostle group on the central tympanum. Like the Perrecy Master, the Plus Master occasionally reduced folds—on the stomach for example ("1")—and unnaturalistically connected them to parts of the anatomy: indeed, he turned pieces of hair into drapery tubes on the arm ("2"). Despite these "advances," however, the drapery of the Plus Master's Ecclesia is most like the drapery of the figures the Perrecy Master carved for the nave capitals (Figs. 111b, 111a, 112b, 112a). Like the Perrecy Master in these nave pieces, the Plus Master projected every third or fourth fold (e.g., "3," "4"), an effect which notably recalls the earliest planar folds of Cluny. Also like the nave pieces, the sides of the drapery ridges are sharply chamfered and their top surfaces are flattened ("5," "6," "7"). Despite the overall linear impression, then, the Plus Master had yet to master the tubular flat drapery used by Gislebertus at Autun (Fig. 135) and by the Perrecy Master for the apostles of the central tympanum at

Vézelay (Figs. 114c, 114a). The carved drapery of the Plus Master's Ecclesia sculpture most resembles the drapery of the Perrecy Master's nave capitals, and these, because of the analogy of style and location, should also be dated after the 1120 fire.

The importance of the 1120 *post quem* date attached to the style of the Ecclesia drapery increases when we realize that below this rondel, on a pier of the bay, the Plus Master executed capitals of a distinctly earlier style (Figs. 126a, 126b) reflecting no contact whatsoever with the flattop technique practiced by the Perrecy Master (for identification of the Plus Master's sculpture, see the excursus to this chapter). Unlike the later style in which he left small flattop ridges with chamfer edges on either side (Fig. 128b), here the Plus Master made fewer, deeper "V"-shaped chamfer wedges and left four or five times the amount of flat drapery surface between folds. Perhaps he reflected, and distorted, the tendency of the Avenas and Perrecy Masters at Cluny to slice thin diagonal wedges into a single plane of drapery (Figs. 96, 102b). The straight "V"-shaped profile he cut on the sleeve ("a") and waist ("b") of Figure 126b contrasts with the small chamfers and raised flattop ridges which dominate the surface of the Ecclesia drapery. Frequently he spaced folds alternately ("c"), ending them in blunted circles ("d") or continuing them around each other as recessed troughs ("e"). In the same manner, he rendered parts of the anatomy as jagged but sharp edges, which can be seen in the muscles of the leg ("f" in Fig. 126b), on the cheek and neck (Fig. 140), and, on a smaller scale, in the hands ("g" in Fig. 126b) and around the mouth (Fig. 140). This is in contrast with the carving on the Ecclesia rondel (Fig. 128b) where ridge folds connect to each other and even to parts of the body ("1," "2").

What is the significance of one master carving different types of sculpture on one bay of the nave? He could hardly have worked simultaneously in two separate styles since he showed no trace of the later tube technique in the nave capitals. On the other hand, traces of the earlier technique are found in the Ecclesia rondel. These include the sharp, chamfer cuts on the hand and chin and, despite the Ecclesia's updated flat ridges, the small "V"-shaped chamfer grooves which occasionally end in a blunted circle ("7," "8" in Fig. 128b). The "late" qualities of the Ecclesia figure, moreover, correspond to qualities in the Perrecy Master's work, which we know from archaeology and masons' marks (see appendix 6 and Fig. 36) changed over time, not simultaneously. Therefore, while the Plus Master apparently carved the nave capitals and Ecclesia rondel at different times, and while strong archaeological evidence dates the nave bay with both sculptures after the construction of the lower aisle and facade, we still are left asking why two works sculpted by the same master at different times appear together and alongside a seemingly random combination of Brionnais and classical bases and imposts throughout the nave. Could the capitals and Brionnais ornaments have been completed but not immediately installed? Or did the Perrecy Master and Plus Master carve certain capitals and rondels after they were in place? Although evidence is confusingly mixed, there is no question that the bases and ashlar of the nave date later than the lower aisles and facade (see appendix 6 and chapter 2) or that the central nave vessel is a new campaign, constructed by twenty new masons who replaced five who departed (Fig. 36).

Perhaps the fire described in the Ecclesia rondel halted the carving of the central portal (see appendix 6) and postponed the installation of certain bases, imposts, and capitals.

This explanation is supported by the evidence from a third series of sculpture carved by the Plus Master on the central tympanum rondels. The style of the drapery of these rondels is intermediary between the style seen on his nave capitals and the style of the Ecclesia figure, with its written reference to a fire. That inscription is important in the context of the stylistic difference between the Ecclesia and rondel figures, for these rondels belonged to the original tympanum program of the Perrecy Master (see appendix 6 and chapter 4) which preceded the obviously unplanned break in construction of the central tympanum (Figs. 235, 104a). Just as the Perrecy Master changed his style in the nave after this interruption on the facade (chapter 4), the Plus Master underwent a parallel stylistic change in nearly the same locations, confirming the archaeological sequence suggested for the central portal (appendix 6). The drapery of the three rondels he signed (Figs. 33b, 127, 104a) fits between his own earliest nave capitals and the Ecclesia rondel and corresponds to the Perrecy Master's first work on the central portal tympanum and lintel (Figs. 108, 107, 109, 104a). But that drapery hardly approaches the rounded tubular style of the Perrecy Master's later tympanum apostles or the top three rondels which Christian Beutler correctly observed were added later when the tympanum was widened (Fig. 238).[3] As on his earlier capitals (Figs. 126a, 126b, 140), in the rondels (Fig. 127) the Plus Master conceived the anatomy of the arm ("a"), hand ("b"), and even an occasional leg muscle ("c") as irregular and sharply raised edges, and he cut the drapery into "V" wedges ("d," "e" in Fig. 127). Yet in the rondel figures he went "beyond" his nave capitals in the direction of his Ecclesia figure and the late work of the Perrecy Master. Rather than isolating individual grooves, he multiplied their number and carved them more closely together. Often he chamfered the edges so closely together that he left nothing but a series of pointed ridges ("f" in Fig. 127), like the work of the Perrecy Master on the lintel; or, when he left slightly more space between the grooves, he created narrow flattop ridges ("g," "h" in Fig. 127) like those he later carved throughout his Ecclesia figure in the nave. He also began to alternate sets of ridge folds in the Cluniac manner, and occasionally even linked isolated ridges together, as on the sleeve ("i"). Both techniques he later systematically applied to the drapery of the Ecclesia figure in the nave.

Comparing these three stages of the Plus Master's work permits us to draw some unusual conclusions. His numerous signature marks on plain ashlar, decorative voussoirs, and figural rondels (Figs. 33a, 33b, 34, 36) reveal a productive mason *and* sculptor, a startling fact for historians who insist on a distinction between these two "professions" in this early period of medieval Burgundian art. The differences between the damaged and incomplete facade carving and the nave sculpture of both the Plus and Perrecy Masters confirm the archaeological break on the facade and tympanum and the direction of stylistic change between this sculpture and their nave work.[4]

Finally, the formal and archaeological (see appendix 6) correspondences between the tympanum rondels of the Plus Master and the second-campaign jambs, lintel, and tympanum of the Perrecy Master give us an indication of the date of this campaign, and help to confirm the date of the Cluny ambulatory capitals. The Perrecy Master's work on the second facade campaign directly followed the style of the Cluny capitals (chapter 4), dated around 1095 from archaeological evidence in appendix 4 and chapter 2. And the drapery of the Perrecy Master's sculpture on the second facade campaign corresponds to the drapery of the Plus Master on the tympanum rondels, which stylistically preceded the Plus Master's Ecclesia with its *post quem* of 1120. Therefore, on stylistic grounds, a date between 1095 and 1120 is appropriate for the second campaign facade sculpture of both masters. These dates are especially plausible because parts of all these sculptures are broken or incomplete—including a topmost rondel, the jamb imposts, the lintel, and the base of the central tympanum (see appendix 6 and Figs. 104a, 105a, 235, 238)—indicating that they were damaged or left unfinished at the same time, possibly when the fire of 1120 ravaged the monastery.

III

No scholar has systematically identified and traced Gislebertus through the various stages of his career, beginning with Cluny, or placed him in the context of artistic changes shared by the other Cluniac artists at Vézelay.[5] Unlike the Perrecy and Plus Masters, Gislebertus is not associated with any in situ Vézelay sculpture, although he underwent the same sequence of stylistic changes they experienced there. On the basis of detailed analysis (see the excursus to this chapter) it would seem that Gislebertus carved the Expulsion capital (Figs. 129a, 129b, 129c, 139a) and two western portal fragments (Figs. 130a, 130b, 130c, 130d, 139b, 131, 139c) at Cluny, as well as the central tympanum at Autun. Until now, neither the Expulsion capital nor the facade sculpture has been directly associated with Gislebertus.[6] Given the changes in Cluniac sculpture (chapter 4), it can be seen that in the Expulsion capital Gislebertus worked in ways that were both "behind" and "ahead" of the Avenas and Perrecy Masters, who completed the ambulatory capitals.[7] Unlike them, he avoided slicing folds into one drapery plane (Fig. 129c), preferring instead to carve strips on the surface in the old belting tradition ("1"); simultaneously, he experimented with forms which came to dominate the later sculpture of the Perrecy and Plus Masters. He began to isolate pointed ("2") and concave ("3") looped ridges above the drapery surface and even extended them into pleats ("4").

These linear techniques, which he used tentatively in the Expulsion capital, had been developed considerably by the time he worked on the western portal (Fig. 131).[8] Perhaps reflecting the work of the Atelier in the ambulatory, Gislebertus increased the undercut and expanded the width of each fold ("1") while lining the surface of the drapery with low projecting dots along the borders ("2") and with a greater number of less-projecting pointed ridges of concentric design ("3"). These small projecting pointed ridges, which the Atelier used only hesitatingly in the Cluny ambulatory (Figs. 103b, 103a), the Perrecy Master later applied systematically to the figures on the jambs and lintel at Vézelay; and together with the Plus Master and Gislebertus, he transformed them into the rounded linear folds which came to dominate sculpture in northern Burgundy and the Ile-de-France after 1130. Judging from the initial steps of Gislebertus in the Cluny Expulsion capital, where he showed little or no contact with the Perrecy Master, it may be that Gislebertus, not the Perrecy Master, first reduced drapery and anatomy to a single linear vocabulary at Cluny. By the time of the western portal, approximately 1120, Gislebertus rendered even the smallest details of the figures with these small pointed ridges (Fig. 131) and a few of these folds suggest his later tubular drapery (Figs. 130d, 130a).[9] He reduced the massive chamfer cuts from the Expulsion figure's hair (Figs. 129b, 129a) and ear (Fig. 139a) to a series of exceedingly small pointed ridges on the Cluny portal figure's hair, eye ("1," "2" in Fig. 130b), ear (Fig. 139b), and even around the nostrils and septum ("1," "2" in Fig. 130c). Indeed, the ridges are so analogous and uniform throughout the figure that Gislebertus could exchange their functions; the upper lip, for example, doubles as a hair of the moustache ("3"). Perhaps Gislebertus, but certainly a mason from the western portal of Cluny, carved the rarely discussed fragments numbered "78" in the Vézelay Lapidary Museum (Figs. 133a, 133b; 132a, 132b).[10] In details like dots and concentric chest folds (Fig. 132a), pointed hair and drapery ridges (Fig. 132b), the sculptor carved in the style of the Cluny portal sculpture and, although I do not mean to imply the direction of influence, he brought it "up-to-date" with changes in the Perrecy Master's work at Vézelay. Like the Perrecy Master, the sculptor practically eliminated undercutting on the hand, sleeve, and chest (Fig. 132a), while reducing planar Cluniac folds to a schematic surface pattern of pointed ridges (Figs. 132a, 133b). Given their similarity to the Perrecy Master's incomplete work on the jambs and lintel of Vézelay (Figs. 104c, 104b; 108, 107), these noticeably pointed ridges (Fig. 132b) may indicate that the mason's work preceded the Perrecy Master's flattop drapery on the nave capitals. In fact, the fragments seem most like the eastern Infancy capitals at Autun (Figs. 133b, 134), where pointed ridges are only occasionally rounded in the technique Gislebertus almost exclusively practiced by the time of the western tympanum at Autun (Fig. 135). Because of the rapid exchange of new artistic ideas apparent from the stylistic parallels in the careers of the Plus and Perrecy Masters at Vézelay, we can speculate that the Autun chevet was begun simultaneously with or even before the nave at Vézelay. This seems so because the drapery techniques of the eastern Infancy capitals at Autun represent an intermediate stage between the pointed facade type and the flattop nave formula of the Perrecy and Plus Masters at Vézelay.[11]

While Gislebertus's career was surely more complex than we describe, on the Expulsion capital at Cluny he definitely started to work in a linear technique which he expanded in the larger planar folds of his western portal pieces, before he went to Vézelay or Autun.[12] To assume that Gislebertus suddenly adapted the linear ridge technique at one of these later sites from media other than sculpture overlooks the course of his masonry career at Cluny.

The changes in his style from the Cluny portal to the Autun tympanum are not unique but correspond to changes in the style of masonry decoration at Autun as well. Just as Gislebertus reduced the Cluniac pattern of drapery to essentially a linear design on a flat surface with the sides of the figure cut by a straight chamfer (Fig. 135), masons at Autun similarly modified the typical Cluniac elevation.[13] They reduced the distinctive classical motifs on the blind arcades and string course to tube-like forms strikingly similar to Gislebertus's folds on the drapery of the facade (Figs. 135, 138). They reduced the projecting pilasters and moldings which were veneered over brick-based construction at Cluny and Paray (Fig. 218) to barely projecting details which they inscribed, actually scratched at times, on uniform beds of ashlar (Figs. 137, 138) with simple, straight-edged reveals.[14]

In addition, the changes in Gislebertus's style from the portal of Cluny to the tympanum of Autun correspond to changes in the styles of two other important sculptors, the Plus and Perrecy Masters, changes documented from their in situ works at Vézelay. Indeed, it is remarkable that after 1120 and thus well beyond the heyday of Cluny, Gislebertus and the Perrecy Master—sculptors of the two major Burgundian tympana of Autun and Vézelay, sculptors who had trained at Cluny and still worked in a Cluniac tradition—reduced the Cluniac planar folds to an alternating linear pattern of rounded ridges based on the pointed ridges as seen in Cluny West sculpture.

In fact, the technique of projecting every third or fourth parallel round ridge, derived from the traditional Cluniac pattern of alternating folds, was carried beyond the latest works of the Perrecy Master and Gislebertus at Vézelay ("f" in Fig. 114e) and Autun ("a" in Fig. 135) and became a part of the drapery technique of the "Headmaster" at Chartres ("a" in Fig. 136).[15] The Headmaster transformed this drapery technique to such an extent that we might even speak in the traditional way of a new Gothic direction rather than a surviving Romanesque style. Unlike the Perrecy Master and Gislebertus, who maintained a uniform dimension for each tube throughout the drapery (Figs. 135, 114c, 114e, 114a), the Chartres master distinguished different folds (Fig. 136). He undercut the more projecting tube, increasing its circumference beyond a semi-circle ("b"); simultaneously, he progressively reduced the size of the more numerous alternating tubes until they disappeared between the larger projecting ones ("c"). In contrast to Gislebertus, he effectively emphasized the outline of the figure by expanding both the projecting and the smaller alternating tubes into wide shallow rolls of drapery on the outer edge of limbs ("d"), by sagging the drapery into scooped folds at the calf ("3"), and by pulling it tightly between joints ("f"). By using such techniques to reveal body outline, the Chartres master altered the vocabulary of analogous linear tubes, which the Burgundian masters had adapted from traditional Cluniac folds and had carved uniformly across all parts of the drapery and anatomy. Thus the Chartres Headmaster largely owed the form of his drapery to Cluny and to changes which occurred within that tradition after 1120. His execution and interpretation of these forms produced startling new effects, but the forms themselves were old and established and can be traced through individual masters and ateliers back to the northern First Romanesque tradition.

NOTES

1. No scholar has systematically identified and traced Gislebertus through various stages of his career, beginning with Cluny, or placed him in the context of artistic changes shared by other Cluniac sculptors, as for example in the different campaigns of construction at Vézelay. The tendency in general is just the opposite: to attribute to his work great individual creativity, separating it from closely contemporary sculpture at Vézelay and Cluny. By dating Autun early, Lücken ("Burgundische Skulpturen," 109–114) observed a "Kluft" between the sculpture of Autun and the "vorangehende Stufe der burgundischen Plastik." "Man kann also nirgends in Burgund eine Vorstufe zum Stil von Autun feststellen." Similarly, Zarnecki (*Gislebertus*, 161ff., 174–175) observed in Gislebertus's work a kind of spontaneous generation. Despite the influence at Autun of "facial types" from the western portal of Cluny, and the attribution of a fragmentary female head at Cluny to the

hand of Gislebertus, Zarnecki distanced the master from Cluniac sources: "he was the only sculptor of that workshop who . . . evolved an individual manner unlike any of his Burgundian contemporaries." His drapery style was "little affected by the characteristic Cluny folds." This belief in the inconsequential role of Cluniac sculpture in the formation of Gislebertus's style echoes the position of Talobre ("La reconstruction," 238), who believed that "le modèle Cluniésien ne semble pas avoir réussi à s'imposer."

Other scholars have observed no direct sculptural antecedents to Gislebertus's style but have suggested indirect sources through other media. Porter (*Pilgrimage Roads*, 110) believed that his style was "largely formed" from Winchester and German manuscripts, while Sauerländer ("Gislebertus," 24) insisted that "die Figurenbildung des Bildhauers Gislebertus von kluniazensischen Wandmalereien in der Art von Berzé-la-Ville ausgegangen sein muss." Sauerländer, who believed that exacting "hand" comparisons were of "durchaus sekundärem Interesse," preferred broader analogies based on the "spitzgliedrig-eckige Beweglichkeit" of "überlängte und dünngliedrige" drapery. Salet ("Review of Zarnecki," 111–112) combined the previous opinions. While he described the Autun workshop as independent of Cluny, "un atelier autonome" with a style unique in Burgundy (*Vézelay*, 164f.), he suggested that Gislebertus may have been trained at Cluny, worked at Autun, copied from Cluniac painting, and then practiced at Vézelay.

2. "Sum modo fumosa, sed ero post haec speciosa."

3. Beutler, "Vézelay," 10f. Despite his accurate observation, he incorrectly concluded that the extra rondels were added when the Christ figure was inserted (see appendix 6).

4. The Plus Master also worked on the outermost voussoirs and rectangular archivolts of the central portal. He sculpted the apostles to the right of Christ on the tympanum, and these figures show the late stylistic characteristics of the Perrecy Master's apostles described in chapter 4. He was joined at times by another mason who signed his work with a triangle.

5. See note 1.

6. In the previous scholarship, neither the Cluny Expulsion capital nor the Cluny facade sculpture has been *directly* associated with Gislebertus. The female head fragment (no. 4811) has been identified as the work of Gislebertus (Zarnecki, *Gislebertus*, 166), but this piece is made of a harder grey stone than the facade sculpture and it was excavated a great distance from the facade—indeed, it was uncovered three bays from the crossing in pit XLVIII. This female head is attributed to the west facade portal in the catalogue, *L'art roman, exposition organisée par le gouvernement espagnol sous les auspices du conseil de l'Europe*, 276.

Among the sculpted pieces at Cluny, the Expulsion

capitals were identified by Kleinschmidt ("St. Peter," 20) as the work of the tympanum master, one of three sculptors she distinguished on the western portal; and Conant (*Cluny*, 88) associated the sculptor of the Expulsion capital with the head fragment no. 4811. Outside of Cluny, R. Oursel (*Les églises*, 93) proposed that the sculptor of the Cluny rondels created the archivolts at Anzy, while Salet (*Vézelay*, 166) believed that an unspecified master from the Cluny western portal worked on the jamb figure of Saint Peter at Vézelay.

7. As Salet noted, the original location of the two engaged capitals, including the Expulsion capital, "reste inconnu" ("Review of J. K. Conant," 185). Conant ("L'abside," 10–11) claimed that the Expulsion and Second Plain Song capitals "furent enterrés dans le remblai, et retrouvés par hasard quand on creusa près du site vers 1880–1890"; Germaine Chachuat, former Director of the Musée Ochier, Cluny, kindly referred me to a letter of 1 October 1850, addressed from the Director of the Haras to the Mayor of Cluny, in which he referred to the Expulsion capital: "le Directeur du Haras émettait à la ville de Cluny quatre chapiteaux (dont l'un représente Adam et Eve chassés du Paradis terrestre)." R. Oursel (*Les églises*, 89) correctly suggested certain links of the Expulsion capital to the tympanum on the facade of Charlieu. Pendergast (*Anzy*, 409) proposed a source for the Expulsion capital in the Donjon region based on an "emphasis on flat surfaces and line," qualities which Conant ("The Apse of Cluny," 337) and I did not find in the capital: "figures there were not relatively flat and calligraphic."

8. From the bases and foliage on the western portal, I assigned the portal figural sculpture to the fourth and final campaign before 1132 (appendixes 5 and 6). In the past, scholars disagreed about the dating of the western sculpture in relation to capitals from other parts of the building. For references and a résumé of these differences, see Walter Cahn, "Romanesque Sculpture in American Collections: II. Providence," 53; Vergnolle, "Cluny," 100–101; Pendergast, *Anzy*, 324; and Scher, *Renaissance*, 28. For different reasons, both Conant and Salet assigned the portal a date around 1110; for Conant, this date corresponded to the final years of vertical construction in the west, whereas for Salet it represented the beginning of the horizontal perimeter construction.

Conant ("Medieval Academy Excavations at Cluny—the Season of 1929," 9) claimed that the debris exploded from the sculpted facade in 1810 was "roughly piled up and then spread indiscriminately over the surrounding streets in order to raise their level."

9. For a justification of this 1120 date, see appendixes 5 and 6.

10. Fragments numbered 78 in the Vézelay Lapidary Museum are presently catalogued numbers 224 and 225 by Lydwine Saulnier (*La sculpture oubliée de Vézelay, exposition permanente des collections lapidaires de Vézelay*,

Auxerre, 1979) who assigns them no specific provenance or attribution. Both pieces were simply "found in the demolitions," and, I believe, belong to the same sculptural group as the unidentified fragment numbered 240. See also figure 1949.47.50, provenance unknown, Harvard Fogg Museum, published by Linda Seidel, "Romanesque Sculpture in American Collections," 76.

11. See chapter 4, note 10.

12. Zarnecki (*Gislebertus*, 174) recognized "without a shadow of a doubt the style of Gislebertus" in the fragments of a triangular gable (known as the *fronton*) in the Vézelay Lapidary Museum. The style corresponds to Gislebertus's work after the chevet of Autun. Two of the three fronton pieces have the pointed and flattop drapery associated with the Autun chevet capitals, while only one fragment, number 222, from the fronton has the rounded drapery ridges like those on the Autun western tympanum. See appendix 6, note 9.

13. For the changes in nave proportions, see Schlink, *Cluny*, 79ff. Zarnecki's theory that the chevet of Autun was built in two campaigns (*Gislebertus*, 57) is incorrect because the stones of what he described as the "earlier" low arcade directly course to the masonry of the "later" pilasters in the choir. Moreover, I hesitate to accept his theory that a Cluniac atelier replaced a Brionnais atelier at the point of the second-story apse. The motifs of the exterior second-story choir corbels are not Cluniac—they do not exist at Cluny—but are common in Brionnais churches such as Charlieu and Anzy. By contrast, a common Cluniac device, the classical doucine molding, already was employed on the first story at Autun—in the outside bays of the apse—before it became standard on the second story, the point where Zarnecki claimed that the Cluniac atelier began. Moreover, while admittedly five of the apse first-story capitals are Brionnais in type, all of the northern first-story capitals are distinctly Cluniac and typical of capitals on the freestanding piers of the nave to the west of the great transept. In addition, the first-story apse voussoirs already exhibit a distinctly Cluniac drilled foliage decoration,

found on the orders of the western tower porch and on the top frieze of the "choir closure" fragments from Cluny.

14. These changes in part may be due to techniques observed on the Roman gates at Autun. See chapter 2, note 28.

15. Many different theories support the Burgundian origins of the Chartres Headmaster and his atelier. They range from Deschamps's ("Notes," 78) broad statement that first generation Gothic in the Ile-de-France "proceeded" from Burgundy, to the specific identification of the source at one Romanesque site, such as the Last Supper tympanum from Saint-Bénigne Dijon by Grodecki ("La 'première sculpture gothique', Wilhelm Vöge et l'état actuel des problèmes," 281) or the central tympanum from La-Charité by Porter (*Pilgrimage Roads*, 126). Recently, scholars have created more complex theories with intermediary stages between Burgundian Romanesque and Chartres. Kerber (*Kathedralskulptur*, 45) associated the Headmaster with the New York Metropolitan Museum Saint-Denis statue column and thereby proposed a "Vorstufe" preceding Chartres; Whitney Stoddard (*The West Portals of Saint-Denis and Chartres*, 52–53) described the relationship between the monumental sculpture of Burgundy and Chartres as "tenuous" despite the fairly direct connection of the ornamental design. In an admitted "jeu d'esprit," Sauerländer ("Sculpture on Early Gothic Churches: the State of Research and Open Questions," *Gesta*, IX, 1970, 35) suggested a "chain" of influence from a small, peripheral handmaiden figure on a minor side-aisle capital at Autun, to the statue columns placed on the extremes of the outside portals of Chartres, to the Headmaster's sculpture from the central portal. The peripheral location of the sculpture he examined at Autun and Chartres, as well as the extreme simplicity and regularity of its drapery in comparison to the folds of the Headmaster, indicate a reduction from these principal sculptors' work rather than an intermediary stage.

Excursus: Identifying Characteristics of Gislebertus and the Plus Master

GISLEBERTUS	THE PLUS MASTER

EAR Figures 139a, b, c, d

Contrary to nature, two separate concha holes appear (1) (2), one above the other. The deep openings are separated by a straight helix leg (3) that ends at the inside surface of the antihelix opposite the tragus (4). A corner (5) is created on the facial side of the upper hole where the helix leg meets the antihelix. Contrary to nature, at the base of the ear the helix replaces the lobe and circles back at least 240 degrees toward the inside of the ear (6). There it extends to a point (7), usually touching the straight underside of the helix leg as the leg crosses the two holes (8). Also contrary to nature, the concave profile of the scapha (9) continues at the base of the ear inside the circling helix (6). The tragus is exceptional for the size of its inside point (10). The width of the tragus almost equals its length. The point frequently merges with the circling helix (6) and ends by touching the straight underside of the helix leg (11).

FACE Figures 140, 141, 142

The eyebrows of the Plus Master are flat chamfers (1), with curved, sharp ridges above (2) and a sharp-edged groove at the base (3). On the medial side, frequently the brow ends in a point well before the canthus of the eye (4). The groove at the base of the brow meets the medial edge of the eye margin at a point (5) from which a diagonal, straight line (6) ascends to the ridge of the brow. The eye ball (7) is extremely round, filling less than half the width of the socket. Unlike the Avenas eye, for example, the iris (8) occupies as much as one half the area of the globe, and the iris is cut almost straight through the ball. The circumference of the iris (9) is interrupted by one of the lid margins. Both lid orbits are visible—the lower orbit (10) stands out away from the ball, while the upper lid orbit (11) overhangs it. While the upper lid (12) is almost a straight horizontal line at right angles to the nose, the lower lid (13) curves downward. The nostrils (14) are narrow, pointed triangles. Because the area of the alar cartilage hardly projects, the nose (15) appears to be the same width throughout its length. Each philtrum ridge (16) ends in a small triangular wedge on the upper lip. The sharp edge of the lower lip (17) depresses in the center to a curve below the area of the philtrum. The mouth (18) is extremely small, indeed, hardly wider than the base of the nose. By contrast, the chin (19) is wide, almost twice the width of the mouth. On the cheeks (20), the outside lower eye margin extends downward as a plane built up away from the face.

Conclusion

Generations of scholars have been attracted to Cluny III because of its beauty, size, and historical significance, only to discover that they lacked the primary evidence necessary to answer elementary questions about its creation: Who built it? What was the background or training of the artists? What were their artistic aims? Such insufficient documentation about the design process led me to search for the necessary information by means of a new method. My objective was to see whether these questions could be answered by careful visual analysis of the architecture and sculpture at Cluny.

To avoid preconceptions about Romanesque and specifically Cluniac practices, I began my visual analysis by closely observing the earliest Romanesque buildings in the region around Cluny. In so doing, I was able to discern distinctive patterns of construction indigenous to the region, patterns which related to two definite craft traditions. The question then became whether such traditional building techniques survived in the architecture of the High Romanesque period. This was the first step in learning about the design practices of the creators of Cluny III.

In examining High Romanesque buildings for signs of an ongoing traditional craft, I discovered new information about these later buildings. I noticed that distinctive features of architecture, such as masonry marks and minutely detailed "hand" characteristics of sculpture, appeared in the same form in a particular group of buildings. The recurrence and accumulation of so many discrete, peculiar, and idiosyncratic features allowed me to determine who created the major works of High Romanesque architecture and sculpture in Burgundy. By integrating the archaeological methodology of architecture and the hand analysis of sculpture, it became possible to identify works by particular masons and sculptors—who in many cases turned out to be the same individuals—and to establish a relative chronology for the different buildings that these masons and sculptors created. The end result of this visual approach allows us finally to appreciate High Romanesque works as the achievements of a man or of a distinct group of men working at specific times in specific places.

With this method combining architecture and sculpture, I discovered new truths about High Romanesque art in Burgundy. It became clear, for example, that artistic excellence was recognized and perpetuated during this period: a very small group of masons and sculptors completed most of the major Cluniac buildings in Burgundy from 1080 to 1120 and, indeed, only two sculptors carved the principal tympana and capitals. In spite of the small size of the Atelier, however, little evidence supports the Renaissance concept of an elite class of sculptors and architects as opposed to a pool of menial masons. The same signatures are found on masonry blocks, masonry sculpture, and tympana, and frequently aesthetic and technical changes occurred simultaneously in architecture and sculpture. We may want to question the theory of architectural dominance in Romanesque art since in Burgundy the sculptors were the builders, and when changes in the two media occurred, they changed in distinctly parallel ways. The changes in the two media, which reached a climax at Cluny III, began, in fact, within northern First Romanesque masonry practices.

By studying architecture and sculpture together, I was able to achieve a more precise understanding of the relative chronology of monuments and the direction of artistic change. This synthetic approach made it possible to identify previous works by Cluny III sculptors and masons in local Burgundian buildings, thus contradicting theories of spontaneous generation, distant sources, and inspired overseers for the abbey church. Now we can see that the origins of Cluniac art lay primarily in traditional, regional architecture and sculpture and not in other media practiced by foreign artists in distant lands. Southern First Romanesque masons, so long denied their proper role in the creation of High Romanesque art, must now be seen to have contributed significantly to the formation of a Cluniac style.

An integrated study of architecture and sculpture not only reveals the size and roles of the work force, the interrelationship of the media, and the sources and direction of artistic change. It also exposes, as if in high relief, the personalities and contributions of individual artists themselves. It was my purposeful effort throughout my research to understand the architecture and sculpture of Romanesque Burgundy in human terms, as the work of individuals. And so I tried, whenever possible, to examine works from the practical perspective of the artists who created them. I hoped to avoid the pitfalls of analyzing architecture and sculpture in abstract and schematic terms by being constantly aware of the hand upon the stone. In the course of such intimate examination of the material labor of art, the physical shaping of stone, the works of art were, as much as possible, allowed to tell their own story. "Innovation" was thus characterized by tangible and often technical changes in ways of working stone, changes that produced new aesthetic effects. Documented by detailed photographs, the approach gives, I think, a more true and vital picture of the creative process, in which specific artists emerge from separate traditions, respond to and interact with each other, explore new approaches, and establish their own legacies.

Identifying ateliers and distinctive artistic personalities who went through growth and change seems a more direct and revealing method for discovering Cluny's sources and influences than matching motifs and general stylistic traits across wide boundaries of time, space, and medium. Once we recognize the roles of individuals in the creation of Burgundian architecture and sculpture, our appreciation of the artistic importance of Cluny is not diminished, but it does change. In sculpture, it has been shown that the Avenas Master was the original and dominant personality in the creation of the Cluniac figural style, a style which developed within a context of northern First Romanesque masonry sculpture. The ambulatory sculpture of Cluny did not mark the beginning of a stylistic tradition, but came at the end of a series of joint projects by the Avenas and Perrecy Masters, two men whose different personalities, shared learning experience, and artistic interaction can be traced in a series of "experiments" prior to their achievement at Cluny. Similarly, the impact of Cluniac sculpture on the course of later Burgundian art can be seen as the influence of individuals who had worked at the mother church. The changes in Gislebertus's style from the west facade at Cluny to Autun paralleled the changes in style of other sculptors—such as the difference between the jamb and tympanum apostles at Vézelay, the work of the Perrecy Master. Observing such changes in the style of individual masters allows us to see a personal dimension of the artistic impact of Cluny during the Romanesque period.

Understanding the role of individuals at Cluny III also allows us to see in specifically human terms the creative and synthetic qualities of this building. The picture that emerges shows that the Cluniacs used the available local talent and that these masons in the course of construction worked out a new relationship among themselves. Their work at Cluny reflects a creative moment when local masons not only applied their distinctive techniques and aesthetics to large-scale religious architecture but merged two previously separate traditions into a new design. The result was something new, combining the subtleties of late eleventh-century ashlar with brick-based construction. The architecture, however, was not new in the way suggested by standard Cluniac theory—not new, that is, in the sense of an architectural revolution, engendered from foreign designs by an overseeing intellectual, and then copied in "vest-pocket" editions. Informing the design of the building were surviving masonry traditions from the local regions of the Mâconnais and Brionnais. Similarly, the impact of the design can be evaluated in human terms: Paray no longer should be seen as a simple copy of Cluny, but rather, in the chevet campaign, as the creation of specific masons who continued to work in the style they already had achieved in earlier portions of the mother church.

This revision of theory does not mean that the important role of Cluny in art history is at all diminished. The role is simply changed: Cluny was an exceptional point of synthesis—a unique and ongoing experiment in style and construction—but not a "revolution from outside" as heretofore thought. As Cluny lost its economic, political, and religious dominance after 1120, the direct impact of its artistic achievement decreased.

The situation wherein a closely knit group of masons almost exclusively created major Burgundian projects suddenly ended. In Burgundy, important artistic centers like La Charité, Charlieu, Dijon, and Autun, sprang up outside the Mâconnais, and artists turned for inspiration to sites far from Cluny, to the Rhône Valley and the Ile-de-France.

ARCHAEOLOGICAL APPENDIXES

Appendix 1

Saint-Bénigne at Dijon, Saint-Philibert at Tournus, and the Regional Theory of First Romanesque Architecture

I

No one has undertaken a systematic review of First Romanesque architecture since the pioneering studies of Porter and Puig i Cadafalch.[1] Waves of revived interest followed Focillon's important study of northern First Romanesque sculpture but even these have diminished to a trickle.[2] We are left with concepts derived from Puig's extreme theory of southern First Romanesque architecture as an international school more geographically fixed than any regional Romanesque school proposed in the nineteenth century and severed from any "foreign" influence: "cet art concret, uniforme, fermé aux influences étrangères, se détermine sur la carte avec une précision que n'ont jamais connue les écoles si discutées de la seconde période romane."

Modern writers rely on his exclusive theory to justify two separate international styles in France in the year 1000. Grodecki spoke of two geographic "blocs," the "'premier art roman du Nord,' distinct, et symétriquement opposé au 'premier art roman' méridional." He believed we were "autorisés, et même obligés" to accept geographic groupings. Deshoulières concurred: "on trouverait alors en France un groupement scindé en deux seules écoles," and Vallery-Radot, without spelling out the boundaries, spoke of a solid southern "bloc préroman" with "un caractère d'uniformité très remarquable et pour ainsi dire international."[3]

While masons from the north and south of France practiced two different stone techniques, they did not quarantine themselves, especially not in Burgundy where the major rivers of southern and northern France, the Saône and the Loire, come together. Puig was a great pioneer, but his theory of a geographically exclusive style can be disproved by showing that masons from both the North and the South worked on the most important First Romanesque buildings of Saint-Bénigne at Dijon and Saint-Philibert at Tournus. Three amateur art historians—a viscount and two clerics—previously noticed northern masonry in Burgundy, although they never fully recognized its significance for the theory of Romanesque art.

In his undated, unpublished, and uncatalogued manuscript in the municipal library of Dijon, a local viscount, Pierre Truchis, recognized that the eastern campaign of Tournus was built by northern masons (Fig. 143a) and that the rest of the church was executed by masons practicing a southern style (Fig. 143b). The names he gave Tournus campaigns (*école franque carolingienne* and *école latine-lombarde*) must not detract from the accuracy of the distinction he made. Truchis was the first not only to observe these two building techniques as they exist at Tournus, but he was also the first to recognize that the techniques were characteristic of northern and southern French styles in the year 1000.[4]

A part-time art historian like Truchis, Abbé Plat mentioned Tournus only briefly in his encyclopedic treatise on the *art de bâtir* from antiquity to the Middle Ages.[5] Nevertheless, he identified the characteristics of northern First Romanesque style which distinguish the crypt of Tournus from the southern First Romanesque construction of the nave and narthex.

Unlike the engravings he published, Dom Plancher's eighteenth-century writings on Saint-Bénigne at Dijon are sadly neglected. In them he observed the same differences that Plat and Truchis recognized at Tournus. Plancher distinguished a brick-based southern masonry in the rotunda and a northern technique in the chevet and eastern chapel which he naively attributed to the sixth century (campaign "VI" in Fig. 144).

These disparate, avocational observations combine with evidence I introduce to suggest a single, new conclusion. Heretofore, southern First Romanesque architecture has been described as a geographically circumscribed, homogeneous style. But that style cannot be exclusive if northern and southern First Romanesque masons were active contemporaneously within one region and even within one building.

II

The features Plat observed throughout northern First Romanesque architecture appear in the crypt of Tournus and indicate a northern origin for its masons. Plat even illustrated northern First Romanesque masonry with occasional examples from the Tournus crypt.[6] There he noted *joints saillants*, the built-up, shaped and polished mortar joints which appear throughout the Loire basin (Figs. 17, 18),[7] and *lames de pierres*, narrow blades of stone which fit vertically between ashlar blocks (Figs. 20, 145).[8] Here, as in northern construction generally, such blades are most often white, the same color as the buttresses (Fig. 146a); or they are pink to imitate brick (Fig. 19); occasionally, they are real bricks as on the south interior wall (Fig. 14a).[9] Plat recognized the mark of the hatchet (*taillant*) by its parallel, long, narrow and flat strokes. Common in Loire buildings (Figs. 15, 18, 145) and throughout the Tournus crypt (Figs. 14a, 17), these marks never occur in southern First Romanesque masonry.[10] Plat further distinguished two types of northern masonry. The exterior of the crypt was built with the first type in which buttresses and corners are constructed of oversized white ashlar (Figs. 146a, 19), joined to walls made of stones ranging from medium ashlar to *opus spicatum*,[11] and set into extremely heavy mortar beds (Figs. 146a, 147), like many northern French churches (Saint-Wandrille, Fig. 21; Saint-Michel-sur-Loire, Fig. 20; Angers, Fig. 23; and Vendôme, Fig. 148).[12] Indicating even closer northern ties is the second type of masonry—more common in the North—which dominates the interior construction of the Tournus crypt (Fig. 14a). All the stones are ashlar of even height and uneven width, but never as large as the oversized stones on the exterior. Closely related to the wall construction is another northern technique, *jambage à boutisse renforcée*, in which horizontal ashlar stones reinforce the sides of window jambs (Figs. 147, 149).[13] Perhaps the most outstanding example of a reinforced jamb occurs in the only fully original window of the crypt ambulatory (Figs. 146a, 146b), where stones of the same size, shape, and color balance each other on opposite sides of the window. The numbers printed on Figure 146b identify the stones which have parallel relationships.[14]

It is clear then that the important features which Plat described dominate the crypt construction at Tournus and point to a northern origin for its masons.

III

Beyond the general characteristics of northern construction defined by Plat, specific features of northern crypts recur at Tournus. These leave little doubt that the masons of the Tournus crypt were familiar with the largest and most important buildings in northern France.

The type of impost molding used in the crypt of Tournus is unique to northern construction and is never seen in a southern First Romanesque building.[15] On the corners of the molding are two chamfered edges filled in by a vertical strip of masonry (Fig. 14a). The strip is the same height as the molding face, but its edge may be sharp (Fig. 150a) or rounded (Fig. 14b); and it may (Fig. 14b) or may not (Fig. 150a) connect to the surfaces above and below it. This same impost molding recurs in the crypts of the most outstanding First Romanesque northern buildings, in the cathedrals of Auxerre (Fig. 16) and Nevers (Fig. 15), Notre-Dame de la Couture at Le Mans (Fig. 150c), Saint-Aignan at Orléans (Fig. 150d), and Saint-Benoît-sur-Loire (Fig. 150b).

These moldings are not only similar in type but also in execution; their edges have a "doughy" quality, as if they were made of unevenly molded, pliable strips. Indeed, the projecting corners closely resemble *joints saillants* which they perhaps imitate (e.g., compare the vertical members of the molding, Figs. 16, 150d, with an actual mortar joint, Fig. 17).[16]

Among the crypts built in the northern First Romanesque style, the Cathedral of Clermont-Ferrand is located the farthest south along the Loire and is constructed in a technique and plan almost identical to the Tournus crypt. Both ambulatories were vaulted by pouring a rubble mix onto short timber boards (Figs. 14a, 151a). Both inner sanctuaries included a double row of columns, straight walls with side entrances, and two eastern niches separated by a large portal (Fig. 151b). Although its moldings have not survived, the masonry of Clermont-Ferrand is almost identical to Tournus. Huge mortar beds separate the stones; and the mortar is covered by a thin layer of polished stucco common in the North.[17] Moreover, the two ashlar types of the Tournus crypt occur at Clermont: the stones in the sanctuary are even and horizontal of the second type Plat described, and around the eastern niches they are oversized and irregular with rubble fill between. As at Tournus, parallel hatchet strokes mark both types of northern ashlar.[18]

The Clermont-Ferrand crypt matches the plan and construction of Tournus, and like Tournus it straddles the Loire and penetrates deep into the province of southern First Romanesque art. The similarity of Tournus to Clermont and the recurrence of a unique molding throughout the crypts at Tournus, Nevers, Auxerre, Saint Benoît, Le Mans, and Orléans, pinpoint the Loire Valley in northern France as the origin of the Saint-Philibert crypt masons.

IV

With Plat's definition in mind, we can easily distinguish the northern First Romanesque construction of the Tournus crypt (Fig. 146a) from the southern First Romanesque construction of the narthex at Tournus (Fig. 152) and the nave in nearby Chapaize (Fig. 41).

> La première espèce de moilon n'a presque rien de semblable dans toutes ses parties, qui sont de diverses grosseurs & de diverses figures; la pierre blanche & tendre y domine, mais elle n'est pas seule; on ne lui donne à ce moilon en l'employant dans le mur, aucun arrangement étudié, on le place indifféremment & sans autre attention que celle de remplir de bon mortier le vuide causé par l'irrégularité des figures de toutes ses parties. La seconde espèce de moilon . . . est de pierres dures de couleur grise ou rougeâtre, presque toutes semblables & plates, de deux à trois pouces d'épaisseur, arrangées dans le mur, non indifféremment & au hazard, mais avec étude; & toujours posées sur leur côté plat, qui se trouve si uniforme dans toutes ses parties, qu'il ne laisse presqu'aucun vuide pour le mortier; en sorte que les murs faits de ce moilon, paroissent aussi propres & aussi unis que des murs de brique.

One of the techniques described above is the standard southern First Romanesque type of construction (Fig. 42, 152). Hard stones either grey or red are worked to resemble the narrow, uniform shape of brick and are laid like brick with little mortar. The other technique is "frame and fill," which is similar to the first technique of northern construction Plat described (Fig. 146a). Stones are not uniform in size; rather stones of different sizes are gathered in a thick mortar bed and braced at the corners by oversized, soft white stone.

Although the above quotation fittingly describes the campaigns of Tournus, it was, in fact, written in 1739 by Dom Plancher to describe the two campaigns of Saint-Bénigne at Dijon.[19] I bring in the problem of Saint-Bénigne at this point because according to Plancher the chevet and eastern chapel of Saint-Bénigne were constructed in an ashlar technique practically identical to the one Plat observed in the Tournus crypt. The significance of this similarity for First Romanesque theory is clear: the eastern ends of the two most important basilicas in Burgundy at the beginning of the eleventh century were constructed in a northern style. Furthermore, both the plan and construction of these parts find precise parallels with other known examples of northern construction in Burgundy cited by Truchis. By combining the observations of Plat, Plancher, and Truchis, we see clearly and for the first time the importance of another style in a southern First Romanesque region.

The three examples of northern construction cited by Truchis (Fig. 143a) are the crypt of Saint-Philibert and chapel of Saint-Laurent at Tournus and the church at Prayes. These all share a similar ground plan and construction technique with the chevet and eastern chapel of Saint-Bénigne which Plancher described as campaign "VI."[20] They all have square-ended chapel apses and masonry where "la pierre blanche & tendre y domine"; almost all the buttresses, windows, and jambs are made from white ashlar stone, at Saint-Philibert (Figs. 146a, 147), at Saint-Laurent (Figs. 22a, 22b, 153) and at Prayes.[21] Also the surfaces between the white stones are as Plancher described them, an "espèce de moilon n'a presque rien semblable dans toutes ses parties, qui sont de diverses grosseurs & de diverses figures." At Prayes, Saint-Laurent (Figs. 22a, 22b), and the crypt of Saint-Philibert (Figs. 146a, 19), the large quoining stones bracket smaller stones of many colors, sizes, and shapes; oval, rectangular, round, even herringbone and reused masonry are brought together. The diversity results in the huge mortar beds Plat described throughout northern First Romanesque masonry and Plancher observed in campaign "VI": "remplir de bon mortier le vuide causé par l'irrégularité." Indeed, the mortar beds are so thick in parts of these Burgundian buildings that the beds extend beyond their individual joints to form a sea of mortar on which the mixed and irregular stones of the wall float (Figs. 19, 22b, 146a, 147).

In summary, Plancher's description of campaign "VI" at Saint-Bénigne characterizes as well the three churches cited as northern in type by Truchis. Moreover, Plancher's detailed observation matches Plat's description of the widespread northern First Romanesque style and provides us with further evidence of northern masons at Dijon. But the clinching argument for their presence is Plancher's account of the other campaign (marked "XI" in Fig. 144) at Saint-Bénigne. He distinguished it in no uncertain terms, isolating the identical features of southern First Romanesque masonry which appear alongside northern masonry at Saint-Philibert at Tournus.[22] As at Saint-Bénigne, the stones of the nave and narthex at Tournus are uniform (Figs. 42, 152): "presque toutes semblables . . . les murs faits de ce moilon, paroissent aussi propres & aussi unis que des murs de brique." In fact, the stones in Plancher's description resemble bricks which are narrow, flat ("plates, de deux à trois pouces d'épaisseur"), hard, and generally colored red or grey. Unlike the irregularities of the northern fill masonry in the Tournus crypt, the even coursing of the narthex precludes huge amounts of mortar. The stones are laid "dans le mur, non indifféremment & au hazard, mais avec étude; & toujours posées sur leur côté plat . . . si uniforme dans toutes ses parties, qu'il ne laisse presqu'aucun vuide pour le mortier." And unlike northern construction where ashlar frames the architectural parts and mortar fills the interstices, these tight and uniform courses extend into doors, windows, and buttresses; even voussoirs are made of the brick-like rectangular stones.[23] The occasional ashlar that occur in the southern masonry at Tournus are horizontal bands that end abruptly, causing lively asymmetrical patterns along the otherwise uniform wall surfaces. These large stones function completely differently from the crypt ashlar which symmetrically frame important architectural parts, punctuate a loose mortar fill, and destroy any impression of uniformity.[24]

Thus Plancher's description of two different stoneworks at Saint-Bénigne corresponds to the significant differences which separate the western campaigns of Tournus from the three examples of northern construction cited by Truchis. A further coincidence sets apart the ashlar campaign of Saint-Bénigne and the buildings cited by Truchis: all have square-ended apses, a feature very rare in Burgundian First Romanesque buildings.[25]

V

Although Plancher clearly described northern and southern First Romanesque masonry at Saint-Bénigne, there remains the question of the accuracy of his description.[26] Fortunately, Plancher's vocabulary is so precise that his comparisons rival those of most twentieth-century archaeologists. That he repeated the same comparisons using different words strengthens our faith in the accuracy of his observations.[27] In addition, we know that Plancher's first purpose in writing about Saint-Bénigne was to leave an exact visual description, something he strongly felt was lacking in previous accounts:

> l'Auteur de la Chronique étant le seul qui ait essayé de nous en donner une idée, mais idée fausse en plusieurs choses & sans aucune exactitude, confondant ce qu'il auroit dû

séparer, prenant la partie pour le tout, & donnant au tout le nom & la figure de la partie; taisant ce qu'il auroit dû dire pour former une idée juste, ou le détaillant avec des termes équivoques; retranchant de ces monuments des parties essencielles, ou leur en attribuant d'autres qu'ils n'eurent jamais; laissant partout son lecteur dans l'embarras & le mettant dans l'impuissance de concevoir les choses comme elles sont. C'est pour ôter cet embarras & pour empêcher que nos lecteurs n'y tombent, que l'on joint à cette description le plan & la représentation des lieux, dont on souhaite donner une idée qui soit juste & la transmettre à la postérité.[28]

Plancher lived up to his role as an archaeological observer and at times overplayed it, never losing a chance to remind us that Mabillon was "trompé par de faux mémoires qu'il a suivis," or that the medieval Chronicler was bad at numbers.[29] The long list of grievances against the Chronicler proves that Plancher was aware of the wide range of pitfalls awaiting accurate observation. He directly stated that his purpose was to eliminate them in order to leave posterity an accurate record. He even bothered to correct by fifteen percent a mistake the Chronicler made in the angle of the turret stairs.[30]

Besides Plancher's reassurance of his purpose—that he meant to be precisely accurate—we have archaeological evidence with which to judge the distinctions he made between the two campaigns. A buttress (marked by white lines on the lower right on Fig. 154) remains from the south transept area marked "VI" on Plancher's plan (identified by an arrow in Fig. 144). The original stonework corresponds exactly to his description of the masonry from this campaign: soft white stones dominate the sides of the buttress while the center is filled with smaller stones of irregular size and shape on thick and uneven mortar beds.[31]

It is an often repeated fiction that none of the original stonework remains from Saint-Bénigne at Dijon. Even Prosper Mérimée, the severest contemporary critic who heatedly withdrew Commission des Monuments historiques funding from the reconstruction, allowed that a "petit nombre de vestiges"[32] survived and these had the appearance of "un appareil très irrégulier, intéressant par cette irrégularité même" like the buttress masonry (Fig. 154).[33] Lending proof to the originality of the buttress, he specifically cites the small niche vault contiguous to it as the only original vault left.[34]

Plancher's description of a separate ashlar campaign ("VI" in Fig. 144) is confirmed further by the resemblance of the Saint-Bénigne buttress to other ashlar buttresses of the northern First Romanesque type. Although repointed, the mortar beds duplicate the uniformly wide northern type (Figs. 18, 151b). The hatchet finish of the stones, their size, and the "frame and fill" construction correspond to the northern techniques defined by Plat and illustrated by Figures 18, 151b. Moreover, the buttress of Saint-Bénigne closely matches local buttresses of northern ashlar in the chapel of Saint-Laurent and the crypt of Saint-Philibert at Tournus (Figs. 14a, 153). Compared to the Saint-Philibert crypt, the buttress stones of Saint-Laurent and Saint-Bénigne range to more irregular sizes including oversized stones, yet all three examples contrast with the southern brick-like masonry described by Plancher and illustrated throughout the narthex and nave at Tournus.

It is evident, then, that Plancher correctly observed two different constructions at Saint-Bénigne. His description is not only precise but the same description is repeated in different words. Moreover, we have his own statement of purpose that his first aim in describing Saint-Bénigne was to leave posterity a totally accurate picture. In addition, the remains of a buttress in the area he distinguished as campaign "VI" match not only his account of that campaign but show close parallels to northern stonework, in Burgundy, and throughout the Loire Valley.

VI

The theory of a geographically exclusive southern First Romanesque style has undergone little change since Puig i Cadafalch first proposed it more than half a century ago. If anything, it recently gained greater currency with the full discovery of northern First Romanesque architecture and the assignment of the Saône River in Burgundy as "une sorte de front de résistance" between the two styles.[35] The area of Burgundy is a good test of the theory of two exclusive "blocs préromans," for it is the northernmost region where southern First Romanesque masons were active and it is the crossroads of the major tributaries of southern and northern France, the Saône and the Loire. There the most important First Romanesque churches of Saint-Philibert at Tournus and Saint-Bénigne at Dijon were built.

By bringing together the observations of diverse antiquarians, I was able to show that both northern and southern First Romanesque masons practiced in both these buildings. Plat described the general characteristics of northern First Romanesque stonework recurring in the Tournus crypt, Truchis spotted similar construction in two smaller Burgundian chapels, and Plancher observed the same masonry at Saint-Bénigne of Dijon. Together with my discovery of a fragmentary northern First Romanesque buttress at Dijon and a molding which Tournus shares with outstanding crypts of northern France, these scattered observations prove conclusively the presence of northern masons in Burgundy. The extent of northern construction in Burgundy is so pronounced that the traditional view of southern First Romanesque as an exclusive domain is no longer valid.

The importance of these discoveries for High Romanesque theory is equally clear. Burgundian Romanesque and especially Cluniac architecture is said to depend for its sources largely on northern models outside of Burgundy, whereas now it is clear that northern masons had reached Burgundy at a very early time. In the text I show how the northern and southern ateliers, which were separate in Burgundy during the First Romanesque period, developed independently and merged to form a High Romanesque style at the end of the eleventh century.

NOTES

1. Porter, *Lombard Architecture*; Puig, *La géographie*.

2. Focillon, *Sculpteurs romans*, and "Recherches récentes sur la sculpture romane en France au XIᵉ siècle"; Francastel, *L'humanisme roman*; Georges Gaillard, *Les débuts de la sculpture romane espagnole*; Grodecki, "La sculpture du XIᵉ siècle"—where he recognized northern First Romanesque sculptural motifs in the crypt sculpture of Saint-Bénigne at Dijon (see chapter 2, note 14); L. Micheli, *Le décor géometrique*.

For recent regional studies of southern First Romanesque architecture, see Armi, "Orders and Continuous Orders," 174, note 6.

3. Puig, *Le premier art roman*, 8; Grodecki, *L'architecture ottonienne*. Although he pointed out the importance of southern First Romanesque architecture for later styles (p. 313, and p. 318, note 4), he defined it as an international bloc, as a widespread style circumscribed in time

and space, separate from a *second art roman* as well as from a *premier art roman du Nord*. Grodecki explicitly assigned the Mâconnais to the area of First Romanesque architecture of the South (see note 13, excursus to chapter 2). Deshoulières, "Séance du 15 Décembre," 17–18; "Le premier art roman," 153.

4. Pierre Truchis, "Architecture-romane-lombarde en Franche-Comté," undated and uncatalogued manuscript in the Bibliothèque municipale, Dijon. The first broad statement of the differences between northern and southern First Romanesque architecture was published by Truchis in 1921 ("Robert-le-Pieux," 37): "le duché de Bourgogne . . . cette région comme ballottée, aux début du XIᵉ siècle, entre deux courants civilisateurs n'ayant ni les mêmes goûts, ni les mêmes tendances." Grodecki stated that the distinction between a northern and southern First Romanesque architecture was rec-

ognized later (*L'architecture ottonienne*, 318–19, note 14).

5. Plat, *L'art de bâtir*. Others have discussed the similarities in type between the ambulatory plan of Tournus and northern crypts: Bréhier, "Les origines de l'art roman," 142; Deshoulières, "Les crypts en France et l'influence du culte des reliques sur l'architecture religieuse"; Focillon, "Les origines des déambulatoires à chapelles rayonnantes." But none of the above distinguished the archaeological construction of the Tournus crypt from southern construction, as did Plat and Truchis. In making this separation, however, Plat supported Puig's theory of a geographically exclusive southern First Romanesque style: "Il faut en fait reconnaître deux premiers art romans, l'un à l'est, l'autre à l'ouest du Massif Central" (pp. 192–93).

6. The fabric of the crypt is largely the same as it was in 1825. Even in the case of the cella, which probably was restored, an engraving in the "Franche-Comté" volume of Nodier, Taylor, and Cailleux, *Voyages pittoresques et romantiques*, makes enough accurate references to details that we may conclude that the appearance of the basic elements is largely unchanged from 1825. Except for transverse arches and engaged columns, all the illustrated architectural details can be seen today. For example, except for slight differences, the present bases and capitals are identical in type to those in the engraving. The third northern capital is the type twice repeated in the present crypt, with a central rosette motif and a heart-shaped palmette. The abacus and upper lip of the present columns are the same as in the engraving, as are the side chapels of the central vessel.

Only one large restoration is known to have been undertaken before 1877, the date of the first Mieusément photograph of the crypt. Although we have no photographic control, it is clear from the *Devis* of September 1845 that little damage was done to the crypt. Expenses list reparation of the floor, the wall, stairs, stucco, and *dalles*. The report from January 1843 (no. 6136) states that the *dalles* refer to window and jamb restoration and not to extensive wall resurfacing. The architect, Questel, intended to commit "grattage et raversement des murs, colonnes et voûtes," but his budget for those restorations was cut from an estimated 2000 francs in 1843 to 14.85 francs by the time of the actual *Devis* in 1845. Some of the cella capitals, however, seem to have been scraped or replaced at this time.

The photograph taken by Mieusément in 1877 verifies that Daumet's restorations of the exterior of the crypt were minor. His first *Devis* was accepted 8 August 1877, and his work continued until 1883. It was limited to the external buttresses and pavement, plus minor refacing.

A Commission des Monuments historiques inspector, Selmersheim, in 1892 proposed that a new architect, Sauvageot, remove stucco and rejoin the masonry of the crypt chapels. The project was not mentioned again, and it is evident from the Lefèvre-Pontalis pho-tograph (no. 8707) taken between 1909 and 1911, that this work was not begun.

By far the most extensive restoration was undertaken by another architect, Ventre, after 1909. Again, the fabric of the crypt was largely preserved. We have an account of the money which was spent, for the estimated *Devis* in Ventre's report of 1909 equals amost exactly the amount, 29,435.40 francs, approved 24 January 1910. We also have the Mieusément photo of 1877 with which to control the changes on the exterior, where almost the entire budget was spent. And we have Ventre's pledge: "nous n'attaquons pas l'ancienne partie fondamentale du monument. Ce sont les parements seuls que nous ragréerons et les couvertures que nous mettrons en bon état. Dans la crypte quelques reprises indispensables seront exécutées seulement sans essayer d'en poursuivre la restauration nous nous contenterons seulement d'en assurer la conservation." Important changes were made to the windows and socles. These changes are evident from the pinkish hue and machine-like finish of the replaced stones on both the windows and buttresses (Fig. 19). Luckily, a few windows—one from the ambulatory (Fig. 146b), one from the crypt chapel, and one from the first story chapel (Fig. 147)—were left totally unrestored. Minor repairs were made to corbels, pavements and *glacis*.

7. Plat, *L'Art de bâtir*, 39: "Ces joints sont sensiblement en saillie sur le nu du mur, chanfreinés sur les bords, garnis en surface d'un mortier plus fin, et polis à la truelle"; and 41: the "joint épais n'est pas, comme on l'a prétendu, une particularité de la région tourangelle. Employé partout sous le Bas-Empire, il demeure partout l'indice de constructions archaïques. . . . Il existe également dans les chapelles de la Crypte de Saint-Philbert de Tournus." Perhaps the joints from the Tournus crypt resemble most closely the example Plat cites from the Cathedral of Blois (*L'art de bâtir*, 40, p. IIa).

8. Plat (*L'art de bâtir*, 39) described *lames de pierres* as "ayant parfois moins de O m. 07 d'épaisseur, posées verticalement pour suppléer à la longueur d'un carreau, à la façon des briques."

9. Blades are a special case where a northern building characteristic appears in the first campaigns of the narthex and nave of Tournus. However, the blades there appear only between the large white stones that make up the horizontal bands. And these bands are almost unique among southern First Romanesque architecture.

10. Toward the end of the tenth century, the hatchet largely replaced the chisel and pick in northern France (Plat, *L'art de bâtir*, 20).

11. Plat, *L'art de bâtir*, 35–38.

12. Virey (*L'église Saint-Philibert de Tournus*, 25–26) observed three zones of construction in the ambulatory and crypt chapels.

13. Plat, *L'art de bâtir*, 86, *jambages à boutisse renforcée*: "sur la face où elle se trouve posée en boutisse, chaque

pierre d'angle est accompagnée d'un carreau assez court. L'assise d'appareil, ainsi garnie, se trouve, par rapport au parement de maçonnerie dans lequel elle s'insère, ramenée à la même longueur que les deux assises entre lesquelles elle s'intercale . . . cette disposition se rencontre en de nombreuses églises, et, notamment, au Xe siècle . . . aux fenêtres latérales de la Basse-Oeuvre de Beauvais et de la crypte de Tournus."

14. Plat, *L'art de bâtir*, 86: "Il convient de noter que les assises de presque tous ces jambages à boutisse renforcée s'opposent symétriquement dans la même fenêtre. C'est-à-dire que la pierre d'angle qui forme parement sur le jambage de droite a pour vis-à-vis sur le jambage de gauche une boutisse renforcée et réciproquement."

15. The only buildings in the South with these moldings are built in northern masonry and are located on the Loire or its tributaries: e.g., Chamalières, Pommiers, Saint-Rambert-sur-Loire, Thiers.

16. The crypts where the molding appears share a second common characteristic: the interior stones are the same size and shape described by Plat as the second type. Frequently, and most notably in the crypt at Le Mans, the interior pilasters contain the same vertical blades of stone as in the crypt at Tournus.

17. Plat, *L'art de bâtir*, 39.

18. Because the stones of the crypt of Clermont-Ferrand are harder than those of the crypt of Tournus, they show hatchet strokes less.

On the basis of the closest analogies with the crypt at Clermont-Ferrand, consecrated in 946, the crypt of Tournus may date after 950, the date given by Plat (*L'art de bâtir*, 68) and Vieillard-Troiekowioff ("La Cathédrale de Clermont"). It was in 960 that Etienne succeeded as the Abbot at Tournus after he served as Prior at Saint-Pourçain, in a suburb of Clermont-Ferrand. The crypts associated with Robert-le-Pieux at Orléans are generally given to the end of the tenth century, as is the south transept crypt at Saint-Benoît-sur-Loire. Probably the latest crypts with Tournus moldings are those at Nevers and Auxerre. The similar characteristics of these last two crypts were noted first by John Bilson ("Cathédrale d'Auxerre") and both are generally dated to 1030: J. Hubert, "Séance du 26 Février"; R. Louis, *Les églises d'Auxerre des origines au XIe siècle*, 111–24; Vallery-Radot, "Cathédrale d'Auxerre."

19. U. Plancher, *Histoire générale et particulière de Bourgogne*, I, 491.

20. Truchis, "La chapelle Saint-Laurent"; Dickson, *Les églises*, 311–313; M. G. Jeanton, "L'église Notre Dame de Prayes"; Virey, *Les églises*, "Prayes," 360–362.

21. For illustrations of Prayes, which is now destroyed, see Virey, *Les églises*, 360–61.

22. Two lithographs of the exterior of Saint-Bénigne, one by Cambon and the other after a painting by P. J. Antoine (both in the Bibliotèque municipale, Dijon),

show pronounced southern Lombard bands on the rotunda stair turrets. Moreover, a recent *sondage* revealed the rotunda stair turret foundations to be built of uniform, brick-like southern First Romanesque masonry.

23. Based on the superficial similarity of *opus spicatum*, it has been common practice to group as one style the crypt of Saint-Philibert, Saint-Laurent, and Prayes, with Saint-Mayeul at Cluny, Notre-Dame at Bonnay, and Saint-Clément-sur-Guye: Virey, *Les églises*, 361; Jeanton, "Prayes," 16; Dickson, *Les églises*, 12–13. It has been shown in the text that the northern technique of construction sets apart the Tournus examples and Prayes from the others.

As all southern stonework, the *opus spicatum* used at Bonnay, Saint-Clément, and Saint-Mayeul dominates the mortar and not the other way around. The size of the stones in relation to the joints creates this impression (e.g., the stones of Bonnay range from 27 to 31 cm.). By contrast, the stones of *opus spicatum* are smaller and the mortar joints larger at Saint-Laurent (Fig. 22b), Saint-Philibert (Figs. 19, 147) and Prayes. An extremely loose coursing in these examples adds to the impression of stones floating on a sea of mortar. *Opus spicatum* of a small size and uneven coursing in a thick mortar bed is common in northern construction, e.g. in Saint-Paul, Cormery, Saint-Mexme at Chinon, Notre-Dame at Château-Landon, and Saint-Saturnin at Saint-Wandrille (Fig. 21). Significantly, the masonry of Cluny II is the uniform southern type and not the "frame and fill" arrangement found in these examples of northern construction.

Although the chapel of Saint-Laurent is lower than the eastern chapels of Saint-Philibert, the side windows in each are very much alike (Figs. 22b, 147). Their similarity in construction as well as overall appearance contrasts with the windows at Saint-Clément. The jamb stones of the windows at Saint-Clément are coursed with the wall masonry, and the "voussoirs" are actually smaller than most stones of the wall. This uniformity with the wall construction recalls the features of the first two campaigns of Tournus (Fig. 152) and contrasts with the construction of Saint-Laurent, where the window masonry stands out as different from the wall stones in type, finish, and arrangement.

24. Like the nave of Tournus, the walls of Chapaize are uniform without quoining and they include the same rows of vertical filler stones standard throughout the Tournus nave. The stones are chipped and laid in a tradition which is derived from brick-laying, e.g., no effort has been made to shape a trapezoidal voussoir; and actual bricks, laid flat, are used in a double row of stones common to southern brick masonry (also visible on the northwest narthex portal at Tournus). By contrast, the voussoir stones from Saint-Laurent are worked with a hatchet; filled with a deep, even bed of mortar piled above the level of the stones; and shaped like trapezoidal vous-

soirs instead of rectangular bricks.

25. Both the eastern chapel at Dijon and the chapel of Saint-Laurent at Tournus were independent rectangular buildings situated well apart from the principal church; however, the chapel at Dijon is symmetrically on axis with the church, while the chapel of Saint-Laurent is not. A contemporary example of an isolated eastern chapel built in the northern technique is La Trinité at Vendôme (Fig. 148). Plat suggested that the chapel at Vendôme was used during the construction of the abbey; he dated it to 1033 ("Vendôme," 273). The function of the chapels at Dijon and Tournus is unknown and rarely discussed. Plancher described the chapel at Dijon as a funerary chapel, whereas Dickson (*Les églises*, 311) and Truchis ("Saint-Laurent," 1) disagree about the use of the chapel at Tournus. The purpose of these square-ended chapels is not clarified in the cartulary passages cited by Th. Chavot (*Le Mâconnais, géographie historique*, Mâcon, 1884).

26. Plancher (*Histoire générale*, 478) interpreted the text of the *Chronicle* to support his claim for two campaigns. And he added further archaeological evidence for his claim, based on a blocked chapel window (pp. 483, 496).

27. Ibid., 496.

28. Ibid., 485.

29. Ibid., 481.

30. Ibid., 491.

31. Unfortunately, both the Commision des Monuments historiques library in Paris and the Archives de Bourgogne in Dijon are missing the plans and "détails graphiques" relating to the reconstruction of the eastern chapel of Saint-Bénigne, which are referred to in a letter from Faucher fils et Fournier of 2 April 1879, and which were "vu et approuvé" by the diocesan architect, Charles Suisse (documents in the Archives de Bourgogne, Dijon). Important discrepancies separate the plan of the present chapel building from the original one published by Plancher (Fig. 144).

Andrew Martindale indicated that original masonry exists in the southern transept chapel and that it is different from that of the rotunda. However, he failed to distinguish the qualities of any of the original masonry or to compare it to stonework from other First Romanesque buildings ("The Romanesque Church of S. Bénigne," 30–31).

Recently Wilhelm Schlink (*Saint-Bénigne in Dijon*, 60) repeated Martindale's opinion, describing "die einzige noch heute erhaltene Mauerpartie des Kryptenquerarmes, die äussere Apsidiole im Süden." Schlink denied the distinction between chevet and rotunda construction observed by Plancher.

Although he had attempted to analyze the historical context of Saint-Bénigne of Dijon, Schlink seemed to be unaware of the important difference between northern and southern First Romanesque architecture in Burgundy. More fundamentally, he seemed not to know—he at least did not cite—most Burgundian First Romanesque buildings, and he failed to cite the major publications of Virey, Truchis, and Gras in which they appear (see references in Armi, "Saint-Philibert," 1973). To substantiate his thesis (p. 163) that Saint-Bénigne is the idiosyncratic "ungewöhnliche Bauleistung" of one man, William of Volpiano, Schlink would have to contrast his reconstruction of the building—itself debatable—with the existing buildings from the same time and place as Saint-Bénigne.

The most recent excavation is partially inconclusive for many of the same reasons. Carolyn Malone ("Les fouilles de Saint-Bénigne de Dijon") failed to uncover definite evidence in the chevet, but she unquestionably showed that the nave was a three-aisled structure built almost uniformly in a southern First Romanesque masonry technique. Despite these important new findings, the very uniformity of the nave's brick-based construction seems to confute the major conclusion of the study, which is that the building represents a synthesis in type. No other examples of a synthesis exist among the numerous First Romanesque buildings in Burgundy, and no later copies of this supposed type exist. Indeed, for a building as important as Dijon we are left with a most unlikely historical situation. The study made almost no effort to compare the excavation with contemporary First Romanesque structures in the area, or even to relate the foundation of Saint-Bénigne with foundations excavated in other Burgundian First Romanesque buildings (see appendix 3). The article made little detailed analysis of basic archaeology—stone technique and moldings, for example—and discards the opinions of Plancher and findings of carbon dating when they do not support a conclusion, as in the case of the crypt (p. 264).

32. Prosper Mérimée, "Rapport à la Commission, Séance du 12 Février 1847," Commission des Monuments historiques.

33. Mérimée, marginal comments on "Extrait du registre des délibérations de la commission départementale des antiquités de la Côte-d'Or," Séance du 2 Janvier 1847, Archives de Bourgogne, Dijon.

34. Mérimée, "Rapport no. 179, 17 February 1847" ("Observations sur les rapports envoyés par la commission des antiquités de la Côte-d'Or de 1846"): "toutes les voûtes exceptée celle de l'apside (Marquée E sur le plan) sont entièrement neuves." The plan he cites is "Plan B," submitted by Henri Baudot, Président de la Commission Départementale des Antiquités de la Côte-d'Or, in 1844 ("Rapport no. 748," Commission des Monuments historiques).

35. Grodecki, *L'architecture ottonienne*, 314.

Appendix 2

The First Romanesque Narthex, Nave, and Cloister of Saint-Philibert at Tournus

I

Cluny II, Saint-Bénigne at Dijon, and Saint-Philibert at Tournus were the most important southern First Romanesque churches in France, and each has been the subject of numerous different reconstruction studies.[1] The studies remain, for the most part, controversial because at Cluny almost the entire nave lies unexcavated,[2] while at Dijon only the reconstructed crypt and scattered remains of the nave exist. The most credible studies of French First Romanesque architecture have relied principally upon findings at Tournus which, alone in the triad, remains standing. Previous attempts to reconstruct the early building history of Saint-Philibert have been so conflicting—and thus inconclusive—that any evidence of new campaigns at Saint-Philibert would have important implications for scholars of First Romanesque and could effectively alter our opinion of First Romanesque architecture in France. My purpose is to isolate the First Romanesque narthex, nave, and cloister from later additions, and thereby to provide the basis for a reevaluation of the First Romanesque basilica in Burgundy.

Archaeologists studying Tournus have not settled upon a single building chronology for several reasons: they have attached precise dates to seemingly logical campaigns without thoroughly exploring the archaeological evidence; moreover, most were hindered by an unfamiliarity with First Romanesque architecture in general and the restoration history of Tournus in particular.

Although no document conclusively dates any part of the eleventh-century church of Saint-Philibert, every scholarly theory assigned specific dates for campaigns (see chart on pages 145–150). Even skilled modern *chartistes* like M. and C. Dickson and R. Oursel, who admitted the hopelessness of drawing exact dates from the texts, still insisted upon exactly dating campaigns.[3]

Although the documents are filled with dates, they are not explicitly related to either the building campaigns or to specific parts of the structure. The most basic questions are hurdles at the starting line. Of what type was the 1007(8) building and does any of it survive, either in the foundations or as parts of the walls? To what architectural parts does the 1019 dedication refer? How can the reference to crypt relics explain the building? Specific textual clues abound, but none helps to confirm a single interpretation of the architecture. Tournus documents, because they are seemingly exact, have stirred generations of competent *chartistes* to propose precise but contradictory campaigns leaving the problems unsolved.

Historically the interpretation of the dates given for Tournus follows a pattern: pre- and post–Ernst Gall. In 1912, Gall redated Tournus to the eleventh and twelfth centuries and revised Henri Curé's tenth-century attribution of the narthex up to the arcade level, the chevet ambulatory and radiating chapels, and almost the entire crypt.[4] After Gall's 1912 study, opinions divided over the different parts of the church but fell *between* the two extremes set by Curé and Gall. Only Puig i Cadafalch contributed a new thought to the range of dating; for him the lower narthex had an even more advanced date than for Gall: 1028–1056.[5]

While assigning precise but unprovable dates for Tournus, scholars were not fully aware of the facts of restoration. Much of the confusion about the original nave campaign has been caused by the pink paint on the piers which until the nineteen-sixties escaped the notice of scholars.[6] Surely, overlooking the paint on the piers vitiates any knowledge of the state of the stones beneath it: the stones are only rarely pink Préty stones and usually are the white and whitish-yellow stones of the quarries of Venières and Lacost. André Ventre, the restorer/painter of 1909, it seems intentionally wished to deceive the observer into believing the stones were pink. He had each stone colored separately so as not to paint over the joints. And in fact we know he even mixed the Préty color himself![7] Moreover, in reporting this somewhat embarrassing activity to the Commission des Monuments historiques, he traded on the double meaning of the word "brushed" to cover up his true intentions: "Ces piles devront donc être nettoyées et brossées de façon à leur rendre leur couleur primitive."[8]

Unquestioned acceptance of the few published excavation reports may have led to other mistakes in reconstructions of the nave. Jean Martin stated that he had proved by his excavation of 1901 that the narthex foundation did not continue into the nave.[9] But he failed to indicate what can be proved by overlapping his excavation ground plan with the "projet d'installation d'un éclairage de gaz," undertaken by the architect Sauvageot (25 June 1900). The overlaying of these two plans reveals that the excavation was entirely limited to the confines of the gas-main channels, as is further indicated by a letter to Virey from the Commission des Monuments historiques on 20 July 1900: "toutefois, cette opération étant subordonnée à l'installation du projet d'éclairage." Limiting his search to openings in the floor left by laying pipes means that Martin's conclusions only touched upon the range of possible evidence and that a definitive conclusion awaits a proper excavation.

Another reason there is no accepted Tournus chronology is that no one has made an in-depth, monographic study of the church since its inside stucco was removed in 1908–1915. Curé's book, the only comprehensive study of the building, was undertaken while the interior was entirely masked with stucco.[10] The impossibility of achieving a correct archaeological analysis with stucco covering the walls is borne out by Ernst Gall's retraction in 1952 of his 1912 conclusions made at a time when stucco still remained on the walls.[11] There have been smaller studies in which experts brought to Tournus knowledge of Romanesque architecture outside the region but little Burgundian experience, or a great deal of Burgundian specialization and little travel abroad. Gaillard, Gall, Hubert, Lesueur, and Puig were experts in regions outside Burgundy, and Virey,

C. Oursel, Truchis, and Vallery-Radot were the best of the early twentieth-century Burgundian specialists—extremely skilled local experts but almost untravelled outside France.[12]

The most important cause of the contradictory reconstructions is art-historical method. Almost every reconstruction of the early building history is typological—that is, it includes only easily defined architectural parts, based on logical structural resting points, arranged chronologically with respect to each other (see chart). Examples of these typological campaigns are single units, like the nave up to the pier moldings, or collective units, like the narthex ground floor and nave.[13] In every case distinct dates are suggested for the limits of such campaigns, although none of the proposed chronologies is the same.

II

By deemphasizing the question of dating individual parts at Tournus and by carefully examining the stonework for archaeological evidence, I have discovered two First Romanesque campaigns. During the first campaign the lower story of the narthex was built; in the second, the lower portion of the nave was built and joined to the narthex. These findings will seem curious because each campaign stops at a seemingly illogical construction level (see Fig. 155). This is especially true of the nave campaign, the key campaign. While it joins the narthex and nave, it terminates neither, acting as an inter-story filler in the narthex, and attaining only the midpoint of the aisle windows and less than half the height of the nave piers. Yet however out of place the mid-aisle-window level seems within the second campaign, it makes good sense within the next campaign where it equals precisely the level of the springing of the aisle vault. Significantly, the same horizontal campaign layout was used to build Cluny III (see appendix 4). Masons at the mother church were trained largely in the southern brick technique of Tournus (see chapter 2) and followed the example of this tallest eleventh-century Mâconnais building by halting the first campaign just below the springing of the aisle walls.

Besides the layout, the construction and aesthetics of the nave campaign of Tournus had a profound impact on the design of Cluny III (see chapter 2). In contrast to the lower narthex (Fig. 157c), where the bands are narrow in relation to the size of the wall between them, in the nave (Figs. 156a, 156f) and upper narthex ("a" in Fig. 46b), the width of the wall bays and bands is relatively equal. A visual confusion appears as these elements approach the same size on the surface of the building. No longer—as was the case in the lower narthex—are appliqué bands clearly added to a primary plane. In the nave and upper narthex, the "bands" also may be read as the primary plane and the "wall" as a recession from it. Either way, the masons at Tournus treated the surface as a series of analogous planes—a fact reinforced in the nave by the disappearance of the corbel table (Fig. 156a). There is no longer even a decorative reference to the earlier use of the band as an applied ornament. Rather, this projecting surface reads as a form analogous to the sheer plane of the wall to either side of it. In the text I explore the impact of this important but subtle change on the southern First Romanesque architecture of the Mâconnais in relation to the aesthetics of Cluny III.

I conclude that the First Romanesque nave of Tournus was designed to incorporate and expand what remained of the earliest campaign in the narthex. Several facts support such a conclusion. The stonework of the second campaign binds into the fabric of the narthex, forming there a 2- to 3-foot section between the first and third campaigns; the eastern surface of the narthex is covered by a complicated veneering in the pattern of the second campaign; and most significantly, the height of the narthex piers is retained in the original building of the nave.

To show how the builders of the nave incorporated the narthex, I will describe the unique and unmistakable second campaign masonry on the exterior and interior of the church. The description of the exterior will begin on the south nave wall, proceed around the narthex and finish on the other side of the nave; the description of the interior will include the western wall of the nave and the original nave piers.

It is not clear whether the original nave campaign (II) is an uncompleted structure or a ruin; however, the fact that from west facade to crossing, the campaign's wall height is uniform and comes just below the level of the side-aisle vaults, and that the level of the original nave piers is uniform, strongly suggests a planned stage of completion (Fig. 155). In both the narthex and the nave, the second campaign wall reaches the same height; it rises to the level of the slit windows of the narthex and the springing of the aisle vaults in the nave. From this level, a third campaign can be clearly distinguished by its coursed, medium-sized rectangular stones (Figs. 155, 156d).

Every bay on the exterior of the nave tells the same story (Figs. 45, 156a–156f).[14] It is only below the midpoint of the aisle windows that second-campaign stonework can be seen. These stones are of varied size, unevenly colored and unevenly coursed (Fig. 156f); the walls of the second campaign are shot through with large, irregular bands of white stones whose sides and corners are often chopped off; but most characteristic of the second campaign are the rows of small, vertically laid stones. Rows of this kind are not treated equally: some stand isolated among other kinds of stonework, and others end abruptly in the middle of a wall (Fig. 156d). The unusual and irregular stonework of the second campaign makes it visually exciting and easily distinguishable from the construction of the first campaign below it in the narthex (Fig. 157b) and from the third campaign above it in the nave and narthex (Fig. 46a). While the height of the courses in the third campaign is irregular (above the dotted line in Fig. 156d), the width of the stones is usually twice the size of the second campaign (below the dotted line in Fig. 156d). The corners of the stones are more squared and the finish is more uniformly regular. Unlike the rows of vertical stones in the second campaign, isolated individual stones shaped like brick headers randomly fill the spaces between the larger third-campaign masonry.

The construction break between campaigns II and III on the south nave aisle wall continues onto its western face (Fig. 156a). At a level equivalent to the middle of the aisle windows, the loose, irregular stonework of campaign II, dominated by rows of vertical stones, gives way to courses of larger and more horizontal masonry from campaign III.

At that level, the construction break continues from the western nave wall into the narthex fabric (Fig. 156a). In Figures 156a and 156b, photographs taken before the recently replaced roof tiles obscured the break, all the telltale characteristics of campaign II appear on the narthex wall up to the same level that the campaign reaches in the nave. Further proof that the second campaign in fact connects the nave to the narthex at this point is the "elbow" stone which nestles into the joint between the nave and narthex and is surrounded by the characteristic rows of vertically laid stones (photographed in its full length before it was partially covered in 1971, and marked as "A" in Fig. 156b). This stone provides specific and decisive evidence beyond that of analogous stone construction techniques that the nave and part of the narthex were both built during the second campaign.

On all sides of the narthex (Figs. 156a, 156b, 157a–157c) the stonework of campaign II continues as a 2- to 3-foot section between stonework characteristic of the first and third campaigns. In Figures 157a–157c, the characteristic features of the campaigns are especially clear. In these figures, the larger ashlar of campaign III, distinguished before on the nave, runs above the second campaign, and the small but regular stonework of the first campaign runs below it. Many more types of stone are used on the second campaign than on the first (Fig. 157a), and these stones are of different colors and sizes.[15] Together with the rows of small, vertically placed stones, they create a heterogeneous wall surface.[16] The rows of vertical stones occur randomly and thereby produce a variegated effect. The white ashlar blocks of campaign II are not set in mechanically even bands as on the facade (campaign I), but are employed in ways unique to campaign II (Figs. 157b, 157c). Often the corners are sliced off; in rare instances, a small stone is inserted into the center portion of a larger stone ("a" in Fig. 157b).[17] The frequent but irregular use of white stones in campaign II contrasts with the absence of white stones throughout most of campaign I, except where they form regular bands on the facade.[18] Also, the size of the stones of the second campaign greatly varies in contrast with the evenly spaced rows of uniformly small stones from the first campaign (Fig. 157b). The close-up photograph of the south narthex wall (Fig. 157a) shows this clear difference between the types of stone used in the two campaigns. A similar distinction in stonework can be seen on the Lombard bands of the narthex (Figs. 157b, 157c), where in campaign I the regular rows of small stones continue across the bands, while in campaign II the wall coursing is interrupted by larger and more irregular stones.

The characteristic stoneworks of the three campaigns on the facade and south flank of the narthex continue onto its north face, although their sutures are sometimes masked by restorations. The break between campaigns I and II remains undisturbed (Fig. 159b), but the line between campaigns II and III is broken by post-medieval windows filled in by Charles Questel in the nineteenth century. Figure 159a illustrates three windows (numbered from the west, bays 4, 6, and 7) as they existed before Questel restored them, and Figure 159b, a detailed photograph of the area formerly occupied by the largest of these windows from bay 4, shows his stone and mortar replacements.[19] By contrast, bay 3 was not restored by Questel, and retains the clear separation between campaigns II and III.

The masons of the second campaign joined the nave to the narthex on the north side with the same techniques they used to remodel on the south. In the nave they built walls to the middle of the present aisle windows (Figs. 45, 156f). In the narthex they built on top of the walls of the first campaign which were left as two vertical stubs one on either side of the nave, visible on the interior (Figs. 160, 161, 162) and exterior.[20] Above these fragments and in line with the height of their nave construction, the masons laid typically irregular second-campaign masonry, including white stones (Fig. 45) on the exterior and telltale rows of vertical stones on the interior. These courses extend from the walls of the nave onto the narthex, where they continue above and beyond the vertical suture of the first campaign (Figs. 160, 161, 162).

From the description it is clear that masons of the second campaign built from the nave over the narthex and onto its three faces. They also covered its east facade by buttresses and a veneer.

On either side of the church, the masons of the second campaign inside built thick horizontal buttresses to brace the long, weak vertical suture which separates the wall stub of the first campaign from the western nave wall of the second campaign (Figs. 160, 161).[21] These buttresses were built during the second campaign since they are joined to the nave walls. The correspondence of the buttress stones to the coursing on the nave walls is especially noticeable on the north side (Fig. 163) and evident on the south from a *sondage*. Moreover, the buttress stones are not coursed with the adjacent walls of campaign I (Fig. 160): a particularly obvious vertical suture separates the buttresses and the projecting wall stubs (Fig. 164). Only at a few random points are the courses from the buttresses chipped into the fabric of the first campaign (Fig. 164).

Where campaign II stonework does not extend above or buttress against the remains of campaign I, it covers it over with a thin tile-like surface. The veneer stretches from the bottom tip of the ground-floor spandrels (Figs. 160, 166) to just above the sill of the open arcades of the Saint-Michael chapel (Figs. 162, 167). The purpose of the veneer may have been to cover unfinished or destroyed vaults which before the nave's construction rested on the narthex piers that now project into the nave (Figs. 43, 160, 164, 166, 168). These four piers and the narthex transverse vaults behind them still exist. However, we do not know why the vaults were terminated suddenly above these piers, which were then left as stubs projecting into the nave. Whatever the reason, if a transverse barrel vault is severed along its perpendicular line of support, what remains is an unplanned and irregular surface that begs to be refinished.

A great deal of evidence supports the fact that the nave facade of the narthex was refinished with a thin veneer of stones. That the outside lining stones of the easternmost narthex soffits were built separately from the soffit itself is evidence of a veneer. The easternmost narthex arcades are lined on the nave side with small brick-like stones ("a" in Figs. 165, 166), which are not found on the western face of the same soffits ("b" in Fig. 165) or on any other soffit in the narthex. However they are similar to the small stones on the veneer face next to them (Figs. 162, 166).[22] Clearly the bricks are not joined to the body of the arcade soffit but were built at another time: they are distinguished from the soffit stones by an almost filed finish and a small, regular, rectangular shape (Figs. 165, 166).

These brick-like soffit liners are not joined to the round piers which project into the nave (Fig. 166). On the piers within the narthex (and even on the opposite side of the easternmost soffits, Fig. 165), the courses of the soffits are the same as the courses of the piers. But on the narthex piers which project into the nave, the small stones of the soffit do not continue the large courses of the pier. The eastern lining of the narthex arcade is joined neither to the arcade soffits nor to the piers which support them, providing double proof of a later resurfacing.

By comparing the width of the narthex soffits with those of the eastern wall, one can detect the veneer, since the soffits lined by bricks are consistently wider than the other soffits. While the four narthex side-aisle soffits are between 82 and 87 centimeters wide, the easternmost soffits (including brick liners) measure from 94 to 99 centimeters in width.[23]

Further evidence that the nave facade of the narthex was resurfaced with a veneer of small stones is discovered by following these stones over the moldings of the narthex piers which project into the nave.[24] Since the courses of the wall arc over the moldings instead of running horizontally into them, the piers must have existed before the wall, and the wall must have been rebuilt to accommodate them.[25]

Knowing the sort of stonework characteristic of the second campaign, one would expect the stonework of the veneer to resemble it. The small, closely packed stones and uneven bands of white ashlar found in the veneer are unlike the mechanically even stonework of campaign I, but are very similar to the nave walls built in campaign II. The veneer surface resembles the stonework above the first campaign wall stubs (compare stoneworks labelled "2" in Fig. 162) and the adjacent walls of the nave. This kind of stonework—small, almost brick-like, with typical rows of vertical stones—reaches the same level on the narthex face as the middle of the nave aisle windows (Fig. 167), the uniform height for the second campaign (Fig. 155).[26]

From the description of the narthex it is clear that the second campaign masons tried to include the previous building in their own program. On three sides they overlapped the prior building with their own masonry and the fourth side they resurfaced with a veneer. They also paid tribute to the narthex structure by building their own piers to the height of those in the narthex. The evidence of short piers in the nave refutes both previously held theories that the entire present nave was finished in a single *jet* or that the nave first was built up to the level of the present high round piers and then roofed with timbers.[27]

Figures 168 through 174 and Figure 43 show that the original piers stopped at the height of the narthex piers. The difference in stonework apparent on the exterior nave walls is visible on the interior piers as well. The change from the second campaign to the third is again seen in a suture separating one course from the next;[28] the technique for working stones in large part changes from chipped to hatchet-cut,[29] and the size changes from smaller to larger stones. Similarly, the moldings from each campaign show similar differences. While the stones from the impost of the nave piers (Fig. 44b) are generally long, sharp, and worked to an even, rippled surface, the stones from the base of the same piers (Fig. 44a) have an uneven size, edge, and finish.

Both the photographs of numerous piers together as well as details of individual piers reveal the characteristic points of difference between the first and second campaigns.[30] The pier nearest the narthex (Fig. 43) shows that the second campaign stopped at the same height as the narthex pier moldings, for beneath this level the stones are smaller and less worked than above. Indeed, in some cases, as in Figure 43, and especially on piers of the south aisle, the first courses of the third campaign are signalled by a bed of oversized rectangular stones. Although stones within the third campaign differ in size and finish,[31] their size is consistently large and their surface is hatcheted, in contrast to the small, chipped stones characteristic of the second campaign on the exterior and interior.

Since the piers of the nave were originally as high as those of the narthex, they provide the best single example of a pattern which emerges from other parts of the building. The second campaign was not simply an addition to the first, but rather it incorporated a standing structure (the partial nature of the earlier structure may have been the result of a devastation of the kind which occurred in 1007). On the exterior and interior walls on both the north and south sides of the church, the masons bound the remains of the first campaign into the fabric of the second; where they could not easily pick up the strand of the preceding structure, they refaced it with a buttress or a veneer. It was quite in line with their other subtle attempts to merge the two buildings for the second-campaign masons to retain the height of the narthex piers in the new nave.

Although specific features of the original nave elevation cannot now be known, the planned structure of the building seems apparent. The even, mid-aisle-window height of the second campaign and the uniform, low level of its piers reveal no intention to build the present high piers and vaulted structure. Indeed, the absence of any trace of a vault or respond above the projecting narthex piers on the western face of the nave strongly indicates that the masons of the second campaign were willing to sacrifice a vaulted structure to gain the advantages of light and space in a widened ground plan. The changes in plan and structure from the narthex, however, did not preclude every effort to join the two parts with congruous piers, wall courses, buttresses, and a veneer.

III

All scholars who discussed the cloister of Saint-Philibert assigned it one campaign from the time of Abbot Ardain (1028–1056), a date gleaned from Ardain's death record which describes his burial in a cloister.[32] Shortly after 1960, the Commission des Monuments historiques had the stucco removed from the walls of the cloister, providing the first opportunity to examine its fabric and re-examine the single-campaign theory.[33] I discovered that the wall and piers of the cloister, like the original nave piers, were remodelled at a later date when the arcade was added. It is important to recognize that the arcade and its molding were the product of a second campaign, for without the later addition of those elements, the original piers are similar in size, shape, finish and molding type to the other First Romanesque piers in Burgundy (discussed in the conclusion).

Four points of evidence indicate that the arcade of the western and northern walls (Figs. 176, 177) was built after the completion of the walls behind them and the piers below them. The arcade is a veneer that covers an earlier construction.

(1) *There is clear evidence that the northwestern door of the cloister was remodelled.* This statement is based on three observations. (a) The piers and wall on the north and west sides of the cloister were built at the same time. A detail of the northern wall and piers shows their coursing (Fig. 176d) to be tightly interlocking. (b) The western face of the western wall of the cloister (Fig. 175) was built at the same time as the eastern face (Figs. 176a–d), as proved by continuous coursing which runs from the western face of the western wall through the doorway jamb to the eastern face. On the *lower* portions of the northern (Fig. 175) and southern sides of the jamb, certain large white stones and smaller stones run continuously from the western face to the eastern face. (c) The round head on the same northwestern door is not original, as proved by traces of the previous door arch below it on the western face of the western cloister wall (Fig. 175). The original arch was a standard southern First Romanesque type, such as exists over the northern entrance to the Tournus narthex. It was constructed of a series of flat stones that arched over brick-like voussoirs.

The remains of an original door arch existing on the western face (c) have been shown to be part of the original cloister wall (b) to which the piers are joined (a). However, the present cloister wall arcade was not placed directly above the traces of the original portal; instead, over the door it was made much higher than the original portal in order to accommodate the greater height of the later remodelled portal (Figs. 176a–c). In fact, the arcade has the same concentric point as the remodelled doorway (Fig. 176a). That the wall arcade not only proceeds above, but is concentric to, a later opening proves that the arcade was built after the original wall of which the first doorway is a part.

(2) *The arcade moldings correspond to the alternating arcade elevation but show no sign of correspondence to the uniform pier moldings.* Indeed, the moldings of the arcade are misaligned either to one side or to the other of the round pier moldings. For example, in the view of three piers in Figure 177, the leftmost arcade molding projects over the left side of the pier molding, while the two other arcade moldings extend far to the right of the pier moldings. Moreover, the alternation of moldings with chamfered and recessed edges has no relation to the uniform ring moldings of the piers below them. On the other hand, the alternating moldings correspond to the alternation of the transverse arches and flat wall spandrels in the elevation above. The molding with recessions supports the multiple orders of the transverse arches and wall arcades (Figs. 52a, 177, 178, 179a), while a molding with no recessions supports the flat profile of the arcade spandrels (Figs. 176c, 177, 179b, 180a, 180b).

(3) *The arcade and its moldings are not joined to the wall of the cloister, while the piers and their moldings are joined to it.* No course runs between the soffits of the arcade and the cloister wall. An open suture visibly separates those two surfaces (Figs. 179b, 180a).

Although the moldings of the piers are coursed to the cloister wall by one of two different methods, the moldings of the arcade are never joined to the wall. Figures 179a–c illustrate the method in which the ring molding of the pier is bedded to the wall. The molding conforms to the height and location of one course. Figures 180a–b illustrate the other method, where a hole has been chipped from one of the large white stones in the wall to accommodate the pier molding. By contrast, the moldings of the arcade never course with the stones of the cloister wall, either by entering directly the small stone beds or indirectly the chipped large white stones;

where an arcade molding lies in front of a large white stone, the molding never pierces it. For example, in Figure 176c the pier molding enters a chipped hole in a large white stone of the door jamb but the adjacent arcade molding veneers over the same stone. And while the pier molding courses below the white stone in Figure 178, the arcade molding simply rests in front of it.

The difference between the arcade moldings, which are not coursed with the cloister wall, and the pier moldings, which are, is emphasized by the treatment of the moldings on the south side of the cloister. There, recessed moldings (marked by an arrow in Fig. 52a) almost identical to the recessed moldings on the north wall (Fig. 179a) serve the same purpose as on the north: to support the transverse arches (Figs. 52a, 177). However, the relation of these moldings to the walls behind them is entirely different on the two sides of the cloister. While moldings of this kind are not joined to the northern wall, the moldings are distinctly bedded with the small stones on the southern wall. Furthermore, the white stones on the southern cloister wall are cut in a semicircular shape to fit exactly the table of the corbel arcade (Fig. 52b), unlike the white stones of the northern wall, which are left uncoursed to the arcade moldings. It is clear then that the arcade moldings on the north cloister wall do not join the beds of small colored or large white stones, while the same moldings on the south wall are part of a wall arrangement obviously conceived at one time.

(4) *A stylistic difference separates the wall arcade from the wall and its piers.* For reasons of workmanship, molding type, size, and shape, the wall piers are a Burgundian First Romanesque type and the wall arcade is not. The molding of the wall arcade which overlaps the width of the pier molding (Figs. 176c, 179a, b) is a characteristic never found in Burgundian southern First Romanesque architecture, where typically the arcade is narrower than the pier which supports it. But the cloister piers themselves are exactly the Burgundian southern First Romanesque type; the size and shape are short and round, and like other Burgundian southern First Romanesque piers, the stones are chipped with a chisel and pick instead of finished with the smooth, even strokes of both hatchet and chisel. Close examination of Figures 176a–c and 180a shows the introduction of a smooth rippled surface in the voussoirs of the wall arcade in contrast to the pocked and irregularly chiseled surface of the piers below. In addition, the moldings of the piers are unevenly worked ring moldings, one of the two standard southern First Romanesque pier molding types in Burgundy. The other First Romanesque molding type is the trapezoidal impost at Chapaize, Saint-Mesmin, and the dorter of Saint-Bénigne at Dijon (Figs. 41, 181, 182).

Although the alternating moldings of the arcade are unlike either of the two First Romanesque Burgundian types, they have numerous later parallels. Even at Tournus, the recessed molding reappears in the third campaign, on the interior tower and tribune windows of the Saint-Michael chapel. The other arcade molding, a flat lintel with diagonally chamfered corners, also finds only a later parallel in the greater Burgundy area. Analogous moldings exist in the nave of Saint-Vincent-des-Prés, the rebuilt crypt of Anzy-le-Duc, the second-story narthex of Romainmôtier, and in Jura churches, for example in the crypt of Lons-le-Saunier and on the portal of Saint-Lupicin.

Other differences in construction separate the cloister wall from the arcade wall and suggest a remodelling later than 1056, the death of Ardain. Typical of late eleventh-century architecture is the complex pattern of correspondence in the cloister, where a simple, chamfered molding corresponds to the square base of the arcade in even bays, and a compound molding supports it and a transverse arch in every other bay. The similarity of the finish of these moldings (Fig. 52a) to the even, superficially marked surface on the nave piers (Fig. 44b, from the third campaign), suggests a late date for the cloister alterations—especially in light of the close analogy (discussed in chapter 2) between the cloister's Lombard decoration (Fig. 52a) and details at Berzé-la-Ville

(Fig. 51c). Another similarity between the remodelled cloister and the third campaign at Tournus is the flat-planed and wedge-shaped corbel type (Fig. 52a) which appears again on the exterior of the Saint-Michael chapel (Figs. 46a,b), on the interior of its tower, and—in a more finished version—on the western interior wall of the nave (Fig. 167). Significantly, from the point of view of dating, this type of corbel reappears on the exterior (Fig. 51c) and interior tables at Berzé.

If the reference to a cloister at Ardain's death may refer to either of two stages of construction, then dating the visually similar nave of Tournus[34] and capitals from Montmajour and Venasque[35] to Ardain's time takes for granted that both cloister campaigns—including sculpture and architecture—were finished by his death. More likely, the cloister was completed later and the capitals were sculpted earlier. The cloister capitals are very similar in type to those in the outer ambulatory at Tournus, and careful analysis shows that their abaci (Fig. 52a) and bases were crudely chipped to fit the present location.[36]

IV

Scholars have proposed a wide range of possible supports, from alternating compound piers to columns with Corinthian capitals, in their reconstructions for the destroyed naves of Saint-Bénigne at Dijon and Cluny II. Exciting as these possibilities are, the fact remains that except for a few narrow foundation trenches beneath the naves of Cluny II and Saint-Bénigne, their elevations remain a matter of conjecture.[37] Therefore, the discovery of new campaigns in the most important standing Burgundian First Romanesque church, Tournus, entirely changes our perspective on the other destroyed Burgundian buildings.

Significantly, the original supports in the cloister and nave of Tournus are piers of short size and round shape as in the dorter of Saint-Bénigne (Fig. 182) and the only other truly First Romanesque basilicas in Burgundy, at Chapaize (Fig. 41), Gigny (choir, Fig. 183), Saint-Hymetière, and Saint-Mesmin (Fig. 181). Moreover, the piers of later eleventh-century Burgundy frequently were modelled after the tall round piers from the third Tournus campaign in the nave. In fact, at Saint-Hymetière (Fig. 184) the exact same remodelling occurred as at Tournus. The original First Romanesque piers are round and short, with moldings like those of the Tournus narthex, and two of them are extended in height as were those of the Tournus nave (compare Figs. 184 and 43). On these two piers, fragments of the Tournus type of double ring molding remain at approximately the height of the Tournus narthex piers, duplicating the shape of the original nave piers at Tournus and their subsequent alteration. Although piers in other later Burgundian basilicas were built in a single campaign, their shape and masonry are like the remodelled Tournus pier. Both Combertault and Sainte-Marie at Chalon (Fig. 185) have round piers of large ashlar stonework, which are two to three times higher than the First Romanesque type. At Combertault the molding is exactly like the Tournus molding, and the molding at Chalon is only slightly different, with a chamfered straight edge.[38] Therefore the original shape of the Tournus piers and their shape after rebuilding find contemporary parallels in the region.

Thus the short round pier was the standard and, as far as I know, the only nave support used in southern First Romanesque buildings in Burgundy. The consistent use of the round pier suggests a number of crucial questions for the theory of First Romanesque architecture: Can Conant's hypothetical reconstruction of the nave of Cluny II without round piers be correct? Is southern First Romanesque architecture an international style, as is so commonly claimed, if the one characteristic Burgundian support reappears almost nowhere else in First Romanesque Europe?[39] Lefèvre-Pontalis warned of the danger of generalizing on the basis of a single architectural device, and that is why I show elsewhere that a particular *parti* frequently accompanies the Burgundian First Romanesque round pier and its later regional copies.[40] But even as a single device, the round pier stands out as exceptionally significant in Burgundian architecture. It usually occupies at least half the height of the elevation, especially in the later buildings, where it continues as a major architectural device well into the eleventh century. One might be tempted to speak of a continuous local tradition beginning in the First Romanesque period and developing throughout the eleventh century. By the twelfth century, the newer designs at Cluny III and Vézelay overshadowed the round-piered basilica, but they should not obscure the early importance of this type. Especially in light of the new evidence from the narthex, nave, and cloister at Tournus, the round pier type can be seen as a consistent, separate variety, perhaps in the nineteenth-century sense even as a "School," within the international tradition of southern First Romanesque architecture.

NOTES

1. The different reconstructions of Cluny II and Saint-Bénigne are well known, but the scholarly debate over Tournus has never been adequately assessed or even charted. For a more complete discussion of the first campaigns of Tournus, see my dissertation, "Saint-Philibert at Tournus and First Romanesque Architecture in the Mâconnais." The research for the dissertation was made possible by a generous grant from the Woodrow Wilson Foundation. I am particularly grateful to the late Robert Branner, and also to Wayne Dynes, Richard Krautheimer, and to the staffs of Columbia University's Avery Library and the library of the Commission des Monuments historiques, Paris.

2. Appendix 3 examines the excavation results from the nave of Cluny II.

3. Dickson, *Les églises romanes*, 316–17: "L'exposé de ces opinions diverses montre assez qu'aucun texte précis ne vient fournir une base solide à l'étude archéologique de Saint-Philibert. . . . A défaut d'indication précise concernant la construction, les faits historiques constituent du moins les points de repère indispensables de la recherche archéologique."

4. Henri Curé, *Saint-Philibert de Tournus*; Ernst Gall, "Die Abteikirche Saint-Philibert in Tournus," 624–36; Jean Virey outlined dates similar to Curé's two years earlier in "Les différentes époques de construction de Saint-Philibert de Tournus," 515–61.

5. Puig, *Le premier art roman*, 81–83.

6. M. Berry, "Tournus l'abbaye de Saint Philibert," 16–17.

7. A worker for André Ventre in the restoration told this account to Jacques Fournier, who was for twenty years the regional architect of the Commission des Monuments historiques. He in turn related the incident to me, at Chalon-sur-Saône, November 1971.

8. Estimated financial statement by Ventre, 24 June 1913 (accepted 4 July 1913).

9. Jean Martin, "Appendice," 559.

10. Curé, *Saint-Philibert*.

11. Ernst Gall, "St. Philibert in Tournus," 179–82.

12. For references, see note 27 and chart 1.

13. Even a most sophisticated archaeological study of Tournus, made by Maurice Allemand ("La construction du narthex de Saint-Philibert de Tournus," 6–21) makes campaign decisions on the basis of intellectually satisfying solutions instead of on the basis of archaeological evidence. Employing "Détailtypologie"—tracking the displacement of windows and the changes in the width of Lombard bands and the correspondence between bands—without examining joints, coursing and construction differences, he concludes that the narthex up to the end of the first Lombard system is one campaign.

14. A distinct horizontal line divides campaign II from campaign III on each bay of the southern nave wall (marked by a line in Fig. 156e). In addition, in the last three southeastern bays, the vertical sections of wall between each pier (visible on the right and left in Fig. 156e) were replaced by a later building program, probably campaign III.

15. For the specific quarries of the stones at Tournus, see P. C. Fournier, "Note sur l'emploi des matériaux," 3–8; and P. C. Fournier and C. Rouyer, *Etude comparée de la nature du sol*, 1–23.

16. Although rare in the north, rows of vertically placed stones are common in brick buildings of Lom-

bardy, e.g., Saint-Vincent at Milan, Pombia, Galliano. Among the northern stone buildings, Chapaize and Combertault are constructed in this technique.

17. The play with white stones in the second campaign at times reaches the prankish level of Visigothic masons. An unusual symmetry exists on the southwestern nave interior buttress, where the upper corners of two large white stones are identically squared to bracket a horizontal filler stone. The space left between the white stones is filled by two square, small stones. The whole appears to be a play at a symmetry of sizes, colors, and corners.

18. The narthex facade, where even rows of white stones separate even rows of small colored stones, is the one place where the first campaign repeatedly uses stones of different size and color; while the effect is in keeping with the regularity of this campaign on the interior and exterior of the narthex lateral walls, it is so mechanically regular that one could suspect restoration. On balance, however, the evidence—although not conclusive—indicates that the regular white bands are original.

Countering this conclusion is the evidence from a Charles Questel ground plan, a Questel bill for reparation, and a request by Questel to the Minister of the Interior. The ground plan (Fig. 158) submitted by Questel 25 January 1843 (Commission des Monuments historiques document no. 2572) proves his intention to replace the wall behind the eighteenth-century porch with new stone. In a bill proposed 25 January 1843, and accepted 7 April 1843, Questel spent 7501 francs for "la taille et ravalements des parements vers l'ensemble [narthex facade] 111.96 mètres à 67.00 le mètre." Furthermore, in his report to the Minister of the Interior (letter no. 6136), January 1843, Questel makes no distinction between the normally uniform stonework of the narthex (campaign I) and the variety of stonework of the nave (campaign II), but insists that they both are the same style of mixed small stones and larger white bands of stone; not realizing that the other faces of the narthex are largely uniform in contrast to the varied surface of the nave, he well might have constructed the present alternating white stone bands.

But the argument against a large-scale facade restoration is strong. In engravings made before the restoration (e.g., Nodier et al., *Voyages pittoresques*, "Façade de l'Eglise de l'Abbaye de Tournus" by Fragonard, pl. 12; Questel, "Façade, état actuel," 25 January 1843, Commission des Monuments historiques document no. 2572) the eighteenth-century porch does not extend to the end of the narthex facade; by contrast, not only do the present white bands extend to the end of the face on both sides, they run for a few feet along the flanks (Figs. 157a and 159b). Questel neither mentions nor illustrates (Fig. 158) any intention to continue his restoration to the flanks, and thus we can doubt that these white bands or the surrounding colored stones are restored.

Neither case can be proved decisively because no "before and after" illustrations of the stonework exist. It was Questel who removed a heavy layer of stucco from the facade, so that all engravings made before the restorations allow no chance to observe whether white stone bands did in fact continue around the flanks of the narthex. When the stucco is shown to be peeling, such as in the Fragonard engraving of the facade (Nodier et al., *Voyages pittoresques*, pl. 12), the level exposed is above that in question. The other narthex illustration from this book, plate 18 by Jorand, also shows exposed stones only higher than those questioned; besides, the accuracy of these engravings is known to be unreliable. In the Jorand, the Lombard bands are incorrectly doubly lined and the wall stones incorrectly worked as ashlar, and in the Fragonard engraving the facade Lombard system includes seven instead of five bands and a nonexistent string course between the two Lombard band systems.

19. We do not know what were the large openings shown on the north side of the narthex in the Fragonard and Cailleux ground plan (Nodier et al., *Voyages pittoresques*, pl. 19). We do not know what the openings illustrated by Questel were, either, but we have a visual record of their appearance (Fig. 159a) and a written record of their restoration. In the third article of a paid bill of 15 July 1850, Questel refers explicitly to the repair of slit windows (*meurtrières*) on the north wall of the narthex:

Reprise principale à la
façade nord de 4.00^m sur
2.00^m et 1.00^m prod. un
cube de 8.00^m Vaut 8.00

Idem. aux meurtrières 8.00

Ensemble   16.00^m

Cubes de maçonnerie de smille joints
compris à 9^{cte} le mètre, vu la hauteur
et la difficulté . . . . 144.00^{cte}

10 dalles pour couronner les
meurtrières à 3.00^{cte} l'une taillées
et posées . . . . 30.00^{cte}

174.00^{cte}

Besides the extensive interior restorations made by the architect P. Gelis on the interior of the Saint-Michael chapel (bill accepted for this work on 27 May 1929), he further spent 800 francs in the accepted bill of 27 September 1930, on the *ébrasements* of the windows for the chapel. Although the second campaign covers two or three feet on the exterior of the upper narthex, the third campaign appears to have refaced the interior on most of the upper story.

20. Illustrated by Dickson, *Chalon*, 318.

21. Because the two eastern doors of the Saint-Michael chapel lead onto empty space, scholars have assumed

that the remains of the narthex below them belonged to a now destroyed stairway serving the doors. However, if the narthex remains are from a campaign terminated before the upper story was built, then using the Saint-Michael chapel door as proof is after-the-fact evidence.

22. Dickson (*Chalon*, 323) makes a passing mention of the bricks, referring strictly to the narthex arcade and not to a veneer. It is clear from the evidence of early photos that these bricks are not modern reconstructions; the peculiar, steep bottom curve which they form (Fig. 164) existed before the removal of the stucco.

23. Left out of these statistical averages are the westernmost transverse arches, which are embedded into the west wall of the narthex.

24. See Vallery-Radot, *Tournus*, p. 49.

25. The statues which were removed from above the narthex piers in the nave were too high above the moldings of the piers to have affected the bedding phenomenon discussed in the text.

26. On the nave facade of the narthex, this suture comes a few courses higher on the south than on the north.

27. Of the proposed building histories of Tournus (see Chart), the most popular theory is that the first nave included the present high piers which were covered by a wooden roof. Only Virey, who switched his position in 1932, and Lesueur reject this idea of a first church (Frédéric Lesueur, "Hypothèse sur la construction de Saint-Philibert de Tournus"; Virey, *Tournus*). Both theories maintain that a first nave structure was built entirely by one campaign.

Although Pierre Truchis ("Les influences," 459–500) and Virey ("Les différentes époques de construction de Saint-Philibert de Tournus") proposed a single campaign that was wooden roofed above the present nave capitals, the first serious statement of this position could come only after the stucco was removed from the nave clerestory in 1911. Ernst Gall gave two reasons for the existence of a high wooden-roofed basilica (*Der Cicerone*, 624–36). The first was an archaeological discovery: he spotted what he considered to be a horizontal construction suture running above the nave arcade; the second was a "structural-aesthetic" reason: the *Raumverhältnisse* of light attached piers, narrow nave arcades, and thin walls excluded the possibility of a vault.

The *Raumverhältnisse* were anything but light, thin, and airy, for the original nave piers were not tall, as Gall thought, but rather were low, the height of the narthex piers. Two explanations rebut Gall's conclusion that a horizontal suture runs through the nave above the arcade level. First, this "suture" is visible only above certain bays. For example, although stones are narrower in shape above the "suture" in the third southern bay, in the second southern bay this is not the case. On the side next to the diaphragm arch, large stones run continuously from the bottom of the wall to the top, while small thin stones lie undisturbed throughout the center of the bay. Neither in the case of the small stones nor in that of the large stones is a suture evident. Secondly, for the bays that are clearly marked by a difference in stone type above the level of the arcades, a different explanation is likely. In both local and Lombard buildings of this period, it was normal building practice to straighten out the courses of the clerestory wall after erecting the nave arcades. Quite often, as in the third southern bay, the stones of the spandrel were jumbled from erecting the arcade, and a leveling process was needed before continuing. This "breather" in bedding gives the appearance of a suture. Chapaize is the most analogous local example where the same process takes place: a level just above the nave arcades is used as a resting point to make alterations. Not only was the cant of the nave walls corrected, but the diameter of the nave responds was reduced above this level. Early Lombard examples that display a shift of construction above the nave arcade level include Lomello, Pombia, Spingò, and Vigolo Marchese.

28. A particular case is the first southern aisle pier, which may owe its uneven suture line (Fig. 172) to heavy restoration by Ventre (see note 30).

29. In studying the surface marks of the stones on the nave piers, one must take care to distinguish the light scrape marks left by the removal of the stucco in 1911, from the flat, longer, rippled hatchet strokes left by the third campaign on the stones above the narthex level.

30. The one exception to a construction break occurring on the nave piers at narthex pier height is the last northern aisle pier. Restored white ashlar stones cover this pier to the height of the narthex piers (Fig. 174). It should also be noted that within the uniform construction break of the other piers a number of variations occur. At the point of break in the last southern aisle pier, the stones change from large to small, instead of the normally opposite pattern (Fig. 174). On the four eastern attached piers of the northern wall, the construction break occurs slightly higher (six to twelve inches) than the narthex pier height. And although the characteristics of the construction break occur on all the piers attached to the southern wall, the situation is complicated by a separate uniform break in all these piers at a level a couple of feet lower than the narthex pier height.

Further evidence for the original nave piers being the height of the narthex piers are the photos taken in 1912 after the stucco had been removed from the four western nave piers but before their restoration. Details from the photos (Commission des Monuments historiques no. A5) prove that old stucco and severe stone damage existed just to the narthex pier height and not above.

31. E.g., the upper stonework of the easternmost piers on the four aisles is unusually large and finely finished. Yet the contrast in finish to campaign II stonework in any of these piers is far more significant than the irreg-

ularities within the third campaign. Also, the regular placement of the traces of scaffold holes on the free-standing nave piers substantiates that these piers were completed in a single campaign above the narthex pier level.

32. Vallery-Radot (*Saint-Philibert*, 15) claims that the vaults are later. The lost eleventh-century chronicle of Falcon was incorporated in Pierre Junien's *Nouvelle histoire de l'abbaye royale de Saint-Filibert, et de la ville de Tournus* (pp. 92–93). See John Cameron, "Early Romanesque Sculpture in Provence," 19, note 9.

33. None of the known restorations to the cloister affected the stonework of the piers or the arcades. See letters in the Tournus dossier at the Commission des Monuments historiques, Paris, dated 24/8/1863, 11/9/1863, 26/1/1864, 30/1/1864, 23/6/1879, 29/6/1879, and 25/6/1900. In his letter of 21/1/1864 to the Ministre des Beaux Arts, the Curé of Tournus admitted his responsibility for bricking in the northern arm of the cloister, a restoration of 1862 which the "Architecte-voyeur," C. Blanc, reported in a 29/6/1879 letter to Viollet-le-Duc at the Commission des Monuments historiques as "sans aucune autorisation." M. Berry, Architecte en chef des Monuments historiques, in an interview on 3 March 1971, indicated that the surface of the stones of the cloister piers is original. The covering he removed from them (*Bulletin, Société nationale des antiquaires de France*, 24 April 1963, 90–94) was whitewash and therefore did not cause the surface damage sometimes produced by the removal of stucco. For published details of the recent cloister restoration, see Berry, "Saint-Philibert," 15–19.

34. Vallery-Radot, *Saint-Philibert*, 15.

35. See chapter 2, note 14.

36. The original chevet of Tournus probably dated after 950. See appendix 1, note 18.

37. Martindale, "The Romanesque Church," 28, and Malone, "Saint-Bénigne," 253ff. See appendix 1, note 31.

38. Other round piers, at Saint-Vincent-des-Prés and Farges, although shorter, reveal the same combination of chamfered molding and large rectangular stones worked as ashlar. And in the stair tower at Saint-Vincent at Mâcon, the round center post is made from ashlar similar to the second nave piers at Tournus.

39. See pp. 58–60 of my "Saint-Philibert" for an examination of the other round pier types in international southern First Romanesque architecture.

40. Lefèvre-Pontalis, "L'école du Périgord n'existe pas"; Armi, "Saint-Philibert," 60–71.

CHART: Building Chronologies of Saint-Philibert of Tournus

AUTHOR	Lower Narthex	Upper Narthex	Nave	East End	Crypt
Henri Curé, *Saint-Philibert de Tournus*, Paris, 1905	before 935 -------------- mid 10th cent. vaults --------------			after 875 lower walls of apsidal chapels	chapels
		ABBOTS HERVE III & ETIENNE I 949–979 --------------------		10th cent. upper walls of apsidal chapels, base of choir, central tower --------------------	10th cent. walls and vaults of ambulatory
		SAINT ARDAIN & SUCCESSORS 1028–1056 (perhaps 1066) vaults of two eastern bays, top story of twin towers --------------------	central and side aisle vaults	11th cent. resurfacing transept --------------------	beginning 11th cent. columns, capitals & vaults of cella
			1080–1119 choir and sanctuary refinished transept chapels --------------		
Paul Frankl, *Die frühmittelalterliche und romanische Baukunst*, Potsdam, 1926	after 1007 --------------------	begun before 1020	completed 1019 with wooden roof --------------------		
			12th cent. vaults --------------------	beginning 12th cent. crossing and choir interior	

Chart, *continued.*

AUTHOR	Lower Narthex	Upper Narthex	Nave	East End	Crypt
Charles Oursel, *L'art roman de Bourgogne*, Dijon, 1928				------------- ABBOT ETIENNE 979 chevet	transforms martyrium of Saint Valerien into crypt -------------
	------------------------------- 979–1007(8) -------------------------------	979–1007(8)	------------------ ABBOT BERNIER 1008–1019 one campaign including diaphragm arches but not including main vessel vaults ------------------		------------- after 1007(8) fire minor reparations
			------------------ ABBOT PIERRE 1er 1066–1107 capitals, diaphragm arches and vaults replaced ------------------	1120 dedication	
Jean Virey, *Saint-Philibert de Tournus*, Collection des petites monographies des grands édifices de la France, Paris, 1932	----------------- end 10th cent. -----------------		------------------ ABBOT ETIENNE or before 980 side aisle walls ------------------		------------- ABBOT ETIENNE or before 980 -------------
		first story	-- ABBOT BERNIER beginning of 11th cent. nave piers and entire clerestory walls --	south transept, ambulatory and radiating chapels	
			------------------ ABBOT PIERRE beginning of 12th cent. diaphragms and vaults --	Choir reconstruction	

Chart, *continued.*

AUTHOR	Lower Narthex	Upper Narthex	Nave	East End	Crypt
J. Puig i Cadfalch, *La géographie et les origines du premier art roman*, Paris, 1935				928–946, 949–970 sanctuary and crypt	
	ABBOT ARDAIN 1028–1056				
			ABBOT PIERRE 1er 1066–1117 main vessel vaults	completed 1120	
Marcel and Christiane Dickson, *Les églises romanes de l'ancien diocèse de Chalon*, Mâcon, 1935	ABBOTS HERVE and ETIENNE 949–981 ground story and facade to second window level			ABBOT ETIENNE 960–981 choir substructure	
	ABBOT BERNIER 1008–1028 vaults	ABBOT ARDAIN 1028–1056 vaults	ABBOTS BERNIER AND ARDAIN 1008–1056 exterior walls	exterior walls and radiating chapels	
			ABBOT PIERRE 1er 1066–1107 all piers, vaults of two western bays		
			1107–1150 ca. vaults of three eastern bays	transepts and choir interior	

Chart, *continued.*

AUTHOR	Lower Narthex	Upper Narthex	Nave	East End	Crypt
Ernst Gall, "Die Abteikirche Saint-Philibert in Tournus, eine kritische Untersuchung zur frühburgundischen Baukunst," *Der Cicerone* 4 (1912):624–636; slightly revised "St. Philibert in Tournus," *Zeitschrift für Kunstgeschichte* 16 (1952): 179–182	1007(8)–1019 to a degree using pre-fire materials, entire narthex and flat roofed nave to base of white capitals	1007(8)–1019	1007(8)–1019 ／ ca. 1050 except for two eastern bays: white capitals and above ／ ca. 1100–1120 two eastern bays: white capitals & above	1090–1120 irregular and changing renewal of the east end from the crypt up	
Jean Hubert, *L'architecture religieuse du haut moyen age en France*, Paris, 1952	1019 begun, but largely completed as one campaign by ABBOT ARDAIN 1028–1056		1007(8) began reconstruction	1120 dedication of transept and interior of choir	end of 11th cent. and beginning of 12th cent.

148

Chart, *continued*.

AUTHOR	Lower Narthex	Upper Narthex	Nave	East End	Crypt
J. Vallery-Radot, *Saint-Philibert de Tournus*, Paris, 1955				pre–1007(8) foundation of transept, choir, & chevet	echelon crypt
	1007(8)–1019				
			ABBOT ARDAIN 1028–1056 nave except for vaults		
				ABBOT PIERRE 1er second half of 11th cent. non-vaulted transept, walls of ambulatory and radiating chapels	structure
			1120 dedication vaults of nave	choir and chevet interior; vaults of transept and ambulatory	
Georges Gaillard, "Sur la chronologie de Tournus," *Revue archéologique* 49 (1957): 47–59			in part reuse of pre–1007(8) walls		pre–1007(8) foundation plan
			beginning 11th cent. nave to below side aisle vaults	1007(8)–1019 unvaulted transept ambulatory and radiating chapels	
		1056 Saint-Michael's	1056 nave to above side aisle vaults		
				end of 11th cent. to 1120 chevet and transept completed	

Chart, *continued.*

AUTHOR	Lower Narthex	Upper Narthex	Nave	East End	Crypt
J. K. Conant, *Carolingian and Romanesque Architecture 800 to 1200*, Baltimore, 1959			begun 950		dedicated 979 with 10th cent. work above it
		about 1020, or perhaps later		after 1007(8) vaults of ambulatory (dedicated 1019)	vaults later
			after 1066 vaults		
				ca. 1120 vaults of sanctuary and crossing	
Frédéric Lesueur, "Hypothèse sur la construction de Saint-Philibert de Tournus," *Mélanges René Crozet*, Paris, 1966	1007(8) PROJECT I first bays of projected nave reused as lower narthex			1007(8)–1019 PROJECT I oldest parts of choir, transept, crypt	
			1028–1056 PROJECT II ABBOT ARDAIN entire present nave		
				12th cent. crossing, transept vaults, choir interior	

Appendix 3

Cluny II

The excavation study of Cluny II proposed that compound piers, square piers, and columns were used for support, not short round piers. I believe that it is more likely that Cluny II did have round piers like every known southern First Romanesque basilica in Burgundy.[1] Although this hypothesis cannot be proven with any certainty, it can be shown that the archaeological evidence for the traditional reconstruction of Cluny II is not definitive.

Conduct and Presentation of Cluny II Excavation. The method used for the Cluny II excavation, 1928–38, was accurate and controlled; for each day, an illustrated journal was kept and then transcribed into measured plan and elevation drawings. In addition, numerous photographs documented each pit. The excavation discovered an echelon plan and brick-based southern First Romanesque masonry. In spite of this valuable work, questions about the excavation remain, questions which are crucial to the study of early Romanesque architecture.

Excavating the entire site of Cluny was a mammoth task, the difficulty of which was compounded by the restricted working conditions: work could only be carried on in the summers, and excavations were restricted to the small stretches of ground between the deep roots of the trees in the yard of the crafts and engineering school at Cluny. Moreover, a cement drainage ledge blocked the complete excavation of the north side of the nave. By contrast, Cluny III was more easily accessible, and consequently this site was more completely exposed.

How little of the Cluny II foundation was actually uncovered is obscured by the presentation, in which the evidence of foundations (Fig. 186a) is published separately from the layout of the excavation trenches (Conant, *Cluny,* figs. 2, 41). Although any hypothetical reconstruction must make explicit its source material, the presentation makes no distinction between what was found and what still lies uncovered. It gives us no way to distinguish the entirety of what remains of Cluny II from the fragments unearthed among the scattered *sondages* and thus leaves one with the impression that the excavation was more extensive than it actually was.

A more serious ambiguity, however, concerns the discoveries themselves. The actual findings are conflated with their assumed implications. The shape of the actual foundations was never published; rather the blackened areas in Figure 186a (Conant, *Cluny*, fig. 41) *indicate the parts of the superstructure for which the author believed there was evidence* in the foundations. If a foundation indeed always determined a specific superstructure and if the foundations were clearly distinct, then this reconstruction technique could be fruitful. But we shall see that no foundation determines a specific superstructure in Burgundian First Romanesque, and that, moreover, no complete foundation remains beneath the piers or columns of Cluny II. Regardless of the relationship of the foundation to the support, we must be able to see what is left of the foundations to judge the accuracy of the reconstruction. Unfortunately this is not possible, because what seems to be primary evidence—the "plan des fouilles" (Fig. 186a)—is in fact not. It presents conclusions about the meaning of the foundations for the elevation: the figure is no more than a hypothetical ground plan that indicates neither essential foundations nor excavation trenches.

For a number of reasons then, we must reconsider the accuracy of the reconstruction of Cluny II. The excavation of Cluny II was limited in time and scope, and by the priority of excavating Cluny III. Moreover, the published evidence is a conflation of the actual findings and their assumed implications. It is never made clear how limited the excavation was and how fragmentary were the discovered remains.[2]

Cluny II Foundations. Instead of the standard Burgundian round piers, a number of other support types have been proposed for Cluny II, five of which can be isolated and are numbered in Figure 186a. These proposals could be valid if there were enough fragments to determine the shape of the foundations at any given point on the ground plan, and if specific foundations determined specific support types.

Unfortunately, not enough has been uncovered to say what any support foundation of Cluny II, in the nave, crossing, choir, or apse, looked like—although cruciform piers, square piers, and columns have been proposed. Cruciform crossing piers were reconstructed under the western face of the tower in Figures 186a, 186b. No photographs of this portion of the excavation survive, but Conant's excavation drawings show that the southeastern crossing foundation is shaped like an "L" instead of a cross, and is insufficient for a foundation of any kind, being less than two feet wide (Fig. 187). An undifferentiated mound in Figure 188 is the basis for the reconstruction of the northeastern crossing. Only the lateral excavation trench was made for the nave columns, so that four of the six columns proposed are extrapolations. By placing question marks ("5" in Fig. 186a) by the amorphous chunk of "column" foundations uncovered (Figs. 192a, 192b), the report expressed doubt even about this fractional evidence. As for the nave pier foundations ("4" in Fig. 186a), the chunk of stone exposed on the north aisle (Figs. 189a, 189b) is less determinate than the amorphous "column" foundation protected by the question marks. As for the south aisle piers, who can say what those rectangular projections are (Figs. 190a, 190b)? Although they are more than four feet wide, they have not been cleared away to expose more than 2′6″ of their length in either direction, not enough to distinguish them as either pit foundations or interrupted trench foundations as claimed. Problems occur, too, in attempting to reconstruct the choir columns. Seeing three blacked-out round spots ("2") in the excavation plan

(Figure 186a), we may assume that the evidence supports at least the existence of three of the four reconstructed columns. It is therefore disconcerting to turn to the 1954 publication of the same plan, where the choir supports are indicated as four piers and two columns on one page and as wall buttresses and two columns on the preceding page.[3] No excavation was carried on between the three different reconstructions, so we can only conclude that Conant found the choir trench foundation (Figs. 191a, 191b) as unrevealing of its superstructure as we do.[4]

Clearly, then, not enough remains of the freestanding portions of the apse, choir, crossing, and nave to describe even the foundations accurately, let alone a possible superstructure. Yet a proposal exists for the elevation of Cluny II with features unlike those found in any Burgundian southern First Romanesque church.

Relation of Foundation to Elevation. What is the relation of the superstructure proposed to the foundations uncovered, however minimal those remains? The parts of the superstructure proposed are inconsistent with the foundations that remain. It is almost as if different foundation types were randomly assigned for the same supports, or the same foundations for different supports. For example, the columns proposed for the apse, choir, and nave are similar (Fig. 186b): they are tall, narrow without entasis, and terminated by articulated capitals and bases. But no similarity exists among what Conant considers to be their foundations: in the apse, no separate foundations were found for the columns; in the nave, a small delicate strip less than a foot wide and 4′11″ in length (Figs. 192a, 192b) is said to support columns; while in the choir a massive 6′1″ wide continuous trench foundation is said to support columns (Figs. 191a, 191b). No single type of foundation supports the same column, and the same is true for the two square piers which were proposed. The square pier that is supported in the galilee by a 4′5″ × 5′6″ rectangular pit foundation (Fig. 193) is supported in the nave by a 4′1″ wide trench foundation (Figs. 189a, 189b).

Clearly, there is no direct connection between the shape of a foundation and the proposed type of support placed above it. Indeed, more similarity exists between the foundations of opposite support systems than among those of a similar type, for example, the trench foundation of the nave piers and the trench foundation of the choir columns. Thus, we must take into account when judging the reconstructed Cluny II that its parts are inconsistent with its foundations and that the foundations themselves are hardly distinct.

But even if a complete set of foundations existed, and if a superstructure were reconstructed over them in a meaningful and consistent way, even then we could not establish the correct superstructure of Cluny II. The reason is simply that in Burgundian southern First Romanesque architecture, no easy correspondence exists between a particular foundation and any one support type. While the round piers of the narthex and nave of Tournus rest on round pit foundations,[5] the round piers of the dorter of Saint-Bénigne rest on square foundations (Fig. 194),[6] and the round piers under the crossing of Chapaize rest on huge pyramid-like platforms (unpublished restoration excavation, undertaken and photographed by Lucien Keller, Fig. 195).[7] Thus, while round pit, square pit, trench, and pyramidal foundations exist for First Romanesque basilicas in Burgundy, only one support type stands on top of these foundations: a round pier. That the foundations of Cluny II were pit or trench foundations by no means determines that square piers or round columns existed in the elevation; rather, by all local contemporary evidence, the probable supports were round piers. Indeed, if we entertain the traditional assumption that Cluny II was the monument that determined the course of Burgundian Romanesque architecture, then we should also assume that it had round piers; how else explain the exclusive use of this device in the regional First Romanesque basilicas and for generations thereafter?[8] One cannot have it both ways: either Cluny II was so important that it determined the course of the regional style, or it had square piers, a developed column type, regular crossing, and belonged to another style of architecture entirely.[9]

Historical Accuracy. Southern First Romanesque basilicas in Burgundy used only round pier supports; the reconstructed Cluny II used columns, square and compound piers, but no round piers; therefore, as basilica supports, those proposed for Cluny are historically unlikely. But putting the basilica aside for the moment, are the columns and regular piers anything like the supports used on other parts of the Burgundian southern First Romanesque churches, for example on towers? Even taken on their own, out of the context of the basilica, the individual support types proposed for Cluny are inconsistent with southern First Romanesque models.

The column type proposed for the apse, choir, and nave is high, narrow without entasis, and terminated by developed capitals and bases (Fig. 196). It did not exist in Burgundian southern First Romanesque architecture and is only rarely seen in other southern First Romanesque buildings (e.g., crypt of S. Vincent, Milan). Almost all southern First Romanesque columns, and every example in Burgundy, have exaggerated entasis, and the base and capital, if there are any, are rudimentary, unlike the developed Corinthian type of Cluny II.[10] A column from the Chapaize tower is typical of Burgundian southern First Romanesque columns: it is stubby, crudely worked, with its parts only slightly articulated.[11] Even later examples, such as the tower columns from Massy and the colonnaded Mâconnais church at Saint-Vincent-des-Prés, in spite of rudimentary capitals and bases, repeat these same features.

Two columns from Cluny II were actually excavated, but the report is not certain that they came from the church: "These may come from the nearby arcade of the back side of the sanctuary of Cluny II [or possibly from the east range (chapter house, etc.) built by Odilo]."[12] If they came from the church, it is more than likely that they are the result of a later campaign, because no colonnaded apse arcade existed in southern First Romanesque architecture, anywhere. Only obviously advanced, second generation churches, dating from after 1050, are so equipped (e.g., Salmaise), and even then the device is exceedingly rare.[13] In fact it was a twelfth-century structure, the east end of Payerne, which was explicitly cited as the model for the reconstruction of the Cluny II apse (Figs. 196, 197).[14] Moreover, the columns claimed to have come from the apse of Cluny II are hatchet marked; yet the hatchet was in use only at the end of the tenth century, almost fifty years after the date assigned the apse.[15] Thus, the workmanship of the apse columns and the reconstructed blind apse colonnade are too late in type to belong to Cluny II.

For the crossing, the model chosen—the regular crossing—was also a type that appeared almost a century after Cluny II (the origin and date of the regular crossing have been carefully chronicled by Hermann Beenken).[16] If neither a square pier nor a cruciform pier existed in Burgundian southern First Romanesque basilicas, then the use of several cruciform piers in the Cluny II crossing is historically most unlikely.[17]

Whereas the supports proposed for Cluny II are inconsistent with the remains uncovered, they are equally inconsistent with the examples of southern First Romanesque buildings that remain standing. In its apse, crossing, and nave supports, the reconstructed Cluny II is unlike the universal Burgundian type of round-piered basilica, and in its column and pier types dissimilar to other European southern First Romanesque buildings.

Conclusion: Cluny II Reconstruction. Significantly, the excavation of Cluny II revealed the actual dimensions of the building, a southern First Romanesque masonry type, and an echelon chevet plan. The excavation, however, was restricted in time and limited in scope; the scope was reduced by the emphasis on the larger Cluny III, and by the shape of the site, which was hemmed in by tree roots and eighteenth-century architecture. In the published report, possible implications of the excavation are not distinguished from actual results of the discoveries. Too little space is devoted to the ambiguous results of the limited excavation (i.e., no foundations were published), and too much emphasis is placed on hypothetical elevation drawings. Moreover, the published reports make explicit neither the degree of accuracy of the original drawings, nor the subsequent changes, nor the reasons for these changes.

The excavation of Cluny II did not determine the shape of the support foundations for the nave, crossing, choir, and apse, and therefore provided little justifiable evidence for the proposed superstructure. The proposed superstructure is inconsistent both with the remains and with standing churches from the period. Although one type of foundation never implies, let alone determines, a specific support type of Burgundian southern First Romanesque architecture, the reconstruction assigned the fragmentary evidence of widely divergent foundations to specific support types. The individual features proposed, from the masonry of the apse "jumelles" and the articulation of the crossing, to the columns and piers and their capitals and bases, differ from southern First Romanesque architecture in the rest of Europe.

An accurate reconstruction of Cluny II is essential for understanding the true course of Romanesque architecture, especially in light of the past forty years when historians have elevated the building to the position of a seminal monument of Romanesque style.[18] In reality, unfortunately, we know very little about the church; its piers probably were round, but we do not know enough even to determine that its pier supports resemble those of other Mâconnais First Romanesque buildings. The evidence for Cluny II, although graphically interpreted, falls short of the necessary proof upon which to base the mainline development of Romanesque architecture.

NOTES

1. Although no text described the piers of Cluny II, the "Chronique de Saint-Bénigne" ambiguously refers to the piers of the other great First Romanesque basilica in Burgundy ("Fulcitur centum viginti et una columnis"). C. Oursel, a most careful researcher of the Saint-Bénigne problem, was unsure of the pier alternation, let alone the shape of the piers (*L'art roman*, 26). Martindale ("Saint-Bénigne," 99) found evidence in the "Chronique" that the piers at Saint-Bénigne were stubby and round, with typical Burgundian moldings—just like the southern First Romanesque piers from the region discussed in appendix 2. This opinion may be supported by the recent excavation in the nave of Saint-Bénigne showing southern First Romanesque brick-based masonry throughout (see appendix 1, note 31).

2. Perhaps simply a different color for the degree of accuracy of each reconstructed part might restore confidence in the drawings. Conant has encountered such criticism before, most notably, as he tells it, when Nicholas Pevsner edited out a number of controversial Cluny

reconstruction drawings destined for his Pelican book. Amusingly, Conant resubmitted the illustrations with a red border—for danger—to which Pevsner reacted by publishing them in an entirely separate section.

3. Conant, "Medieval Academy Excavations at Cluny" (1954), 23, fig. a; 25, pl. VII.

4. In the excavation drawing of pit LV, 21 August 1932 (Fig. 191b), Conant was unsure of the date of the choir foundations: "whitish sandstone-like drums but may be Gothic or Renaissance" (Archives Conant, Musée Ochier, Cluny).

5. Martin, "Appendice," 556–61. The foundation for the attached round piers of the Tournus cloister is a trench; see Curé, *Tournus*, fig. 433.

6. Numerous sondages revealed square foundation bases, as shown in Figure 194. The piers are approximately 420 cm. in circumference and the bases average 145 cm. on the side.

7. Lucien Keller, in conversation at Chalon-sur-Saône (24 March 1971), described the foundation of each

crossing pier of Chapaize as a square pyramid of three steps, each of 40 cm. in height, and the bottom steps contiguous on the same level.

8. See Conant, "Cluny II and St.-Bénigne," 183, 185; and note 18 of this appendix.

9. See chapter 2 and appendix 1 for the impact of northern First Romanesque architecture in Burgundy.

10. See for example the columns in the crypts of Lons-le-Saunier, Saint-Dalmas at Valdeblore, and Ivrea Cathedral, and in the nave of S. Vincenzo at Galliano di Catù.

11. The southern face of the upper level of the Chapaize tower contains perhaps the earliest known statue column (Figure. 38b). The figure is worked in the same style as the capital heads on the other faces at the same level. See chapter 2, note 16.

12. Conant in an excavation drawing of Cluny II, pit LX, 3 September 1936 (Archives Conant, Musée Ochier, Cluny). Conant's reconstruction reflects the undated columns shown in the plan of the apse of Cluny II in the anonymous drawing from 1700–1710, Musée Ochier, Cluny.

13. Virey, *Les églises*, 38.

14. Conant, "Les rapports architecturaux entre Cluny et Payerne," 134–38.

15. Plat, *L'art de bâtir*, 19–20.

16. Hermann Beenken, "Die ausgeschiedene Vierung, kritische Bemerkungen zu einigen Rekonstruktionen karolingischer Kirchenbauten," 209–31. To assign the foundations with compound crossing piers beneath the final church at Charlieu to the ninth or tenth century, as my friend Elizabeth Sunderland suggested, would make it a unique exception in France before the eleventh century. Given its advanced regular crossing, this earlier work and not the final foundation may well be the church identified by the eleventh-century monk Jotsaldus with Saint Odilo, Abbot of Cluny from 994 to 1048. Even if Sunderland correctly dated the earlier foundation to the ninth or tenth century, that earlier building would have been an unlikely source for Cluny since she showed that the masonry and plan are based on Loire Valley practices. Cluny II, by contrast, was built by craftsmen trained in the entirely different southern First Romanesque brick-based technique. For the three editions of Jotsaldus, see Sunderland, "St. Fortunatus at Charlieu," 64–68.

17. The church of Saint-Point near Cluny is not analogous to Cluny II. Indeed, southern First Romanesque masons did not build it, as is proven by the ashlar construction of its piers. See the restoration of E. Gelis, documented by unnumbered, undated photographs in the "Travaux Dossier" of Saint-Point, Commission des Monuments historiques, Paris.

18. Conant, *Cluny*, 55: "Sans qu'on puisse le prouver d'aucune manière, nous croyons que l'église Cluny II a marqué de son empreinte les églises plus modestes de la région, telles Massy, Saint-Vincent-des-Prés, Saint-Point, Chapaize (pour ne nommer que les plus anciennes). Toutes sont plus récentes que Cluny II, mais d'une architecture traditionelle. On sent l'influence d'un monument auguste qui ne peut être, à notre avis, que Cluny II"; E. Sunderland, "Symbolic Numbers and Romanesque Church Plans," 98: "Such a number system can also explain many of the puzzling differences in dimensions between churches which are considered to have a common prototype, such as Chapaize, Baume-les-Moines, Gigny, Romainmôtier, Bourbon-Lancy, Anzy-le-Duc, and Charlieu, which are all thought to be derived from Cluny II. The general type of plan of Cluny II has been worked into essentially individual creations by the use of different sets of numbers"; Evans, *Romanesque Architecture*, 61–65; Grodecki, *L'architecture ottonienne*, 64, 65, 68; R. Oursel, *Les églises*, 110–11.

Appendix 4
Cluny III

I

For the last half century and especially in recent publications, French and Americans have disputed the dates and building campaigns for the abbey of Cluny (see chapter 1). In spite of these disagreements, both sides based their arguments on typological differences and on reconstructions made from engravings, textual evidence, and excavations. In an endeavor to overcome the art-historical impasse, I turn away from disputes over texts and dates to specific visual problems and evidence: pains are taken to distinguish sutures, masonry differences, and changes in bases, plinths, corbels, moldings, and capitals; these details then are documented with photographs and charts.

The purpose of this method is to distinguish Cluny's initial campaign of construction—definitively—so that in the text we may establish its relative as opposed to its absolute chronology. The same masons who created the ashlar of the first campaign also constructed numerous other important Burgundian churches (see chapter 2). By discovering their first campaign at Cluny, therefore, we can evaluate it in light of their achievements before and after. This method allows us to understand for the first time the real complexities of Cluny III: to judge its sources from the initial stage of construction rather than from the later completed building; to place its sculpture in the proper chronology; to review its relationship to southern architecture as it changes over the course of the building's construction; and to recognize Cluny's impact on Paray and Berzé, which were begun after the first campaign was completed.

II

The initial campaign runs horizontally throughout all the remaining northern outside walls of the building, from the minor transept through to the side portal of the nave. From evidence especially clear in bases, it seems that the campaign includes none of the bays to the west of the nave side portal or any freestanding piers in the nave or choir; rather the campaign begins along the low-lying outside walls and only crosses over to the main vessel at the sanctuary, in the pattern of the chevets at Anzy (Fig. 198a) and Paray (Fig. 76).[1]

The height of the first campaign remains relatively constant, with differences occurring at logical structural resting points. In the nave (Fig. 65) and choir (Fig. 63a), it stops at the springing of the aisle vault and formeret and consequently divides the window jambs approximately in the middle (Figs. 65, 62e). Significantly, this repeats the pattern of building found in the nave of Tournus, the largest eleventh-century church still standing in the area, where the masons halted construction in the middle of window jambs in order to achieve an even resting point at the springing of the formeret and aisle vault (appendix 2). As seen in the chapel on the eastern face of the great Cluny transept, the first campaign suture occurs at a structurally logical point above the quarter barrel vault on the interior and above the window voussoirs on the exterior (Fig. 64a); and on the interior of the minor transept it rises above the vault and voussoirs of the chapel arcade, and just below the level of the string course in the transept (Figs. 62b, 63a).

Fill Masonry. The arrangement of fill masonry is distinctive in the ground story of the first campaign largely due to the restricted use of ashlar. Unlike masonry on the upper stories, ashlar courses never run between the dosserets and responds of each bay (Figs. 62d, 64d, 202);[2] and veneering—a common characteristic of the upper stories in which exterior fill is covered by ashlar on the interior—almost never occurs on the ground stories (Figs. 62a, 63a, 65).

In addition to the relation of fill masonry to ashlar, the placement and finish of the stones distinguish the first campaign from all other parts of the standing building. Despite a greater variety in size than in later construction, the stones all approximate the shape of bricks, with narrower stones of the proportion 1:4 or 1:5 alternating every two or three courses with squarer stones of an approximate 1:3 proportion. These characteristic alternating courses appear throughout the first campaign from the easternmost minor chapel (Fig. 62d), through the minor transept (Fig. 62a) and choir (Fig. 63b), to the eastern (Fig. 199) and western (Fig. 50) walls of the great transept and nave aisle (Fig. 65). Frequently, isolated individual stones shaped like brick headers randomly fill the spaces between the horizontal stones in the western portions of the first campaign (Figs. 64d, 65). A similar combination of masonry characteristics can be found in the chevet construction at Saint-Hippolyte and may suggest an atelier connection between these buildings. The eastern portions of the first campaign, including the chapels of the great (Fig. 199) and minor (Fig. 62d) transepts, appear to have been constructed after the western walls of the great transept (Fig. 64e) and nave aisles (Fig. 65). The eastern masonry (Figs. 62a, 63a) includes more alternating courses of the smaller, narrower stones which dominate the next stage of construction (Fig. 200).

Both types of fill stones are worked in much the same way in all parts of the first campaign building. Unlike later masonry, a chipped percussive technique dominates the surface of the stones, although traces of pick and axe blade occasionally appear. The irregular, chipped quality is best seen on the earliest stonework of the western face of the great transept (Fig. 64e) and nave aisles (Fig. 65), but it also is evident throughout the building from the great transept chapel (Fig.

64a) to the minor transepts (Figs. 63a, 62b). Where the axe is occasionally used—again most evident in the east as on the choir wall—blade marks are deep, up to a quarter of an inch, and irregular, without any of the uniform surface strokes typical of the later masonry.

After the first campaign, a different type of fill masonry covers a relatively short area up to the level of the aisle vaults. Unlike the earlier campaign (Fig. 199), these stones, as seen on the eastern face of the great transept (Fig. 200), are uniformly narrow in type and are laid in smaller mortar beds. While still largely chipped, the surface depressions are less deep and more regular. These characteristics of construction and finish are visible above the first campaign throughout the standing building and are particularly distinct on the western face of the minor (Fig. 63a) and major (Figs. 64e, 64d) transept and along the nave aisle wall (Fig. 65). Slight shifts in the alignment of plug holes confirm the other changes in construction: above the first campaign, the holes on the eastern wall of the minor transept (Fig. 62b) move slightly to the right, those farthest from the responds on the western face of the same transept (seen in Fig. 63a) move to the left, while certain plug holes on the western face of the great transept (Fig. 50) move radically to the left above the level of the first campaign. In sum, the evidence of the masonry of the first campaign, as well as the consistently different characteristics of masonry above it, indicates that the entire structure of Cluny as it remains today to the east of the nave side portal was laid out first as a low horizontal wall. It could neither have been the separate series of horizontal and vertical divisions Salet proposed nor the vertical sections Conant suggested.

The transition to a third level and type of fill masonry once again occurs at a structurally logical point, above the major lower vaults throughout the building: above the chapel vault at the level of the first string course on the interior of the great transept; above the outside aisle vaults in the nave; and above the ambulatory vaults in the sanctuary. Unlike the distinction between the first and second levels, the transition to the third is not a suture, as is clear on the western face of the great transept (Fig. 201). The lightly chipped and narrow stones of the second level ("2") first alternately mix with larger stones of more square dimensions before they are largely replaced by stones of this type ("3"). Unlike earlier masonry, all these later stones are finished by an axe with more uniform, parallel, and lighter strokes. Because these masonry differences continue horizontally from the aisle bay through both northern bays of the great transept (Fig. 201) they cast doubt on the theory that the three-story bay on the left, and the central bay to the right, were built in separate vertical campaigns.[3] Significantly, the transition from the first to the third level—from largely narrow, chipped stones to more rectangular, worked stones—parallels a general change already apparent in southern First Romanesque masonry from the end of the eleventh century, as seen for example in the difference between the two nave campaigns at Saint-Philibert of Tournus (Fig. 170).

Finally, on the last level of the three-story elevation, the fill stones become so much longer that in one instance only two of them fill an entire bay (Fig. 66). This change corresponds to the increased size and horizontal dimensions of the buttress stones in the same level of the three-story elevation (Fig. 66) and in the fill masonry from the narthex (Fig. 215).[4]

Ashlar: Responds, Buttresses, and Voussoirs. Important differences in material, size, and finish distinguish the ashlar of the first campaign from later work. That these differences occur at the level of the fill-masonry changes further supports the theory of a horizontal, low, first campaign along the outside walls.

The way in which the ashlar dosserets and buttresses were joined to fill masonry distinguishes the first campaign from later construction. While the ashlar blocks penetrate the wall, as seen in the ruined section of the minor transept (Fig. 62b), they never extend laterally into the courses of brick-based stones. This characteristic is consistent in the buttresses on the exterior and the dosserets on the interior and continues throughout all the parts of the first campaign, from the minor transept to the nave (Figs. 62a, 62d, 63a, 64a, 64d, 64e, 57, 65). It contrasts with later campaigns, where ashlar blocks sometimes extend from the dosserets and buttresses laterally into fill areas (Fig. 66), and conversely, where the ashlar blocks, carved open on the sides, receive the brick-like stones which literally course into them (Figs. 66, 59).

The unique appearance of voussoirs also distinguishes the first campaign from later construction. The traditional southern First Romanesque technique of placing arcade stones laterally above voussoirs only occurs in the first campaign—and it occurs twice, on the western face of the great transept (Fig. 50) and above the choir portal (Fig. 63b). Moreover, where ashlar replaces regular brick-like stones as voussoirs, the blocks vary widely in size (Figs. 62c, 62a), and harking back to the older technique, they frequently are accompanied by an order of brick-like stones (Fig. 62c). This contrasts to later construction at Cluny, where laterally placed brick-like voussoirs disappear and the irregularly shaped voussoirs become regular trapezoids (Fig. 63a, 203b). An example of the change is the remarkable contrast which exists in the formeret on the exterior of the choir, where the chipped brick-like stones at the second level suddenly change to large regular trapezoids.

Further confirming the existence of the first campaign, the shape and type of stones in buttresses, dosserets, and responds change throughout the standing building at the levels noted for the fill masonry. In general, the buttress stones in the first campaign vary widely in size: their dimensions are frequently vertical, unlike the predominantly horizontal shape of the second level stones, and at their extreme they are double the size (Figs. 50, 64a, 64d). Moreover, the shape and size of stones distinguish the piers of the first campaign from the freestanding piers constructed later. Throughout the building, from the minor transept chapel (Fig. 62d) to the nave aisles (Fig. 202), the earlier, attached supports are made up of irregularly sized stones with horizontal colonnette drums of greatly reduced size. Frequently several dosseret stones make up each course on either side of the colonnette. By contrast, the dosseret stones of the freestanding piers (Fig. 203a), like the voussoirs above them (Fig. 203b), are predominantly regular. In the vast majority of cases, only one stone is used in each course on either side of the colonnette. When more than one stone is used, they are separated by a narrow vertical "blade" only a few inches wide. These differences at Cluny between the freestanding and attached piers also distinguish the nave freestanding piers in the eastern bays at Vézelay (Fig. 227) from the freestanding piers in the western bays (Fig. 28). The difference may well be explained by the influx of new masons from Cluny after the sixth bay at Vézelay (see Fig. 36).

Besides the differences in shape, the first-campaign buttresses, dosserets, and responds are soft yellow limestone which oxidizes to a grey color and frequently flakes;[5] by contrast, the ashlar above this level is purple-grey, porous, and pitted, with a hard surface that does not flake. The difference is remarkably consistent throughout the building and corresponds to the level of change of the fill masonry, seen, for example, on the exterior buttresses (Fig. 62e) and interior dosserets (Fig. 62b) of the minor transept. An added distinction can be drawn from the eastern dosseret of the choir (Fig. 63a): while the bottom two grey, pitted stones of the transverse arch fail to course with the top two yellow, flaking stones of the first campaign dosseret, the remaining grey arch stone not only courses to a drum and respond on the second level of the dosseret but it is made of the same grey material as these upper stories. At least in this location, it is clear from the coursing that an interruption followed the laying of first campaign masonry. A possible explanation for the time interval is that the masons waited for a large part of the aisle walls to be completed before vaulting them. This hypothesis is supported by the changes in masonry which occurred as soon as the vaults of the ambulatory, aisles, and chapels were finished.

On both sides of the great transept, the same important differences occur in ashlar on the exterior buttresses, for example on the southeastern corner and central western bay (Figs. 64a, 64e), and on interior responds and colonnettes, for example on both faces of the central bay (Figs. 57, 64c, 64d).[6] One sees a clear interruption in both dosserets and responds from larger, soft, flaking yellow stones to harder, porous stones at the second level, and these distinctions carry over to both faces of the pier on the nave aisle (Figs. 57, 65).[7]

The marked horizontal change between the two types of ashlar occurs consistently throughout the standing structure. Seen together with the horizontal break in fill masonry and the evidence to come from architectural details, the difference casts doubt on proposals of vertical construction and even on the theory which limits construction to certain bays of the transept.[8] Indeed, aside from any validity in these new observations, two major archaeological mistakes cast doubt upon the theory limiting vertical construction to the transept. First, the theory proposed that the central western buttress was added as part of later construction on the western face of the transept (Fig. 50). The buttress, however, courses to ashlar pilasters that actually support the arcaded orders (Fig. 50) of the western transept which the theory claimed was built before the buttress. Second, this theory proposed that the northern bay of the transept—that is, the entire three-story elevation on both faces—was built after the unvaulted portions of the central bay, although it can be shown that parts of the northern and central bays were built simultaneously. On the northern bay, on either side of the top story (Fig. 66), beds of ashlar ("b") continue uninterruptedly from the transept face into each buttress; and rows of fill masonry ("a") occasionally continue directly from the transept face into openings behind the ashlar blocks on the buttresses. On the central bay, small beds of filler stones ("a" in Fig. 59) repeat the same pattern, extending into the same buttress stones from the other side. Thus, as ashlar, or fill masonry, or both, stones from one buttress course to masonry on two sides—on both the northern and central bays—proving that these separate bays were built simultaneously.

Bases. Differences in bases confirm the distinction of construction between the outside wall and freestanding piers. The chart of base profiles (Fig. 68) lists only in situ bases and plinths with a definite provenance—no unattached examples are included. It combines profiles taken by the author, largely unpublished profiles in the Cluny Archives collected by Conant from his excavations, and three plinth profiles, "oN," "1N," and "SANCT N," which Conant copied from the "Bound Book of the 1913 Excavation" into the "Sanctuary Yellow Packet" (Archives Conant). In the chart, bases of the central nave vessel are distinguished by the letters "N" for north and "S" for south, while the bases on the aisles are labelled "NN" or "SS" if they are freestanding, and "NNN" or "SSS" if they are attached to the outside walls.

Despite gaps in information, particularly between bays 6 and 10 SSS and NNN, the chart reveals three distinctively different types of base profile corresponding to three locations on the building: the outside walls (NNN and SSS) from the sanctuary to bay 5; the freestanding piers from the ambulatory to bay 6; and the outside and freestanding piers from bay 7 to the facade, bay 15. The bases and plinths within each of these three locations are so similar and so consistently different from those of both other locations that, together with other evidence, they suggest separate campaigns of construction for each location.

Let us first compare the difference between the bases and plinths on the outside walls (NNN and SSS) and on the freestanding piers (N, NN and S, SS) from the sanctuary up to the southern portal on bay 7: (1) the scotias of all the bases and plinths on the outside wall are more open, comprising a smaller circle segment than any profile among the bases of the freestanding piers; (2) the bases on the outside walls are higher than any other bases on the ground story—for example compare 3SSS to 3SS, and 4NNN to 4SS; (3) the relative height occupied by the scotia compared to the top torus is greater on all the bases and plinths along the outside walls. For example, compare plinths 5NNN and 5SSS to plinths 5S, 5SS, and 5NN.

While every in situ example from the outside walls from the sanctuary up to the fifth bay is different from any freestanding pier profile in ways just described, within each of the two series a *general* but consistent progression seems to occur. What is most striking is that the progression runs in opposite directions: from west to east for the first series of bases on the outside walls, and from east to west in the second series of freestanding piers. Plinth 5NNN on the west of the first series is taller and its scotia relatively higher and more open than the easternmost freestanding plinth, on the northern pier of the sanctuary colonnade shown in the upper left-hand corner on the chart. In turn, on the freestanding piers of the second series, although the size of the easternmost plinths only minimally decreases by the sixth bay (5NN, 6S, 6SS), the scotia radically compresses and loses height in relation to the upper torus.

The consistent differences between the bases and plinths on attached and freestanding piers strongly suggests separate campaigns for these parts up to the seventh bay portal. Speculating one step further on the basis of the reverse progression in each campaign and from the fact that the "beginning" of the second series almost overlaps with the "end" of the first series in the sanctuary, I believe that the chevet with its ambulatory capitals acted as the cross-over point, where building on the outside walls turned in the opposite direction down the center of the nave. Indeed, the reduced "copy" at Paray shows a similar process, where a low-level exterior wall campaign in the west, in the aisles and transepts, builds up to a three-story elevation throughout the eastern chevet (see appendix 5). If this was the pattern of construction at Cluny, then the achievement of the east end extended in time beyond the first laying of stones in 1088 to a somewhat later date, perhaps 1095, when Pope Urban II is known to have consecrated the altars of the chevet.[9]

Previously, another theory used the bases of Cluny III to understand the campaigns and direction of construction. The observation was made that in any particular portion of the building the bases on the outside walls and the bases attached to freestanding piers were the same.[10] The differences which existed derived from a uniform "evolution of attic column-base profiles from end to end of the building" in which the profiles become "progressively blockier to the west, with the scotia diminishing in height."[11] As part of this east-to-west evolutionary theory, it was believed that the "heavy through-stones mounting ladderwise toward the east in the wall indicate that the minor transept was built before the choir bays" (Fig. 63b).[12] A series of stepped ashlar stones can be laid from bottom up or from top down depending on the manner of construction with no directionality implied from the steps themselves. In this case, however, the last full-sized ashlar step ("4") supports the easternmost filler stones ("5") and therefore the ashlar block must have been laid before them to the west. The second-to-last full-sized stepped ashlar stone ("2") is corbelled left more than fifty percent of its length from the fill stones beneath it ("3") to the east and therefore must have been laid upon the stepped stone ("1") below it to the west. Finally, and seemingly overlooked in the discussion, the bottommost western steps course directly to the jamb stones of the choir portal. By the law of gravity, if each stepped stone is preceded to the west by another stepped stone, and if the westernmost stepped stones are coursed to a portal, then the portal must have preceded all the stepped stones to the east of it. Clearly in building a wall, it is best to construct the portal first and not punch it through the wall later on. By this logic, it would make sense to start with the portal and build up to the height of the wall in the direction of construction. And this reasoning would explain why the steps which mount from west to east wind up at the height of the first campaign.

Besides these first two campaigns, I believe a further phase of construction included the western bays of the nave from the south side portal. The conclusion that this final work, unlike the previous campaigns, included both the outside walls and freestanding piers is based on numerous types of evidence, including changes in bases, changes in the profile and level of exterior plinth moldings, shifts in the original pavement and axis, and alterations in capital foliage design.

Two proofs of a separate western campaign emerge from studying the bases after bay 7 to the west. First, the outside wall base 11NNN is more like the free-standing pier bases from the western bays (7NN, 9SS) and central facade portal (15 GT PT) than any other base from the first or even second campaigns. Although only a fragmentary sample exists, as a group the bases on the freestanding piers and on the aisle and facade walls in the western bays are markedly similar compared to any other bases from the ground floor of Cluny III: (1) their overall size is smaller; (2) their overall profile more diagonal; and (3) the scotia is compressed, with its lower margin more horizontally extended than before.

The second feature of this western group of bases is that they extend further the changes within the second campaign. We saw that from east to west within this campaign, the freestanding pier bases decrease in overall height as their torus becomes larger in relation to the increasingly compressed scotia. Then, as a western base attached to a wall, base 11NNN differs radically from other wall bases of the first campaign, but like all bases in the west, freestanding and attached alike, it follows "progressively" from the changes found from east-to-west in the second campaign. It seems natural to assume that because these bases, found in all the western bays, follow the "direction" of change among the freestanding bases of the second campaign, they therefore were built after it.[13]

Outside Plinths. The profiles of original plinth moldings taken from the standing building and found in Conant's excavation records support two positions outlined before. First, the changing plinth profiles charted in Figure 204 parallel the west-to-east construction of the first campaign. The profile becomes increasingly diagonal as its convex curves become more segmental from the side portal of the nave (7SS) and great transept (4SS, 3NN) to the western buttress and eastern apse of the minor transept. Second, a shift in the plinth molding profile corresponds to a similar shift in the profile of bases, which, as we have seen, changes significantly beginning with the third campaign to the west of bay 7. From the eastern buttress of the side portal, a molding with a straight diagonal profile (Fig. 205) replaces the pronounced double torus and scotia molding which appears throughout the eastern portions of the standing building. This new type of plinth molding continues west beyond the southern aisle wall to the other portions of the building where the latest base type is used: templets from the Conant Archives show two of the new moldings on the tenth and eleventh bays on the northern aisle wall (Fig. 204); and two photographs in the Conant Archives, numbers 478 and 1475, show the new plinth molding appearing on the northwestern corner and along the western face of the facade. From the evidence of an older torus-scotia plinth molding in the fourth northern bay (Conant Archives photo number 1035), a change corresponding to the new molding type on the southern side portal seems to have occurred on the northern aisle wall at a point to the west of the fifth nave bay.[14]

The changing level of these plinth moldings as measured by Conant supports the evidence that the plinths changed alongside the bases in the western bays of the nave (see "Cluny III, Levels, Top of Water Table Plinth Moldings," Archives Conant). In the bays from the great transept to the nave side portal, the height of the plinth moldings varies little, remaining level on the south and climbing only .015 m on the north; but suddenly in the bay to the west of the side portal the molding on the south gains .296 m and adds another .106 m by the facade, while the molding on the north adds .693 m over the last eight western bays.

Pavement and Axis. Changes in the pavement and axis correspond to those in the level of the plinth moldings. These changes support the evidence of a different final campaign to the west of the nave side portal.[15] The pavement dramatically rises to the west of the portal. While it varies relatively little, only .295 m from the ambulatory to the nave side portal, over a distance half as long from the portal to the facade the pavement rises an impressive .492 m. Moreover, the nature of the change is radical at first and then gradual within the campaign itself: while the two bays surrounding the portal remain level, the next bay (10) abruptly differs by .197 m, and the difference progressively increases to .492 m by the facade.

The axis shifts at the location of other final campaign changes and may be part of the collective adjustments carried on at this time.[16] Both aisle walls of the first campaign, although they regain the central axis by the western face of the great transept, begin by deviating considerably in the southern direction. The northern wall starts with a maximum deviation of .12 m to the west of pier 10NNN, a figure which is reduced to .03 m by pier 7NNN and is eliminated by the greater transept. The angle of deviation is greater on the *southern* wall, although the axis shift is smaller; that is, the wall originates deviating .08 m in a southern direction at pier 8SSS, just to the east of the nave side portal, although that axis difference is reduced to zero over the shorter distance between the portal and the great transept.

While the masons of the first campaign progressively eliminated the misalignment in both nave walls as they built eastward from the nave side portal to the transept, the masons of the final campaign were left with the same problem as they built westward to the facade. Compensating for the southern deviation described above, the masons to the west of the nave side portal suddenly veered the southern wall in a *northern* direction, indeed, gaining so much in this direction that by the facade the wall actually deviates .09 m to the north. A parallel correction occurs further to the west on the northern wall—before pier 11NNN—and by the facade produces a northern misalignment of .08 or .09 m, paralleling the deviation on the southern wall.

Corbels and Moldings. On the whole, changes in corbels and moldings correspond to the different campaigns of construction described before. In general, the nature of these changes parallels the chronological changes in the bases at Cluny: over time (1) the profile becomes more diagonal, (2) the concavity in the middle compresses as (3) the tip of the molding or corbel extends more horizontally, and (4) the convex curve on the bottom becomes more segmental.

Only four in-situ moldings remain from the first campaign (Figs. 3, 8, 62c, 206a). Their profile is more vertical than any others found in the church, and, like the bases from the first campaign, it becomes increasingly diagonal from west (Fig. 206a) to east (Fig. 8), presumably following the direction of construction.[17] On the impost molding from the western face of the great transept (Fig. 206a), the cyma curve descends almost vertically, its top edge barely projecting into a tip, and its bottom edge rolling into a full quarter circle; by contrast, the cyma profile on the portal molding from the minor transept (Fig. 8) is more diagonal, its concave curve more compressed, and its tip more horizontally projecting.

The easternmost in situ molding from the first campaign is found on the exterior of the minor transept chapel. Significantly for dating Cluniac sculpture, its intact left profile (Fig. 3) resembles closely the imposts uncovered in the excavation and assigned by Conant to the ambulatory capitals (Fig. 206b).[18] Like the base profile from the sanctuary, both these moldings from the minor transept chapel and ambulatory stand between earlier western examples from the first campaign on the great transept and later examples from the second campaign. Compared to a second-campaign molding from the first string course in the southeastern corner of the great transept (Fig. 206c), the molding in Figure 206b is more vertical, its tip less horizontal, and its bottom convex curve more circular. Yet compared to the first-campaign molding from the great transept (Fig. 206a) it is "ahead" on all three counts. Following the evidence from masonry and bases, the comparison of moldings underscores the transitional position of the ambulatory chevet, including the colonnade, between the first two campaigns.

Differences in corbels parallel the changes between the first- and second- campaign moldings. The only remaining corbels from the first campaign are on the minor transept chapel and consist of an abacus block and torus above a slightly curved cavet with an almost vertical profile (Fig. 207). The first campaign was built from west to east; in the second the direction was reversed. Significantly, therefore, the same type of molding exists further west on the part of the great transept chapel built by the second campaign (Fig. 64b), but its diagonal profile and concave curve indicate a later date. In turn, the original corbels from the third campaign, on the southeastern bay of the great transept (Fig. 208a), are even more diagonal, with a more compressed opening and more segmental lower curve. When an example (Fig. 208b) from the final stage of construction of the three-story elevation is compared to these corbels, it shows an even more diagonal profile, a more compressed concave curve, and an upper tip extended fully in the horizontal direction.

The changes from the second to the third level in corbels are paralleled by similar changes in moldings. Compared to moldings from the second campaign (Fig. 206c), moldings from the upper stories, including the Saint-Gabriel chapel (Fig. 206e) and the southeastern corner of the transept (Fig. 206d), reveal an increased diagonal profile, a more extended horizontal tip, and a bottom convex curve more segmental in shape.

Foliage Sculpture. Enough in situ capitals remain at Cluny III for us to conclude that the differences among them correspond to changes in construction. The first campaign aisle wall capitals share qualities distinct from the remaining freestanding pier capitals, and these in turn differ from sculpture on the upper transept and western portal. In general over the course of construction: (1) the size of each leaf cluster increases in relation to the capital as a whole, and therefore there are fewer branches per capital; (2) the foliage projects less from the core and projects more uniformly throughout the capital; each leaf becomes (3) flatter, (4) narrower, and (5) more narrowly pointed.

The similarities between the first campaign foliage—on the exterior capitals of the great and minor transept chapels (Figs. 209a, 3) and on the interior capitals of the choir walls (Fig. 209b)—and the foliage on the ambulatory capitals of Cluny by the Avenas Master (Fig. 97c) indicate once again that the ambulatory capitals were sculpted during the first campaign. Indeed, the similarities are so close in every case, and include so many characteristics of the Avenas Master described in chapter 4, that I believe he carved almost all the in situ capitals from the first campaign. As a group they stand apart from the freestanding pier capitals in the choir and nave (Figs. 210, 211). Although each branch or cluster of leaves from the first campaign is noticeably smaller, each leaf is wider and its pointed tip is more blunted. Compared to the freestanding capitals, much deeper and wider areas are left uncarved, creating a chiaroscuro effect enhanced by the relatively broader drill holes at the base of each stem. Around these holes the wider leaves twist radically, unlike the freestanding capital leaves, which remain flatter. While perhaps correct, the traditional attribution of a freestanding choir capital (Fig. 210) as the work of the other ambulatory sculptor does not account for these differences, which are due as much to the time separating the first campaign from the freestanding piers as to a possible difference in artists.[19] The proof comes in a comparison of the second master's (Perrecy Master, see chapter 4) ambulatory foliage sculpture (Fig. 102c) to this capital (Fig. 210): the ambulatory capital corresponds to the earlier first campaign in which the clusters are smaller, the uncarved spaces relatively wider and deeper, and the leaves broader and more twisting.

Further changes in the carving of foliage parallel the shift to the third level of masonry construction. The differences which distinguish remaining capitals of the freestanding piers of the nave (Fig. 211) and choir from the first-campaign sculpture (Fig. 209b) are accentuated throughout the sculpture of the great transept—for example on the capitals above the first string course on the eastern (Figs. 212, 213) face, and above the second string course on the western face in the chapel of Saint Gabriel (Fig. 214). By the time of the transept sculpture on the upper stories, an almost uniformly flat background replaces deeper areas found occasionally on the freestanding pier capitals. Similarly, the occasionally chamfered groove separating leaves gives way to a more uniformly incised line, and the slightly cupped depressions on the surface of the leaves flatten out. Reinforcing a "cookie-cutter" effect, the depth of relief decreases and a straight chamfer replaces any slight undercutting which exists in the earlier examples.[20]

Fragments (Fig. 72), known by engravings and an eye-witness description to be from the west facade, parallel other changes in the final western campaign of the nave.[21] As we saw with bases, plinths, and masonry, changes made after the first campaign are further accented in the western construction: the background of foliage sculpture flattens almost completely, chamfers cut less deeply, while inscribed lines separating the leaves extend farther down to the base of the stem. These changes correspond directly to those found on the foliage of the Perrecy Master in the nave of Vézelay (Fig. 112c) and may further indicate the time parallel between the nave of Vézelay and the facade of Cluny (chapter 5).[22] Moreover, the increasing emphasis on the surface in the foliage at the Cluny facade, on its shallow relief, flat top, and lengthy inscribed lines—especially with the introduction of built-up linear ridges on the face of the leaves (Fig. 72)—parallels the changes in the figural sculpture at Cluny from the ambulatory to the west facade (chapter 4). These changes, which both figural and foliage sculpture share, reinforce the distinctive character of the western campaign. In addition, the characteristics of western campaign foliage reappear alongside late Cluniac articulation, masonry, capitals, and bases in the chevet at Paray (appendix 5; Fig. 73). By analogy, then, the first campaign of Paray can be seen as contemporary with the final campaign at Cluny.[23]

The purpose of this appendix has been to distinguish Cluny's initial campaign so that in the text we may establish its relative chronology. Because the same masons who built the first campaign also constructed other important Burgundian churches, by analyzing their work at Cluny we can evaluate it in light of these other achievements.

The first campaign runs horizontally throughout all the remaining outside walls of the building, from the minor transept to the side portal of the nave, and it stops at the level of the springing of the aisle vault. The unique character of the first campaign is shown by the arrangement, lay, and finish of the fill masonry, as well as by the ashlar responds, buttresses, and voussoirs. Moreover, study of the bases reveals not only the unique character of the outside aisle wall—from the sanctuary to at least bay 5—but also a progression in the bases on the wall from west to east. The chevet with its ambulatory capitals acted as the cross-over point, where building on the outside wall reversed direction down the center of the nave. The capitals of the ambulatory correspond to the capital type of the first campaign, and like the bases they changed radically as construction moved in the opposite direction down the center of the nave during the second campaign. Built from west to east, the construction of the first campaign aisle wall reached the east end somewhat after the time of the first laying of the stones in 1088, perhaps when Pope Urban II consecrated the chevet altars in 1095.

Distinguishing the first campaign allows us to judge sources of Cluny III from the initial stage of construction rather than from the later completed building. With a clear understanding of the church at the beginning of construction, we can see the changing role of southern architecture in the later parts of the building and recognize that Paray and Berzé reflect these later stages and not the first campaign. Finally, assigning the ambulatory sculpture to a part of one distinctive campaign constructed by a known Atelier that built other churches helps place the capitals in a chronological context.

NOTES

1. Through a series of steps, both transepts of Anzy were built up from a low-lying wall on the western face to the height of the transept chapels in the east. The suture line can be traced on the southern transept, in Figures 198a and 198b, where the buttress stones change from an average 1:3 proportion to a ratio of less than 1:2 above the height of the chapels. Significantly, this pattern of a low-lying wall which builds up to vaulted parts in the chevet is repeated at Cluny and Paray (appendix 5); moreover, the parallel buildup of both transepts to the height of the chapels supports Elizabeth Sunderland's contention ("Les fenêtres murées du chevet d'Anzy-le-Duc," 24–26) that the chevet including the chapels were created at one time. Other scholars believed that the transept chapels were added later: Edouard Jeannez ("L'église et le prieuré d'Anzy-le-Duc"), Rhein ("Anzy," 288), R. Oursel (Les églises, 140).

2. At the base of each bay, an ashlar plinth molding runs between the dosserets.

3. Alain Erlande-Brandenburg, the editor of the *Bulletin monumental*, discerned stone sutures from an eighteenth-century drawing in the J. Vanuxem collection ("Iconographie de Cluny III"; "Un dessin inédit du XVIIIᵉ siècle"). From this drawing he determined the existence of a "rupture des supports entre le premier et le second niveau" which "permet d'affirmer que les travaux de construction ont été effectués par tranches horizontales." There are obvious dangers in determining building campaigns from drawings, let alone from eighteenth-century renderings. He himself admitted that "la plupart de ces dessins ou de ces gravures sont décevants." In addition, there is a clear difference between parts which do not correspond, walls which recede, orders without supports, and masonry sutures due to campaigns. Perhaps if it were accompanied by an ex-

amination of the standing building, this writer's method would deserve the serious consideration which Conant gave it in "Sur des pas de Lallemand à Cluny" (p. 6) and "Medieval Academy Excavations at Cluny, X" (p. 33). Salet ("Cluny III," 250) engaged in similar archaeological speculation based on the Vanuxem drawing. He observed an oversized space between the first piers and the nave facade, and this distance he interpreted as a lack of "précision pour retrapper exactement une façade déjà située." Yet when faced with an oversized first bay, in an actual, standing building at Vézelay, he preferred to remain silent, dismissing it as a "disposition dont j'ignore la raison" (*Vézelay*, 50).

A shift in the ashlar on the western interior of the three-story elevation corresponds to the change in fill masonry described on the exterior. Between the levels of the second and third campaigns: the ashlar changes from irregular rows of large and small ashlar of varying widths to uniform courses of regular, medium-sized rectangular blocks; the ashlar changes from being by and large coursed to the round respond on the face of the elevation to being uncoursed up to the triforium level; the material of the stones changes from dominantly porous purple stone to a dominantly grey color with an even axe finish that at times gives the impression of being filed. Some of the stones, especially just below the triforium level, are restored and others have suffered a great deal of erosion.

Despite heavy restoration, especially on the western face of the three-story elevation, the ashlar buttresses largely change at the third level described for the fill masonry. The stones become a more uniformly rectangular shape and change from a largely purple color and porous texture to a fine grey finish. On the western face, at the level of the shift from the second to the third campaign masonry, the small strips coursed to the buttresses narrow in a tapered *glacis* and their unrestored stones become more horizontal in shape.

4. Conant observed no difference or changes in filler stones throughout the building as it remains today (*Cluny*, 84): "les pierres encore en place présentent la même facture partout, sans conteste."

5. Conant, "The Season of 1928," 291: "The stone came from the Carrière des Moines near Cluny. It is cream-colored when quarried, but turns buff and pale orange-brown on exposure."

6. The restored stones are clear at the base of the buttresses.

7. Conant (*Cluny*, 102) observed no horizontal sutures in the ashlar masonry. Rather, he believed that through a series of vertical campaigns, one stone type progressively replaced another from the east to the west of the building. The "petit marbre" from the chevet and choir mixed in the great transept with another stone "plus dure," "rarement employée à l'est" which "remplacera complètement le petit marbre."

8. Salet, "Cluny III," 259.

9. First excursus to chapter 1.

10. Conant, "Medieval Academy Excavations at Cluny, X," 33.

11. Although he drew different conclusions, Salet accepted Conant's evidence that the bases uniformly flatten from east to west in Cluny III ("Cluny III," 246–47).

12. Conant, "Medieval Academy Excavations at Cluny, X," 28; also see Conant's opinion about the function of these stepped stones in "La chronologie," 343: "Ils avaient évidemment pour emploi d'étayer le transept mineur avant la construction de travées du choeur."

13. A discriminating approach must be taken in the study of bases because they offer treacherous pitfalls. I consider only bases which are attached to an extant part of the building. Cluny III was dynamited and therefore any small, unattached fragment was easily dispersed. Under the angelic guidance of Germaine Chachuat, anyone who has foraged through the *réserves, caves, Farinier,* and *Cellier* at the Musée Ochier, Cluny, knows the great diversity of styles which mark the loose sculpted fragments from the same excavation pit.

It is understandable, even logical, to find bases which are *retardataire* or "behind the times," especially in buildings which reflect the "mainstream" work of the Atelier (like the Paray nave). What is exceptional in the work of the tightly knit *équipe* of the Atelier and of more provincial masons, is to find a base which is "ahead of its time," which points toward the future. In general, then, especially when judging "backwater" works or bases on peripheral parts of the Atelier's buildings, it is a sound policy to use the most advanced base or molding as a gauge of the relative date.

14. Archives Conant, Musée Ochier, Cluny, photograph no. 1475, pit XLVII, 22/VI/32; photograph no. 478, pit XI, 4/VII/29; photograph 1039, pit XXVIII, 9/VI/31.

15. Archives Conant: "Pavement Levels of the Great Church Originally Studied in 1956," "Slope of Nave Pavement; Levels of Pier Bases (part by J. C. B.)," "Deviations of Main Axis, Cluny," "Deviations of Main Axis, Cluny III," "Cluny III—Nave Dimensions and Deviations, 1965," "Cluny III—Axis Study, 1965," "Cluny III—West Axis, 1965 Calculations." Conant published only the briefest summary of the axis shifts and devoted most of his discussion to possible conclusions. At first, in 1939 ("The Third Church," 329), he argued that the axis shifts supported "two major campaigns," but by 1963 ("Medieval Academy Excavations at Cluny, IX," 8), he suggested that the bends may have been "consciously laid out to avoid rigidity in the interior effect of the building."

16. See note 15 and the penciled words, initialed by K.J.C., on the Master Plan, Archives Conant, Musée Ochier, Cluny.

17. Deshoulières, "Tailloirs," 28–29. While discussing the widespread use of the doucine molding in Burgundy, he did not explain any changes over time within the type. Conant believed that the moldings of Cluny III changed like the bases from east to west through a series of vertical campaigns (*Cluny*, 102): "l'épure évolue lentement pendant la trentaine d'années." Unlike bases, however, the moldings changed in ways seemingly hard to describe: "La delicatesse des épures est rehaussée par la belle netteté des moulures dont la surface a été lissée par frottement."

18. Both impost no. 3825 (6/V/32) and impost no. 3827 (9/V/32) were found in the same pit XXXVIII *outside* the ambulatory. Conant, "Replica of the Arcade of the Apse at Cluny," 7: "one of the old impost blocks, found in a basement wall near the side of the apse." Similarly, Conant freely attributed a fragment found in the south minor transept (pit VIII) to the ambulatory colonnade ("The Season of 1929," 8): "fragment (814) which must be identified as a portion of an impost block for one of the great ambulatory capitals."

19. Conant, "The Season of 1928," 25.

20. Conant believed that the in situ foliage capitals at Cluny were "entirely similar" ("The Season of 1929," 24). Specifically, he observed in the attached choir capitals "la même facture que les grands chapiteaux" (*Cluny*, 91). See chapter 1, note 14.

Deschamps ("L'âge des chapiteaux," 165) distinguished the late Cluniac foliage sculpture as "délicatement traités et si différents de la stylisation sèche de l'ornament floral en usage dans l'art roman primitif." Words like "delicately treated" help little to distinguish the late Cluniac sculpture because the words connote different meanings to different people. Indeed, the words are so imprecise that they describe objects other than sculpture from countless historical periods.

In analyzing Cluniac foliage, Jalabert ("La flore sculptée," 63, 69) in part of one sentence combined biological, anthropomorphic, and teleological approaches ("l'évolution d'un art qui, ayant cherché pendant une longue période l'éxpression de la vie") but finally expressed no definite opinion ("les feuilles d'acanthe varient à l'infini"). See also *La flore romane*, 195f.

21. Although fragmentary, pieces of foliage can be identified as belonging to the western portal from visual and written records. In 1792, a local Cluniac antiquarian, Philibert Bouché, noted the demolition of Cluny III, and he also copied a manuscript of Dr. Dumolin, physician to the monks, who described the western portal and its decoration. See Cahn, "Providence," 52, and Scher, *Renaissance*, 26ff. Le Maitre left a visual record of the decoration on the portal in an engraving, after a lost engraved sketch by Garneray, in N.-X. Willemin, *Monuments français inédits pour servir à l'histoire des arts*. Cahn cites the later copies based on this engraving.

22. These characteristics as well mark the early foliage sculpture from the chevet of Autun (Fig. 223) and reinforce the similarities between Gislebertus's work there and his sculpture from the western portal of Cluny (chapter 5).

23. Conant's teacher, Porter, formulated the theory of continuous construction (*Pilgrimage Roads*, 85): "The existing church is entirely homogeneous; there are no breaks nor reconstructions visible in the masonry." Charles Oursel (*L'art roman*, 77) similarly believed in a continuous building, concluding that the "rapidness of construction" would make the "hypothesis of an interruption hardly likely." Conant ("The Third Church," 329) in turn argued for a single building project with "little or no real interruption." He conceived of "three nearly equal parts" as vertical sections built consecutively from east to west.

Salet ("Cluny III," 250) proposed that the entire "exterior perimeter" was laid out before the central nave was completed. He believed (pp. 270–71) that the exterior walls of the ambulatory "perhaps" were begun at the same time as the "first project" of the great transept. The ambulatory then was enveloped ("retrappé") by a second campaign.

Appendix 5

Paray-le-Monial

I

The buildings of Paray-le-Monial and Cluny not only look alike, they present many of the same problems. Dates from texts are disputed, and according to Salet no in-depth archaeological study exists.[1] The specialist on Brionnais churches, R. Oursel, abandoned any attempt to study the building because he claimed "on ne pourrait que répéter mot pour mot" Virey's *petite monographie* on Paray, and Porter similarly described Virey's conclusions as "indisputable."[2] In his pioneering book, however, Virey observed no important changes throughout the construction of Paray and Cluny, and as a consequence he was unable to relate one part of one building to a part of the other without speaking of each building as a whole. He spoke of Cluny and Paray as having "the same masonry," "the same buttresses," "the same half-columns with bases and capitals in the apse," and as a result he concluded that they were just about contemporary.[3]

Only by first isolating the campaigns at Cluny and Paray can we precisely compare the different parts of these buildings. First we must carefully distinguish the masonry, buttresses, bases, moldings, and capitals within each building and between both churches. Only then can we position one campaign relative to another and recognize Paray as a limited version of only certain portions of the mother church. In the past, the entire building of Paray has been seen as a reduced and lesser copy of Cluny, while in fact the word "copy" is a misnomer: five of the masons who worked on the chevet campaign of Paray were among the six who left marks on the first campaign at Cluny, an overlap which insures a direct standard of comparison in lieu of a vague model-copy relationship.[4]

Two distinct campaigns emerge from studying the archaeological details of Paray. The first campaign is signed by sixteen members of the Atelier who worked on the most important Romanesque buildings in Burgundy, including Cluny and Vézelay (see Figs. 36, 67). Significantly, members of this Atelier finished only the most important parts of the building, the perimeter construction of the nave and transepts and the complete chevet. Their signatures cannot be found on the rest of the building. The procedure for building Paray, then, apparently involved a hierarchy of ateliers in which the mainline Cluniac Atelier was assigned the outside plan, choir, and sanctuary, while the construction of the nave vessel and the upper part of the transepts was left to local masons. Moreover, the pattern of the first construction—starting in the west at a low level and building up at the choir in the east—repeats the system employed in the first campaign at Cluny. Likewise at Cluny, the construction crossed over in the choir, from a west-east direction along the nave aisle walls and chevet, to the east-west direction of the freestanding piers in the nave (see appendix 4).

The discovery of two campaigns at Paray causes us to reconsider the theory of Paray as a provincial copy of Cluny. Only the transepts and freestanding nave of the second campaign correspond to this previous notion. The first campaign was executed by Cluniac masons who did not *copy* but *continued* their own manner of construction at the mother church. In fact, by comparing the masonry, buttresses, moldings, and bases at Paray and Cluny, we can establish a consistent connection between the first campaign at Paray and the last western campaign at Cluny (appendix 4); similarly, the articulation and execution of the first campaign at Paray correspond to the later campaigns of Cluniac construction, as described in chapter 2.

Then, while the layout of Paray follows the arrangement of the first campaign at Cluny, its style and execution reflect Cluny's final phase of construction. By showing the consistent overlap of the details of Paray's first campaign with this fourth campaign at Cluny, we can date Paray more precisely to the time of a distinct portion of the mother church; in turn, the recurrence of so many unique details from one part of Cluny III confirms the existence of a distinctive, last campaign at the mother church.

II

Fill Masonry. By comparison with the later campaign, the fill masonry from the first campaign is largely grey instead of beige, its size is more irregular, and its shape more horizontal. Its surface is more pitted, with deep chips and regular pick marks setting it off from the shallow and regular blade strokes which dominate the masonry of the second campaign. These differences are consistent and follow a distinct suture line, vertically down the eastern face of each transept (Fig. 74) and horizontally across all three sides of the transepts at the height of the nave aisle walls (Figs. 75, 76) where the first campaign began (Fig. 216).[5] Details from all parts of the first campaign, for example from the central ambulatory chapel (Fig. 67), northern transept (Fig. 217) and nave aisles (Fig. 216), link it directly with the fill masonry from the final campaign at Cluny. Although the western bays of Cluny are no longer standing, the southern aisle wall of the narthex courses directly into the masonry of the facade and therefore gives us a good sample of the masonry from the fourth phase of construction (Fig. 215). While smaller and more irregular than the Cluny narthex masonry, stones from the Paray first campaign (Figs. 216, 217) frequently exhibit the uniform pick marks and increased horizontal shape and size which distinguishes the final campaigns of fill masonry at Cluny (Figs. 66, 215) from earlier construction (Fig. 199).[6]

Ashlar. Corresponding to this difference in fill masonry, the ashlar buttresses, dosserets, and responds change between the two campaigns (Figs. 75, 76). The first-campaign ashlar is more irregular, predominantly smaller in height and thus more horizontal in shape; frequently two or three filler stones ("a") wrap around the sides of the buttresses on the exterior and the dosserets on the interior (Fig. 75), distinguishing them from ashlar stones above the level of the first campaign.[7] In places like the lower portions of the ambulatory chapels (Fig. 67), horizontally shaped ashlar extend over three feet and approximate a three-to-one proportion, confirming the late quality of Paray ashlar in relation to Cluny where ashlar of this kind appears only in the final stages of construction (see appendix 4 and Fig. 66).

Differences in ashlar on jambs likewise distinguish the two campaigns at Paray. Usually no more than two large stones line each first-campaign jamb on the second story in the choir ("3" in Fig. 58) and transept ("3" in Fig. 219a, and on the right in Fig. 218); by contrast, three or more ashlar stones occupy the same place in the second campaign (Fig. 220, and on the left in Fig. 218); moreover, in the first campaign, these jamb stones usually are single ashlar blocks (Fig. 218), while in the transepts and nave of the second campaign (Fig. 220) single stones form the curved molding on the inside surface of the jambs but frequently are replaced on the flat outside edges of the jambs by vertically shaped stones three to six inches wide. The division of ashlar by irregular smaller stones corresponds to the generally irregular finish and blemished appearance of the corners and surfaces of many architectural details throughout the second campaign (Fig. 220), including moldings, corbels, pilasters, string courses, and arcades.[8]

Like jamb stones, ashlar voussoirs change radically in type between the campaigns. In both transepts (Figs. 218, 219a), the profiled voussoirs ("4") of the second story and the squared-off voussoirs ("7") from the third story both change from segments of irregular size—often as large as a quarter of the semi-circular arch—in the first campaign, to voussoirs rarely exceeding a tenth of its size in the second.

String Courses, Arcade Moldings, Pilasters. Differences among other architectural details correspond to the differences among ashlar and fill masonry between the first and second campaigns. The string course molding from the first campaign at Paray ("2" on the right in Fig. 218) repeats the characteristic profile with segmented torus and compressed scotia from the freestanding nave of Cluny (below the line in Fig. 68), whereas the molding from the "less advanced" second campaign at Paray repeats characteristics of the earliest plinths and bases of Cluny (above the line in Fig. 68). In the second campaign at the vertical suture on both transepts (on the left in Fig. 218, on the right in Fig. 219a) the first string course molding changes immediately to a more vertical profile, a more open scotia with smaller and less segmental tori ("2"). Remarkably, on the north side of the transept the change is made within one molding ("2" in Fig. 218), where the larger and more segmental torus of the first campaign is abandoned in mid course. The sequence of this change from right to left, along with evidence from fill masonry and voussoirs on the transepts, proves that the first campaign preceded the second. On the exterior of the southern transept, as seen, for example, in Figure 74, the fill masonry of the second campaign must have been laid last because it continues from the vertical suture above and across the level of the first-campaign masonry under the eaves of the roof. Similarly, on each transept (Figs. 218, 219a) the campaign suture for both profiled ("4") and square-edged voussoirs ("7") occurs closer to the springing of the arch on the side of the first campaign; if the second campaign had been built first, this division, which leaves a majority of the arch on the side of the second campaign, would have left many voussoirs hanging in mid-air awaiting the next construction. Clearly for the reasons shown from moldings, fill masonry and voussoirs, the second campaign followed the completion of the chevet. After the first, west-to-east campaign was completed in the choir, the second campaign continued westward along the freestanding piers of the nave.[9] This sequence of construction, which reverses directions and crosses over the main vessel in the choir, follows precisely the pattern set at Cluny (appendix 4).

A change analogous to the first string course molding occurs in the arcade molding of the third story ("8") at the point of the vertical suture on both transepts (Figs. 218, 219a). The classically paired torus and scotia of the first campaign give way after the suture to a torus almost fifty percent larger and scotia correspondingly smaller.

Similarly, the involved details the Atelier created on fluted pilasters are different from copies in the second campaign. In the choir (Fig. 58), the pilaster capital ("9") is roughly square, while in the second campaign of the nave (Fig. 220) and transept the horizontal dimension extends as much as three times the height of the capital. In the choir (Fig. 58), the astragal ("10") of the pilaster combines a fillet and torus, while in the second campaign of the nave (Fig. 220) and transept (Fig. 218) only the torus remains. Similarly, the dots ("11") which aid the transition from pilaster to astragal at the end of the fluted channels in the choir (Fig. 58) disappear in the nave (Fig. 220) and transept of the second campaign.

Especially as seen in details like the string-course molding and pilaster astragal, the complicated relationship between different shapes, based on convex and concave classical designs, disappears along with the unblemished appearance of ashlar as masons from the second campaign "reduced" the model the Cluniac masons left behind.

Corbels, Imposts, Moldings, and Bases. Features of these architectural devices show important differences between the two campaigns. In light of the changes in masonry and the profile of the first string course, it should not be surprising that the local masons of the second campaign, although building later than the Cluny Atelier, adopted a profile in these architectural parts that the Cluny Atelier had abandoned and probably considered passé after the first stage of the mother church.[10] The corbels ("5" in Fig. 220) of the second campaign in the nave and transepts are chipped and blemished like the ashlar from the second-story jambs described before. By comparison with corbels of the first campaign in the choir (Fig. 58) and transept (on the right in Fig. 218), second-campaign corbels (Fig. 220, and on the left in Fig. 218) have a more vertical profile and more open doucine curve. The abacus is relatively taller but the width of the corbel is usually narrower. Underneath the lowest projecting curve, the fillet frequently found on the first-campaign corbel disappears in the second campaign. By contrast, the corbels of the first campaign are marked by features which associate them with the final phase of construction at Cluny. The pronounced diagonal profile and extended horizontal tip of their doucine curve place the first-campaign corbels from the exterior of the chevet among the latest examples on the great transept of the mother church (Fig. 66).[11] Similarly, the cyma profile of imposts and string courses distinguishes the first campaign of Paray and relates it to the final stages of construction at Cluny III: imposts from capitals in the first chevet campaign of Paray (Fig. 222) attain the diagonality and horizontal corbelled extension achieved only by the third campaign of Cluny (Fig. 206d); and the cyma string-course moldings, seen for example on two levels of the transept ("6" right of the suture in Fig. 218, left of the suture in Fig. 219a), have a more diagonal profile, a more projecting tip, and a more segmental bottom curve than moldings from the second campaign adjacent to it in the transept and throughout the nave (Fig. 220). This exaggerated profile begins in the second campaign of Cluny (appendix 4; Fig. 206c) and becomes typical only later in the third (Fig. 206d).

Finally, even the bases link the first Paray campaign to the final phase of construction at the mother church (Figs. 67, 69). All the bases from the Paray first campaign have a more diagonal angle, more compressed scotia, and more horizontally extended bottom scotia edge than any example from the first three campaigns of Cluny (described in appendix 4). Yet, they are almost indistinguishable from the five westernmost bases in the fourth Cluny campaign (bases 7NN, 9SS, 9SS, 15 GT PT, 11NN, in Fig. 68).

Foliage Capitals. Like so many other elements of the second campaign at Paray, its capital sculpture is distinct. Local talent created many figural capitals—for example, the Curbigny Master completed capitals in the southern clerestory of the south transept (Fig. 221). Typically, by contrast, the first-campaign Atelier followed the example of Cluny III and carved almost exclusively foliate sculpture.[12] These foliate designs offer another opportunity to place Paray's first campaign in relation to the changing construction of Cluny III, for the very differences which distinguish the later sculpture at Cluny also characterize these earliest examples at Paray. Sculpture from all parts of the first campaign at Paray, including the ambulatory (Figs. 73, 222) and the eastern (Fig. 71) and northern (Fig. 55) faces of the transept, shares features which distinguish the fourth-campaign foliage (Fig. 72) from sculpture in the first (Fig. 209b), second (Fig. 210), or even third (Fig. 212) campaigns at Cluny. Compared to the earliest sculpture at Cluny, at Paray the background flattens out and the relief carving becomes more straight and diminishes in depth. The number of leaf clusters decreases as the size of each one increases; the surface of each leaf is flatter, its width narrower, and the tip more narrowly pointed; the inscribed lines on and between the leaves are longer and more numerous. And linear, built-up ridges mark the surface (Fig. 73) as they did for the first time on the western portal foliage at Cluny (Fig. 72). Both these linear surface effects and the flatter and shallower carving of the foreground and background parallel what we observed from the western portal sculpture of Cluny (chapter 4; appendix 4; Figs. 72, 130c, 131), the nave sculpture of Vézelay (chapter 4; Figs. 112b, 112c, 128), and the chevet sculpture of Autun (chapters 4, 5; Figs. 134, 223).[13] On the basis of the completion date of 1130–32 for the Cluny facade,[14] a *post quem* of 1120 for the nave of Vézelay,[15] and the widely accepted 1120–1130 date for the nave of Autun, I propose a late date, between 1120 and 1130, for the first campaign of Paray.[16]

NOTES

1. Chapter 1, first excursus (Salet, "Cluny III," 281). Despite this disclaimer, Salet believed that the church was built from east to west around the year 1100.

2. R. Oursel, *Les églises*, 248. Porter, in C. Oursel, *L'art roman*, 3, explained that C. Oursel and Virey independently arrived at the same conclusions, which he considered "indiscutables."

3. Virey, *Paray*, 26–29. In the text I dispute Virey's claim that Paray was built in one campaign from east to west contemporary with his date for Cluny, "à peu près" 1100. Lefèvre-Pontalis (*Etude historique*, 11; "Paray," 53) believed that the nave, transept and choir of Paray were built in one campaign from 1130–1140.

4. For the model-copy theory of Cluny, see the second excursus to chapter 1 and the opinions of specialists cited in the text. Other specific statements on Paray include Lefèvre-Pontalis ("Paray," 54): "chacune des travées doit être considerée comme une réplique de celles de l'abbatiale de Cluny"; Evans (*Romanesque architecture*, 115): "Paray is a lesser imitation of Cluny"; Branner (*Burgundian Gothic Architecture*, 11): "local following at first consisted of reduced versions of the mother church, such as Paray"; see also Conant, "L'abside," 8.

5. The first campaign courses rest on ashlar block "a" in Figure 76. This block extends farther to the south than these courses, proving that the first campaign was built from west to east.

On the western face of the northern transept, the first

campaign mounts approximately six courses in a stepped pattern at the northwestern corner of the transept (Fig. 76). This level then is maintained on the northern face all the way to the northeastern corner of the transept (Fig. 75), where it once again drops approximately six courses to its previous height.

6. The 1856 restoration by the architect Millet included the ground story of the porch, two towers of the facade, and the tower of the central crossing (Lefèvre-Pontalis, "Paray," 54). In the east, the restoration was largely restricted to individual stones, except for obvious areas like the southern bays of the choir joining the transept.

7. The characteristic ashlar of the first campaign appears on the transverse arches only in the ambulatory and choir, the only spaces I believe the Atelier vaulted.

8. R. Oursel, (*Les églises*, 252) correctly observed "certaines anomalies" in the nave such as the "inachèvement des rares chapiteaux," but he attributed them to the need to finish the building with haste rather than to differences in the work of separate ateliers or campaigns.

9. Unlike the stepped suture on the Cluny choir wall, which indicates a west-to-east construction (see appendix 4), the parallel series of stepped sutures on the Paray nave clerestory only could have been constructed from east to west because of the corbel angle of the overlapping beds. This fact further supports an east-to-west direction for the construction of the second campaign.

10. See appendix 4 for a description of the changes in corbels between the campaigns of Cluny III.

11. The characteristics of the corbels on the first campaign also appear on the corbels on the exterior of the chevet from the level of the ambulatory to the clerestory. Especially visible at the suture on the eastern face of the south transepts, the exterior corbels of the first campaign contrast with the exterior corbels of the second campaign. The second-campaign corbels are

generally more vertical in profile and horizontally less extended.

12. R. Oursel, *Les églises*, 199–202. Exceptions are the two corbel figures in the northern ambulatory and the figural capital in the southeastern crossing bay. These as well as the single bearded head on the interior, eastern face of the facade may have been carved by the master of the Paray Hieron Museum tympanum.

13. Rather than relate the chevet capitals to specifically late sculpture at Cluny, or distinguish them from the Brionnais sculpture in the nave of Paray, scholars in the past have emphasized the difference of all of Paray's sculpture from work at the mother church. Schapiro ("Review of C. Oursel," 227) described the capitals of Paray as "unlike those of Cluny." Conant ("The Apse," 27) explained the difference as a lack of finish caused by the intention to paint them. Deschamps ("L'âge des chapiteaux," 169–70) attributed the difference to time, with Paray having an earlier date than Cluny; while previously installed, the Cluny ambulatory capitals were not carved until after those at Paray. Like Porter before him, R. Oursel (*Les églises*, 93) suggested that the difference was a qualitative one: the best artists remained at Cluny while lesser ones worked at Paray, where "un bon maçon peut répéter les leçons du maître architecte."

14. Salet, "Cluny III," 282, especially note 5.

15. See appendix 6.

16. Indeed, based on the crocket capitals in the second-campaign northern nave clerestory (Fig. 224), and their analogy to sculpture at Beaune Cathedral (Fig. 225), I would assign the later second campaign a date of 1140. At Beaune, Rhein ("Beaune," 271) believed that "une décoration de crockets qui, à eux seuls, permettraient d'assigner une date à cette partie" of the thirteenth century. Schlink's more telling archaeological arguments place Beaune after 1150 (*Cluny*, 79ff.). See also, Salet, "Les chapiteaux de Beaune," 220.

Appendix 6
Vézelay

I

The three different styles of Vézelay sculpture outlined in the text correspond to archaeological changes within the building. The earliest sculpture, including all the lower jamb capitals and both side tympana, belongs to an early low-perimeter campaign of the type observed in the architecture at Cluny (appendix 4) and Paray (appendix 5). The campaign reached the level of the first imposts on the nave facade (Figs. 28, 226a) and continued at this level of approximately 8 ashlar courses through the smaller fill masonry on both aisle walls of the second bay (Figs. 28, 226a, 226b). On the northern and southern aisle walls, the first campaign dropped off slightly in the third bay through a small step in the western fill masonry ("a" in Fig. 226c), and dropped off radically in the fourth bay, reaching a level of approximately 5 ashlar courses through a stepped suture (Fig. 226d).

Changes in masons' marks correspond to the differences in sculpture. From marks compiled in Figure 36, it is clear that only members of the Brionnais Atelier built the lower facade and laid out the lower courses of the aisle walls, while a much-expanded workforce completed the nave, upper aisles, and facade above the string course. Specific evidence confirms the close connection of the first architectural and sculptural campaigns at Vézelay: (1) all of the marks found on the facade below the imposts (Fig. 31) and on the aisle walls below the eighth course within the first campaign belong to masons from the Atelier who worked at Anzy, Mâcon, Perrecy, Montceaux, and on the first campaigns at Cluny and Paray;[1] indeed, fourteen of the nineteen members worked at Anzy, Mâcon, and Perrecy, the buildings which I determined in the text were built before Vézelay. However, (2) the marks of the first campaign include none of the twenty new, non-Atelier masons who worked in the nave and above the first campaign in the aisles and facade.

For example, on the facade, seventeen masons, all from the original Atelier, worked up to the level of the imposts, while above that point eight new masons joined thirteen of the older group.

Masons' marks on the facade below the first imposts match the marks on the aisle masonry from the first campaign, just as the marks on the facade above the imposts correspond to the marks on the remaining nave construction at Vézelay. (3) All but two of the thirteen Atelier members who marked the first campaign of the aisles worked on the facade below the imposts, and five of the eleven worked at Perrecy, the building which immediately preceded the construction of Vézelay (see chapter 2). By contrast, the facade above the imposts on all three bays undergoes the same change as the nave and upper aisle walls: (4) the same four masons among the original Atelier who marked the masonry from the first campaign in the aisles and below the imposts of the facade disappeared from the facade above the imposts, and three of the four did not reappear throughout the nave and above the eighth course, or first campaign in the aisle. (5) Conversely, of the twenty new masons not found in the Vézelay first campaign or in any of the Atelier's Brionnais churches, fully six appeared above the first imposts on the side portals of the facade. (6) Of these six, five joined the other new masons finishing the central nave vessel, and two were among the three new masons (the other was an Atelier member previously absent from Vézelay) working above the eighth course or first campaign on the aisle walls. Therefore, the connection of the workforce on the upper facade to the builders of the nave vessel and upper aisle walls is convincingly close: the same group of men disappeared from all these parts, and another group of men, who did not work on the first campaign, appeared there together at these locations to replace them.

The decided difference between the first campaign and later construction at Vézelay contradicts both the Anglo-American-Burgundian and Parisian opinion that the nave was built in a single, uniform campaign.[2] The distinction in the nave campaigns apparent from masons' marks is reinforced by other information: the difference in bases from the first campaign on the aisle walls and the bases on the freestanding nave piers (chapter 2);[3] the outstanding distinction between sculpture from the lower and upper facades (chapters 4, 5); and the changes in masonry between the two campaigns on the aisle and facade walls. The fill masonry almost doubles in height between campaigns, as seen, for example, on the aisle walls of the western bays (Figs. 226a, 226b, 226c); and the deep and irregular blade strokes on the lower aisle walls (Fig. 24f) become more numerous, superficial, and regular (Fig. 226d). The ashlar on the facade also changes dramatically at the level of the first impost (Fig. 28). Above that point, the normal dimensions of ashlar are approximately two feet long and one foot high ("C" in Fig. 28); on the level of the capitals just below the imposts, however, the wall on both sides along all three bays is interrupted by a continuous bed of stones with pronounced vertical dimensions, matching precisely the height of the first-campaign capitals at that level ("B"). Below this interruption, the ashlar largely conforms to the pattern of the first-campaign fill masonry as seen on the aisles, with stones frequently half the size of the second-campaign blocks seen above the imposts ("A").

While the first construction was laid out as a low horizontal wall, the final construction consisted of a continuous series of vertical sections from the western to the eastern part of the nave. Once again, while the direction of building at Vézelay was different from that at Paray and Cluny[4]—conditioned probably by the preexisting crossing observed by Viollet-le-Duc—the pattern of laying out the construction was the same. The construction of the freestanding nave followed only after a low perimeter wall was set in place. It is my opinion, based on the marks of the original first Atelier who continued working in the freestanding nave, that it was built without important interruptions.[5] Of the nineteen original Atelier men, sixteen continued in the nave, and of these only two (T, A) did not work consistently from the western to eastern bays on both levels of the piers and spandrels.

This fact is especially important because of the radical shift among the new masons after bay six, which I will now discuss in light of the evidence of a vertical pattern of construction in the nave. Unlike the first campaign on the aisles, the evidence of new masons in the piers and arcade spandrels of the nave indicates that, at least up to the string course, the main vessel was built in vertical sections from west to east. A clear vertical shift occurs on both pier and spandrel levels to the east of bay six. Of the twelve new, non-Atelier masons in the first six bays of the nave, only four continue in the last eastern bays. Conversely, of the eleven non-Atelier masons working on the last four bays, only four were among the group of the masons who worked on the first six bays. Therefore, from the reduced but consistent number of members from the original Atelier who worked on two levels of the nave, we can assume that it was built continuously. And from the departure of a majority of the non-Atelier masons and the arrival of a new set after bay six, we can conclude that they built in vertical rather than in horizontal sections, at least up to the level of the nave string course. On the ashlar of the piers to the east of bay six (Fig. 227), the vertical dimensions increase while the number of smaller, horizontally shaped stones decreases (see appendix 4; Fig. 203a).

The three chronologically different groups of facade sculpture described in chapters 4 and 5, and their relationship with the changing horizontal and vertical campaigns of construction, can best be understood in light of three archaeological changes within the facade itself. I shall discuss these changes in the context of the theories of Salet and Beutler, to date the only serious archaeological studies of the facade sculpture.[6] On the basis of style, I observed three campaigns for the facade sculpture. The first included the side tympana and the capitals on all three bays below the first impost molding. The tympana rest directly above the masonry of the first architectural campaign and the capitals course directly into that masonry (Fig. 32).[7] The same two sculptors who carved the first-campaign sculpture (chapter 4) and the masonry Atelier who built the first-campaign architecture (chapter 2) also carved the ambulatory sculpture and first-campaign architecture at Cluny (Fig. 36). Thus, by comparing the bases, imposts, and masonry they made for the first campaigns at the two sites (chapter 2), I could determine that the first Vézelay sculpture preceded the ambulatory capitals at Cluny (chapter 4). The second group of facade sculpture included the central trumeau and lintel, the Christ figure of the central tympanum, and a majority of the rondels, which were installed during the expanded last campaign. In addition to the old rondels, the last sculptural campaign added new rondels, archivolts, and the tympanum apostles to either side of Christ (chapter 5).

Aside from disputing dating and architectural campaigns, I disagree with the sculptural analysis found in the major study of Vézelay, especially its assigning the jamb and pilaster capitals and tympana of the side portals to a second campaign.[8] In the text, I show that all these sculptures, together with the colonnette capitals of the central portal, belong to the same stylistic phase, which preceded the ambulatory capitals of Cluny (chapter 4). The evidence for attaching the tympana and jamb and pilaster capitals to the later construction of the upper walls of the western facade is not convincing for reasons I shall now discuss.

Salet claimed that during the first campaign, the eastern face of the side portals (Figs. 228, 229) was built with an opening to accommodate stairs to a proposed upper chapel, while the western face of the same wall was left undressed above the western string-course level. In this way both side tympana could be included in a later campaign, when the western face of the side portals was veneered over in a "single jet."

A number of questions arise about the theory of the side tympana belonging to a later campaign. The statement that the tympana have "the wrong proportions for the narrowness of the bay," and the opinion that the stones filling the wall openings on the western face (Fig. 230) "do not in any sense have the effect of being filled in on a wall that was standing for a long time," are impressions and nothing more.[9] Specific inconsistencies bedevil the archaeological argument. First, the remains of the springer stones, which were intended, it is said, to support the Saint-Michael chapel in the original campaign, course directly with the ashlar next to the tympanum ("a" in Fig. 231), claimed to be from a second campaign. The coursing, however, proves that the wall next to the tympanum is contemporary with, not later than, the springers from the "first" campaign.[10] Second, the theory claimed that during the first campaign, wall openings were made in the eastern face of both side portals with the intent of providing an access to the Saint-Michael chapel from the nave (Figs. 228, 229). Today, the jambs of both openings continue without any sign of interruption or change from the eastern side to the western face (Fig. 230), which is claimed to be from a separate, second campaign when a decision was made to eliminate the Saint-Michael chapel.[11] We might ask whether masons would have made and then filled in two special openings on the later western facade with no purpose in mind but to continue an already abandoned scheme (Fig. 230).

Indeed, evidence disproves the claim that a single second campaign veneered the western face of both side portals above the string course. While both the northern and southern bays appear analogous, their construction in fact is quite different; because these differences recur on both eastern and western faces of the same portals, they prove that both facade and nave faces were completed simultaneously. On the southern bay, uniform ashlar above the string course covers both the eastern (Fig. 229) and western (Fig. 230) faces, coursing with the jamb stones of the opening on both sides of the wall. By contrast, the ashlar stones on the northern bay shift to *petit appareil* both above the tympanum on the western face (Fig. 232) and at the equivalent level three ashlar beds above the string course on the eastern face (Fig. 228). Moreover, on both faces of the northern bay, the jamb continues as ashlar around the opening (Fig. 228) despite this horizontal shift to smaller fill. Thus, distinctive differences in the treatment of wall and jamb stones repeat on both faces of the northern bay but appear on neither face of the southern bay. The fact that the wall construction on both sides of each bay shifts simultaneously makes it most likely that both faces of each portal were constructed together—and most unlikely that the western face of each portal was veneered over a preexisting wall.

Besides these arguments against a later veneering which included the side tympana, it is clear that the ashlar immediately surrounding the northern tympanum on the western face belong to the structural layout of the central bay and not to a uniform "single jet" of construction from a second veneering campaign. The larger ashlar surrounding the tympanum on the northern portal are not only horizontally interrupted by *petit appareil* above the level of the archivolts (described before), but continue vertically as an isolated, narrow strip on the side of the portal behind the later dosserets of the central bay ("B" in Fig. 232).

The second large group of sculpture completed during the first campaign was the column, jamb, and pilaster capitals below the first imposts which I related stylistically to the side tympana sculpture (chapter 4). The accepted opinion has been that only the capitals above the central portal columns were completed during the first stage. According to this theory, sculptors from a second campaign, realizing that the side portals were "too simple," carved figures onto the inside jambs and applied capitals with pilasters to their bare faces (Fig. 30a). To assign all these sculptures to one period, I first should evaluate the merits of the previous theory, which proposed that pilasters were installed later than the embrasure wall behind them based on the impression that "too much plain stone" was left after the first campaign.[12] It was argued that the pilasters are *en délit* and monolithic and therefore they and their capitals must have been installed after the stones behind them. The monolithic character and sequence of installation of this one form are correctly observed but they do not constitute evidence of separate campaigns. While the pilasters are *en délit*, the capitals above them on the south side of both portals are not. Clearly, the figure of the Tones on the northern portal (Fig. 32) is carved from a stone which courses directly into the core of the embrasure wall. If the point at issue is the chronology of the pilaster capitals, then the evidence from the pilasters beneath the capitals is not as convincing as the evidence from the capitals themselves. Besides, if this argument were consistent, then the bases and capitals of the lower columns on the central portal, claimed to belong to the first stage of construction, should join the embrasure wall, which they do not (Fig. 10e). It is difficult to accept an *en délit* shaft as a sign of later additions on the side portals if it is interpreted in a contrary sense on the central portal at the very same level of construction.

In the standard theory, a second argument proposed that fluted columns and pilasters with decorative masonry buttons at the ends can be found in works only after the first stage of construction.[13] By this logic, the pilasters with buttons on the side portals and their accompanying capitals (Figs. 30a, 32) date from the second stage, and the Saint-John trumeau column, being bereft of buttons, dates earlier; in this system, masonry buttons—without any further definition or distinction—establish the relative date of a work of art. Whatever the potential of this method, it relied on correct observation yet overlooked the existence of buttons on the lower columns of the central portal and on the trumeau column of Saint John ("A" in Figs. 233, 234). Both columns were placed in the first campaign despite the logic of a method which assigned them to a later category.

It was argued further that the ground-story jamb capitals were carved during the second campaign at the same time as the pilaster capitals in front of them (Fig. 30a). This conclusion was based on an unusual space ("A" in Fig. 230) separating the outside edge of the impost molding from the side face of the pilaster capitals. According to this reasoning, the curved sides of the jamb sculpture ("B" in Fig. 230) forced the impost molding above it to project, overlapping the side face of the pilaster capitals next to the jamb sculpture. There are a number of archaeological discrepancies in this argument. First, on the southern portal, the imposts ("C" in Fig. 230) above the outermost uncarved jambs are isolated—that is, they are made of separate stones from the imposts under discussion, and they do not touch the curved jamb sculpture two orders away inside the portal. Yet these outside imposts project on both sides of the southern portal as much as the other imposts which overlap the pilaster capitals. It is hard to believe that the curved jamb carvings on the inside of the portal ("A") would affect the projection of imposts on the outside jambs ("C") with which they are not in contact. Second, it was claimed that the curved jamb sculpture on the north portal had been carved during a later second campaign. But unlike their counterparts on the south portal, these jamb figures, if they were carved later, caused none of the impost moldings to overlap any of the capitals and jambs on that side. It is indeed a case of selective evidence to argue that the curved surface of sculpted jambs determined an overlap on one portal, when the same hypothetical recarving had no effect whatsoever on the other portal.

Even if the discrepancies between impost moldings and sculpture had occurred consistently in both portals above both pilasters and jambs, and if the discrepancies had been caused by newly carved inside jamb sculpture, what does it prove? In this theory, all the lateral portal capitals, jamb sculptures, and impost moldings date from a second campaign, so that a discrepancy between any one of them proves nothing about a break from a previous stage of construction. The lack of correspondence between the impost molding and pilaster capitals, then, hardly constitutes "the detail which attests to the truth of the changes carried out in the original conception."[14]

II

In the text I describe two changes in style on the central portal above the level of the first campaign (Fig. 104a). The second stage of construction consists of the two blocks on the central tympanum Christ, the apostle jambs and their imposts, the trumeau, lintel, and most of the rondels. While most of these blocks were installed permanently and were then damaged or left bare, without companion pieces, the rondels were rearranged during the final campaign when three extra rondels were added at the top and rectangular archivolts and tympanum apostles were added to each side of the portal.

I accept in the main the standard proposal for two late campaigns for the central portal, although I assign the trumeau and all but three of the rondels to a second stage that also included the tympanum Christ. The separation of the tympanum Christ and the lintel into two campaigns can be dismissed, as Beutler pointed out, because the human-sized Peter and Paul figures which extend through both these parts are carved half on the tympanum and half on the lintel.[15] Similarly, as explained in chapter 5, the drapery of the Saint-John trumeau corresponds to the sculpture on the lintel and to other jamb figures (Figs. 105a, 105b, 107) and not to the lower level first-campaign sculpture. Therefore, while I partially accept the standard theory for the final stages of construction of the central portal, I fundamentally disagree with the dating and stylistic analysis (chapters 4 and 5).

Along with many telling new archaeological findings, the recent analysis of the Vézelay sculpture by Beutler suggested two new central portal campaigns, a hypothesis which, if true, would disprove my own conclusions about the changes in style of Cluniac sculpture.[16] This straightforward new theory proposed two campaigns instead of three, and assumed that construction continued between them; it allowed for no interruptions for artisans to go to or from Cluny and cited no drapery differences between figures on separate stages; moreover, the theory limited artistic activity to typologically separate parts of the building. It assumed, for example, that the tympanum was completed only after the nave was finished. By contrast, I observed that the nave was begun on its outside walls at the time of the first-campaign sculpture and completed in its central vessel at the time of the final sculpture campaign. In the text, I show that the Perrecy Master created nave sculpture after the style of the second tympanum campaign (chapter 4; Fig. 111b), and that the Plus Master carved nave sculpture similar in style to the first and last phases of the central portal (chapter 5; Figs. 126b, 128b). Indeed, the recent analysis straightaway admitted its intention was not to discuss style or individual artists' differences. In the process, however, it may have given up an important control against which to verify the archaeological and iconographic findings.

I will try to demonstrate that the archaeological disturbances accurately observed for the first time in Beutler's study do not necessarily justify two new campaigns based on iconography. The theory proposed a first campaign combining the present jamb and trumeau figures, all but the top three rondels, and the tympanum apostle figures—which according to the hypothesis originally included a Pentecostal Lamb where Christ's arms and hands are now. The artisans of a second campaign added the two slabs of the tympanum Christ, the top three rondels, the rectangular archivolts, the lintel, and the supports beneath and alongside the Saint-John trumeau, and then they recarved the hands of Christ on the existing tympanum.

If masons from the last campaign added the central figure of Christ (Figs. 104a, 109), instead of the side apostle figures (Figs. 114a, 114c) as I claim, it would defy all the evidence of stylistic changes between these parts (chapter 4). And it would contradict the direction of stylistic change seen in works of the Perrecy and Plus Masters from other parts of the central portal and nave (chapters 4 and 5; Figs. 110b, 127). The evidence of archaeological alteration is as follows. A rectangular section at the base of the mandorla remains unworked (Fig. 235). To my mind, this unworked portion of one of the Christ slabs must be seen in the larger picture: its side edges ("A," "B") correspond to the inside edges of the two lintel stones ("C," "D"); its center is a jagged hole ("E") which extends below and penetrates the outside edges of both lintel stones as well ("F," "G"). It appears that the central tympanum slab and both lintel stones were assembled together when a fourth sculpture, now removed, penetrated the middle of all three pieces. Given that the section at the feet of Christ remains incomplete and a hole from a previous project affected both the Christ slab and lintel, it seems illogical to argue that both these parts were created as final additions in the last campaign.

More evidence of an abandoned project can be found on the Christ mandorla and lintel pieces (Fig. 235). A rectangular border ("I") on the left of the unworked stone does not continue in the stones of the tympanum apostles but changes to a wavy border ("J") on either side. If the central Christ slabs had been inserted during the final campaign, would it have been logical to start a new border design for a couple of feet ("I") at the base of the slabs and to include in the new design a bare and unfinished block ("A") with a chipped hole in the bottom ("E")—especially if the opening of the hole corresponds to the same abandoned opening ("F," "G") on the lintel stones immediately beneath it?

Let us examine the undulating border attached to the tympanum apostles (Fig. 114a) which, it is claimed, was created before the lintel. Figure 236 very clearly shows that the heads of many lintel figures, had they survived, would have collided with this undulating border and the bottom edge of the archivolts. When the heads were severed cannot be determined. From the height of the lintel figures, however, it is definite that they were designed for a different top border than the present undulating one, and therefore they must have been carved before the tympanum apostles. Significantly, figures on the right lintel (Fig. 104a) with heads well below the apostle border (like those around the ladder, and those right lintel figures which project beyond the plane of the archivolt border) survive with their heads intact.

It is logical to include the flat face of the impost blocks behind and to either side of the reused trumeau as part of the abandoned lintel and central Christ project (Fig. 105a).[17] A completely flat and uncarved surface would have extended (Fig. 235) from the base of Christ's feet ("A") down the front of the lintel ("C") to the face of the impost blocks behind the present trumeau, with at least one large hole in the center ("E," "F," "G") for attaching a major piece of sculpture. That the western face of the imposts was left flat and uncarved implies that what was meant to go in front of them was changed, but it specifies little about any hypothetical changes within the tympanum above. What is significant, however, is that the uncarved and continuously flat area on the central portal includes the three levels of sculpture I ascribe to the second campaign in the text: the jamb apostles, the lintel, and the central Christ figure.

Other evidence within the tympanum indicates that the Christ figure was carved before the apostles. At the suture between the lower stone block of Christ and the slab of the apostles (Fig. 237), three horizontal decorative grooves (beneath Christ's right arm) were abruptly discontinued on the apostles' slab. Moreover, in contrast to the finish of the apostles at this point, the deep and irregular chisel marks on, above, and below the grooves of the Christ slab indicate an unfinished or possibly reworked state. An unplanned, ragged break at the suture between two sculpted blocks is more convincing evidence of the sequence of changes within a sculptural program than the existence of simple undercutting which appears throughout the tympanum and not just at the selected points around the Christ figure described in the new theory. In fact, the argument appears to be inconsistent on this score: although it claimed that the mandorla was undercut on the top of the apostle slabs to compensate for the replacement of a Pentecostal Lamb by the projecting hands of Christ, in fact the mandorla only recedes above the *top* of Christ's right hand, while below that hand the mandorla projects as much as almost any place on the tympanum.

Other pieces of information from the tympanum indicate that the Christ figure was carved before the tympanum apostles. The drapery of the apostle figure which overlaps the left edge of the lower Christ slab is made of stucco ("H" in Fig. 235). If, as the theory suggested, the Christ slabs were carved last, would the sculptors have left the bottom edge to be stuccoed later? More likely the Christ figure was carved first, then later the apostles were added on either side, and the overlap from these new figures onto the central slab was added in stucco.

The new theory proposed that the introduction of a new elongated Christ figure in the final campaign determined an increased size for the portal circumference and caused rectangular archivolts with triangular filler stones to be added between the original rondels and tympanum on either side of the portal (Fig. 104a). Beutler accurately observed that three new rondels with an iconography and typology different from the others were added above Christ's head (Fig. 238), and he suggested that these were carved to make up for the increased circumference. As discussed in the text, stylistically the Christ figure, lintel, and original rondels predate the rectangular archivolts, side tympanum panels, and three new rondel figures, and therefore I propose another explanation for the archaeological evidence.[18] The cause is very practical and has to do with the need to coordinate the third-campaign sculpture with the present narthex vault, which was not foreseen originally (see Salet's convincing evidence) when the jamb imposts, Christ, lintel, and original rondels were carved. The imposts above the side jambs project in a pronounced stepped pattern (Fig. 104a) that would have corresponded to a pronounced stepped series of archivolts, typical of the late work of the Atelier. When the decision was made to attach a groined narthex vault to the facade, the masons realized that the circumference of these projecting orders would have cut into the webs of the groins—indeed, even the springers of the present groin vault are severed (Fig. 104a)—and so they flattened the portal design. Instead of building out stepped archivolts, they substituted flat rectangular archivolt panels on the plane of the tympanum and recessed the single order of original rondels back into a shallow splay. The change in the plan left a large space above the projecting steps on the impost molding, and these projections no longer corresponded to the recessed orders above. I mentioned previously that traces of unfinished construction and damage only appear on pieces from this altered design— that is, to the lintel, central impost, original rondels, and Christ slab—and this evidence tends to link these pieces together and to explain why they had to be modified in a later design. Further evidence of alteration to an original design that included the figure of Christ can be seen in the cavet molding above Christ's head. It clearly was conceived as part of the early arrangement and not inserted during a final campaign, as the new theory suggests, because the cavet formed a section of a continuous tympanum molding, with its original circumference still visible in the curved projecting outline and curved rectangular profile of its top edge (Fig. 238).

What purpose would it have served in the final campaign to create a continuous cavet molding with a curved circumference, and then abut this curved profile on either end with the vertical frame of the rectangular archivolts which, according to this theory, were designed at the same time as the cavet and the Christ figure? Instead, the Christ figure was designed before these rectangular archivolts, and its cavet molding was intended to continue—as the archivolts do now—in a circumference ending above the outside edges of the lintels. The cavet is a transitional molding that projects three dimensionally and—just as the restored cavet on the Autun tympanum—would have marked a transition from the plane of the Christ figure to what would have been stepped orders, including the rondels. When the groin vault and decorative formeret were added to the facade at the impost level, the original rondels were sunk as far back as possible to allow the webs to descend closer to the springing above the impost without being interrupted by the stepped projections of the archivolts. The result, clearly visible in Figure 104a, is that the steps of the impost do not correspond to the splayed orders above them, and a large and otherwise unexplained void occupies the area above the impost molding originally planned for the projecting archivolts.

The question, then, is what originally was intended to fill the space directly above the projecting stepped imposts, and how does it relate to the need to add three rondels at the top of the tympanum? The suggestion that the circumference of the original rondels minus the three new rondels corresponds to the diameter of the tympanum minus the central Christ block is geometrically impossible. The rondels fit very tightly, so that their circumference is the same with or without the added rondels. The segment of the circle has simply been enlarged—that is, the rondels were designed to occupy their present location and circumference (although surrounding an original cavet molding) but to stop *above* the level of the lintel, which, like Perrecy (Fig. 1a) and the side portal at Charlieu, would have projected forward on the sides in keeping with the stepped imposts below.[19] When these stepped wings of the lintel were eliminated to make room for the springing of the groin and formeret above the impost, the recessed rondels were dropped to the level of the impost and that segment of the circle previously occupied by the projecting side lintels was added at the top in the form of three new rondels. Without interfering with the groin, the additional scenes of the four corners of the earth eliminated from the projecting lintels were then added in the form of flattened rectangular archivolts above the newly carved tympanum slabs to either side of the Christ figure.[20]

The sequence in which the Christ figure preceded the apostles instead of the reverse makes more iconographic sense even if one accepts the theory that the Mission of the Apostles replaced an earlier subject. First: placed together with the Pentecostal Lamb in an original campaign, the Saint-John trumeau figure would have made an inappropriate precursor or companion piece; Saint John, however, couples ideally to the tympanum Christ, and I maintain that the two were designed for the same second campaign.[21] Second, nothing in the iconography of the lintel is more appropriate to the subject of the Mission of the Apostles than to any number of other possible subjects which could have been intended for the location where the Christ is now. Rather the weight of non-iconographic evidence—the earlier style of the Christ and lintel figures (chapter 4), the archaeological connections between these parts, as well as the non-correspondence of the apostle slab border with the heads on the lintel—indicates an earlier date for the lintel and Christ than for the apostles. Third: let us assume for the sake of argument that a switch was made to the subject of the Mission of the Apostles. Then it would be far more appropriate to this new iconography if the large-scale figures of the major apostles like Peter and Paul were added in the final campaign to either side of Christ. According to the new theory, however, in the final campaign the figure of Christ was inserted between these preexisting apostles on the tympanum and the extra figures of Peter and Paul were sandwiched between Christ's feet and the lintel (Figs. 104a, 105a). If images of the same apostles already were in place and held predominant positions on the tympanum, what was the iconographic point of adding these extra little apostles at the feet of the Christ figure, especially given the third representation of Peter and Paul (Fig. 104b) on the earlier life-sized jamb figures of the central portal? Fourth, the argument proposed that the clouds above Christ's left hand were recarved to appear calm to correspond to the new iconography of the Mission. If the clouds were recarved when the two Christ slabs were installed, why does the new design stop at the suture line between the two left apostle slabs, both of which the recent report considered to be from the original first campaign? More pertinent, why are clouds with many waves to be considered more calm than the rest of the clouds with fewer undulations?[22]

III

None of the three stages of facade sculpture I propose can be precisely dated, although circumstantial evidence indicates an 1110–1120 date for the second campaign. First, the only damage and repair to the facade appear in the work of the second campaign on the incompletely carved or reworked sculpture of the trumeau, central imposts, rondels, lintel, and central Christ slab. Second, while the date of 1120 is not definitely associated with these parts, it is definitely associated with damaged architecture at Vézelay of which these parts are the only significant examples. A fire in 1120 destroyed enough of the church or monastery to kill innumerable women, children, clergy, and pilgrims on the feast day of the Madeleine.[23] Third, the Abbot of Vézelay in 1120, Renaud de Semur, is known from his epitaph as a repairer, the "reparator monasterii Vezeliacensis."[24] Fourth, a unique Ecclesia rondel (Fig. 128a) in the second southern bay of the nave is inscribed with these words implying damage from fire: "I am rather covered with smoke but later I shall be resplendent."[25] The Ecclesia figure was created by the Plus Master in a style later than his facade rondels, which were carved during the second campaign (appendix 6; chapter 5 and the excursus). Because of these stylistic differences and the incomplete and damaged portal sculpture in the second campaign, we may conclude that the smoky fire with its presumed 1120 date disrupted the construction of the facade before the portion of the nave with the Ecclesia rondel was begun. Fifth, the Perrecy Master's nave capitals and the Plus Master's nave Ecclesia changed direction, away from the second-campaign work on the central portal, toward the style of the final campaign sculpture on the tympanum (chapters 4, 5). However, because the Perrecy Master's nave capitals do not exhibit certain qualities standard to his latest tympanum sculpture (chapter 4), they support the theory, based on the work of the Plus Master, that masons constructed the central nave after the fire interruption on the facade and before the completion of the tympanum in the third campaign. Sixth, we know from masons' marks that masons who joined the Atelier only at the end of nave construction, after the sixth eastern bay, were among those who completed the facade masonry covering the back of the tympanum slabs ("Int. cent. portal btw. impost and string," in Fig. 36). Therefore, the installation of the final tympanum sculpture paralleled or followed the latest nave construction, while the nave sculpture of the Perrecy and Plus Masters followed the damage from the 1120 fire on the portal.

Seventh, a final date of 1120 for the second campaign is especially attractive given the sculptural changes at Cluny and the likely dates associated with them. The western portal sculpture of Cluny most closely compares to the sculpture from the Vézelay second campaign (chapter 5). From archaeological evidence, it is clear that these works from Cluny date to the final fourth campaign (appendix 4) known to have been completed by 1130 or 1132.[26] Because the sculpture was presumably installed at the beginning of the campaign—the portal was placed at a low level of construction—and because the final construction took time to build—extending five aisles in width and seven bays in length—it is not unreasonable to assign the western portal sculpture a date somewhat earlier than the latest 1132 date. Perhaps an appropriate date is 1120, the time of the Vézelay second-campaign works which it parallels stylistically (chapter 5).

The evidence for dating the second campaign thus can be established from inscriptions describing damage and repair, from in situ archaeological repairs, from changes in masons' marks between the three stages of construction, and from stylistic changes by two sculptors on the different parts of the building. The stylistic changes of these men are parallel at Vézelay and correspond to possibly simultaneous changes in sculpture at Cluny.

The less-definite dating of the first campaign benefits from the more secure dates of the second stage of construction. Comparisons to Cluny are especially telling, because many of the same masons and sculptors, including both the Perrecy and Avenas Masters, worked on the first campaign at both sites (chapters 2, 4). On the basis of architectural details and drapery style, I determined that the first Vézelay sculpture preceded the ambulatory capitals of Cluny (chapter 4). From the pattern of construction and direction of change within the Cluny first campaign, I concluded that the Cluny choir and ambulatory probably dated from the time of the consecration of certain chevet altars in 1095, well after the initial laying of stones in 1088 (appendix 4). The close resemblance of the first Vézelay facade sculpture to the Cluny ambulatory capitals (chapter 4) makes an approximate date of 1095 logical for it as well, while the wide difference which separates the style of the initial Vézelay sculpture from works of the second Vézelay campaign supports a time lapse of perhaps 15 years between them.

Given the date of the first facade sculpture, the dedication of 1104 ("Dedicatio ecclesiae Vizeliaci") may well have applied to the perimeter layout of the first nave campaign, which included the earliest facade sculpture as well as the crossing from an immediately preceding chevet.[27] At Vézelay fragments remain of a crossing built in the earlier style of Charlieu, dated approximately 1094, and these crossing piers preceded the layout of the nave aisle walls.[28] An interruption following the first-campaign construction of low-lying aisle walls is not at all unlikely given the similar pattern in the nave at Tournus (appendix 2), Cluny (appendix 4), and Paray (appendix 5). If it seems unreasonable that the break between the first and second campaigns would have lasted from the dedication in 1104 to the return of the Perrecy Master from Cluny about 1110, remember that Abbot Artoud was assassinated in 1106, and political unrest and economic difficulties preceded and followed the event.[29]

NOTES

1. The description of courses is approximate because of the variation in the height of the ashlar blocks in the responds. The masonry on the last three eastern bays on both aisle walls is disturbed and therefore does not correspond to the campaign division described in the text. Further evidence of the first campaign in the nave can be found on the interior of the southeastern wall of the narthex where, starting just below the string course, a diagonally stepped masonry suture ends by the middle of the first bay. The colonnette base coursed to the dosseret of this wall on the southeastern corner of the narthex is of the early campaign type, while the colonnette base just to the west of it on the southern wall is of the late narthex type. Some of the other details and masonry fill

on the southeastern corner of the narthex were restored in the nineteenth century. My thanks to Whitney Stoddard for his advice on the masonry of the narthex.

Salet (*Vézelay*, 49) without comment acknowledges the existence of masonry marks at Vézelay. For the types of stones used at Vézelay, and a brief discussion of the marks, see Cotteau, *Bulletin de la société des sciences historiques et naturelles de l'Yonne*, 18, 1864, 153–59; Guillon, *Bulletin de la société des sciences historiques et naturelles de l'Yonne* 46, 1892, 493–502.

2. As early as 1873, in his *Monographie de l'ancienne église abbatiale de Vézelay*, Eugène Viollet-le-Duc observed no sign of an interruption in the nave, a position recently reiterated by Diemer (*Vézelay*, 34–38, 197), who

observed an "ununterbrochene Arbeit" of "erstaunliche Einheitlichkeit" in the nave. Similarly, Salet ("La Madeleine," 18, 22) observed no trace of a "reprise" in the "parfaite unité" of the nave. In the preceding generation, both Deschamps ("Notes," 72) and Porter (*Pilgrimage Roads*, 90) observed an entirely homogeneous nave construction.

Recently, two scholars suggested that a break occurred in the nave construction. R. Oursel (*Bourgogne romane*, 284) speculated that an 1106–1120 nave campaign may have been interrupted by fire, with the last western bay capitals forming a separate group after the fire. Conant ("Deux traditions," 101) proposed that the Church of the Madeleine was built like Saint-Denis around a preexisting Carolingian nave. He speculated that an atelier first joined a new transept to the Carolingian nave between 1106 and 1111, and then in 1112 began the facade, where they were joined by Cluniac sculptors. By 1114–1119, they had completed the facade as well as the first bay and the lower parts of the second bay of the nave when the fire of 1120 destroyed the remaining Carolingian nave.

A number of inconsistencies detract from this theory. Conant may have misinterpreted Neil Stratford's observations upon which he based his argument. In a letter (10 October 1976), Stratford explained that he observed no burn marks and only a difference in masonry on the southern wall of the nave under the aisle lean-to roof east of the third bay. He suggested that the masonry difference *may be* the result of a break caused by the fire of 1120, in which case work may have begun on certain parts of the church before the fire, especially on "door or doors—the outer walls of the open porch—some of the nave arcade of the west end."

Regardless of the possibility of breaks in the nave wall, it is clear from masonry differences (Figs. 28, 226b, 226c) and masons' marks (Figs. 31, 36) that the aisle wall on both sides runs in horizontal campaigns throughout the western bays, eliminating the possibility of a vertical suture between a Carolingian and Romanesque nave at this point.

3. See chapter 2, note 3.

4. See appendixes 4 and 5.

5. For the historiography of the discovery of the earlier crossing campaign, see Vallery-Radot, "Les analogies," 264–265. Lefèvre-Pontalis observed the different axis and masonry of the western crossing piers. Deschamps recognized the older "facture" of the eastern bay capitals. See chapter 3, note 2.

6. Salet, *Vézelay*, and "Notes sur la façade"; Beutler, "Vézelay." C. Oursel ("Problèmes de filiation") criticized Salet's archaeological examination of the Vézelay facade for "une telle lenteur de démonstration" and "un certain luxe d'hypothèses."

On the basis of comparisons to the "geschossüber-greifende Gestaltung" of the Perrecy western portal facade, Diemer (*Vézelay*, 197) suggested an altered Vézelay narthex plan but an unchanged and continuous facade construction ("in seiner vollen Höhe geplant gewesen," p. 56). He dismissed any significant architectural shifts on the central portal simply as "schlampige Arbeit" (p. 55), preferring not to deal with the many keen observations of Beutler ("Hier ist nicht der Ort," p. 489, note 186). He dismissed the significance of individual artists' differences as "ganz ungünstig" because the portal "in einem stilistisch unauflösbaren Durcheinander und Miteinander einer grösseren Anzahl von Mitarbeitern entstanden" (p. 76). He did not attempt to prove this concept of medieval craftsmanship nor did he attempt to show that the stylistic differences within the "Hauptportalstil" were due to contemporary variations (p. 86) rather than to changes over time. He perceived the Saint-John trumeau to be an "ungeklärtes," "unbefriedigendes Resultat," despite the fact that it is the one most important piece which all scholars agree was not meant for its present location.

While unable to identify a single Vézelay master among the sculpture at Perrecy (p. 95), Montceaux (pp. 100, 195), or Mâcon (p. 204), he did not hesitate to classify all these works as "Nachfolger" of Cluny. He charted the stylistic changes over time at Vézelay as "evolving" from the more "natural" and "ideal" to the more "functional," and finally achieving the "inhaltliche Element" as expressed most completely in the "Trockenheit" of the "Petrusstil" (pp. 184–186).

7. Each side tympanum is an exception among the jamb sculpture of the first campaign. Although the tympanum may well have been set in place at the time of carving, it was surrounded by masonry from the second stage of construction.

8. Salet ("Notes sur la façade," and *Vézelay*) proposed four campaigns for the Church of the Madeleine, three of which involved changes to the facade sculpture. Following a Carolingian nave and an eleventh-century crossing, the facade was begun in 1120. For the first stage of the twelfth-century building, he proposed a massive central tympanum, a transverse barrel-vaulted narthex porch and a Saint-Michael chapel above it with access from the nave. He believed that these parts were never built, unlike other portions of the first campaign, including: the facade wall up to the level of the side tympana on the western face, and the facade up to the level of the aisle vaults on the eastern face; in the central portal, the lowest level facade columns, and the Saint-John trumeau column; the triangular *fronton*, intended originally for the location of the present semi-circular side tympanum, but surviving in fragmentary condition in the Vézelay Lapidary Museum. Salet modelled this first project on the narthex chapel of Saint-Philibert of Tournus, which is not known to have had access from

the nave (see appendix 2), and on the porch sculpture of Tonnerre, which is stylistically dissimilar and undated (see Salet, "Tonnerre," 214).

Salet believed that masons of a second facade campaign abandoned the idea of a transverse vaulted narthex with a Saint-Michael chapel, and replaced the lower triangular tympana with the present semicircular ones, extending the height of the side bays of the facade on the western face with newly dressed stones. The second campaign filled in the windows on the eastern face of the facade side bays, carved new sculpture on the rectangular jambs, and covered their bare surface with pilasters. In the central bay of the facade, the masons of the second campaign increased the height of both the dosserets and attached colonnettes, inserting an intermediary story, raising the Saint-John trumeau, and created a new lintel and a series of apostle figures above the previous embrasure columns. The nave was completed in a third campaign after 1135, and the central tympanum was executed as part of the final campaign, which also included the narthex.

9. Salet ("Notes sur la façade," 231) claimed that the triangular *fronton* now in the Lapidary Museum originally was carved for a side portal. However, no specific evidence can be found for this claim. The piece has no provenance, for it was discovered by Viollet-le-Duc in the course of demolishing an altar in the upstairs' narthex. The drapery type is later than that of the first and second levels of the facade, as described in chapters 4 and 5 (see especially notes 10 and 12 in chapter 5). And Salet's position on the early date of the *fronton* seems to be contradicted by his more recent opinion ("Review of Zarnecki," 11–12) agreeing with Zarnecki's attribution of the sculpture to Gislebertus. Salet said that "it is not impossible that he had been formed at Cluny and took part in the Autun facade before coming to Vézelay."

10. Viollet-le-Duc previously claimed that the four severed arches on the west facade originally were intended for low narthex vaults (*Dictionnaire*, I, 264). Salet cited the transverse barrel vaults in the narthex of Perrecy as a reflection of his first Vézelay narthex project (*Vézelay*, 48).

11. By analogy to a similar opening at Tournus, Salet ("Notes sur la façade," 230) assumed that the side portal facade windows were intended for stairs to reach the upper narthex chapel. However, the function of the openings and accompanying "stair stubs" in the nave of Tournus are not established (see appendix 2).

12. Salet, "Notes sur la façade," 232ff.

13. Ibid., 229, especially note. 2.

14. Ibid., 235.

15. Beutler, "Vézelay," 19.

16. Ibid., 7–30.

17. It is generally agreed that the Saint-John column was reused. The column supports nothing, and its top

edge molding overlaps figures in the lintel, and its base is not concentric to its support. While the drapery of the figure belongs to the second campaign (see chapter 4), the exact original location and purpose of the column remains uncertain.

18. See chapter 4, pp. 96ff., and chapter 5, p. 107ff.

19. Included in this reconstruction is the keystone which probably was cut in half when the three additional rondels were installed. Beutler, "Vézelay," 10f; Salet, *Vézelay*, 178.

20. Thanks to Elizabeth Bradford Smith for her help in reconstructing the central portal sculpture at Vézelay.

21. Thanks to my colleague Jaroslav Folda for his help in discussing the iconography of the portal. See A. Katzenellenbogen, "The Central Tympanum at Vézelay," 141.

22. The importance of the extra December rondel and the presence of one stone with one and a half rondels to either side of the lintel should not be exaggerated. The one and a half rondels on the left begin the calendar with January in the normal paired arrangement with a zodiac figure found throughout the portal; the style of the one and a half rondels on both sides matches the other original rondels (see chapter 5); and the number of rondels per block is inconsistent throughout the portal.

23. First excursus to chapter 1.

24. For the texts describing the fire of 21 July 1120, see Salet, "La Madeleine," 5ff. It seems more concrete to relate the fire to evidence of repairs on the present building than to apply it to parts of buildings for which there exists no evidence. Salet, like Deschamps and Lasteyrie before him, suggested that the fire destroyed a hypothetical Carolingian nave, clearing the way for the entire nave to be rebuilt in one campaign after 1120. In assessing this theory, we must remember that no textual or archaeological evidence remains of a Carolingian church; moreover, the present nave was built in more than one uninterrupted campaign—as the archaeology, sculpture, and masonry show.

Salet claimed that the epitaph of Renaud of Semur, Abbot from 1106 to 1128, and the recollections of Arnould, Bishop of Lisieux, establish that Renaud "demolished and replaced the building destroyed by the fire" (Salet, "La Madeleine," 18ff; *Vézelay*, 24, note 5). This may be an overreading of the texts which at no time referred to complete destruction, either by fire or Renaud's hand. The epitaph described him simply as the "reparator monasterii Vezeliacensis," while Arnould's recollections portrayed a building "parietum ruinas," not levelled or razed, and its return "ad innovandum" neither precluded a partial reconstruction nor suggested a complete replacement (Migne, *Patrol. lat.*, CCI, col 180).

25. See the first excursus to chapter 1 and chapter 5, note 2. The various interpretations of the nave rondel

have been summarized best by Diemer (*Vézelay*, 197, 37), who observed from its curved borders that it was intended as an arcade voussoir after the fire of 1120 ("eine Art von Hinweisschild 'Travaux'"). This is a widely accepted position: for example, Charles Porée ("Vézelay," 31) and Porter (*Pilgrimage Roads*, 90) accepted the reference on the rondel as a specific allusion to the fire of 1120, although they believed that the rondel was intended from the start for its present location. Indeed, Porter cited the rondel as "a dated monument of 1120." Pierre Meunier (*Iconographie de l'église de Vézelay*) believed that the inscription on the rondel referred to a later fire of 1165, while J. Walter ("La clef de doubleau de Vézelay," 402) believed that it had no specific historical reference but a general one to the Allegory of the Church. C. Oursel (*L'art roman*, 117) accepted Walter's position that the Ecclesia rondel is of no chronological value beyond a "figuration purement symbolique." For a discussion of the paleography on the rondel and its relation to the Cluny ambulatory capitals, see Lloyd, "Cluny," 349.

26. Conant, *Cluny*, 110; Aubert, "Cluny," 514.

27. See Vergnolle, "Recherches," note 13, where she discussed the bases in the crypt beneath the crossing.

28. Salet, *Vézelay*, 41; "La Madeleine," 18.

29. Salet, *Vézelay*, 23; "La Madeleine," 5f.

Selected Bibliography

Allemand, Maurice. "La construction du narthex de Saint-Philibert de Tournus." *Travaux des étudiants du groupe d'histoire de l'art de la Faculté des lettres de Paris* (1928), pp. 6–21.

Anfray, Marcel. *L'architecture religieuse du Nivernais au moyen-âge.* Paris, 1951.

Armi, C. Edson. "Saint-Philibert at Tournus and First Romanesque Architecture in the Mâconnais." Ph.D. dissertation, Columbia University, 1973.

———. "Orders and Continuous Orders in Romanesque Architecture." *Journal of the Society of Architectural Historians* 34 (1975): 178–81.

———. "Charlieu and the Origins of Romanesque Sculpture in Burgundy." *Symposium Honoring Elizabeth Read Sunderland,* Duke University, 28 March 1980.

Arslan, Edoardo. "L'architettura da 568 al Mille." *Storia di Milano,* vol. 2 (Milan, 1954), pp. 501–608.

L'art roman, exposition organisée par le gouvernement espagnol sous les auspices du conseil de l'Europe. Barcelona, 1961.

Aubert, Marcel. "Les clochers romans bourguignons." *Bulletin monumental* 80 (1921): 38–70.

———. *La Bourgogne, la sculpture.* Paris, 1930.

———. "Le choeur de l'église de Cluny au début du XIXᵉ siècle d'après une aquarelle de la collection de M. le comte de Rambuteau." *Bulletin monumental* 94 (1935): 375–76.

———. "Eglise abbatiale de Cluny." *Congrès archéologique* 98 (1935): 503–21.

Banchereau, J. "Orléans, Saint-Avit." *Congrès archéologique,* 93 (1930): 72–77.

Barbier, L. "Etudes sur les voûtes du premier étage du narthex de Saint-Philibert de Tournus." *Bulletin monumental* 92 (1933): 51–57.

Bard, Joseph. *Manuel général d'archéologie sacrée burgundo-lyonnaise.* Paris, 1844.

Barrès, H. *Perrecy, son prieuré, son église.* Perrecy, 1957.

Beenken, Hermann. "Die ausgeschiedene Vierung, kritische Bemerkungen zu einigen Rekonstruktionen karolingischer Kirchenbauten." *Repertorium für Kunstwissenschaft* 51 (1930): 209–31.

Bénet, A., ed. *Inventaire sommaire des archives départementales antérieures à 1790,* "archives ecclésiastiques," 1887; "archives civiles," 1896.

Berenson, Bernard. *Rudiments of Connoisseurship.* New York, 1902.

Bernard, Auguste, and Bruel, Alexandre. *Recueil des chartes de l'abbaye de Cluny.* Paris, 1876–1894.

Berry, Maurice. "Les travaux récents exécutés à l'abbaye de Tournus." *Bulletin de la société nationale des antiquaires de France.* (1963), pp. 90–94.

———. "Tournus l'abbaye de Saint Philibert." *Les monuments historiques de la France* 2 (1973): 16–17.

Beutler, Christian. "Das Tympanon zu Vézelay. Programm, Planwechsel und Datierung." *Wallraf-*

Richartz-Jahrbuch 29 (1967): 7–30.

La Bibliotheca Cluniacensis. trans. Dom A. l'Huillier. *Vie de saint Hugues.* Solesmes, 1888.

Bilson, John. "Cathédrale d'Auxerre." *Congrès archéologique* 74 (1907): 170–71.

Bony, Jean. "La chapelle épiscopale de Hereford et les apports lorrains en Angleterre après la conquête." *Actes du XIXᵉ congrès international d'histoire de l'art.* Paris, 1959.

Borg, Alan. *Architectural Sculpture in Romanesque Provence.* Oxford, 1972.

Bouché, Philibert. *Description historique et chronologique de la ville, abbaye et banlieue de Cluny.* Bibliothèque Nationale, Ms. nouv. acq. fr. 4336, 1787.

Bouquet, Dom Martin, ed. *Recueil des Historiens des Gaules et de la France.* Vol. 12. Paris, 1877.

Bourdon, Léon. "Les voyages de Saint Mayeul en Italie." *Ecole française de Rome. Mélanges d'archéologie et d'histoire* 42 (1926): 61–89.

Branner, Robert. *Burgundian Gothic Architecture.* London, 1960.

———. "Gothic Architecture 1160–1180 and Its Romanesque Sources." *Studies in Western Art* 1 (1963): 92–104.

Bréhier, Louis. "Les origines de l'art roman. Naissance des écoles régionales d'architecture." *La revue de l'art* 38 (1920): 130–43; 231–48; 265–80.

———. "Thiers, église du Moûtier." *Congrès archéologique* 87 (1924): 287–323.

———. "Questions d'art roman bourguignon." *Revue archéologique* 29 (1929): 291–316.

———. *L'art en France des invasions barbares à l'époque romane.* Paris, 1930.

Cahn, Walter. "Romanesque Sculpture in American Collections: I. Hartford." *Gesta,* 6 (1967): 48–49.

———. "Romanesque Sculpture in American Collections: II. Providence." *Gesta* 7 (1968): 51–53.

Calmette, Joseph. "Les éléments communs et les éléments spéciaux dans l'architecture romane de Bourgogne." *Revue bourguignonne* 16 (1906): 1–22.

Cameron, John B. "Early Romanesque Sculpture in Provence and the Dauphin Capitals." *Gesta* 17 (1978): 15.

Carlson, Eric. "Religious Architecture in Normandy, 911–1000." *Gesta* 5 (1966): 27–33.

Charmasse, André de. *Origine des paroisses rurales dans le département de Saône-et-Loire.* Autun, 1909.

Chavot, Th. *Le Mâconnais, géographie historique.* Mâcon, 1884.

Chomton, Abbé L. *Histoire de l'église Saint-Bénigne de Dijon.* Dijon, 1900.

"Chronique de Saint-Bénigne de Dijon." Ms. 591, Bibliothèque Municipale, Dijon.

Clapham, A. W. *The Monastery of Cluny, 910–1155.* Oxford, 1930.

Cluny, Saône-et-Loire. Archives Conant, Musée Ochier.

Colombert, Albert. "L'art 'Lombard' en Bourgogne." *Pays de Bourgogne* 2 (1953): 12–15; 9 (1955): 10–11.

———. "Problèmes autour de l'art dit 'lombard' en Bourgogne." *Premier colloque du centre international d'études romanes.* Paris, 1954.

———, and Gras, Pierre. "L'église de Combertault." *Mémoires de la commission des antiquités du département de la Côte-d'Or* 24 (1954): 141–58.

Commission des Monuments historiques. Archives et catalogue des relevés, dessins et aquarelles. Paris.

Conant, Kenneth J. "La chapelle Saint-Gabriel à Cluny." *Bulletin monumental* 87 (1928): 55–64.

———. "Five Old Prints of the Abbey Church of Cluny." *Speculum* 3 (1928): 401–4.

———. "Medieval Academy Excavations at Cluny— the Season of 1928." *Speculum* 4 (1929): 3–26; 168–75; 291–94.

———. "Les fouilles de Cluny." *Bulletin monumental* 88 (1929): 109–23.

———. "The Significance of the Abbey Church." *Speculum* 4 (1929): 443–50.

———. "The Date of the Ambulatory Capitals of Cluny." *Speculum* 5 (1930): 77–94.

———. "The Iconography and Sequence of the Ambulatory Capitals at Cluny." *Speculum* 5 (1930): 278–87.

———. "Medieval Academy Excavations at Cluny— the Season of 1929." *Speculum* 6 (1931): 3–14.

———. "Replica of the Arcade of the Apse at Cluny." *The Fogg Art Museum* 3 (1933): 5–8.

———. "Excavations at Cluny." *Résumés du XIIIᵉ congrès international d'histoire de l'art* (Stockholm 1933), pp. 104–6.

———. "The Third Church at Cluny." *Medieval Studies in Honor of Arthur Kingsley Porter* (Cambridge, 1939), pp. 327–38.

———. *A Brief Commentary on Early Medieval Church Architecture with Especial Reference to Lost Monuments.* Baltimore, 1942.

———. "Two New Books about Cluny." *Speculum* 17 (1942): 563–65.

———. *Benedictine Contributions to Church Architecture.* Latrobe, 1949.

———. "Medieval Academy Excavations at Cluny." *Speculum* 29 (1954): 1–43.

———. "Cluniac Building During the Abbacy of Peter the Venerable." *Studia Anselmiana* 40 (1956): 121ff.

———. *Carolingian and Romanesque Architecture.* Baltimore, 1959.

———. "Données de l'abbaye de Cluny," *Bulletin de la société nationale des antiquaires de France* (1960), pp. 88–91.

———. "Medieval Academy Excavations at Cluny, IX: Systematic Dimensions in the Buildings." *Speculum* 38 (1963): 1–43.

———. "Cluny II and St. Bénigne at Dijon." *Archaeologia* 99 (1965): 179–94.

———. "Les rapports architecturaux entre Cluny et Payerne." *L'abbatiale de Payerne* (Lausanne, 1966), pp. 134–38.

———. *Cluny, les églises et la maison du chef d'ordre.* Mâcon, 1968.

———. "Medieval Academy Excavations at Cluny, X." *Speculum* 45 (1970): 27–32.

———. "Sur les pas de Lallemand à Cluny." *Gazette des beaux-arts* 65 (1970): 1–10.

———. "La chronologie de Cluny III, d'après les fouilles." *Cahiers de civilisation médiévale* 14 (1971): 341–47.

———. "Early Examples of the Pointed Arch and Vault in Romanesque Architecture." *Viator* 2 (1971): 203–9.

———. "L'abside et le choeur de Cluny III." *Gazette des beaux-arts* 79 (1972): 5–12.

———. "Deux traditions dans la chronologie du roman bourguignon." *Annales de Bourgogne* 44 (1972): 94–103.

———. "Le portail monumental en Bourgogne." *Actes des journées d'études d'histoire et d'archéologie* 72 (1972): 23.

Consuetudines Farfenses. In Mortet, V., ed., *Recueil de textes relatifs à l'histoire de l'architecture et à la condition des architectes en France au Moyen Age XIe–XIIe siècles,* vol. I (1911), pp. 132–40.

Contenson, L. de. "L'église de Mt. St. Vincent." *Bulletin monumental* 69 (1910): 285–90.

Cotteau, G. *Bulletin de la société des sciences historiques et naturelles de l'Yonne* 18 (1864): 153–59.

Courajod, Louis. *Leçons professées à l'Ecole du Louvre.* Paris, 1899.

Crozet, René. "A propos de Cluny." *Cahiers de civilisation médiévale* 13 (1970): 149–58.

Cucherat, François. *Hugues de Poitiers, le prieuré, l'église et les peintures murales d'Anzy-le-Duc.* Mâcon, 1862.

———. *Les origines du Beaujolais et l'autel d'Avenas.* Lyon, 1886.

———. *Guide historique et archéologique du pélerin à Paray-le-Monial.* Lyon, 1895.

Curé, Henri. *Saint-Philibert de Tournus.* Paris, 1905.

Dard, Charles. "Calamités à Tournus à travers les âges." *Société des amis des arts et des sciences de Tournus* 47 (1947): 1–60.

Dartein, Ferdinand. *Etude sur l'architecture lombarde et sur les origines de l'architecture romano-byzantine.* Paris, 1884.

Decloitre, L. "Les véritables dimensions de la cathédrale Saint-Vincent de Mâcon." *Annales de l'academie de Mâcon* 25 (1940): 63.

Desbordes, Jean-Michel. "La troisième campagne de fouilles sous le choeur de la cathedrale de Meaux." *Bulletin monumental* 127 (1969): 27–33.

Deschamps, Paul. "Les deux tympans de Saint-Bénigne de Dijon et de Til-Châtel." *Bulletin monumental* 81 (1922): 380–86.

———. "Notes sur la sculpture romane en Bourgogne." *Gazette des beaux-arts* 7 (1922): 61–80.

———. *La sculpture romane.* Paris, 1924.

———. "A propos des chapiteaux du choeur de Cluny." *Bulletin monumental* 88 (1929): 514–16.

———. *Etude sur la paléographie des inscriptions lapidaires de la fin de l'époque mérovingienne aux dernières années du XIIe siècle.* Paris, 1929.

———. "L'âge des chapiteaux du choeur de Cluny." *La revue de l'art ancien et moderne* 53 (1930): 157–76; 205–18.

———. *La sculpture française à l'époque romane.* Paris, 1947.

———. Review of F. Salet, *La Madeleine de Vézelay. Bulletin monumental* 106 (1948): 229–34.

Descroi, J. "Inscription de l'autel d'Avenas. Réponse à M. le docteur Loison," cote 1221, Archives de Saône-et-Loire, Mâcon, n.d.

Deshoulières, François. "Essai sur les bases romanes." *Bulletin monumental* 75 (1911): 77–101.

———. "Souvigny." *Congrès archéologique* 80 (1913): 182–223.

———. "Essai sur les tailloirs romans." *Bulletin monumental* 78 (1914): 5–46.

———. "La théorie d'Eugène Lefèvre-Pontalis sur les écoles romanes." *Bulletin monumental* 84 (1925): 197–252; 85 (1926): 5–65.

———. "Eglise Saint-Philibert Dijon." *Congrès archéologique* 91 (1928): 96–109.

———. "Le premier art roman d'après M. Puig i Cadafalch." *Bulletin monumental* 87 (1928): 101–5.

———. *Au début de l'art roman.* Paris, 1929.

———. "La date des chapiteaux du choeur de l'église de Cluny." *Bulletin monumental* 90 (1930): 83–89.

———. "Farges." *Congrès archéologique* 98 (1935): 540–54.

———. "Le rôle de Cluny." *Bulletin monumental* 94 (1935): 413–34.

———. *Eléments datés de l'art roman en France. Evolution du style.* Paris, 1936.

———. "Souvigny, église Saint-Pierre." *Congrès archéologique* 101 (1938): 115–52.

———. "Les cryptes en France et l'influence du culte des reliques sur l'architecture religieuse." *Mélanges en hommage à la mémoire de Fr. Martroye* (Paris, 1941), pp. 213–38.

———. "Séance du 15 Decembre," *Bulletin de la société nationale des antiquaries de France* (1943), pp. 146–51.

Dickson, M. and C. *Les églises romanes de l'ancien diocèse de Chalon.* Mâcon, 1935.

Diemer, Peter. *Stil und Ikonographie der Kapitelle von Ste. Madeleine, Vézelay.* Heidelberg, 1975.

Dijon. Bibliothèque Municipale. Collection Epercy.

Duby, Georges. *La société aux XIe et XIIe siècles dans la région Mâconnaise.* Paris, 1953.

Duckett, G.F. *Record Evidences from among Archives of the Ancient Abbey of Cluny.* Lewis, 1886.

Dumolin, Benoît. *Histoire et description de la ville et des environs de Cluny, 1749–78.* (unpublished manuscript).

Enlart, Camille. *Manuel d'archéologie française,* vol. 1. Paris, 1902.

———. "Le porche de Charlieu." *Millénaire de Cluny* (Mâcon, 1910), pp. 232–34.

Erlande-Brandenburg, Alain. "Iconographie de Cluny III." *Bulletin monumental* 126 (1968): 293–322.

———. "Un dessin inédit du XVIIIe siècle figurant la nef de l'abbatiale de Cluny III." *Bulletin de la société nationale des antiquaires de France* (1968), pp. 119–20.

Evans, Joan. *The Romanesque Architecture of the Order of Cluny,* Cambridge, 1938.

————. *Cluniac Art of the Romanesque Period.* Cambridge, 1950.

————. "Travaux du congrès à Cluny." *Congrès scientifique* (Dijon, 1950), p. 44.

Février, P.-A. "Venasque." *Congrès archéologique* 121 (1963): 348–64.

Focillon, Henri. *L'art des sculpteurs romans.* Paris, 1931.

————. "Les origines des déambulatoires à chapelles rayonnantes." *Notes et documents d'archéologie.* Paris, 1937.

————. "Recherches récentes sur la sculpture romane en France au XIᵉ siècle" *Bulletin monumental* 97 (1938): 49–72.

————. *Peintures romanes.* Paris, 1938.

————. *The Art of the West.* Jean Bony, trans. Greenwich, 1963.

Fournier, P.C. "Note sur l'emploi des matériaux et spécialement de la pierre dans la restauration des édifices anciens, en particulier des églises romanes dans le sud de la Bourgogne." *Centre international d'études romanes* 2 (1958): 3–8.

————, and Rouyer, C. *Etude comparée de la nature du sol et de la réparation des édifices anciens dans le département de Saône-et-Loire.* Mâcon, 1941.

Francastel, Pierre. *L'humanisme roman. Critiques des théories sur l'art du XIᵉ siècle en France.* Paris, 1942.

Francovich, Geza de. "La corrente comesca nella scultura romanica europea." *Revista del R. Instituto d'archeologia e storia dell'arte* 5 (1935): 244ff.

Frankl, Paul. "Die Entstehung der romanischen Formengattungen." *Die frühmittelalterliche und romanische Baukunst* (Potsdam, 1926), pp. 57–63.

Gaillard, Georges. *Les débuts de la sculpture romane espagnole.* Paris, 1938.

————. "Sur la chronologie de Tournus." *Revue archéologique* 49 (1957): 47–59.

————. "L'abbaye de St. Philibert de Tournus: naissance de l'art roman." *Principe de Viana* 106 (1967): 5–10.

Gall, Ernst. "Die Abteikirche Saint-Philibert in Tournus, eine kritische Untersuchung zur frühburgundischen Baukunst." *Der Cicerone* 4 (1912): 624–36.

————. "St. Philibert in Tournus." *Zeitschrift für Kunstgeschichte* 16 (1952): 179–82.

Garnier, J., ed. *Chartres de communes et d'affranchissements en Bourgogne.* Dijon, 1868.

Gaudilliere, André. *Eglise d'Avenas.* Undated mimeograph, cote 1174, Archives de Saône-et-Loire, Mâcon.

Gelis, E. "Saint-Point—Travaux Dossier." Commission des Monuments historiques, Paris.

Ginet-Donati, F. "Notes épigraphiques." *Bulletin de la société d'études du Brionnais* (March 1926), p. 117.

Girond, Frédéric. "Etude archéologique sur le vieux St. Vincent de Mâcon." *L'union architecturale de Lyon* (1889), p. 2.

Grabar, André. "Peintures murales, notes critiques." *Cahiers archéologiques* 6 (1952): 177–91.

Grodecki, Louis. "Le 'transept bas' dans le premier art roman et le problème de Cluny." *Cluny congrès scientifique* (1950), pp. 265–69.

————. Review of W.S. Stoddard, *The West Portals of Saint-Denis and Chartres. Bulletin monumental* 111 (1953): 312–15.

————. *L'architecture ottoniene.* Paris, 1958.

————. "La sculpture de XIᵉ siècle en France, état des questions." *L'information d'histoire de l'art* 3 (1958): 98–112.

————. "La 'première sculpture gothique', Wilhelm Vöge et l'état actuel des problèmes." *Bulletin monumental* 117 (1959): 265–89.

————. "Guillaume de Volpiano et l'expansion clunisienne." *Centre international d'études romanes* 2 (1961): 21–31.

Guillon, A. *Bulletin de la société des sciences historiques et naturelles de l'Yonne* 46 (1892): 493–502.

Hearn, M.F. *Romanesque Sculpture.* Ithaca, 1981.

————. "Le moyen âge occidental." *Revue de l'art* 42 (1978): 22ff.

Heitz, Carol. "Réflexions sur l'architecture clunisienne." *Revue de l'art* 15 (1972): 81–94.

Héliot, Pierre. "L'ordre colossal et les arcades murales dans les églises romanes." *Bulletin monumental* 115 (1957): 241–61.

————. "Remarques sur la cathédrale d'Autun et sur l'architecture romane de la région bourguignonne." *Bulletin de la société nationale des antiquaires de France* (1963), pp. 182–99.

————. *Du carolingien au gothique. L'évolution de la plastique murale dans l'architecture religieuse du nord-ouest de l'Europe.* Paris, 1966.

Horn, Walter. "On the Origins of the Medieval Bay System." *Journal of the Society of Architectural Historians* 17 (1958): 2–23.

Hourlier, Dom Jacques. "St. Odilon bâtisseur." *Revue Mabillon* 51 (1961): 303–24.

————. *Saint Odilon abbé de Cluny.* Louvain, 1964.

Hubert, Jean. *L'architecture religieuse du haut moyen âge en France.* Paris, 1952.

————. "Séance du 26 Février—date de la construction de la crypte de la cathédrale d'Auxerre." *Bulletin de la société nationale des antiquaires de France* (1958), pp. 41–45.

l'Huillier, Dom A. *Vie de saint Hugues.* Solesmes, 1888.

Hunt, N. *Cluny under Saint Hugh, 1049–1109.* London, 1967.

Jalabert, Denise. *La sculpture romane.* Paris, 1924.

————. "La flore romane bourguignonne." *Gazette des beaux-arts* 55 (1960): 193–208.

————. *La flore sculptée des monuments du moyen âge en France.* Paris, 1965.

Jeannez, Edouard. "Le colonnade romane de l'abbaye de Charlieu." *Bulletin de la Diana* 6 (1891): 55 ff.

————. "L'église et le prieuré d'Anzy-le-Duc." In *L'art roman à Charlieu et en Brionnais*, Félix Thiollier, ed. Montbrison, 1894.

Jeanton, M.G. "L'église Notre Dame de Prayes." *Société des amis des arts et des sciences de Tournus* (1908), pp. 11–18.

————. "Comment le grand clocher de Tournus fut sauvé à la fin du XVIIIᵉ siècle." *Annales de l'académie de*

Mâcon 26 (1928–1929): 28–32.

Junien, Pierre. *Nouvelle histoire de l'abbaye royale de Saint-Filibert, et de la ville de Tournus*. Dijon, 1733.

Katzenellenbogen, A. "The Central Tympanum at Vézelay." *Art Bulletin* 26 (1944): 144–51.

Kerber, Bernhard. *Burgund und die Entwicklung der französischen Kathedralskulptur im zwölften Jahrhundert*. Recklinghausen, 1966.

Kleinschmidt, Helen. "The Cluny St. Peter." *Studies: Museum of Art* (Rhode Island School of Design, Providence, 1947), pp. 19–33.

Kubach, Hans, and Verbeek, Albert. "Die vorromanische und romanische Baukunst in Mitteleuropa. Literaturbericht 1938 bis 1950." *Zeitschrift für Kunstgeschichte* 14 (1951): 124–48.

Lacroix, F. "Le vieil évêché de Mâcon." *Annales de l'académie de Mâcon* 7 (1890): 46–51.

Lassalle, V. "L'origine antique de l'appareil polychrome roman dans la région lyonnaise." *Bulletin des musées et monuments lyonnais* 3 (1962–1966): 55–66.

Lasteyrie, Robert de. "La sculpture de Bourgogne au XIIᵉ siècle." *Millénaire de Cluny* (Mâcon, 1910), pp. 227ff.

———. *L'architecture religieuse en France à l'époque romane*. Paris, 1929.

Lefèvre-Pontalis, Eugène. "Etude historique et archéologique sur l'église de Paray-le-Monial." *Mémoires de la société Eduenne* 14 (1885): 333ff.

———. *Etude historique et archéologique sur l'église de Paray-le-Monial*. Autun, 1886.

———. "Essai sur quelques particularités des églises romanes bénédictines," *Millénaire de Cluny* (Mâcon, 1910), pp. 220–30.

———. "Châtel-Censoir." *Congrès archéologique* 80 (1913): 425–30.

———. "Paray-le-Monial." *Congrès archéologique*, 80 (1913): 53–65.

———. "L'école du Périgord n'existe pas." *Bulletin monumental* 82 (1923): 7–35.

Lelong, Charles. "La nef de Saint-Martin de Tours." *Bulletin monumental* 133 (1975): 205–31.

Lemaitre, Henri. "Romanische Kirchen in Frankreich. St. Philibert von Tournus." *Antares* 4 (1957): 51–52.

Lenoir, Alexandre. *Monuments des Arts libéraux, mécaniques et industriels de la France*. Paris, 1840.

Lesaing, M. "Le prieuré de Perrecy-les-Forges." *Annales de l'académie de Mâcon* 16 (1911): 251ff.

Lesueur, Frédéric. "Saint-Martin d'Angers, La Couture du Mans, Saint-Philibert de Grandlieu et autre églises à éléments de briques dans la région de la Loire." *Bulletin monumental* 119 (1961): 230–42.

———. "Hypothèse sur la construction de Saint-Philibert de Tournus." *Mélanges René Crozet* 1 (Paris, 1966): 215–22.

———. *Les églises de Loir-et-Cher*. Paris, 1969.

Lex, Léonce. "Congrès archéologique de France—Mâcon." *Annales de l'académie de Mâcon* 4 (1899): 447–92.

———. "Paray-le-Monial." *Annales de l'académie de Mâcon*, 1899.

———. "Peintures murales de la chapelle du Château des Moines de Cluny à Berzé-la-Ville." *Millénaire de Cluny* (Mâcon, 1910), pp. 248–56.

Ley, L. *Histoire de Saint-Point*. Mâcon, 1898.

Leiss, Reinhard. *Der frühromanische Kirchenbau des 11. Jahrhunderts in der Normandie*. Munich, 1967.

Lloyd, Richard W. "Cluny Epigraphy." *Speculum* 3 (1932): 336–49.

Lorain, M.P., and Sagot, Emile. *Essai historique sur l'abbaye de Cluny*. Dijon, 1839.

Lorton, A. *Mazille et Sainte-Cécile*. Chalon-sur-Saône, 1943.

Louis, R., *Les églises d'Auxerre, des origines au XIᵉ siècle*. Paris, 1952.

Lücken, Gottfried von. *Die Anfänge der burgundischen Schule, ein Beitrag zum Aufleben der Antike in der Baukunst des XII. Jahrhunderts*. Basel, 1913.

———. "Burgundische Skulpturen des XI. und XII. Jahrhunderts." *Jahrbuch für Kunstwissenchaft* 1 (1923): 103–24.

Lyman, Thomas. "Terminology, Typology, Taxonomy: an Approach to the Study of Architectural Sculpture of the Romanesque Period." *Gazette des beaux-arts* 88 (1971): 223–27.

Mabillon, Jean, ed. *Acta Sanctorum Ordinis S. Benedicti*. Venice, 1733.

Magni, Mariaclotilde. "Sopravvivenze Carolinge e Ottoniane nell'architettura romanica dell'arco alpino centrale." *Arte lombarda* 14 (1969): 35–44, 77–87.

Magnien, Emile. "Les plus anciennes églises de la région de Cluny." *Annales de l'académie de Mâcon* 36 (1942): 47–48.

———. *Histoire de Mâcon et du Mâconnais*. Mâcon, 1971.

Mâle, Emile. *L'art religieux du XIIᵉ siècle en France*. Paris, 1922.

Malo, Christiane. "Les églises romanes de l'ancien diocèse de Chalon-sur-Saône." *Bulletin monumental* 90 (1931): 370–435.

Malo, Edmond. "Les voûtes de la chapelle haute de l'église abbatiale de Tournus." *Bulletin monumental* 98 (1939): 73–84.

Malone, Carolyne. "Les fouilles de Saint-Bénigne de Dijon (1976–1978) et le problème de l'église de l'an mil." *Bulletin monumental* 138 (1980): 253–91.

Margand, A. "Les églises et clochers mâconnais: région du sud-est." *Annales de l'académie de Mâcon* 36 (1942–1943): 35–36, 63–64.

Martin, Jean. "Découvertes archéologiques dans les dépendances de l'église abbatiale de Tournus." *Congrès archéologique* 66 (1899): 223–232.

———. "Appendice." *Bulletin monumental* 67 (1903): 556–61.

———. "Nouvelles découvertes archéologiques faites en 1910 autour de l'église abbatiale de Tournus." *Annales de l'académie de Mâcon* 16 (1911): 239–49.

Martindale, Andrew. "The Romanesque Church of S. Bénigne at Dijon and MS. 591 in the Bibliothèque Municipale." *Journal of the British Archaeological Association* 25 (1962): 21–55.

Masson, H. *Saint-Philibert de Tournus. Essai sur la con-*

struction de l'église. Tournus, 1936.

Mayeux, Albert. "Le tympan du portail de Montceaux-l'Etoile." *Bulletin monumental* 80 (1921): 239–45.

Mercier, Fernand. "Berzé-la-Ville." *Congrès archéologique* 98 (1935): 485–501.

Mérimée, Prosper. Marginal comments to "Extrait du registre des déliberations de la commission départementale des antiquités de la Côte-d'Or." Séance du 2 Janvier 1847, Archives de Bourgogne, Dijon.

———. "Rapport à la commission, Séance du 12 Février 1847"; and "Rapport no. 179—17 Février 1847." In "Travaux Dossier, Saint-Bénigne Dijon," Commission des Monuments historiques, Paris.

Meulien, E. "Notice sur une inscription murale de l'époque romane dans l'église abbatiale de Tournus." *Annales de l'académie de Mâcon* 1 (1896): 83–89.

Meunier, Pierre. *Iconographie de l'église de Vézelay.* Avallon, 1858.

Michel, André. *Histoire de l'art.* Paris, 1905.

Micheli, L. *Le décor géometrique dans la sculpture de l'Aisne et de l'Oise au XIe siècle.* Paris, 1939.

Migne, J.-P., ed. *Patrologiae cursus completus,* series Latina. Paris, 1844–1864.

Morelli, Giovanni. *Italian Painters.* J.F. Ffoulkes, trans. London, 1892.

Morey, Rufus. "The Sources of Romanesque Sculpture." *Art Bulletin* 2 (1919): 10–16.

Nicolas, Fernand. *Le vieux St.-Vincent de Mâcon.* Publication du Groupe 71, Dijon, cote br. 1109, Archives de Saône-et-Loire, Mâcon, n.d.

Nodier, Ch.; Taylor, J.; and Cailleux, Alph. *Voyages pittoresques et romantiques dans l'ancienne France.* Paris, 1825.

Oursel, Charles. "Le rôle et la place de Cluny dans la renaissance de la sculpture en France à l'époque romane." *Revue archéologique* 17 (1923): 255–89.

———. "Paray-le-Monial et Cluny." *Art Studies* (1926), pp. 81–100.

———. "La genèse monumentale de l'église abbatiale de Vézelay." *Art Studies* (1927), pp. 31–50.

———. *L'art roman de Bourgogne.* Dijon, 1928.

———. "Comptes-rendus critiques: congrès archéologique de France—XCI^e session tenue à Dijon," *Annales de Bourgogne* 2 (1930): 188–96.

———. "Les églises Martiniennes de l'école romane de Bourgogne—remarques et observations." *Annales de Bourgogne* 3 (1931): 293.

———. "A. Kingsley Porter et la Bourgogne." *Medieval Studies* 17 (1939): 323–25.

———. "Les étapes de la construction de la grande abbatiale de Cluny." *Annales de Bourgogne* 12 (1940): 7–10.

———. "Une grande mission archéologique americaine en Bourgogne." *Mémoires de l'académie des sciences, arts et belles-lettres de Dijon* 60 (1945): 58ff.

———. "La chronologie de la chapelle du Château des Moines à Berzé-la-Ville." *Annales de l'académie de Mâcon* 38 (1947): 222–24.

———. "Problèmes de filiation en histoire de l'art roman; à propos d'un livre récent. La Madeleine de Vézelay." *Annales de Bourgogne* 21 (1949): 59–69.

———. "La Bourgogne dans l'art roman." *Revue du moyen âge latin* 6 (1950): 347–54.

———. *L'art de Bourgogne.* Paris, 1953.

Oursel, Raymond. "A propos de l'autel d'Avenas." *Annales de Bourgogne* 20 (1948): 204.

———. "Anzy-le-Duc, Cluny, Vézelay." *A Cluny. Congrès scientifique. Fêtes et cérémonies liturgiques en l'honneur des saints Abbés Odon et Odilon,* 9–11 (July 1949 (Dijon, 1950), pp. 270–73.

———. "La Bourgogne dans l'art roman, essai de mise au point." *Revue du moyen âge latin* 6 (1950): 347–54.

———. "Berzé-la-Ville." *Bulletin des Amis de Cluny,* 1955, pp. 1–8.

———. *Les églises romanes de l'Autunois et du Brionnais.* Mâcon, 1956.

———. *Evocation de la Chrétienté romane.* La Pierre-Qui-Vire, 1968.

———. "A propos de la reconstruction de l'abbatiale Saint-Martin d'Autun aux XVIIIe siècle." *Comptes rendus du 40e congrès de l'association bourguigonne des sociétés savantes* (Autun, 1969).

———. *Floraison de la sculpture romane.* La Pierre-Qui-Vire, 1973.

———. *Bourgogne romane.* La Pierre-Qui-Vire, 1974.

———. "La sculpture romane de Tournus." *Bulletin de la société des amis des arts et des sciences de Tournus* 78 (1978): 1–40.

Pendergast, Carol. *The Romanesque Sculpture of Anzy-le-Duc.* Ph.D. dissertation, Yale University, 1974.

———. "The Lintel of the West Portal at Anzy-le-Duc." *Gesta* 15 (1976): 135–42.

Penjon, A. *Cluny, la ville et l'abbaye.* Cluny, 1872.

Perrat, Charles. *L'autel d'Avenas, la légende de Ganelon et les expéditions de Louis VII en Bourgogne (1166–1172).* Lyon, 1933.

Petite Chronique de Vézelay. Bibliothèque d'Auxerre. Ms. 227.

Plancher, Dom Urbain. *Histoire générale et particulière de Bourgogne,* vol. 1. Dijon, 1739.

Plat, Gabriel. "La Touraine, berceau des écoles romanes du sud-ouest." *Bulletin monumental* 78 (1913): 375–77.

———. "Vendôme." *Congrès archéologique* 88 (1925): 271–78.

———. *L'art de bâtir en France des romains à l'an 1100 après les monuments anciens de la Touraine, de l'Anjou et du Vendômois.* Paris, 1939.

Poinssot, Claude. "Le bâtiment du dortoir de l'abbaye de Saint-Bénigne de Dijon." *Bulletin monumental* 112 (1954): 304–30.

Porée, Charles. "Vézelay." *Congrès archéologique* 74 (1907): 24–44.

Porter, Arthur Kingsley. *Medieval Architecture, Its Origins and Development.* New Haven, 1912.

———. *Lombard Architecture.* New Haven, 1917.

———. "La sculpture du XIIᵉ siècle en Bourgogne." *Gazette des beaux-arts.* 62 (1920): 73–94.

———. *Romanesque Sculpture of the Pilgrimage Roads.* Boston, 1923.

Pradel, P. "Les sculptures de l'église de Souvigny." *Monuments Piot* 2 (1944).

Puig i Cadafalch, José. "Procès-verbaux, séance du 26 Mai." *Congrès archéologique* 73 (1906): 220–22.

———. "Decorative Forms of First Romanesque Styles." *Art Studies* 4 (1926): 11–25.

———. "Decorative Forms of the First Romanesque Style: Their Diffusion by Moslem Art." *Art Studies* 6 (1928): 15–27.

———. *Le premier art roman.* Paris, 1928.

———. *La géographie et les origines du premier art roman.* J. Vrellard, trans. Paris, 1935.

Quarré, Pierre. "La date des chapiteaux de Cluny et la sculpture romane en Bourgogne." *Annales de Bourgogne* 39 (1967): 156–62.

Questel, Charles. "Façade, état actuel." 25 January 1843. M.H. no. 2572, Saint-Philibert Tournus, "Travaux Dossier," Commission des Monuments historiques, Paris.

———. Plan and *Devis.* 25 January 1843, 5 July 1850, Saint-Philibert Tournus, "Travaux Dossier," Commission des Monuments historiques.

Quicherat, Jules. *Mélanges d'archéologie et d'histoire.* Paris, 1885.

Raeber, R. *La-Charité-sur-Loire.* Berne, 1965.

Ragut, M.C., ed. *Cartulaire de Saint-Vincent de Mâcon,* Mâcon, 1864.

Ranquet, H. du. "Les fouilles du chevet de la cathédrale de Clermont." *Bulletin monumental* 73 (1909): 311–16.

Rhein, André. "Anzy-le-Duc." *Congrès archéologique* 80 (1913): 269–91.

———. "Charlieu." *Congrès archéologique* 80 (1913): 242–57.

———. "Beaune." *Congrès archéologique* 91 (1928): 267–89.

———. "Anzy-le-Duc et Semur-en-Brionnais, *Congrès archéologique* 98 (1935): 422–30.

Richard, Jean, ed. *Le cartulaire de Marcigny-sur-Loire 1045–1144: essai de reconstruction d'un manuscrit disparu.* Dijon, 1957.

Rivoira, Giovanni. *Le origini della architettura lombarda e delle sul principali derivazioni nei paesi d'oltr'Alpe.* Rome, 1901–1904.

Saint-Paul, Anthyme. *Annuaire de l'archéologie française,* 1 (1877), 96ff.

Salet, Francis. "La Madeleine de Vézelay et ses dates de construction." *Bulletin monumental* 95 (1936): 5–25.

———. "La Madeleine de Vézelay. Notes sur la façade de la nef." *Bulletin monumental* 99 (1940): 223–37.

———. *La Madeleine de Vézelay.* Dijon, 1948.

———. "Une sculpture du portail de Cluny." *Bulletin monumental* 106 (1948): 168–69.

———. "Les dates de Notre-Dame de Beaune." *Bulletin monumental* 107 (1949): 168–69.

———. "Les chapiteaux de Notre-Dame de Beaune." *Bulletin monumental* 108 (1950): 220–21.

———. "Tonnerre." *Congrès archéologique* 116 (1959): 214ff.

———. "La sculpture romane en Bourgogne—à propos d'un livre récent." *Bulletin monumental* 119 (1961): 325–43.

———. Review of R. Raeber, *La Charité-sur-Loire.* *Bulletin monumental* 123 (1965): 345–49.

———. Review of D. Grivot and G. Zarnecki, *Gislebertus sculpteur d'Autun.* *Bulletin monumental* 124 (1966): 109–12.

———. "Cluny III." *Bulletin monumental* 126 (1968): 235–92.

———. Review of K.J. Conant, *Cluny, les églises et la maison du chef d'ordre.* *Bulletin monumental* 127 (1969): 183–86.

———. Review of Elizabeth Sunderland, *Charlieu à l'époque médiévale.* *Bulletin monumental* 130 (1972): 73–75.

Saône-et-Loire. *Album historique et pittoresque du département de Saône-et-Loire par une réunion d'artistes et d'écrivains,* vol. 1. Mâcon, 1840.

Sauerländer, Willibald. "Gislebertus von Autun. Ein Beitrag zur Entstehung seines künstlerischen Stils." *Studien zur Geschichte der europäischen Plastik* (1965), pp. 17–29.

———. "Über die Komposition des Weltgerichts-Tympanons in Autun." *Zeitschrift für Kunstgeschichte* 29 (1966): 261–94.

Sauvageot, C. *Devis* 15 December 1901, *Rapport* 15 March 1901, cl. 284.293, Saint-Philibert Tournus, "Travaux Dossier," Commission des Monuments historiques, Paris.

Schapiro, Meyer. Review of C. Oursel, *L'art roman de Bourgogne.* *Art Bulletin* 11 (1929): 225–31.

———. Review of P. Deschamps, *Etude sur la paléographie des inscriptions lapidaires.* *Art Bulletin,* 12 (1930): 101–2.

———. "A Relief in Rodez and the Beginnings of Romanesque Sculpture in Southern France." *Acts of the Twentieth International Congress of the History of Art* 1 (1963): 40–66.

———. *The Parma Ildefonsus.* Florence, 1964.

Scher, Stephen. *The Renaissance of the Twelfth Century.* Providence, 1969.

Schlink, Wilhelm. *Saint-Bénigne in Dijon.* Berlin, 1978.

Sedlmayr, Hans. "Spätantike Wandsysteme. Das erste mittelalterliche Architektursystem." *Epochen und Werke* (Munich, 1959).

———. "Die Ahnen der Dritten Kirche von Cluny." *Das Werk des Künstlers,* (Stuttgart, 1960), pp. 49–71.

Seidel, Linda. "Romanesque Sculpture in American Collections: II. The William Hayes Fogg Art Museum." *Gesta* 11 (1972): 76.

Selmersheim, M. *Devis* 15 February 1883, "Rapport de l'architecte sur la nature et l'importance des travaux prévus," *Devis* 22 April 1898, cl. 22744, Saint-Philibert Tournus, "Travaux Dossier," Commission des Monuments historiques, Paris.

Serbat, Louis. "La Charité," *Congrès archéologique* 80 (1913): 374–94.

Sevelinges, J.-B. de. *Histoire de la ville de Charlieu.* Roanne, 1856.

Sheppard, Carl D. "Romanesque Sculpture in Tuscany: a Problem of Methodology." *Gazette des beaux-arts* 54 (1959): 97–108.

Stoddard, Whitney S. *The West Portals of Saint-Denis and Chartres.* Cambridge, 1952.

———. "The Eight Capitals of the Cluny Hemicycle." *Gesta* 20 (1981): 51–58.

Stratford, Neil. "Un bas-relief roman de Nevers." *La revue du Louvre et des musées de France* 27 (1977): 304–6.

———. "Chronologie et filiations stylistiques des sculptures de la façade nord du porche de Charlieu." *Actes des journées d'études d'histoire et d'archéologie* 72 (1972): 7–12.

Stüve, Holger. "Burgundian Romanesque Groin Vaults in "travée simple" Basilicas." *Symposium Honoring Elizabeth Read Sunderland,* Duke University, 28 March 1980.

Sunderland, Alice L. "Saint-Bénigne at Dijon and the Roman Foot." *Journal of the Society of Architectural Historians* 16 (1957): 12–15.

———. "The Legend of the Alternate System at Saint-Bénigne of Dijon." *Journal of the Society of Architectural Historians* 18 (1958): 2–9.

Sunderland, Elizabeth R. "The History and Architecture of the Church of St. Fortunatus at Charlieu in Burgundy." *Art Bulletin* 21 (1939): 61–88.

———. "Charlieu: the First Ambulatory Colonnade?" *Journal of the Society of Architectural Historians* 12 (1953): 3–6.

———. "More Analogies between Charlieu and Anzy-le-Duc." *Journal of the Society of Architectural Historians* 16 (1957): 16–21.

———. "Feet and Dates at Charlieu." *Journal of the Society of Architectural Historians* 16 (1957): 3–5.

———. "Symbolic Numbers and Romanesque Church Plans." *Journal of the Society of Architectural Historians* 18 (1959): 94–103.

———. "Les fenêtres murées du chevet d'Anzy-le-Duc." *Compte rendu annuel* (Société des amis de Charlieu, 1973), pp. 24–26.

Talobre, Joseph. *La construction de l'abbaye de Cluny.* Mâcon, 1936.

———. "La reconstruction du portail de l'église abbatiale de Cluny." *Bulletin monumental* 102 (1944): 225–40.

———. "La place du chevet à déambulatoire de Tournus dans l'histoire de l'art français. Les méthodes de contrôle des maçonneries anciennes." *Premier colloque du centre international d'études romanes* (Paris, 1954).

Terret, Victor. "Cluny centre et foyer artistique de la sculpture bourguignonne au XIIᵉ siècle." *Millénaire de Cluny* (Mâcon, 1910), pp. 1–32.

———. *La sculpture bourguignonne aux XIIᵉ et XIIIᵉ siècles, ses origines et ses sources d'inspiration—Cluny.* Autun, 1914.

Thiollier, Felix, ed. *L'art roman à Charlieu et en Brionnais.* Montbrison, 1894.

Thirion, Jacques. "L'église Saint-Dalmas de Valdeblore." *Bulletin monumental* 111 (1953): 157–71.

———. "L'église de la Madone del Poggio à Saorge." *Nice historique* (1959), pp. 45–60.

———. "Un témoin du premier art roman en Provence: la Madone de Levens." *Bulletin monumental* 119 (1961): 345–51.

———. "L'influence lombarde dans les Alpes françaises du sud." *Bulletin monumental* 128 (1970): 7–40.

———. "Au début de l'architecture romane en Provence. L'ancienne église de Saint-Donat." *Bulletin monumental* 123 (1965): 278–92.

———. "La cathédrale de Nice." *Cahier archéologique* 17 (1967): 121–60.

Thümmler, Hans. "Die Baukunst des 11. Jahrhunderts in Italien." *Römisches Jahrbuch für Kunstgeschichte* 3 (1939): 141–226.

Triger, Robert. "Le Mans, église de la Couture." *Congrès archéologique* 77 (1910): 281–87.

Truchis, Pierre de. "La chapelle Saint-Laurent." *Mémoires, société nationale des antiquaires de France* 65 (1904–1905): 1–16.

———. "Eléments barbares, éléments étrangers dans l'architecture romane de l'Autunois." *Mémoires de la société Eduenne* 35 (1907): 279–303.

———. "Les influences orientales dans l'architecture romane de la Bourgogne." *Congrès archéologique* 74 (1907): 459–500.

———. "L'architecture de la Bourgogne française sous Robert-le-Pieux." *Bulletin monumental* 80 (1921): 5–37.

Vallery-Radot, Jean. "Les analogies des églises de Saint-Fortunat de Charlieu et d'Anzy-le-Duc." *Bulletin monumental* 88 (1929): 244–67.

———. "Le premier art roman de l'occident méditerranéen." *La revue de l'art ancien et moderne* 55 (1929): 153ff.

———. *Eglises romanes, filiations et échanges d'influences* Paris, 1930.

———. "Saint-Paul de Varax." *Congrès archéologique* 98 (1935): 249–60.

———. "La limite méridionale de l'école romane de Bourgogne." *Bulletin monumental* 95 (1936): 273–316.

———. "Le domaine de l'école romane de Provence." *Bulletin monumental* 113 (1945): 5–63.

———. *Bulletin de la société nationale des antiquaires de France.* 3 May 1950, pp. 75–76.

———. "Note sur le mur oriental du transept de St.-Philibert de Tournus." *Premier colloque du centre international d'études romanes,* (Paris, 1954).

———. *Saint-Philibert de Tournus.* Paris, 1955.

———. "Cathédrale d'Auxerre." *Congrès archéologique* 116 (1958): 44–45.

———. "Avallon." *Congrès archéologique* 116 (1958): 307–8.

———. "L'iconographie et le style des trois portails de Saint-Lazare d'Avallon." *Gazette des beaux-arts* 52 (1958): 23–34.

———. *Jean Virey 1861–1953*. Mâcon, 1959.

———. "Saint-Hymetière." *Congrès archéologique* 118 (1960): 133–65.

———. "Introduction." *Congrès archéologique* 121 (1963): 9–43.

———. "L'église de Aime." *Congrès archéologique* 123 (1965): 121–32.

———. La Charité-sur-Loire." *Congrès archéologique* 125 (1967): 43–83.

Vassas, Robert. "Travaux à la Madeleine de Vézelay: voûtes de la nef." *Les monuments historiques de France* 14 (1968): 56–61.

Ventre, André. *Devis* of 24 June 1913 (accepted 4 July 1913), Saint-Philibert Tournus, "Travaux Dossier," Commission des Monuments historiques, Paris.

Vergnolle, Eliane. "Les chapiteaux du déambulatoire de Cluny." *Revue de l'art* 15 (1972): 95–101.

———. "Recherches sur quelques séries de chapiteaux romans bourguignons: I. Le bloc et son décor." *L'information d'histoire de l'art* (1975), pp. 55–79.

———. "Autour d'Anzy-le-Duc." *Gesta* 17 (1978): 3–13.

Vieillard-Troiekowioff, May. "La cathédrale de Clermont du Ve au XIIIe siècle." *Cahiers archéologiques* 11 (1960): 199–247.

Viollet-le-Duc Eugène. *Dictionnaire raisonné de l'architecture française du XIe au XVe siècle.* Paris, 1858–1868.

———. *Monographie de l'ancienne église abbatiale de Vézelay.* Paris, 1873.

Virey, Jean. *L'architecture romane dans l'ancien diocèse de Mâcon.* Paris, 1892.

———. "Les différentes époques de construction de Saint-Philibert de Tournus." *Bulletin monumental* 67 (1903): 515–61.

———. "Excursion à Charlieu et à Châteauneuf." *Annales de l'académie de Mâcon* 12 (1904): 287–93.

———. *Paray-le-Monial et les églises du Brionnais.* Paris, 1926.

———. "Saint Hugues et la chapelle de Berzé-la-Ville." *Annales de l'académie de Mâcon* 25 (1927): 445–50.

———. "Les fouilles américaines à Cluny, en 1928." *Annales de l'académie de Mâcon* 27 (1929): 127ff.

———. "Berzé." *Congrès archéologique* 93 (1930): 91–93.

———. *L'église Saint-Philibert de Tournus.* Paris, 1932.

———. "Les travaux du professeur K.J. Conant à Cluny." *Revue Mabillon* 23 (1933): 69–70.

———. "Le travaux du Professeur J. Conant, à Cluny." *Annales de L'académie de Mâcon* 28 (1933): 407ff.

———. "Bois-Sainte-Marie." *Congrès archéologique* 98 (1935): 451–63.

———. *Les églises romanes de l'ancien diocèse de Mâcon, Cluny et sa région.* Mâcon, 1935.

———. "Mâcon, ancienne cathédrale Saint Vincent." *Congrès archéologique* 98 (1935): 464–72.

———. "Disposition archäiques dans les églises du premier art roman en Saône-et-Loire." *Mémoires de la société Eduenne* 48 (1936): 122–23.

Vita Sanctissimi Hugonis Cluniacensis Abbatis. Bibliothèque Nationale, Saint-Germain, fol. 197v.–224v.

Vöge, Wilhelm. *Die Anfänge des monumentalen Stiles im Mittelalter.* Strassburg, 1894.

Walter, J. "La clef de doubleau de Vézelay." *Bulletin monumental* 83 (1924): 399–403.

Willemin, N.-X. *Monuments français inédits pour servir à l'histoire des arts.* Paris, 1839.

Wixom, William D. "A Manuscript Painting from Cluny." *The Bulletin of the Cleveland Museum of Art* (April 1961), p. 133.

Worringer, W. *Über den Einfluss der angelsächsischen Buchmalerei auf die frühmittelalterliche Monumentalplastik des Kontinents.* Halle, 1931.

Zarnecki, George. *Art of the Medieval World.* New York, 1975.

———, and Grivot, Denis. *Gislebertus, Sculptor of Autun.* London, 1961.

Index

Numbers printed in boldface type indicate the principal discussion of a subject; numbers in italics refer to figures.